D0849646

American Jewish Landmarks

a travel guide and history

Foreword by
Jacob R. Marcus
Director
American Jewish Archives

American Jewish Landmarks

a travel guide and history
by
Bernard Postal and Lionel Koppman
volume II

fleet press corporation/new york

Published by Fleet Press Corporation, 160 Fifth Avenue,
    New York, N. Y. 10010
Library of Congress Catalogue Card No.: 76-27401
ISBN: Hardcover: 0-8303-0155-0
    Paperback: 0-8303-0157-7
Manufactured in the United States of America

Research for this work was supported in part by a grant
from the Memorial Foundation for Jewish Culture.

Foreword

In this period of the American Bicentennial Celebration I am delighted to welcome the appearance of *American Jewish Landmarks,* by the team of Bernard Postal and Lionel Koppman. The book contains valuable historical data on all 50 states, Washington, D.C., Puerto Rico, and the Virgin Islands. For people interested in the Jewish landmarks of the United States and her territorial possessions, this work is invaluable; it is the only guidebook of its kind; there is nothing else like it.

It is worth bearing in mind that this book is more than a manual for the tourist; it is an important book for students of American Jewish history. America's present-day Jewish community is the largest the world has yet known. Jewish Palestine at her zenith could probably never have boasted more than two million or three million Jews; today America shelters a Jewish population of nearly six million. This is a Jewry of some 5,000 to 10,000 Jewish clubs, societies, synagogues, and organizations, a community which has sprung up in the memory of men and women still living, for in 1880 there were only some 250,000 Jews in the United States.

This is not only the largest Jewry in the Diaspora, it is the most affluent, the most generous, the most cultured, the most advanced in the arts and sciences. It is obvious, therefore, why historians, both Jews and Gentiles, will want to know more about a community which has made such a great career for itself in the last two generations. *American Jewish Landmarks* supplies the information people seek. Because it is a ready reference book, adequately indexed, replete with an infinity of important detail, the student will keep it on his desk next to his Jewish encyclopedias.

When I pick up my telephone in my study to answer a call and think of Emile Berliner who invented the first practical telephone microphone, I know that the authors have described the work and personality of Berliner. And when I need data about Frederic William Wile, the author of a large-scale biography of Berliner, the assurance is mine that this book will tell me something about Wile and even inform me that his father, Jacob Wile, was the lay rabbi of LaPorte, Indiana, where the latter's achievements are memorialized in the name of Wile Street.

In a way this volume by Bernard Postal and Lionel Koppman is the only complete history of the American Jew, for it deals not only with the great and the mighty; it deals as well with the men and women of the towns and villages. Here are the annals of Jews whose communities reach from Portland, Maine, to San Diego, California—and on into the northernmost reaches of North America and into the Pacific and the Caribbean.

This is real history, grass roots history, the chronicle of an old people in a new world. It is also a delightful book, carefully researched, and well written. We are truly grateful for *American Jewish Landmarks: A Travel Guide and History.*

Jacob R. Marcus

Director
American Jewish Archives
Cincinnati, Ohio

Introduction

This book is part of a three-volume work that is a guide to and description of American Jewish landmarks and other places of Jewish interest or association in the United States, Puerto Rico, and the Virgin Islands.

It is the only book of its kind in this country. Its purpose is to identify, locate, and describe the thousands of landmarks, sites, shrines, memorials, public buildings, institutions, and other places whose collective story constitutes the chronicle of over three centuries of Jewish life in America.

Alphabetically arranged by states, cities, and towns within the states, and by places within the cities and towns, the three volumes are divided into 54 chapters, one for each state, the District of Columbia, Puerto Rico, the Virgin Islands, and one for New York City and environs.

Each chapter has two parts: an introductory essay devoted entirely to the highlights of Jewish history in the state or area covered, and a travel section listing and describing specific places.

Thirty-six categories of places have been included: shrines of Jewish history; monuments and memorials to Jews and portraits or bas-reliefs of Jews in public places; geographical places named for, founded by, or discovered by Jews; sites of early Jewish agricultural colonies; historic residences and other historic sites or buildings erected by, owned by, or named for Jews;

monuments and statuary having some Jewish connection; places of general historic importance having some Jewish association; monuments and memorials to non-Jews who were philo-Semites; interfaith shrines; historic places and buildings preserved by or donated to the public by Jews; graves of Jewish personalities celebrated in American or Jewish history; works of art depicting Jewish themes or characters on display in public places; Jewish religious objects in non-Jewish places; public collections of Judaica; Jewish museums; general museums housing Jewish artifacts; major Jewish libraries; housing complexes for aged Jews; public buildings or institutions donated by, named for, or dedicated to Jews; Jewish art collections; major libraries and art collections established by Jews for public use; major public works designed, built, or named for Jews; Holocaust memorials; institutions of Jewish higher learning; Hillel Foundations; Chabad Lubavitcher Student Centers; Jewish book and gift shops; major local Jewish institutions and agencies such as Jewish Community Centers, Homes for the Aged, Bureaus of Jewish Education, Jewish Federations and Welfare Funds, Jewish hospitals, and Jewish Vocational Services; synagogues; kosher eating facilities; selection of Jewish communally-sponsored camps; streets, avenues, and boulevards named for Jews; historic Jewish cemeteries; educational institutions named for, or founded by Jews; Israeli consulates; and Jewish community newspapers.

We have produced what we hope is a book that will be readable as well as useful. Our objective was a work that would provide pleasurable reading to armchair tourists, add to the enjoyment of the convention, business, or pleasure-bound traveler, answer the questions of all who seek hard-to-find information about Jewish beginnings, growth, and contemporary status in every state, and serve as supplementary reading in classes on American Jewish history and civics.

Each historical section is a fusion of information culled from countless sources—scholarly and popular, published and unpublished, familiar and newly-tapped.

The biographies that dot each travel section of each chapter lift from obscurity countless forgotten figures in American Jewish history, place in new settings numerous, well-remembered figures of yesterday, and describe the beginnings of many Jewish institutions, local and national.

We had a wonderfully exciting time making this armchair journey through the past and present of the American Jewish community, now well into its fourth century. En route we corresponded with several thousand people in nearly 1,000 different towns and cities. On the way, we read or consulted some 850 books, directories, city and state guides, histories, diaries, memoirs, biographies, almanacs and other reference works, and a vast collection of newspaper and magazine articles. Scattered through the three volumes are thumbnail biographies of more than 500 men and women, details about some 2,000 sites and landmarks, facts about over 800 national and local Jewish institutions, and information about nearly 2,000 synagogues.

American Jewish Landmarks is the successor to *A Jewish Tourist's Guide to the U.S.*, which was published in 1954.

The traveler who makes all or any part of the journey mapped out in the three volumes of *American Jewish Landmarks* is sure to stub his toe on American Jewish history wherever he goes. The reader who dips into these pages will find answers to his increasing curiosity about the Jewish past in America and its tenacious connection with the Jewish present.

Bernard Postal
Lionel Koppman

About the authors

BERNARD POSTAL, editor, journalist, and author, is
associate editor of *The Jewish Week,* editor of *The
Jewish Digest,* and co-author of ten other books on travel,
Jewish history, and Israel. He was the director of public
relations of JWB for 25 years. Prior to that he was
national public relations director of B'nai B'rith for eight
years. He is a member of the executive council of the
American Jewish Historical Society and the Jewish Historical Committee of B'nai B'rith. In 1954 he received the
National Jewish Book Award (together with Lionel Koppman) for his contributions to American Jewish history.
He was similarly honored by the American Jewish Historical Society.

∿

LIONEL KOPPMAN, editor, writer, and publicist, is
director of public information and publications for JWB.
He is a former newspaperman in Texas; medical editor
for the United States government; and winner of the
National Jewish Book Award in 1954 (together with
Bernard Postal) for his contributions to American Jewish
history. He was also the recipient of the Outstanding
Filmstrip of the Year Award for his filmstrip on Sholom
Aleichem in 1970. He is the author of a number of
manuals and plays on various aspects of American Jewish
life. He has received a grant for a textbook in American
Jewish history.

We tip our hats

Years of independent research went into this book, but much of the material in the landmark sections was distilled from correspondence with thousands of people. Since we do not pretend to have visited all the places we describe, we saw large numbers of them through the eyes of good friends and correspondents in every state and Washington, D.C.

A torrent of material came from the staffs of Federal, state, and municipal agencies, Jewish and non-Jewish organizations, museums, libraries, synagogues, historical societies, universities, scholars, researchers, rabbinical seminaries, Jewish Community Centers, B'nai B'rith Hillel Foundations, Jewish Welfare Federations and Jewish Community Councils, Boards of Jewish Education, Jewish schools, and editors of American Jewish newspapers. The editors were a particularly fertile source both for historic data and contemporary information.

To this small army of men and women who cheerfully furnished information, patiently checked data, helpfully undertook local research, resourcefully unearthed new facts, and graciously answered our incessant inquiries, we tip our hats and record their names.

Among the nearly 2,000 individuals with whom we were in contact, a number made unusually distinctive contributions to this book:

Harold E. Katz, Birmingham, who checked out the data for Alabama; Bernice Bloomfield, Anchorage, who helped avoid errors of omission and commission for

Alaska; Pearl Newmark, Phoenix, whose information was of great help for Arizona; Rabbi Ira Sanders, Little Rock, answered all questions about Arkansas.

Julius Bisno, Los Angeles, the unfailingly helpful source of data on Los Angeles; Dr. Robert Levinson, San Jose, who contributed an immense volume of facts about Northern California and mobilized the help of Stephen D. Kinsey, Suzanne Nemiroff, and Ruth Rafael of the Judah L. Magnes Memorial Museum in Berkeley, California, whose help was priceless; Seymour Fromer, of the Judah L. Magnes Memorial Museum, who put his staff's know-how at our disposal; Dr. Norton B. Stern, Santa Monica, who provided a large volume of data on Southern California; and Henry Schwartz, our valuable source on San Diego.

Mrs. Sam Uchill, Denver, who added much to the accuracy of the facts about Colorado; Mrs. Morris N. Cohen, West Hartford, who checked out everything for the Hartford area of Connecticut; Rabbi Arthur A. Chiel, Woodbridge, who did the same for the New Haven area; Rabbi David Geffen, Wilmington, who added greatly to the data on Delaware; Lillian Barsky and Robert Shosteck, whose expertise on Washington, D.C., was put at our disposal; Richard Rosichan and Vivian Becker, Miami, who updated the data on the Greater Miami area and other fast-growing parts of Florida.

Vida Goldgar and Adolph Rosenberg, Atlanta, who were unfailingly cooperative on Georgia; Mrs. Rachel Heimovics, Evanston, whose knowledge and resourcefulness were an invaluable asset in preparing the Chicago segment and the rest of Illinois; Joseph Levine, Fort Wayne, who had all the answers for Indiana; David Berman, Lexington, who checked out the data on Kentucky; Rabbi David Lefkowitz, Jr., Shreveport, who responded to our queries on Louisiana.

Dr. Moses Aberbach, Baltimore, who provided much information about Baltimore and the rest of Maryland; Bernard Wax, Boston, executive director, American

Jewish Historical Society, and Robert Brauner, of "Jewish Boston," who checked out the entire Massachusetts chapter and provided much new data; Irving Katz, Detroit, who contributed much information about all of Michigan; Leo Frisch, Minneapolis, who checked out all of Minnesota; Rabbi Leo E. Turitz, Meridian, who added considerable data on Mississippi; Frank J. Adler, Kansas City, who checked out the Greater Kansas City area in the Missouri chapter; and Dan Makovsky, who checked out the St. Louis area and added much new material.

Carol Gendler, Omaha, who provided data on Nebraska; Saul Schwartz and William Pages, South Orange, who checked all data for Essex County, New Jersey; Rabbi M. Reuben Kesner, Whiteville, and Dr. Abram Kanof, who added much data on North Carolina; Sarah Grossman, Cincinnati, who checked out all the data for Cincinnati; Judah Rubinstein, Cleveland, who checked out all data for Greater Cleveland; Nathan Loshak and Julius Livingston, Tulsa, who provided much Oklahoma material; Rabbi Joshua Stampfer, who added greatly to the data on Oregon; Maurie H. Orodenker, Philadelphia, who checked out all data on Greater Philadelphia and added much new information; Mrs. Ida Cohen Selavan, Pittsburgh, who checked out all data on Pittsburgh and Western Pennsylvania and added much new material; Mrs. Seebert J. Goldowsky, Providence, who checked out all Rhode Island data and provided new information.

Stanford M. Adelstein, Rapid City, who reviewed all South Dakota data and added considerable new information; Jack Lieberman, Memphis, who checked out all of Tennessee data; Mrs. Perry Kallison, San Antonio, who reviewed the entire Texas chapter, adding much new data and helping to avoid errors of omission and commission; Seymour Siegel, Houston, who checked out the Texas data; and Edward B. Eisen, Salt Lake City, who reviewed the Utah data.

Fred W. Windmueller, who checked out all the Richmond, Virginia, data; Mrs. Jeanette B. Schrieber, Aberdeen, who checked out all the Washington material; Jocelyn Cooper, Wheeling, who added much to the West Virginia chapter; Rabbi Manfred E. Swarsensky, Madison, who checked out all the Wisconsin material.

To all of the following, we also tip our hats in thanks:

ALABAMA
Board of Education, Birmingham
Friedman Library, Tuscaloosa
Rabbi Harrold A. Friedman, Mobile
* Rabbi J. S. Gallinger, Birmingham
Mendel P. Goldstein, Mobile
Ralph G. Holberg, Jr., Mobile
John A. Newfield, New York City
University of Alabama, Birmingham

ALASKA
Anchorage Public Library
E. L. Bartlett, Nome
Chaplain Israel Haber, Anchorage
Dr. Isaac Knoll, Sitka
Chaplain Theodore H. Staiman, Anchorage
State Department of Community and
Regional Affairs, Nome
U.S. Department of Interior, Anchorage

ARIZONA
Dr. Merrill M. Abeshaus, Flagstaff
Arizona Highway Department, Phoenix
D.A. Gershaw, Yuma
Rabbi David B. Kaplan, Yuma
Rev. Francis J. O'Reilly, Chandler
Hyman B. Parks, Sun City
Rabbi Albert Plotkin, Phoenix
Tucson Public Schools
Stewart L. Udall, Tucson
Henry F. Unger, Phoenix

ARKANSAS
Alan Altheimer, Chicago
Lewis T. Apple, Little Rock
Sam Levitt, Jonesboro
Hugh Park, Van Buren
* Rabbi Samson A. Shain, Lancaster, Pa.

CALIFORNIA
Hal Altman, Sacramento
Brandeis Camp Institute
Calavaras Publishing Co., Angels Camp
City of Hope, Duarte
Cottage of Israel, San Diego
Sidney Eisenshtat, Los Angeles

Geoffrey Fisher, San Francisco,
San Francisco Jewish Bulletin
Rabbi Joseph Gitin, San Jose
Rabbi David L. Greenberg, Fresno
Herbert Luft, Beverly Hills
Judas L. Magnes Memorial Library
Dr. A.P. Nasatir, San Diego
Rabbi Bernard D. Rosenberg, Stockton
Santa Barbara Museum of Natural History
Santa Barbara Public Library
Santa Rosa-Sonoma County Free Public
Library, Santa Rosa
Save-the-Redwoods League, San Francisco
Skirball Museum, Los Angeles
Ephraim Spivak, Sacramento
Stanford University, Stanford
Tom Tugend, Los Angeles
University of California, Berkley
University of California at Los Angeles
University of Southern California,
Los Angeles
Rabbi Isaiah Zeldin, Los Angeles

COLORADO
Robert Gamzey, Denver,
Intermountain Jewish News
Mrs. Miriam Goldberg, Denver,
Intermountain Jewish News
Mrs. Harry Hoffman, Denver
Ida Hurwitz, Denver
National Jewish Hospital, Denver
Oscar Sladek, Denver
University of Colorado, Boulder
University of Denver

CONNECTICUT
Rabbi Abraham N. AvRutick, Hartford
Connecticut College, New London
Berthold Gaster, Hartford,
Connecticut Jewish Ledger
Rabbi Melvin Jay Glatt, Stratford
Rabbi Theodore Gluck, Derby

CONNECTICUT
Jewish Historical Society of Greater
Hartford
Rabbi Samuel M. Silver, Stamford
Submarine Library, Groton
University of Bridgeport
University of Hartford
David P. Ward, Hartford
Yale University, New Haven

DELAWARE
Mrs. Nina Roffman, Wilmington
Winterthur Museum, Winterthur

DISTRICT OF COLUMBIA
A.F. of L.—C.I.O.
American University
Architect of The Capitol
Armed Forces Institute of Pathology
Meyer Brissman
Seymour S. Cohen
Department of State
Julian Feldman
Albert Friedman, *Jewish Week*
Saul Goldberg
Rabbi Joshua O. Haberman
Moe Hoffman
Samuel Holland
Jewish Historical Society of
Greater Washington
Jewish War Veterans of the U.S.A.
Library of Congress
Military Chaplains Association of U.S.A.
National Historical Wax Museum
National Park Service
Rabbi Stanley Rabinowitz
Bernard Simon
Smithsonian Institution
Supreme Court of the U.S.
United States Board of Geographic Names
U.S. Department of Commerce
U.S. Postal Service
Veterans of Foreign Wars of U.S.
Harry S. Wender

FLORIDA
I. Edward Adler, West Palm Beach
Rabbi Herbert Baumgard, Coral Gables
Harold H. Benowitz, Maitland
Myron A. Berezin, Miami
Myron J. Brodie, Miami
Department of Parks and Recreation,
Miami Beach
Rabbi David Max Eichhorn,
Satellite Beach
Mrs. Norman Elson, Coral Gables
Florida Department of Transportation,
Tallahassee

Florida State Chamber of Commerce,
Jacksonville
International Swimming Hall of Fame,
Fort Lauderdale
Rabbi Sidney M. Lefkowitz, Jacksonville
H. Irwin Levy, West Palm Beach
Seymour B. Liebman, Miami
Isadore Moskowitz, Jacksonville
Leonard Neuman, Hollywood
Palm Beach Atlantic College, Palm Beach
Palm Beach Times, West Palm Beach
Fred K. Shochet, Miami, *Jewish Floridian*
Nathan Skolnick, Miami
Rabbi David J. Susskind, St. Petersburg
University of Florida, Gainesville
University of Miami, Coral Gables
University of Tampa
Samuel W. Wolfson High School,
Jacksonville

GEORGIA
D.A. Byck, Savannah
Irwin B. Giffen, Savannah
Rabbi Alfred L. Goodman, Columbus
Paul Kulick, Savannah
Rabbi Abraham I. Rosenberg, Savannah

HAWAII
Jacob Adler, Honolulu
Morris N. Freedman, Honolulu
Bernard H. Levinson, Honolulu
Rabbi Roy A. Rosenberg, Honolulu
Rabbi Alexander Segel, Honolulu
Chaplain Samuel Sobel, Fort Belvoir, Va.
Kenneth C. Zwerin, Honolulu

IDAHO
Boise Public Library
Secretary of State, Boise
Sun Valley Travels, Sun Valley
Temple Emanuel, Pocatello

ILLINOIS
Board of Education, Waukegan
Chicago Board of Rabbis
Hebrew Theological College, Chicago
Illinois Institute of Technology, Chicago
Illinois State Historical Society,
Springfield
International Museum of Surgical
Science, Chicago
Julian Jablin, Skokie
La Salle Public Library
Howard B. Lazar, Northfield
McCormick Place, Chicago
Maywood Public Library
Northwestern University, Evanston
Hyman Ruffman, East St. Louis
Walter H. Sobel, Chicago
University of Chicago
University of Illinois at Medical Center,
Chicago
Village of Skokie

INDIANA

Alexandrian Free Public Library,
Mt. Vernon
Hammond Public Library
Indiana Harbor Public Library
Frank H. Newman, Indianapolis
Terre Haute Public Library
Valparaiso Public Library
Whiting Public Library

IOWA

Burlington Public Library
Cedar Rapids Public Library
Gerald S. Ferman, Des Moines
Fort Dodge Public Library
Rabbi Jay B. Goldburg, Des Moines
Herbert Hoover Library, West Branch
Oscar Littlefield, Sioux City
Mason City Public Library
Musser Public Library, Muscatine
Temple B'nai Jeshurun, Des Moines

KANSAS

Baker University, Baldwin
Boot Hill Museum, Dodge City
Dodge City Chamber of Commerce
Humboldt Public Library
Kansas State University, Manhattan
Pittsburgh Public Library
Salina Public Library
Rabbi Elbert S. Sapinsley, Topeka
Frank B. Stiefel, Salina
University of Kansas, Lawrence

KENTUCKY

Ashland Public Library
Moses Bohn, Hopkinsville
Herman Landau, Louisville
William W. Orbach, Louisville
Owensboro Public Library
Paducah Public Library
St. Joseph's Church, Bardstown
Southern Baptist Theological Seminary,
Louisville
University of Louisville

LOUISIANA

Rabbi Murray Blackman, New Orleans
B'nai Israel Synagogue, Alexandria
Daily Iberian, New Iberia
Morton J. Gaba, New Orleans
Jewish Welfare Federation, Baton Rouge
New Orleans Public Library
Orleans Parish School Board, New Orleans
Rabbi Marvin M. Reznikoff, Baton Rouge

MAINE

Rabbi David Berent, Lewiston
Colby College, Waterville
Barnett I. Shur, Portland

MARYLAND

Dept. of Economic Development of
State of Maryland, Annapolis
Johns Hopkins University, Baltimore
Samuel Lichtenstein, Silver Spring
Maryland Institute College of Art,
Baltimore
Maryland Jewish Historical Society,
Baltimore
Enoch Pratt Free Library, Baltimore
Secretary of State, Annapolis
Mrs. Abraham D. Spinak, Pocomoke City
Samuel S. Strouse, Baltimore
Lowell E. Sunderland, Columbia
Dr. Daniel Thursz, Baltimore
United States Naval Academy, Annapolis
University of Maryland, College Park
Joseph Weinstein, Baltimore
Wheaton Public Library

MASSACHUSETTS

American Jewish Historical Society,
Waltham
Ashland Public Schools
Boston Public Library
Boston Symphony Orchestra
Boston University
Brandeis University, Waltham
Isaac Fein, Boston
Genesis 2, Cambridge
Eli Grad, Brookline
Harvard University, Cambridge
"Jewish Boston," Boston
Jewish Community Council of Greater
Boston
Gerald A. Kleinman, North Dartmouth
Naismith Basketball Hall of Fame,
Springfield
Mrs. David Rappaport, Oak Bluffs
Dr. Samuel Rosenfeld, Burlington
Rabbi H. David Rutman, Milford
Robert E. Segal, Boston
Rabbi Herman E. Snyder, Springfield
State Library of Commonwealth of
Massachusetts, Boston

MICHIGAN

William Avrunin, Detroit
Stanley J. Elias, Trenton
Mrs. J.M. Fivenson, Traverse City
Rabbi Richard C. Hertz, Detroit
John Henry Richter, Ann Arbor
Irwin Shaw, Detroit
Philip Slomowitz, *Jewish News*, Detroit

MINNESOTA

Rabbi Allen Bennett, Rochester
Norman Gold, *American Jewish World*,
Minneapolis

MINNESOTA

Rabbi Arnold M. Goldman, Minneapolis
St. Paul Public Library
State of Minnesota Dept. of Business
Development, St. Paul

MISSISSIPPI

Cong. Beth Israel, Biloxi
Hebrew Union Congregation, Greenville
Rabbi Benjamin Schultz, Clarksdale
Society of the Divine Word, Bay Saint
Louis
Temple B'nai Israel, Natchez
Karl Weil, Port Gibson

MISSOURI

Rabbi Stephen A. Arnold, St. Joseph
Cape Girardeau Public Library
Robert Cohn, *Jewish Light*, St. Louis
Culver-Stockton College, Canton
Division of Parks and Recreation of the
City of St. Louis
Milton Firestone, *Jewish Chronicle*,
Kansas City
Rabbi Morris B. Margolies, Kansas City
Dr. Mitchell J. Rosenblatt, Columbia
Rabbi Alvan D. Rubin, St. Louis
Rabbi Jeffrey Stiffman, St. Louis
Washington University, St. Louis

MONTANA

Rabbi Samuel Horowitz, Butte

NEBRASKA

Rabbi Kenneth Bromberg, Omaha
Mrs. Morton Greenberg, Tustin, Calif.

NEVADA

Rabbi Erwin L. Herman, Los Angeles
Rabbi Harry Sherer, Las Vegas
Jack Tell, *Las Vegas Israelite*, Las Vegas

NEW HAMPSHIRE

Dartmouth College, Hanover
Rabbi Bela Fisher, Nashua
Rabbi Oscar Fleishaker, Portsmouth
Kevin Lowther, Keene
Manchester City Library
Portsmouth Public Library

NEW JERSEY

Rabbi Aaron Chomsky, West New York
Fairleigh Dickinson University,
Rutherford
Dr. Harold Gabel, Oakhurst
Arthur A. Goldberg, Jersey City
Sam Hatow, Paterson
Zev Hymowitz, West Orange
Howard A. Kieval, Highland Park
Dr. Harry B. Lasker, North Brunswick
Rabbi Pesach Z. Levovitz, Lakewood
Rabbi Ely E. Pilchik, Short Hills
Mrs. Adolf Robinson, Teaneck

Rutgers University, New Brunswick
Rabbi Sidney Schulman, Asbury Park
Israel Silver, Perth Amboy
Rabbi Abraham Simon, Bridgeton
Rabbi Howard A. Simon, Margate
Rabbi Sheldon J. Weltman, Morristown

NEW MEXICO

Mrs. Melwin J. Klein, Las Cruces
Rabbi Abraham I. Shinedling,
Albuquerque
Rabbi David D. Shor, Albuquerque
Judge Lewis Sutin, Santa Fe

NEW YORK CITY

Samuel H. Abramson
American Jewish Committee
American Veterans of Israel
Board of Jewish Education
Brooklyn Museum
Sam Brown
Central Conference of American Rabbis
City College
Columbia University
Rabbi Wayne D. Dosick
Encyclopedia Judaica
Federation Employment and Guidance
Service
Federation of Jewish Philanthropies
Dr. Louis Finkelstein
Rabbi Joseph Gelberman
Leonard Gold
Rabbi Harold H. Gordon
Leslie Gottlieb
Sam Hartstein
* Harry Herbert
Jewish Association for Services for the
Aged
Jewish Theological Seminary of America
Mae Koppman
Rabbi Yehuda Krinsky
Brenda Leibowitz
Sesil Lissberger
Metropolitan New York Coordinating
Council of Jewish Poverty
National Council of Young Israel
New York University
New York Board of Rabbis
Susan Nueckel
Pace University
Rabbinical Assembly
Rabbinical Council of America
Ramah Camps
George Salomon
Morris U. Schappes
Abner Sideman
Belle Sideman
Henry B. Stern
Rabbi Malcolm Stern
Union of American Hebrew
Congregations

NEW YORK CITY
Union of Orthodox Jewish Congregations
United Jewish Council of the East Side
United Synagogue of America
Professor Gerard R. Wolfe
Workmen's Circle
Marjorie Wyler

NEW YORK STATE
Albany Medical Center
Amsterdam Public Library
Beth El Synagogue, New Rochelle
B'nai Israel Congregation, Olean
Buffalo and Erie County Public Library
Sam Clevenson, *Jewish World,* Albany
Cornell University, Ithaca
Rabbi Herman Eisner, Ellenville
Ellenville Journal
Finkelstein Memorial Library,
  Spring Valley
Rabbi Samuel Z. Glaser, Elmont
Gloversville Chamber of Commerce
William Grossman, Amherst
Harrison School District
Jewish Community Federation of
  Rochester
Marian Kramer, Rockville Centre
Samuel Kurzon, Albany
Long Island State Park & Recreation
  Commission, Babylon
Merchants Association of Sag Harbor
Nassau County Museum, Syosset
National Baseball Hall of Fame,
  Cooperstown
National Museum of Racing, Saratoga
  Springs
New York State Court of Appeals,
  Albany
Greater Newburgh Chamber of Commerce
New York State Dept. of Law, Albany
New York State Office of General
  Services, Albany
Orange County Historian, Goshen
Norman Pallay, North Bellmore
C.W. Post Center of Long Island
  University, Greenvale
Pound Ridge Public Library
Mrs. Arthur H. Printz, Hampton Bays
Rochester Public Library
Franklin D. Roosevelt Library, Hyde Park
Sagamore Hill National Historic Site,
  Oyster Bay
St. Bonaventure University,
  St. Bonaventure
Saranac Lake Free Library
Schenectady Museum
Mrs. Morris Shimansky, Amityville
State Education Dept., Albany
State University of New York
  at Purchase

Ella Stuzin, Monticello
Suffolk County Historical Society,
  Riverhead
Sullivan County Historian, Hurleyville
Sullivan County Publicity and Tourist
  Dept., Monticello
Syracuse University
Town of Bedford, Bedford Hills
Town of Huntington
Town of Monroe
Town of Wawarsing, Ellenville
Union College, Schenectady
U.S. Military Academy, West Point
University of Rochester
Donald Wolin, *Jewish Ledger,* Rochester
Yonkers Dept. of Parks and Recreation

NORTH CAROLINA
I.D. Blumenthal, Charlotte
Irving S. Cheroff, Fayetteville
Rabbi Martin M. Weitz, San Diego,
  California

NORTH DAKOTA
Rabbi Jeffrey Bearman, Fargo
Toba Geller, Fargo
OHIO
Antioch College, Yellow Springs
Rabbi Morton M. Applebaum, Akron
Aviation Hall of Fame, Dayton
Stanley Chyet, Los Angeles, Calif.
Cleveland Public Library
Rabbi Gordon L. Geller, Elyria
Mrs. Anne Hammerman, *Jewish Chronicle,*
  Dayton
Ben Mandelkorn, Columbus
Dr. Jacob R. Marcus, Cincinnati
Ohio Historical Society, Columbus
Ohio State University, Columbus
Sidney J. Silvian, Cincinnati
Rabbi Gerald Turk, Kent
Julius Weil, Shaker Heights
OKLAHOMA
Fort Sill Information Office, Fort Sill
Melvin Moran, Seminole
Muskogee Public Library
Walter Neustadt, Jr., Ardmore
Oklahoma Hall of Fame, Oklahoma City
Oklahoma State University, Stillwater
Meyer Sobol, Oklahoma City
Tulsa City-County Library System, Tulsa
OREGON
Sylvan F. Durkheimer, Portland
Rabbi Louis Neimand, Eugene
Oregon Museum of Science & Industry,
  Portland
Oregon State University, Corvallis
Portland Art Museum
Arthur C. Spence, Portland

PENNSYLVANIA
Albert W. Bloom, Pittsburgh,
  Pittsburgh Jewish Chronicle
Leon Brown, *Jewish Times*, Philadelphia
Bucks County Dept. of Parks &
  Recreation, Doylestown
Cambria County Library System,
  Johnstown
Rabbi Robert Chernoff, Chambersburg
Commissioner of Fairmount Park,
  Philadelphia
Drexel University, Philadelphia
Dropsie University, Philadelphia
Federation of Jewish Agencies,
  Philadelphia
Mrs. Lillian Mermin Feinsilver, Easton
Franklin Mint, Franklin Center
Freedoms Foundation, Valley Forge
Hebrew Sunday School Society,
  Philadelphia
Thomas Jefferson University,
  Philadelphia
Juniata College, Huntingdon
Dr. Bertram W. Korn, Philadelphia
Lions Club, Glassport
Mikveh Israel Cong., Philadelphia
Leon J. Obermayer, Philadelphia
Pennsylvania Historical and Museum
  Commission, Harrisburg
Pennsylvania State University,
  Middletown
Philadelphia Jewish Archives
Philadelphia Museum of Art
Philadelphia '76 Inc.
Philadelphia Union of Jewish Students
Pittsburgh Baseball Club
Sayre Public Library
Rabbi Elihu Schagrin, Coatesville
School District of Philadelphia
A. Singer, Middletown
Temple University, Philadelphia
University of Pennsylvania, Philadelphia
University of Pittsburgh
Rabbi David H. Wice, Philadelphia
Rabbi Leonard Winograd, McKeesport
Wolfsohn Memorial Library, King of
  Prussia
Rabbi Gerald I. Wolpe, Philadelphia
Frank F. Wundohl, Philadelphia,
  Philadelphia Jewish Exponent
York School District

RHODE ISLAND
Brown University, Providence
Jewish Community Relations Council of
  Rhode Island, Providence
Rhode Island Jewish Historical
  Association, Providence
Jesse M. Smith Memorial Library,
  Harrisville

SOUTH CAROLINA
City of Rock Hill
College of Charleston
Cong. Beth Elohim, Charleston
Mrs. Herbert A. Rosefield, Sumter
South Carolina Confederate Relic Room,
  Columbia
University of South Carolina, Columbia

SOUTH DAKOTA
Manny Feinstein, South Aberdeen
University of South Dakota, Vermillion

TENNESSEE
Churchmen's Sports Hall of Fame,
  Tullahoma
Harriet Cohn Guidance Center, Clarksville
Memphis Eye, Ear, Nose and Throat
  Hospital, Memphis
Oak Ridge Institute of Nuclear Studies,
  Oak Ridge
Siskin Memorial Foundation, Chattanooga

TEXAS
Seymour Cohen, Houston
El Paso Public Library
Rabbi Harold A. Friedman, Waco
Rabbi Newton J. Friedman, Beaumont
Mrs. I.B. Goodman, El Paso
Philip Hewitt, San Antonio
Harry R. Rosen, Dallas
David M. Seligman, Edna
Southern Methodist University, Dallas
Shimshon Zeevi, San Antonio

UTAH
Rabbi Abner L. Bergman, Salt Lake City

VERMONT
Rabbi Max B. Wall, Burlington

VIRGINIA
Mrs. Ruth Sinberg Baker, Alexandria
Leroy S. Bendheim, Alexandria
Department of Defense, Arlington
Fort Monroe Casemate Museum,
  Fort Monroe
Thomas Jefferson Institute for Study
  of Religious Freedom, Fredericksburg
Mrs. Murray Loring, Williamsburg
Mariners Museum, Newport News
Rabbi Philip Pincus, Virginia Beach
Chaplain Samuel Sobel, Fort Belvoir
Saul Viener, Richmond
Virginia Military Institute, New Market
Virginia Museum of Fine Arts, Richmond

WASHINGTON
Seattle Chamber of Commerce
Murray Shiff, Seattle
State Capitol Museum, Olympia
University of Washington Libraries,
  Seattle

WEST VIRGINIA
Rabbi Philip M. Aronson, Huntington
Rabbi Samuel Cooper, Charleston
Edward I. Eiland, Logan
Kanawha County Public Library,
Charleston
WISCONSIN
Edwarde Perlson, Milwaukee
Mrs. Norton Stoler, Madison
University of Wisconsin-Milwaukee,
Waukesha Chamber of Commerce
Jack Wiener, Milwaukee
Wisconsin Society for Jewish Learning,
Milwaukee
Melvin Zaret, Milwaukee

WYOMING
Mrs. Martin Bernstein, Cheyenne
Mrs. Joseph Feldman, Cheyenne
Laramie County Library, Cheyenne
Laramie County School District No. 1,
Cheyenne
Steve Weinstein, Laramie
University of Wyoming, Laramie
Wyoming State Archives and Historical
Department, Cheyenne

* Deceased

Contents

note

A new national program to provide Orthodox Jewish
travelers with local information centers for their
unique needs while traveling has been instituted by
Agudath Israel of America. Information encompassing
many areas of the United States, Canada, and Mexico,
regarding kosher food, synagogues, and other pertinent
information can be obtained by writing: Agudath Israel
of America, 5 Beekman Street, New York, N. Y. 10025.

JEWISH LANDMARKS SERIES

American Jewish Landmarks

a travel guide and history

Alabama

Montgomery, which became the capital of Alabama and the first capital of the Confederate States of America, was founded by a colorful Jewish character known at times as "Old Mordecai," "Muccose," or "The Little Chief." His full name was Abraham Mordecai and he was not only the first-known Jewish settler in what is now Alabama, but also the first native-born American to take up residence in the area now occupied by Montgomery. When he died in 1850, the *Montgomery Evening News* proposed that the city erect "a monument to the name and memory of Old Mordecai, the cradle-rocker of Montgomery's infancy," on City Square, the city's most beautiful plaza.

Born in Pennsylvania in the 1750s (1751 or 1755), Mordecai came to Montgomery County in 1785 after having served in the American Revolutionary army for three years. Before coming to Montgomery County, he lived in Tallapoosa County, where he built a log storehouse and embarked on a career as an Indian trader.

In 1800, Mordecai moved his headquarters to the west shore of the Alabama River, on the present site of Montgomery, in order to expedite his trading with Mobile and New Orleans. From both cities he received goods which he bartered with the Indians for furs, skins, and hickory nut oil, a special delicacy to the Spanish who controlled New Orleans until 1799.

From Tallapoosa and Montgomery Counties, Mordecai penetrated the wilderness beyond the Pensacola Trail in his trading with Indians, among whom he spent much of his life. In the 20 years during which he carried on extensive business with the Indians, he went on special missions for James Seagrove, the Indian agent of the region. Once Mordecai went into the heart of the Chickasaw Nation on a peace mission, and on another occasion, he visited Creek tribal chiefs to arrange for the ransom of settlers whom the Indians had taken captive in what is now Kentucky. Over the years, he acquired a thorough knowledge of Spanish, and was equally conversant in the languages of the Creeks and the Chickasaws.

In 1802, Mordecai established the first cotton gin in Alabama, on the eastern half of the bluff below the junction of the Coosa and Tallapoosa Rivers. Soon after, a band of Coosawada Indians raided his property and burned down the gin after beating Mordecai and amputating his left ear. One version of the attack is that some of Mordecai's horses had trampled the Indians' cornfields and Chief Towerculla used this as an excuse to drive out the white man. Another version claims that the Indians were angry because Mordecai engaged in a liaison with an Indian woman. In 1813, Mordecai married an Indian woman, who went with him to Georgia when he served with General Floyd's Militia in the Indian wars. In 1836, he returned to Alabama without his Indian wife, who was separated from him when the United States Government ordered the Indian tribes in the area to move westward.

Mordecai settled in an abandoned Indian hut in Dudleyville, a hamlet on the outskirts of Montgomery. There, Albert James Pickett, a journalist and historian, found him in 1847, living alone, a pauper dependent on neighbors for support. When Pickett talked to him, Mordecai had already built his own coffin. It stood in the hut beside an old chest and a rough table on which rested a Hebrew Bible.

According to Pickett, Mordecai firmly believed the Indians to be descendants of the "Ten Lost Tribes of Israel," and never despaired of hearing a Hebrew answer from some Indian to his repeated Hebrew questions. Mordecai's belief in the Indians' Hebraic ancestry was bolstered by their chants of *Yavohoya, Yavohoya*, during their green corn dances. This, Pickett said, reminded Mordecai of Jehovah, and the Indians told him that the chant referred to the Great Spirit to whom they gave thanks for an abundant harvest. Of course, no Jew with even the most elementary knowledge of Hebrew would use anything but *Adonai* for the name of God, so it is likely that this episode was in part a creation of Pickett's imagination.

"Old Mordecai" was not the first Jew to do business in Mobile, which was the capital of the Louisiana Territory when it was French controlled. Under the French Black Code of 1724, all Jews were barred from the colony. However, one Rodriguez, a member of the West Indiana firm of Julien and Rodriguez, conducted business in Mobile in July, 1763. Actually, as Dr.

Bertram W. Korn, the eminent historian, has pointed out, neither law nor custom prevented Jews from settling in Mobile under the French, but the fact that New Orleans was a more prominent location for the trading ventures through which the early Jews in that area made their living, attracted them to the city at the mouth of the Mississippi.

When Mobile became part of British West Florida in 1763, at least three Jewish merchants—Joseph de Palacios, Samuel Israel, and Alexander Salomon—acquired considerable real estate in the city, and also dealt in money, merchandise, livestock, commodities, and slave ownership. De Palacios was imprisoned for debt for nearly two years before he left Mobile. Israel left in 1770, and Salomon appears to have followed in 1774. The latter's brother, Haym (not the celebrated Philadelphia patriot of that name), remained in Mobile until it was seized by the Spanish in 1780-1781, according to Korn.

No permanent Jewish settlement occurred in Mobile until the 1820s, although Jewish merchants continued to travel in and out of Mobile on business. One of these was Samuel Myers of Pensacola. Another was a Mr. Judah, who arrived in April, 1822, and gave recitations and dramatic readings. He became a theatrical impresario and also conducted a private school in Spring Hill, just outside Mobile, in 1822.

In 1823, Dr. Solomon Mordecai established himself as a physician in Mobile where he became a leading figure in the city's civic life. A year later, George Davis, an English Jew who had owned a store in Tuscaloosa since 1820, moved to Mobile. There, at various times, he owned a store, kept a livery stable, operated an inn, and was the city's first auctioneer. He was also the local agent for a New Orleans Jewish slave dealer named Levy Jacobs.

Jacobs himself turned up in Mobile in 1827. That same year, Isaac Lazarus, a former *schochet* for Mikveh Israel Congregation in Philadelphia, and his brother, Henry, opened a store in Mobile, bought and sold land, hawked patent medicines, and acted as agents for Isaac's wealthy brother-in-law, John Moss, the Philadelphia merchant shipper. Isaac's son, also named Henry, emancipated a slave in Mobile in 1834.

Solomon Jones, an English Jew, came to Mobile in 1830 and operated a cleaning and dyeing shop. Two years later, his brother Sol arrived. By 1837, the Jones brothers were operating an auction house. Sol later became a trustee of Congregation Shaari Shomayim, the first synagogue in Alabama. His wife, however, was not Jewish, and their daughter was reared as a Christian. In the register of Mobile's St. John's Episcopal Church, however, Mrs. Jones and her daughter were listed as "Jewish."

Solomon Jones became a city alderman, a lieutenant colonel in the state militia, and treasurer of the Grand Lodge of Masons of Alabama. His brother, Israel, also served as an alderman and acting mayor. He was the founder of the Mobile Musical Association, organizer of the city's first streetcar line, and the first and perennial president of Congregation Shaari Shomayim. In 1860, he was elected a vice-president of the Board of Delegates of American Israelites, the first national Jewish body. His youngest daughter married Rabbi James K. Gutheim, who was such a strong supporter of the Confederacy that he closed the doors of his New Orleans synagogue, Congregation Nefutzoth Yehudah, when the Union forces captured the city in 1862. Gutheim then filled pulpits in Montgomery, Alabama, and Columbus, Georgia, until the Civil War ended.

In the 1830s, Simon and Cauffman Oppenheimer of New Orleans bought and sold land in Mobile. A Mrs. Cohen conducted a school in the city from 1833-1837. Mrs. Jane da Costa and her sister and brother-in-law owned a drygoods store in Mobile from 1833-1842. Abraham Wolff opened a wine and liquor store in 1834.

Solomon Andrews, one of the many grandsons of the Revolutionary War patriot, Haym Salomon, moved his cotton factoring business in 1835 to Mobile from Huntsville and Tuscaloosa, where he had been established with his brothers. Sol left Mobile in 1837 after the panic of that year, but his brother Eliezer Lewis Andrews, arrived in the city in 1839.

Ezekiel Salomon, another grandson of the Philadelphia patriot, migrated to Mobile from Philadelphia in 1836. His first son, Lewis Judson Salomon, was a prominent Mobile civic figure until he moved to New Orleans in 1849. He became the first Rex (king) of the city's famed Mardi Gras in 1872. His brother, David, who settled in Mobile in 1839, was also a civic leader, and served as the first vice-president of Shaari Shomayim.

Other Jewish settlers in Mobile in the late 1830s and early 1840s were Moses Harris, a cotton factor; Isaac Isaacs, a dealer in provisions; Isaac Kohn, a locksmith; Dr. Joseph Bensadon, a dentist; Jacob S. Cohen, a city marshal; L. Goldsmith, a tailer; Isaac Moses, a tobacconist; Dr. Aaron Lopez, a physician; and Solomon Heydenfeldt and Philip Phillips, lawyers.

Dr. Lopez, a member of the class of 1822 of Columbia College of Physicians and Surgeons, opened an office in Mobile in 1841. He was one of the founders of the Mobile Medical Association, as well as the Alabama Medical Association, of which he became president in 1849. Lopez was a delegate to the founding convention of the American Medical Association in 1848, and was elected a vice-president in 1850.

Philip Phillips, described by Bertram W. Korn as "perhaps the most accomplished and respected American Jew of the first half of the 19th century," moved from Mobile in 1835 to Charleston, South Carolina. In Charleston he was one of the founders of the Reformed Society of Israelites, the first Reform congregation in the United States, of which he was secretary.

Phillips became a successful and influential member of the bar and leader of the Democratic party in Alabama. In 1844 and again in 1852, he was elected to the state legislature. In 1855 he was elected to Congress, serving one term, after which he settled down in Washington, D.C. Although there is no record of his having joined Congregation Shaari Shomayim in Mobile, he did contribute to a benefit for a new Torah Scroll for the Washington Hebrew Congregation. In 1857 he was the spokesman for a Jewish delegation that called on President James Buchanan to protest against the decision of the United States to sign a commercial treaty with Switzerland which permitted the Swiss cantons to discriminate against American Jews traveling in that country. In 1866, Phillips was the principal speaker at the cornerstone-laying ceremonies of a New Orleans synagogue.

In Congress, Phillips authored the bill that established the Court of Claims. His *Digest of Cases Decided and Reported in the Supreme Court of Alabama in 1844, 1846 and 1849,* was a legal classic. Phillips and his wife were among the handful of Southerners who opposed secession, but were nevertheless obliged to move within the Confederate lines in 1861. While in New Orleans, Mrs. Phillips was imprisoned for three months by General Benjamin Butler for an alleged insult to Union troops after they captured the city in 1862. After her release, she was received as a heroine in the South. Following the Civil War, Phillips returned to Washington where he practiced until his death in 1884. His book, *The Statutory Jurisdiction and Practice of the Supreme Court* went into five editions.

Solomon Heydenfeldt, like Phillips a native of South Carolina, arrived in Alabama in 1837. Three years later he was a judge of the Tallapoosa County Court. Later, he practiced law in Russell County, and in 1842 he was an unsuccessful candidate for judge of the Mobile County Court. A strong opponent of slavery on economic grounds, Heydenfeldt wrote the governor of Alabama in 1849 to protest the further importation of slaves into the state. He was, however, an ardent "states rights" man, believing that the South would solve the problem of slavery without the interference of the Federal government. He left for California in 1850 where he became a justice of the California Supreme Court in 1852.

Among the few Alabamians who opposed slavery, were the brothers Joseph and Isaac Friedman, merchants in Tuscumbia and Mobile. They bought a slave by the name of Peter Still, and then led him through the underground railway to freedom.

The growth of Mobile's Jewish population in the 1830s and 1840s led to the formation of a Jewish community. Jewish worship services had first been held in the home of Bernhardt L. Tim, who had come to Mobile from New York with letters of recommendation from Jewish congregations there certifying his concern for Jewish observance. In Mobile he went into the shoe business. A deed dated June 22, 1841, records the purchase by "Congregation of Israelites of Shara Shuhmayim of Mobile" of four lots for a cemetery, thus indicating that the synagogue was founded in 1841 or somewhat earlier. In 1843 the congregation was incorporated as Shaari Shomayim U-Maskil El Dol—Congregation of the Gates of Heaven and Society of the Friends of the Needy.

Prior to 1841, the Mobile Jews buried their dead in a Jewish section of the Church Street Graveyard, the oldest non-sectarian cemetery in the city. In the section marked off as "The Oldest Jewish Graves in Alabama," is the grave of Isaac Davis, infant grandson of George Davis, who was buried there in 1829.

Another Jewish community took root in Montgomery. The first Jewish settler there was Jacob Sacerdote, who operated a restaurant at the corner of Montgomery Street and Court Square in the early 1840s. Other pioneer Jewish residents included Henry Isaac, Joseph Young, Isaiah Weil, Freedman Gans, and S.K. Gans, who were among the many German Jewish immigrants who settled in the South in the two decades before the Civil War.

On November 17, 1846, the small Jewish community of 12 families formed the Chevra Mevaker Cholim—Society for Visiting the Sick. One of the founders was Emanuel Lehman, uncle of Herbert H. Lehman, the future Governor of New York and United States Senator. This welfare society acquired a cemetery and conducted worship services. In 1849, the society transformed itself into Congregation Kahl Montgomery, which later changed its name to Temple Beth Ohr.

One of the early members was Jacob Kohn, who arrived in 1848, and the following year opened a shoe store under the name of J.Kohn & Sons. During the Civil War, Kohn and his brother Alexander ran a Confederate shoe factory in Montgomery for the commissary department of the Confederate army.

During the war, some 130 Alabama Jews served in the Confederate forces. Thirteen Mobile Jews enlisted as a group in the 12th Alabama Regiment. The most prominent of them was Adolph Proskauer, the uncle of Judge Joseph M. Proskauer, a New York State Supreme Court Justice, who was the closest political advisor to Governor Alfred A. Smith when he ran for President in 1928, and president of the American Jewish Committee.

Adolph Proskauer enlisted as a corporal and rose to the rank of Major. Badly wounded several times, he was famed for his fearlessness. One fellowsoldier, a non-Jew, paid him this tribute: "I remember him as a brave soldier and a courtly and gallant gentleman. I can see him now as he nobly carried himself at Gettysburg, standing cool and calm with cigar in his mouth, at the head of the 12th Alabama, amid a perfect rain of bullets. He was the personification of courage and gallantry."

When Montgomery became the first capital of the Confederacy, Judah P. Benjamin (see Louisiana) lived there as the Confederacy's first attorney-general. Rabbi Jacob K. Gutheim, who had closed his synagogue in New

Orleans in 1862 rather than live under the Union flag, became the first rabbi of Montgomery's Congregation Kahl Montgomery in 1862. About that time, too, Mayer Lehman, brother of Emanuel, and father of Governor Herbert H. Lehman, was sent to Europe on a secret mission by the Confederate government to sell their bonds.

After the war, Major Proskauer returned to Mobile where he became a leader in the Jewish community. During the tragic Reconstruction era, he was twice elected to the Alabama legislature. Another Jewish soldier from Mobile, Leopold Strauss, who became a captain, also served in the legislature and as a delegate to two Democratic National Conventions. Daniel Bloch, of Mobile, helped redeem Wilcox County from the "carpet-baggers."

Besides Mobile and Montgomery, the only pre-Civil War Jewish communities were: Huntsville (1850); Claiborne, where a short-lived congregation was formed in 1855; and Uniontown. The other older Jewish communities are Selma (1867), Eufala (1870), Birmingham (1882), Sheffield (1884), Demopolis (1886), Bessemer (1891), and Anniston (1893). Virtually all of the older Jewish congregations became Reform by 1890. The East European immigrants who began to settle in Alabama towns and cities after 1880 established their own Orthodox, and later, Conservative synagogues. The Moses brothers of Montgomery were prime movers in establishing the town of Sheffield in 1884.

Alabama's Jewish population grew form 2,045 in 1880 to 6,000 in 1897, 11,086 in 1917, and 12, 891 in 1927. There was a small drop to 12,148 by 1937 and then a sudden increase to 16, 290 in 1948. This was due in large part to the influx of Jews from the North who had trained during World War II at Alabama camps and airbases and came back to settle there, giving new life to many of the smaller Jewish communities facing disintegration through assimilation and intermarriage among the older families.

These older families had important roles in the lives of their communities, as evidenced by the public offices they held. Mobile has had two Jewish mayors, Leon Schwarz (1926, 1932, and 1933), and Lazarus Schwarz (1911-1915). Montgomery has had two Jewish mayors, Henry Faber (1875), and Morris Moses (1884-1888), and Solomon Maas was mayor of Selma (1896-1908). Samuel Ullman (1893-1888) and Benjamin Jacobs (1921-1923) were presidents of Birmingham's board of education. Moses Jacobs was grand master of the Alabama Grand Lodge of Masons in 1906.

In more recent times, Charles N. Feidelson was a municipal judge in Birmingham, and for some years, chief editorial writer of the *Birmingham Age-Herald*. Simon Wampold served as probate judge of Montgomery County. In 1972, Ben Erdreich, whose grandfather, Benjamin Leader, was one of the earliest Jewish residents of Birmingham, lost the Democratic nomination for Congress from the Sixth District. He also served in the State Legislature.

In the 1930s, Rabbi Benjamin Goldstein of Montgomery's Temple Beth Ohr spoke out strongly against the railroading of the Scottsboro Boys —nine young blacks accused of raping two white women. Ultimately the boys were freed, but not before a good deal of anti-Semetic feeling was generated by Goldstein's stand and the involvement of Samuel Leibowitz, the defending attorney form New York. When Goldstein refused to end his protests against the court verdict, the congregation forced his resignation. Though many of his congregants agreed with his stand, they considered his views an open threat to the welfare of the Jewish community.

In 1934, when the Ku Klux Klan was a power in Alabama, State Senator Hodges introduced a bill to invite an interfaith trio of clergymen to address a special session of both houses of the State Legislature. When Rabbi Philip S. Bernstein of Rochester, New York, was presented to Hodges, the Senator greeted him with a "Sholom Aleichem." "I'm a Litvak from Suvalki, Lithuania," Hodges said. His original name was Choydesh and he had come to the town of Fayette around 1900 as an immigrant peddling from house to house, as did many of the Jews in Alabama's small towns before 1914.

One of those who joined the KKK in the 1930s was a young member of the Legislature—Hugo L. Black, later one of the most liberal members of the United States Supreme Court. In a 1967 interview *The New York Times* published after his death, Black said, "It was a Jew, my closest friend, Herman Beck, who asked me to join it (the Klan). He said they needed good people in it. He couldn't be in it, of course, but he wanted me to be in it to keep down the few extremists."

The segregation crisis of the 1950s and 1960s, following the Supreme Court's decision ordering all public schools desegregated, created a terrible dilemma for the Jews in Alabama, as it did for all Jews in the South. The pro-integrationist stand of the national Jewish organizations made Southern Jews fearful that it would threaten the good relations they had with their Christian neighbors. When Rabbi Samuel Atlas of Montgomery participated in a Brotherhood Week program and *Life* Magazine published a picture of him standing next to a black, the trustees of the synagogue asked their rabbi to demand a retraction from *Life*, and a statement in a future issue informing its readers that Brotherhood Week was not involved with blacks, the Supreme Court decision, or the Montgomery bus strike led by the Reverend Martin Luther King, Jr.

One of the first buildings to be bombed by racist bigots in the South was a Birmingham synagogue. The Gadsden synagogue, which had also been fire-bombed, refused in 1958 to contribute to the reward fund for apprehending the criminals.

In the summer of 1963, while Sheriff Bull Connor of Birmingham arrested and herded hundreds of blacks into barbed wire enclosures and turned powerful water hoses on them, a delegation from the Rabbinical Assembly arrived in the city to join the Reverend King's protest against police brutality. Already suffering from the black boycott of white stores, the Jewish community tried vainly to persuade the rabbis to go home, fearing they would make matters worse. Few Jews took a public stand in support of blacks in Alabama, believing they could be of little help and would only leave themselves vulnerable to attack by the White Citizens Councils and reactionary politicians allied with segregationist Governor George Wallace.

Martin Luther King, Jr., commented on the virtual absence of Jewish support for black rights in Alabama. One notable exception was Harold Katz, the executive director of the Birmingham Jewish Community Center, who was later awarded an honorary degree by a black college.

Governor Wallace never disavowed the support of the John Birch Society or the KKK, but no one could point to anything patently anti-Semitic in his utterances or in his attitude toward Jews. In Wallace's 1968 run for the Presidency as the candidate of the American party, all five Jews in the Alabama Legislature campaigned for him. He won only 20 percent of the Jewish vote in Alabama, whereas he had received 90 percent of the Jewish vote ten years earlier when he ran for governor against an avowed Klansman. In the 1972 Presidential primaries, Wallace lost some of the Alabama Jewish vote to Richard Nixon, even though Wallace had announced that he had Jewish relatives by marriage and was a supporter of Israel.

The fight over desegregation and the violence that accompanied it, led many Jews to leave Alabama in the 1960s. By 1970, the Jewish population had fallen to 9,456, an almost 42 percent decline over 1948. In 1975, the Jewish population was 9,850. Birmingham had the largest Jewish community, with 4,160. Other communities were Montgomery, 1,800; Mobile, 1,300; Huntsville, 700; Tuscaloosa, 350; Dothan, 255; Gadsden, 185; Selma, 175; and smaller numbers in Bessemer, Demopolis, Eufala, and Jasper.

* * * * *

ANNISTON
Anniston Hebrew Cong., Quintard at 13th St.

AUBURN
Auburn Hillel Foundation, Auburn University, 442 Cary Dr.

BESSEMER
Gilmore-Cherner Municipal Airport is named in part of the late Bennett L. Cherner, a member of the State Legislature from Jefferson County, who was voted the hardest working member of that body before his death in 1972.
Temple Beth-El, 600 N. 17th St.

BIRMINGHAM

Birmingham Jewish Federation, P.O. Box 9157.

Cong. Beth-El, 2179 Highland Ave.

Jewish Community Center, 3960 Montclair Rd., has a large outdoor sculptured Menorah, 5ft. six inches tall and 9ft. 6 inches wide, on the portico over the main entrance. The Jewish Federation of Birmingham is in the same building. Also there is the Ullman Memorial Library.

Knesseth Israel Cong., 3225 Montevallo Rd.

Miles Library in the Charles Andrew Rush Learning Center of Birmingham-Southern College, 800 8th Ave., W., is named for Dr. N. E. Miles, a Birmingham physician and philanthropist.

Louis Pizitz Junior High School, 2020 Pizitz Dr., in the Vestavia Hills section, is named for a local Jewish philanthropist whose family made extensive gifts of land for public use.

Temple Emanu-El, 2100 Highland, is the oldest congregation in Birmingham, having been founded in 1882. The Morris Newfield Educational Building memorializes Rabbi Morris Newfield, who served the congregation from 1895-1940.

Ullman High School, 625 S. 12th Ave., is named for Samuel Ullman, a Confederate War veteran who served with a Mississippi regiment before settling in Birmingham where he was twice elected president of the board of education (1893-1900 and 1902-1904). His portrait hangs in the lobby. In the Jewish Community Center there is a plaque memorializing him. Ullman and Rabbi Newfield were the principal founders of Birmingham's early YMHA.

University of Alabama

•William P. Engle Psychiatric Day Treatment Center, 1632 7th Ave., S., is named for Birmingham's most prominent Jewish leader, who raised nearly a third of the Center's cost.

•Smolian Psychiatric Clinic, N.E. corn. 7th Ave. and 17th St., S., is named for Mr. and Mrs. Joseph Smolian, Birmingham philanthropists. Smolian House, a student center, is also named for this couple.

•Mervyn H. Sterne Library, 917 S. 13th St., is named for the late civic leader and philanthropist.

CLAIBORNE

Old Jewish Cemetery, on the Alabama River, has graves dating from the early 1850s when there was a flourishing Jewish community here.

DEMOPOLIS

Temple B'nai Jeshurun, Main and Monroe Sts., was founded in 1858. The Jewish community has shrunk to only a handful of families.

DOTHAN

Temple Emanuel, 111 N. Park Ave.

DUDLEYVILLE

Abraham Mordecai's grave lies in the shade of a hickory-nut tree. A roadside memorial marker, erected by the Daughters of the American Revolution, reads: "To the Memory of Abraham Mordecai Soldier of the Pennsylvania Line, American Revolution. Indian Trader and Early Settler in Montgomery County. Scout in Floyd's Georgia Militia, 1814. (Erected by Capt. John Bacon Chapter and Topoheka Chapter.)" Mordecai, the first native-born citizen of the U.S. to settle in what is now Montgomery County, was born in Pennsylvania and when he died in Dudleyville in 1850, he was almost 100 years of age (see introduction).

FALKVILLE

This town on Highway 31, 15 miles south of Decatur, is named for Louis Faulk, a Civil War veteran who opened a store in 1874 at what was then a crossroads in Morgan County. He came here after three years as a prisoner of war. He became the first merchant and postmaster of the town that grew up around his store. His grandson, Louis F. Oberdorfer, who had served as law secretary to Supreme Court Justice Hugo Black, later served as an Assistant U.S. Attorney General in the administration of President John F. Kennedy.

FLORALA

Florala Memorial Hospital, off U.S. Highway 331, on the border of Alabama and Florida, was erected by the Israel Gitenstein , Samuel Green, and the Rose Bralower Gitenstein Foundation, established by Seymour and Anna Green Gitenstein in memory of their parents. The 28-bed hospital stands on the site of the old Covington High School. When that building was razed, the Gitensteins bought the site for the hospital. The seven huge stained glass windows on either side of the hospital's entrance were salvaged from the old Beth Ohr Temple in Montgomery, Ala.

FLORENCE

Louis Rosenbaum Room in the Florence-Lauderdale Public Library, North Wood Ave., memorializes a civic leader and synagogue officer whose $40,000 gift was the incentive toward the fulfillment of the city's 60-year dream of a library building. A plaque in the lobby reads: "In appreciation, Louis Rosenbaum and Stanley Rosenbaum whose original gifts presented the challenge accepted by the citizens of our community which made possible the erection of this building."

Temple B'nai Israel of the Tri-cities Jewish Congregation, 201 Hawthorne St., serves the Jewish communities of Florence, Sheffield,

Tuscumbia, Athens, Decatur, Haleyville, Moulton, and Russellville. An etched glass memorial to the victims of the Nazi Holocaust can be found in the door connecting the sanctuary and the library.

Tri-Cities Jewish Federation Charities.

GADSDEN

Temple Beth Israel, 761 Chestnut St.

HUNTSVILLE

Cong. Etz Chayim, 7705 Bailey Cove Rd., S.E., was founded in 1962 as a Conservative congregation by a group of Jewish scientists at the Marshall Space Flight Center of the National Aeronautics and Space Administration.

Temple B'nai Sholom, 103 S. Lincoln St., S.E.

JASPER

Temple Emanu-El, 1501 Fifth Ave.

LANETTE

Temple Beth-El.

MOBILE

Cong. Ahavas Chesed, 1717 Dauphin St., also known as the Dauphin St. Synagogue, has a unique hand-carved mahogany bas-relief sculpture memorial to the 6,000,000 martyrs of the Nazi Holocaust. Designed by John Shaw, a non-Jew, it was carved by Abner Smiles of Pascagoula, Miss., a survivor of a death camp.

Beatrice Bernheim Hall, 701 Government St., was presented by Eli K. Bernheim in memory of his wife.

Bernheim Hall of Mobile Public Library is an auditorium for recitals and other cultural activities created as a memorial to Eli Bernheim by his family.

Frolichstein Fountain, in the Fearnway residential section, is a memorial to Esau Frolichstein, a member of the crew of the USS *New Hampshire*, who was killed during the Battle of Vera Cruz in 1914. Frolichstein was the first American casualty of the Mexican Expedition. The fountain and plaque were a gift to the city from the American Legion which raised the funds through public subscription.

Mobile Jewish Welfare Fund, 1509 Government St.

Old Church Street Graveyard, a common burial ground in the early days of Mobile, has a marker that reads, "Oldest Jewish Graves in Alabama." It was erected by the National Council of Jewish Women.

Old Magnolia Cemetery, has a Jewish section where the dates of the gravestones show when the yellow fever epidemic hit the community, as the graves are set in chronological order rather than in family lots.

Laz Schwarz Station, the city's central fire station, is named for

Lazarus Schwarz, who served as mayor of Mobile.

Schwarz Street is named for Henry Schwarz, Jr., who was killed in World War I.

Temple Shaaray Shomayim, 1769 Springhill Ave., is the oldest congregation in Alabama, tracing its beginnings to 1841. Sidney Staples, a former president of the congregation, which is also known as the Springhill Avenue Temple, was the father of Mobile's colorful Mardi Gras floral parade.

MONTGOMERY

Cong. Agudath Israel, 3525 Cloverdale Rd.

Cong. Etz Hayim, 725 Augusta St., a Sephardic congregation founded in 1912 by Jews from the island of Rhodes.

Rubin Morris Hanan Annex of the Lister Hill Health Center, 1000 Adams Ave., is named for a prominent Sephardic Jew born on the island of Rhodes, who headed the drive that raised $5,000,000 for the Lurleen B. Wallace Memorial Hospital and Tumor Center, named for Gov. George Wallace's first wife, and whose efforts on behalf of the aged won him appointment as chairman of the State Commission on the Aging.

Jewish Federation of Montgomery, P.O. Box 1150.

State Archives and History Building, Washington St., houses a new Torah Scroll presented to the state of Alabama by Montgomery's three synagogues on July 4, 1976, in honor of the American Bicentennial.

State Capitol Building has a small brass six-pointed star sunk in the marble tile on the front portico. Unveiled on May 20, 1897, the six-pointed star is on the spot where Jefferson P. Davis stood when he took the oath as President of the Confederacy. The Sophie Bibb chapter of the Daughters of the Confederacy ordered the star from a manufacturer and when it arrived it was found to be six-pointed rather than five-pointed. It has no Jewish connotation, although some wags have said it was "the mark of Judah P. Benjamin on the Confederacy."

Temple Beth Or, 2246 Narrow Lane Rd., is an outgrowth of a "sick and burial society" founded in 1846. Its original name was Kahl Montgomery but the present name was adopted in 1902. The congregation was the recipient of a $2,000 bequest from Judah Touro, the New Orleans philanthropist (see Louisiana), to be used as a building fund for a synagogue. When its first sanctuary was dedicated on March 8, 1862, it was believed to be the only synagogue erected in the South during the Civil War.

SELMA

Cong. Mishkan Israel, 503 Broad St.

TUSCALOOSA

B'nai B'rith Hillel Foundation at University of Alabama, 728 10th Ave., is housed in a building named for William P. Bloom, B'nai B'rith and civic leader. Friedman Hall, an athletic dormitory, is named for Victor Hugo Friedman, a University alumnus who was manager of the school's athletics while an undergraduate.

Friedman Library, 1305 24th Ave. (Greensboro Ave.), the public library of Tuscaloosa County, is named for the late Victor Hugo Friedman, businessman and philanthropist, who presented the building as well as the Central YMCA building. The Friedman Home at 1010 24th Ave. (Greensboro Ave.) and the Rosenau Home on 9th St., are among Tuscaloosa's finest surviving examples of Southern architecture.

Temple Emanu-El, 2320 E. Skyland Blvd. In the lobby is a wood sculpture carving representing the Tree of Life, the work of Dr. Michael Dinoff, in memory of his father.

Tenth Street Cemetery contains the graves of a number of Jews who fled from other parts of the state during the yellow fever epidemic of 1879. They are located in the Christian section of the graveyard near the entrance.

The Jewish Monitor, 46 Riverdale.

Arizona

Ownership of the Grand Canyon, Arizona's most famous natural site, was once claimed by Solomon Barth, a Jewish Indian trader, by virtue of an agreement he had made with an Indian chief. Pony express rider, miner, and gambler, Barth was typical of the adventuresome, enterprising, and youthful handful of Jews, most of them immigrants, who were among the earliest American settlers in the Arizona Territory.

Charles H. Meyer, a pharmacist who came to what is now Tucson in 1858, five years before the Arizona Territory was separated from New Mexico, became widely-known for his wise and salty decisions while serving as a justice of the peace.

Another early arrival was Polish-born Michael Goldwater (Goldwasser), who turned up at La Paz, scene of a major gold strike, in 1860. There he set up a freighting business with Ben Cohen, hauling provisions and supplies to army posts guarding Arizona against the Apache Indians. He opened his first store in 1864 and the town that grew up around it, Goldwater named for his friend, Herman Ehrenberg, a German-born explorer and mining engineer, who has been mistakenly described as a Jew in some books. Goldwater's store served as the town hall, post office, and general meeting place. His brother, Joe, was Ehrenberg's first postmaster.

In 1872 the Goldwaters decided that the new village of Phoenix held promise, and they opened a store there, with Mike in charge, while Joe stayed on at Ehrenberg. Joe later established stores at Tombstone, when a rich silver strike was made there, and in Bisbee, Yuma, and Benson.

Mike had eight children, five boys and three girls. Ben was a professional gambler, Sam was a tobacco salesman, and Henry was a wanderer searching for the pot of gold. Morris and Baron picked up where Mike left off. Morris began working for his father in La Paz, Ehrenberg, and Phoenix. After four years in Phoenix, Morris and Baron closed the business and moved to Prescott, which was the capital of Arizona until 1889. In Prescott the Goldwaters opened a store in the town's first brick building. Morris, who brought the first telegraph line to the territory, was mayor of Prescott for 20 years. He remained a faithful Jew all his life. Baron, who stayed in Phoenix where he developed a wide-ranging mercantile and industrial empire, married a Christian woman, and fathered Barry Goldwater, who was elected to the United States Senate in 1952. Barry, who was raised as an Episcopalian, never denied his Jewish origin. In fact, he has gone out of his way to express pride in it. When he was nominated for President of the United States at the 1964 Republican National Convention, Senator Everett Dirksen presented him as "the grandson of a Polish-born Jewish peddler." He was reelected to the Senate after losing his bid for the Presidency. The American Jewish Archives in Cincinnati has a Barry Goldwater Research Fund, established by some of Goldwater's Jewish friends to acquire and copy archival materials about the role of Jews in building the Southwest.

When Prescott marked its centennial in 1964, Morris Goldwater was named man of the century. For 63 years he had been a leader in countless civic and business affairs. He was the father of the city's water system, a founder of its volunteer fire department, secretary of the Prescott Rifles, member of both houses of the territorial legislature, a prominent banker, and a booster of roads and railroads. A leader of the territory's Democratic party, Goldwater was elected vice-president of the 1910 constitutional convention where he helped draft Arizona's first constitution, a preliminary to statehood. The last surviving member of that convention was the late United States District Court Judge Jacob Weinberger of San Diego, California, who died in 1974 at the age of 92. He was a 24-year old lawyer practicing at Globe when he was elected a convention delegate.

The 1864 census in Tucson listed Mike Goldwater, Philip Drachman, Henry Marks, Isaac Goldberg, Louis Heller, Ben Block, Ben Cohn, Louis Rosenbach, Elias Cohen, Aaron Westheimer, Max Solomon, and Jacob Goldman. The census takers overlooked Abe Lazard who had arrived in 1858.

Discovery of gold at La Paz in 1860 first drew white settlers to Arizona, including many Jews, most of whom came from California where they had been in business in the gold rush mining camps. When the La Paz gold mines petered out, many of the miners moved to Tucson, the state's oldest existing city. Among the first of these was Phil Drachman, who had come to La Paz in 1863 and with his partner, Hyman Goldberg, set up a freighting business. He later served in the 4th territorial legislature and on the city council. Drachman named one of his ten children Harry Arizona because he was said to be the first white child of non-Spanish extraction born in Tucson. Harry figured prominently in the territory's growth as county treasurer and a member of the territorial senate. Mose Drachman, who went into banking and also served in the legislature and on the city council, is the father character in Rosemary Taylor's novel, *Chicken Every Sunday*.

Samuel Drachman, Phil's brother, who settled in Tucson in 1867, opened a store that became headquarters for politicians and merchants. He, too, served in the territorial legislature and on the school board, and is honored as the father of the territorial public school system. Sam was often called "the rabbi" because he led the earliest informal Jewish worship services. In his diary he refers to having said his Rosh Hashanah prayers in bed because he was ill. He also speaks of praying alone or with others on Yom Kippur and Sukkot. From a store he expanded into other enterprises, including mail supervisor between Tucson and Apache Pass, Arizona lottery agency, and purveyor of supplies to army posts. Drachman's diary mentions a Hebrew Benevolent Society in 1886 and a Purim ball it gave at which his wife won a prize for her costume.

Hyman Goldberg, brother-in-law of the Drachmans, was another La Paz pioneer. He swung a pick-axe, rode a burro, stood behind a counter, drove cattle, and engaged in placer and quartz mining. Later, he owned stores in Ehrenberg, Phoenix, Prescott, and Yuma. In 1873-1874 he was on the Yuma town council and a delegate to the territorial legislature.

Lionel and Barron Jacobs opened a retail store in Tucson in 1867 when it was a town of 1,300, mostly Mexicans. Already there in addition to Drachmans were Louis, Aaron, and William Zeckendorf, whose firm became the largest retail and wholesale merchandising establishment in the entire Southwest. William Zeckendorf, who once headed a committee of vigilantes and served in the territorial legislature, was the grandfather of William Zeckendorf, who made real estate history in New York. Albert Steinfeld, a nephew of the Zeckendorfs, who came to work for them in 1872, took over the business when the Zeckendorfs moved to New York, and established the Steinfeld name as a major mercantile firm.

Lionel Jacobs served on the Pima County board of supervisors, in the territorial legislature, on the Tucson city council, and was elected territorial treasurer. His home was the center of Tucson's early social life. He founded the Tucson Literary Society and was a charter member of the Arizona Social Union.

Other pioneers at La Paz who subsequently moved to other towns were

Isaac Goldberg, brother of Hyman, who carried mail for the government, and later engaged in storekeeping, bartending, freighting, well-digging, and gold mining, and Abe Lewis, whose son, Larry, was born in La Paz in 1867. He lived to be 106 and when he died in San Francisco in 1974 he had behind him two careers, one as a circus performer and magician, and the other as a hotel waiter. Abraham Lyon was the first Indian agent at Tucson. Selim Franklin, who was only 25 when he was elected to the 13th territorial legislature from Tucson, was the father of the state university. He later served as one of the university's regents and as superintendent of the university agricultural experiment station.

Settlement in Phoenix, the state capital and largest city, began soon after it was founded in 1870. The first known Jew in Phoenix was probably Dr. Herman Bendell, a Civil War army surgeon from Albany, New York. He was appointed superintendent of Indian Affairs for the territory in 1871 by President Ulysses S. Grant. Another early arrival was Michael Wormser, a French-born Yiddish-speaking peddler, who staked out gold mining claims in La Paz in 1862 with his cousin Ben Block. Later he opened stores at Walker, Hassayama, Big Bug, Turkey Creek, and Bradshaw. In 1870 Wormser joined a general mercantile business in Phoenix operated by a banjo-playing French Jew, Aaron Barnett, before the townsite had been laid out. Barnett and Block were among the signers of the articles of association establishing Phoenix. Block had been the first postmaster at Wickenberg before coming to Phoenix.

Wormser's activities took him all over the territory. At Lynx Creek, in 1864, his store was the scene of a miner's meeting to establish an informal government. In Prescott, where he turned up soon after a gold strike near the then territorial capital, he opened the town's first store and built its first structure on the plaza with his partners Henry Wunderlich and Aaron Westheimer. The latter, one of the founders of the Arizona Pioneers Historical Association, ranged widely over the territory. Wormser and Block took over the Barnett-Block enterprise in Phoenix in 1873, but in 1876 Wormser liquidated his stores and went into farming, irrigation, and real estate. He helped introduce new crops, including sugar, into the Salt River Valley. The Mexicans called Wormser "el Judio Miguel" (the Jew Michael). Many anecdotes were told about him, stressing his Jewishness, and not always favorable. Nevertheless, he was well regarded, and in 1880 was elected to the Maricopa County board of supervisors. He also served as superintendent of the county poorhouse. Wormser is a leading character in Clarence Budington Kelland's novel *Sugarfoot*.

Other Jewish settlers in Phoenix in the 1870s included Hyman Goldberg, who had been a tailor in Yuma; his two sons, Aaron and David; and his brother Isaac. Hyman sat in the 1875 territorial legislature and Aaron was elected in 1899. The latter authored the bill which created Phoenix as the capital of Arizona. Emil Ganz, who fought in the Confederate army during the Civil War, was twice wounded and captured. He came to Phoenix in 1879 where he became a hotel owner, served on the city council, and was elected mayor three times.

Ganz's contemporaries included Adolph, Leo, and Charles Goldman (1879); Wolf Sachs, a farmer; Charles and Adolph Goldberg, storekeepers (1879); Gus Hirschfield, saloonkeeper; Harry Friedman, saddler; Phineas Kalman, tailor; Isaac Rosenzweig, jeweler; Selig Michaelson, postmaster of Phoenix from 1908-1912; I.J. Lipson; Abe Frank, who later moved to Arizona City, now known as Yuma, where he was elected mayor and delegate to the territorial legislature; Joe Melczer, saloonkeeper; and Sam, Abe, and Charles Korrick, merchants.

There was also a scattering of Jews in other Arizona towns. One of the first discoverers of the territory's rich copper lodes was David Abraham, who arrived in Arizona in 1869. While engaged in building one of the first wagon roads, he carried with him a complete set of Shakespeare. Henry and Charles Lesinsky operated a major copper mine at Clifton in partnership with Phoebus and Morris Freudenthal. They built the territory's first copper smelter and its first railroad, a narrow gauge line that served the mine.

Isador Solomon, a brother-in-law of the Freudenthals and cousin of the Lesinskys, came to work for them in 1876. When the copper smelter had used up all the wood around, Solomon discovered that mesquite, which grew in profusion around the upper Gila Valley, made fine charcoal. He bought it from Mormon farmers who were eager to have the mesquite cleared away. After burning the mesquite in pits, he had a good grade of charcoal which he sold for $30 a ton.

Solomon settled in the tiny hamlet of Pueblo Viejo at the confluence of the San Francisco River and San Simon Creek. The only other residents were Mexicans and a wandering peddler who had built a tiny store. Solomon bought out the store and developed a major trading post around which a town developed. It was called Solomonville, and in 1883 it became the seat of Graham County, with Solomon as county treasurer. He was also the town's first postmaster and founder of a bank that later became the Valley National Bank of Prescott, the state's leading banking institution. During the 1880s there were enough Jews in and around Clifton to form a short-lived congregation.

Solomon Barth, the prospector who claimed ownership of the Grand Canyon, had been in La Paz in 1862, working for Mike Goldwater. In 1864 he won a contract to carry mail between Prescott and Albuquerque, New Mexico via pony express. Two years later he obtained the mail contract for the Prescott-Maricopa Wells and Fort Stanton-Albuquerque routes.

Jack Isaacson, who began as a peddler in the Santa Cruz Valley near the Mexican border, opened a store in Tubac in the 1870s and found that several Jews had preceded him—Nathan Appel, a member of the first territorial legislature; Joe Goldtree, a hay and grain dealer; and Isaac Goldberg, hotel keeper. The restless Isaacson kept pushing closer to the border, ignoring Apache Indian threats. At Nogales Pass, a stopping off point for stagecoaches between Sonora, Mexico, and Tucson, Isaacson settled down and built a trading post. At first the crude settlement of tents and shacks surrounding the trading post was called Isaacson, but the name was changed to Nogales. In 1883 Isaacson was named postmaster.

After selling his mail routes to Louis Zeckendorf, Barth also founded a town, St. Johns, in the northeast corner of the state, while he was engaged in Indian trading and running stores at Rich Hill and Weaverville. Jake Marx, a redoubtable Indian fighter and La Paz miner, participated in the Pitt River battle with the Indians in 1876 and helped build Fort Crook. In 1894 he was appointed receiver of the United States Land Office in Prescott by President Grover Cleveland.

By 1880 there were hardly more than 100 Jews in the entire territory. The first organized Jewish community is believed to have developed in Tombstone, the mining town celebrated in films and fiction. While Jewish worship services had been held in Prescott in 1879 and 1880 for the High Holy Days, the earliest known Jewish organization was probably the Tombstone Hebrew Association, founded in 1881, with Samuel Blace as president. A meeting to form the association was advertised in the *Tombstone Epitaph*. That same year a Jewish cemetery was dedicated in Tombstone and Yom Kippur services were held in a turnverein hall.

In 1880, the *Epitaph* gave considerable space to a description of a soiree given by Mr. and Mrs. Mendel Myers and Mr. and Mrs. Herman Solomon at the Tombstone Club, indicating that there were Jews in the rough gold mining camp before 1881. The community went out of existence in the 1890s, but High Holy Day services were held as late as 1891. One of the best known citizens of Tombstone in those days was Sam Aaron, whose father had a store in Charleston, 15 miles from Tombstone. A faro dealer nicknamed "the lucky kid Jew," Aaron was a deputy United States marshal at the age of 17.

One of the rare Jewish dance hall girls was Josephine Sarah Marcus, daughter of Henry and Sophie Marcus of San Francisco. She ran away from home in 1880 and joined a troupe of dancing girls touring the Arizona Territory. She fell in love with Wyatt Earp, one-time gun fighter who became sheriff of Tombstone. She later married him. Earp, who was not Jewish, is buried beside her in the Hills of Eternity Jewish Cemetery, San Francisco, California.

Organized Jewish life developed slowly in Arizona because there were only a handful of Jews in the territory until the 1880s and they were widely dispersed. By the turn of the century the Jewish population had grown to

2,000. Impoverished Jews from the East who began coming to Phoenix for their health about 1915 substantially increased the Jewish population. There was a ten-fold growth from 1940-1960 as the state became a haven for winter residents from all parts of the United States. By 1977 there were 32,500 Jews in the state, 25,000 in Phoenix, 7,500 in Tucson, and 1,000 scattered in such places as Scottsdale, Mesa, Flagstaff, Coolidge, Fort Huacchuca, Nogales, Paradise Valley, Prescott, Yuma, Winslow, and Tempe.

Tucson's oldest Jewish congregation, Temple Emanu-El, was founded in 1910, two years before Arizona became a state. Its first president was Samuel Drachman, who had also been president of the Hebrew Benevolent Society, Emanu-El's first name. This was the same Drachman who had conducted services in Tucson for more than 30 years. Temple Emanu-El was the successor to an earlier congregation founded in 1880 by Isadore Gotthelf, who began to lead High Holy Day services soon after he arrived by covered wagon. A B'nai B'rith lodge with 22 charter members had been organized in Tucson in the 1880s.

In Phoenix, Temple Beth Israel, founded in 1918 as the Phoenix Hebrew Center, is the oldest Jewish congregation. Informal services and Hebrew classes had been held in the early 1890s in homes and the back-rooms of stores. Wolfe Lukin, who had studied for the rabbinate in Europe before coming to Tempe, officiated at some of those early services held over Joe Melczer's saloon. A Hebrew Cemetery Association established in 1900 dedicated the first Jewish cemetery in Phoenix on lots once owned by Michael Wormser, whose grave is the center of the cemetery. A congregation called Emanuel predated Beth Israel. Though never able to build or acquire a synagogue, it did bring to Arizona the first rabbi, David Liknaitz of California, who also rode to other Arizona towns.

The early days of the present Phoenix Jewish community were shaped by Barnett Marks, a newly-graduated lawyer from Chicago, who moved to Phoenix in 1905. Informal services were held under his leadership beginning in 1906, and a rabbi was brought in occasionally from El Paso, Texas. Marks also organized a Sunday school and delivered sermons with the help of a collection of rabbis' sermons in English he had sent for.

The influx of many poor Jews from the East who made their way to Arizona between 1915 and 1920 in search of dry air to cure their tuberculosis and arthritis, stimulated the formation of a B'nai B'rith lodge, with Marks as president. A $2,000 grant from the Supreme Lodge of B'nai B'rith helped the still tiny Phoenix Jewish community to care for their needy coreligionists. The Phoenix section of the National Council of Jewish Women, founded in 1917, teamed up with B'nai B'rith to raise the funds that made possible the erection of the first synagogue in 1922. The building was at first known as the Phoenix Hebrew Center and then it became the first home of Temple Beth Israel.

Marks' wife was elected to the state legislature in 1922, one of the first women in the United States to be so honored. Flora Cohen of Phoenix was among the first Jewish school teachers in the state. One of the first women doctors in Arizona was Dr. Anna Reznikov, who practiced in Globe from 1915-1922.

The election of Charles Korrick, who came to Phoenix in 1899, as the first president of the newly formed Phoenix Jewish Community Council in 1940, bridged the end of the pioneer period and the beginning of the modern era of Arizona Jewry. Today Phoenix and Tucson have a network of Jewish social service and cultural agencies and there are one or more synagogues in 10 different communities.

The early political eminence of Jews in the Arizona Territory has been renewed in the last 20 years. In 1958 Charles C. Bernstein became the first Jew elected to the State Supreme Court. In 1970 the state chairmen of both the Democratic and Republican parties were Jews—Herbert Ely and Harry Rosenzweig, respectively. In that same year Sam Grossman, a supermarket builder and newcomer to Arizona, came very close to being elected to the United States Senate as a Democrat. Sam Steiger, who was elected to Congress as a Republican in 1972, the first professing Jewish member of Congress from Arizona, won the Republican nomination for the Senate in 1976 in a campaign marked by anti-Semitism, but lost the election.

Tucson has had two Jewish mayors—Lew Davis in 1970, and Charles Moses Straus in 1883. Sigmund Liberman, who was elected mayor of Coolidge in 1967, served as president of the League of Arizona Cities and Towns. Herman Lewkowitz, city attorney of Phoenix in 1935, was state commander of the American Legion. In 1974, Jonathan Marshall, a Scottsdale newspaper publisher and grandson of Louis Marshall (see Syracuse, N.Y.) was the Democratic candidate for the United States Senate who ran against Barry Goldwater. Other Jews have served as city councilmen, county officials, state legislators, and judges throughout the state. Charles C. Bernstein of Phoenix was justice of the Arizona Supreme Court in the 1960s.

Martin Goodfriend, a former councilman in Santa Monica, California, who visited the Grand Canyon in 1956, became so interested in the plight of the Havasupi Indians living near the bottom of the canyon, that he spent the next 12 years in a one-man battle to improve life on the reservation.

* * * * *

CHANDLER
Convent of St. Mary's Church, 158 E. Cleveland, has a *mezuzah* on the inner doorpost of the main entrance. The Convent of the Sisters of Charity was built and paid for by Mr. and Mrs. Adolph Weinberg of Downey, Calif.,

in 1967. The sisters take pleasure in explaining the significance of the *mezuzah* to visitors. At the convent's entrance door is a prominent plaque explaining that the convent was a gift of the Weinbergs.

CIRCLE CITY
An all-Jewish retirement community in the Arizona desert 38 miles northwest of Phoenix, is named for the Workmen's Circle, a Jewish fraternal and cultural order. Its residents are mostly retired members of the order. All the streets, laid out in circles, are named for Jews prominent in the labor movement. The town was founded by Ben Schleifer, a Phoenix developer, who also built Youngstown, another retirement village near Phoenix.

EHRENBERG
Yuma County ghost town on the Colorado River was founded in 1864 by Michael Goldwater on the site of one of his first stores and named for his friend Herman Ehrenberg, mining engineer and explorer. The town was once the most important in the Arizona Territory.

FLAGSTAFF
Heichal Baoranim (Temple in the Pines), a young congregation founded in 1973, meets in the home of Dr. and Mrs. Merrill M. Abeshaus, 524 Deanne Dr., the first and third Friday nights of the month. It draws its members from faculty at the Northern Arizona University, and scattered Jewish residents in Cottonwood, Lake Montezuma, Winslow, and Jerome. The congregation works closely with the Hillel Foundation at Northern Arizona University where there are 60 Jewish students (Box 5808).

MESA
Temple Beth Sholom, 104 W. 1st St., founded in 1949 when the town had fewer than a dozen Jewish families, also serves Tempe.

NOGALES
Isaacson was the original name of this Santa Cruz County city when it was established in 1880 by Jacob Isaacson, a merchant and peddler. The town grew up around Isaacson's trading post where he did business with the Mexicans just across the international border in Sonora, and with Indians on the American side. When the railroad reached the town in 1882, to join with a new line coming from Mexico, Isaacson helped drive the traditional gold spike. In 1883 President Grover Cleveland appointed him the town's postmaster, but by that time its name had been changed to Nogales, the Spanish word for "walnuts," which grow in profusion around the city. Isaacson went deep into Apache country to trade with the Indians, and despite periodic warfare with the Apaches, he was never molested.

Ephraim Canyon, which stretches from the northwest corner of Nogales about a mile to the Mexican border, is named for Leopold Ephraim, who arrived in Nogales in 1882 when it was still known as Isaacson. Ephraim established the town's first waterworks, engaged in mining, and built the Ephraim building, which is still standing. Ephraim Canyon contained the city cemetery and Camp Stephen D. Little, a U.S. Army post during the U.S.-Mexican border trouble in 1912-1913.

Temple Emanu-El, had as one of its founders the late Charles J. Bracker, a pioneer merchant who settled here in 1924. Although it has no building of its own, it maintains a religious school and a cemetery.

PARADISE VALLEY

Har Zion Cong. of Scottsdale, 5929 E. Lincoln Dr.

PHOENIX

Beth El Synagogue, 1118 W. Glendale, has a large free-standing electric Menorah on its roof. Beth El Youth House is next door.

Beth Hebrew Congregation, 4002 W. Orangewood.

Cong. Haverim, meets at Shepherd of the Hills Congregational Church, 5524 Lafeyette.

Hebrew Academy, 515 E. Bethany Home Rd.

Jewish Community Center, 1718 W. Maryland Ave.

Jewish Family & Children's Service, 2029 N. 7th St.

Jewish Federation, 1718 W. Maryland Ave.

Jewish News, 1530 W. Thomas Rd.

Jewish War Veterans Memorial, a monument at the Arizona State Capitol listing the names of deceased Jewish veterans of World Wars I and II from Arizona, was erected by Jewish War Veterans Post 194.

Kivel Geriatric Center and Nursing Home, 3040 N. 36th St. There is a Kivel Manor East and a Kivel Manor West, adjoining each other at 3040 N. 36th St. The second complex is named for Horace W. and Grace Goldsmith toward which they gave $300,000.

Luke-Krohn Homes, 500 N. 20th St., a low-income housing project named in part for the late Rabbi Abraham Lincoln Krohn, of Phoenix's Temple Beth Israel, who was active in a wide array of civic agencies.

Justine Spitalny School, 46th Dr. and Osborn, is a public school named for a pioneer PTA leader who created a school public library.

Temple Beth Israel, 3310 N. 10th Ave., the second oldest congregation in the state, has an excellent Judaica library, museum, and historical archive.

Temple Chai, Shea Middle School, 10849 N. 27th St.

Ten Commandments Monument, a granite monument on the south side of the Arizona State Capitol, resembles the slabs on which the Ten

Commandments are usually represented. The entire Decalogue is inscribed on the monument, a gift to the state in 1964 of the Fraternal Order of Eagles.

Tiphereth Israel Cong., 1411 N. 3rd Ave.

Torah Moshe Minyan, 337 E. Bethany Home Rd.

Valley Jewish Day School, 2902 E. Campbell.

Yeshiva Ohr Hamidbar (boys division), 400 W. Pasadena; (girls division), 5750 N. Central Ave., is the first residential Hebrew school in the southwest.

PRESCOTT

Lake Goldwater, five miles south of Prescott, is named for Morris Goldwater.

Morris Goldwater Portrait, an oil painting which hangs in Prescott's City Hall, built on the site of the first Goldwater store opened in Prescott in 1876, memorializes a pioneer settler who was mayor of the city for 22 years. He was an uncle of Senator Barry Goldwater.

"Bucky' O'Neill equestrian statue, at the north entrance to the courthouse on Gurley St., between Montezuma and Cortez Sts., has inscribed on it the name of all the 528 men and officers who served in Theodore Roosevelt's Rough Riders during the Spanish American War, including those of the 14 Jews who served in this famous regiment. It was the first volunteer unit formed, equipped, and armed during that war, the first to land in Cuba, the first to fire on the enemy, and the first to receive the enemy's fire. The monument is named for O'Neill, who, while serving as mayor of Prescott, was the first man to enlist in the Rough Riders.

Although the Rough Riders were drawn mostly from the ranks of hunters, cowboys, Indian fighters, ranchers, and college athletes, the regiment reflected the heterogeneous character of the American people. The Jews in the regiment were also a varied lot. Some had served in the regular army, some were the sons of pioneer settlers in Arizona and New Mexico where they had first met Roosevelt, and a few were recent immigrants.

The youngest name on the monument is that of Jacob Willensky, a 16-year old from Chicago, who enlisted under the name of Jack Berling. He was killed in the first engagement at Las Guasimas. Samuel Goldberg, another immigrant, was affectionately known as "Porkchop" to his comrades because he steadfastly refused to eat non-kosher food. A clerk in a Santa Fe, N.M. store when he joined up, Goldberg was wounded at San Juan. Samuel Greenwald of Prescott, who signed up as a private, was promoted to captain for gallantry at San Juan and El Caney, the only Rough Rider to win a battlefield promotion.

First hand knowledge of the bravery of the 14 men who served under him motivated Theodore Roosevelt to accept honorary membership in the

Hebrew War Veterans of the War with Spain, which later merged with the Jewish War Veterans of the U.S. Roosevelt twice paid tribute to his Jewish comrades-in-arms. On June 15, 1903, during his Presidency, Roosevelt received the executive committee of B'nai B'rith in the White House. The committee had called on the President in connection with the Kishnev pogrom. During the course of that meeting, Roosevelt said:

"When in Santiago, when I was myself in the army, one of the best colonels among the regular regiments, who did so well on that day and who fought beside me, was a Jew. One of the commanders who in the blockade of the Cuban coast did so well was a Jew. In my own regiment I promoted five men from the ranks for valor and good conduct in battle. It happened by pure accident, for I knew nothing of the faith of any one of them, that these included two Protestants, two Catholics and one Jew. And while that was a pure accident, it was not without its value as an illustration of the ethnic and religious make-up of our nation and of the fact that if a man is a good American that is all we ask, without thinking of his creed or his birthplace."

The following is the list of Jews whose names are memorialized on the O'Neill Monument:

Sol Drachman of Prescott, son of Samuel Drachman who was lay rabbi for the early settlers; Samuel Goldberg; Samuel Greenwood; Samuel Grier of Albuquerque, N.M.; Hyman Lowitzki, of San Antonio, Tex.; Benjamin Woog, a lawyer from Washington, D.C.; Leo Brauer, a merchant from Richmond, Va.; Albin Pollak, San Francisco, Ca.; Joseph Kansky of Tacoma, Wash.; Hyman Rafalowitz, an immigrant from Russia, who signed up in San Antonio; Adolph Wertheim of San Antonio, Tex.; Samuel Fischell of Chicago; Samuel Okin of Brooklyn; Jacob Willensky of Chicago; and Jacob Allaun of Chicago.

SCOTTSDALE

Marshall Garden, at Scottsdale Mall, across from City Hall, was donated to the city by Jonathan Marshall, publisher of the *Scottsdale Daily Progress*. Marshall is a grandson of the famed jurist, Louis Marshall.

Temple Solel, 3535 E. Lincoln Dr.

SELIGMAN

This town of 900 on U.S. Route 66 is named for Jesse Seligman, New York banker and philanthropist (see Missouri), who financed the old Atlantic and Pacific Railroad, on whose line the town stands. Now part of the Santa Fe Line, the town was founded in 1886.

SOLOMONVILLE

This Graham County town of 1,000, once the county seat, is named for

Isador Elkan Solomon, who settled here in 1876. On Highway 70, at mile-post 344, there is a state historical marker memorializing Solomon who came here as a laborer in the copper mine owned by his relatives, the Lesinky and Freudenthal brothers. Solomon was the town's first post-master and the first treasurer of Graham County. Solomon was respected by both white men and Indians. Marauders would often grant safe-con-ducts to members of his family traveling by stage, when others were rob-bed or killed. Solomon is the hero of a number of popular Wild West stories.

ST. JOHNS
This Apache County town of 1,300 on the Coronado Trail (U.S. Route 66), was founded in 1874 by Solomon Barth, who arrived in Arizona in 1862. In 1868 he was captured by the Apaches, stripped, and threatened with tor-ture. When he was set free, he walked barefoot to a nearby friendly Zuni village. In a card game in 1873 at a place called El Badito (the Little Cross-ing), Barth won a herd of sheep and several thousand dollars in cash. Sud-denly weathy, he established a trading post which he named for the region's first white woman resident, Senora Maria San Juan (St. John) de Padilla de Baca. In 1880 a group of Mormons established a colony near Barth's village and also named it St. Johns. Later, the two settlements merged.

SUN CITY
Cong. Beth Shalom, 101st Ave., between North Coggins and Alabama Aves.

TEMPE
Charles and Edith Getz Elementary School, 900 S. 56th St., which trains handicapped children, is named for a Jewish couple who were in-volved in many Jewish, civic, and communal activities for more than 40 years.

Hillel Foundation, Arizona State University, 1245 E. 2nd St.

Temple Beth Sholom of Mesa, 104 W. 1st St., also serves Tempe.

Temple Emanual holds services in the Church of the Epiphany, 222 S. Price Rd.

TUCSON
Arizona Jewish Post, 102 N. Plummer St.

Berger Memorial Fountain, in front of the old Main Building of the University of Arizona, is named for Alexander Berger, who donated funds for a memorial to faculty members and alumni who were killed in World War I.

Bloom Elementary School, 8310 E. Pima, memorializes the late Clara F. Bloom, who was born in Tucson in 1881, taught school for 11 years, and, with her husband, was a charter member of Temple Emanu-El. Her portrait hangs in the school's main lobby.

B'nai B'rith Hillel Foundation at the University of Arizona, 1245 E. 2nd St. Berger Memorial Library is a memorial to the late Rabbi Marcus Berger, for many years spiritual leader of Cong. Anshei Israel, who founded the university's Judaic studies program after his retirement in the 1970s.

Cong. Anshei Israel, 5550 E. 5th St., has a 23-foot bronze Menorah in its Ginsburg Memorial Garden. The Menorah is designed to allow for the addition of two extra arms during Chanukah. Viewed from any angle, the Menorah looks like the Hebrew letter *shin*. The synagogue also has a mosaic mural dedicated to the 6,000,000 victims of the Holocaust.

Cong. Chaverim, P.O. Box 6807.

Drachman Elementary School, 549 S. Convent, is named for Samuel H. Drachman, one of the early Jewish settlers and a member of the territorial legislature who authored the bill that created the territorial school system.

Drachman Street is also named for Samuel Drachman.

Handmaker Jewish Nursing Home, 2221 N. Rosemont.

Jewish Community Center, 102 N. Plumer, has in the lobby a 24-foot mosaic mural depicting figures in the Warsaw Ghetto Uprising, as a memorial to the Holocaust's 6,000,000 victims.

Jewish Community Council, 102 N. Plumer, Sylvia and Harry Liese Bldg.

Jewish Family Service, 102 N. Plumer.

Mansfield Junior High School, 1300 E. 6th St., is named for Jacob S. Mansfield, pioneer and first trustee of the Tucson Public Library. He was also a member of the first board of regents of the University of Arizona.

Meyer Avenue, in the downtown section of the city, is named for Dr. Charles H. Meyer, a German-born Jew who is believed to have been the first Jewish resident of Tucson. The city's first pharmacist, he also served as a justice of the peace.

Temple Emanu-El, 225 N. Country Rd., is the oldest existing Jewish congregation in Arizona, having been founded in 1910. Its first president was Samuel H. Drachman, one of the pioneer settlers.

Tucson Hebrew Academy, 5550 E. 5th St.

Young Israel Cong., 2443 E. 4th St.

YUMA

Jewish Community Center, P.O. Box 724.

Jewish Community Council, serves both Yuma and neighboring Imperial, Ca., which together have 120 Jewish families. Sabbath services are held at the Marine Corps Air Station. For information, phone Dr. Alan Winfield, 344-1902, and check the *Yuma Daily Sun* on Fridays.

Arkansas

Ownership of part of Hot Springs, the best known site in Arkansas, was once claimed by Jacob Mitchell, the first Jew of record in Arkansas. After France ceded the Louisiana Territory to Spain in 1763, the Spanish military commanders gave land grants, albeit with little authority, in the hope of encouraging settlement in that portion of the region which is now Arkansas. It was one of these dubious grants which came into Mitchell's possession some time in the 1830s following his arrival in the area.

Mitchell settled in Little Rock shortly after the city was chartered in 1831 and, together with his brothers, Hyman and Louis, established a general merchandising firm, with branches in Fort Smith and across the border of the American frontier in the Indian Territory. As a sideline, the Mitchells operated one of the pioneer stagecoach lines between Little Rock and Hot Springs. The latter had already become one of the country's leading spas because of the unusual heating properties of the thermal waters that flowed from the depths of Hot Springs Mountain. Certain of the community's future as a health resort, Mitchell planned one of the first hotels in Hot Springs in 1839.

Exactly how Mitchell acquired an interest in part of "the hot mountain" whose health-giving waters had been discovered by De Soto in 1541, is not certain. It could have been from a debtor who discharged an obligation by signing over to Mitchell the title to one of the old Spanish land grants. There were others who owned similar claims. To prevent private exploitation of the waters, the United States Government set aside four sections of land around the springs as a Federal reservation in 1832. But Mitchell and the other claimants took their grants seriously and for 40 years they and their heirs were engaged in legal actions to sustain them. The litigation continued until 1876 when the United States Supreme Court ruled that all private property titles around the spring were void.

Although the Mitchell brothers, emigrés from Poland, were the only known Jews in Arkansas when the state was admitted to the Union in 1836, further research may yet reveal that there may have been others who had good reason for not proclaiming themselves to be Jews.

Before the Louisiana Purchase of 1803, Jews were not permitted to live, do business, or worship freely in Arkansas or any place in the French colony of Louisiana. Under the Black Code promulgated by the French in 1724 as the governing charter of the colony, Jews were subject to expulsion, and the only recognized religion was Catholicism. Under such circumstances, Jews were hardly likely to identify themselves in the Louisiana Territory. Nevertheless, there were Jews in New Orleans, Mobile, and Natchez, all part of the Louisiana Territory, before 1800. It is not inconceivable, therefore, that other Jews may have found their way up the Mississippi to Arkansas, trading along the Indian trails and the roads hacked out by the French and the Spanish.

It is possible that among these unknown Jews were two Arkansas pioneers. One was a Mr. Raphael who, according to Thomas Nuttall, one of the first travelers to write about Arkansas, was managing a Cherokee trading post in 1819 at what is now Dardanelle on the Arkansas River. The other was Jacob Wolf who built a cabin and blacksmith shop in 1809 at Norfolk, at the juncture of North Fork and the White River, on the Old Salt Trail to Missouri. There is no connection between this Jacob Wolf and a man of the same name who was the first Jewish settler at Pine Bluff in 1845. Nor do we have any evidence that Mr. Raphael and Jacob Wolf of Dardanelle were Jews, except the fact that their names may be Jewish. Morris Bern was a settler in Jonesboro in 1832.

Not long after the Mitchells opened their business at Little Rock, the capital of the new state began attracting other venturesome Jewish immigrants. By 1845, there were enough to organize the state's first *minyan*, although 21 years were to pass before the organization of Temple B'nai Israel, Arkansas' pioneer Jewish congregation. Among the leaders of this first Jewish community were Jonas Levy and Jacob Kempner. Levy was elected to the city council in 1857, and became mayor of Little Rock in 1860. He was the city's chief executive all through the Civil War, guiding the community's destiny during its occupation by the Union Army. Kempner, who owned a stagecoach line that linked Little Rock and Hot

Springs, later became the first Jewish resident of Hot Springs. His descendants are still prominent businessmen and leaders of the city's Jewish community.

Before opposing armies devastated Arkansas during the Civil War with pitched battles, guerrilla warfare, and looting, Jews had established themselves also at Fort Smith, Pine Bluff, DeValls Bluff, Van Buren, Jonesboro, and Batesville.

The new stone fort which gave Fort Smith its name was still unfinished and the city itself, then a town of less than 500, had only just been incorporated, when Edward and Louis Czarnikow and Charles and Leopold Lowenthal arrived there in 1842. When Jacob Wolf arrived at Pine Bluff in 1845 the town consisted of only a few cabins. The Gates family, three of whose sons fought with Arkansas regiments in the Confederate Army, helped make DeValls Bluff a busy steamboat port in the early 1840s. Discovery of gold in California converted Fort Smith, and Van Buren across the river, into key starting points in 1849 for pioneers taking the southern route across the plains and brought a number of Jewish families into those towns.

Van Buren's first Jewish settlers were the Adlers and their kinfolk, the Baers, some of whom also established themselves in Fayetteville and Fort Smith. Bernard Baer built the Fort Smith and Little Rock Railroad, one of the first in the state, now part of the Missouri Pacific Line. The Adlers included Jonas, an Alsatian who had fought under Napoleon, and his two sons. One son, Samuel, became the father of the celebrated Dr. Cyrus Adler, who was born in Van Buren. The Adlers did well in their merchandising and Indian trading business and soon acquired a cotton plantation and a large tract of timber land.

Sober and hard-working folk, the Adlers were typical of many of the first Jewish settlers in the ante-bellum South. Samuel Adler employed slave labor only because there was no other labor supply, but he refused to own slaves.

Far removed from a Jewish community, Adler made the long journey to New York and Philadelphia once a year for the High Holy Days. On one of these trips he met Sarah Sulzberger, daughter of Leopold Sulzberger, a Philadelphia *shohet*. The couple were married in 1858, but before Sulzberger would allow Adler take his bride to what was still a raw frontier town, the *shohet* made sure his daughter would be able to observe the dietary laws. This he did by giving Samuel Adler a short course in the elementary practice of *shehitah*. From 1859 until 1864, when the Adlers, nearly bankrupted by the war, left Arkansas, the family ate kosher poultry slaughtered by Adler.

Although there were probably not more than 300 Jews in Arkansas when the state seceded from the Union and joined the Confederacy, 53 of them, including Mrs. Samuel Adler's brother, David Sulzberger, who had come from Philadelphia to be with his sister, fought with the Confederates. Another was Isaac Gleitzman, who served with General Nathan Bedford Forrest's cavalry and was decorated on the field of battle by the man who later founded the first Ku Klux Klan.

Shortly after the war, a considerable number of Jewish merchants, planters, and storekeepers began moving into the river towns, as well as to Hot Springs and Little Rock, bringing with them capital and commercial connections in St. Louis, Cincinnati, Memphis, and Louisville urgently needed to rebuild the state's economic life. In 1866, four of the six Main Street stores in Little Rock were Jewish-owned. As the state slowly recovered from the chaos of war and Reconstruction, Jewish enterprise played a considerable role in establishing saw mills, railroads, and small industries, and in opening up the inland counties to trade and commerce in the 1870s and 1880s. At one time there were 14 towns and villages named for and founded by Jews in the postwar period.

One village founded by Jews had a brief and tragic history. This was the agricultural colony for Russian Jews established in 1883 on a densely wooded virgin tract in Newport. The land was almost worthless for agriculture even by experienced farmers. The only visible means of eking out a living was to cut down the trees and convert them into staves which could be sold at $20 a thousand. The staves had to be floated down a stream but during flood conditions, delivery became almost impossible. Since floods were a regular occurrence, the colony's tenuous source of income was cut off. Heat, insects, malaria, and inexperience, plus the floods, defeated the settlers and wrote an early end to another of the 19th century's Jewish agricultural experiments. The Industrial Removal Office, however, was more successful with the 261 Jews it settled in 17 different Arkansas towns and cities a generation later.

The first Jewish congregation, Temple Israel, was established in Little Rock. Temple Beth El in Helena and Congregation Anshe Emeth in Pine Bluff were founded a year later. A Hebrew Cemetery Association formed in Fort Smith in 1871 paved the way for the organization of the United Hebrew Congregation in 1881. In Hot Springs, Congregation House of Israel was founded in 1878. Other congregations were organized in Texarkana (1884), Jonesboro (1897), a second congregation, Agudas Achim, in Little Rock (1904), Newport (1905), Eudora (1912), and Forest City (1904). The newest congregation in the state, Temple Beth Israel, dates from 1926.

When the first rabbi arrived in Arkansas in the 1870s, it was discovered that under a statute dating from 1838, only the governor, judges, justices of the peace, and regularly ordained ministers or priests of "any Christian sect" could perform marriage ceremonies. After the Jewish community called this to the attention of the legislature in 1873, the law was amended to read, "any regularly ordained minister or priest of any religious sect or denomination. . . "

Jews have played a comparatively small role in the state's politics. Jonas Levy, the first Jewish officeholder, was elected to the Little Rock city council in 1857 and served as mayor from 1860-1864. After the Civil War, Aaron Meyers was mayor of Helena (1878-80); Joseph Wolf and Jacob Erb served on the Little Rock board of aldermen from 1889-1903; Jacob Fink was mayor of Helena (1906); and Joseph Gates held a similar office in Roanoke in 1909. Simon Bloom served as mayor of Pine Bluff from 1900-1912. Rabbi Louis Wolsey was president of the Little Rock board of education in 1906. Charles Jacobson, who settled in Texarkana in 1884, was secretary to Governor and Senator Jeff Davis from 1901-1908, was elected to the state legislature in 1909, and was named a municipal judge in 1922.

Louis Joseph served in the state assembly from 1912-1916 and on the Texarkana municipal court from 1927-1932. In more recent times Samuel Levine of Pine Bluff was a member of the state legislature for more than 20 years and was once a candidate for lieutenant governor. Samuel Seligson of Little Rock was a member of the state assembly from 1939-1943. In 1974 during the Democratic primary a rumor spread that Arkansas Jews, a tiny minority, and "Jewish money" from New York, were supporting the opponent of Senator William Fulbright, long-time chairman of the Senate Foreign Relations Committee, who had been unfriendly to Israel. Fulbright was defeated and the rumor was exposed for what it was, an election canard.

In 1917 the state's Jewish population topped 5,000. Ten years later it had grown to 8,850, but in the 1930s a decline set in that has continued unchecked. In 1937 Arkansas had 6,510 Jews. By 1960 their number had dropped to 3,400 and in 1977 the figures showed another loss to 3,245. Despite their reduced numbers, the Jews continued to be widely dispersed. Little Rock, with 1,380 Jews, accounted for about a third of the state's total, followed by Hot Springs with 600, Pine Bluff with 300, and Fort Smith with 200. Elsewhere in the state there are 75 towns and cities with some Jewish residents: four with at leat 100; six with about 50 each; 22 with ten or less; and 40 with only two or three Jewish families. Much of the population decline is attributable to the departure from the small towns and cities of the grandchildren of the early settlers and Jewish concern in the 1950s and 1960s over the violence that marked the racial conflict.

James Mendel Kempner, grandson of Jacob Kempner, one of the founders of the Little Rock Jewish community in the 1850s, was one of the state's leading merchants from 1920-1971. He helped found the Little Rock Urban Progress Association and was a prime mover in the formation of the Little Rock Air Force Base Community Council. Howard Eichenbaun, an architect who built some of Little Rock's most impressive structures, headed the Little Rock Planning Commission in the 1970s.

* * * * *

ALTHEIMER

Louis and Joseph Altheimer founded this cotton town in Jefferson County in 1884. Their plantation was long the principal business of the area. Louis Altheimer, who had settled in Pine Bluff in 1869, was responsible for the Cotton Belt Railroad, building a spur line from Altheimer to Little Rock in 1886. In 1892 he was a delegate to the Republican National Convention. Joseph Altheimer's son, Ben, later a lawyer in St. Louis and Chicago, is one of those credited with being the father of Flag Day.

BERGER

Henry Berger, who, with his brother Benjamin, settled in Arkansas in the early 1870s, were memorialized in 1907 in the name of this town just south of Little Rock. The Bergers were in business in Rockport and Malvern, where Henry Berger was city attorney for four terms. Berger Street on Malvern's northside is also named for him.

BERTIG

This town is named for Saul Bertig, once known as "prince of merchants" in Green County (a town on the St. Louis-San Francisco Railroad).

BLYTHEVILLE

Temple Israel, 15th and Chicasawba Sts., owns two Torahs rescued from German synagogues when the Nazis sacked them on November 10, 1938. Both Torahs are dedicated to the famed Rabbi Leo Baeck.

CONWAY

Frauenthal House, 631 Western Ave., one of the town's showplaces, was built by and named for Max Frauenthal, a German-Jewish immigrant who became one of the heroes of the Confederate Army. In business at Port Gibson and Summit, Mississippi in the 1850s, Frauenthal joined the Confederates in Summit as a private in A.P. Hall's Corps. Although he was assigned as a drummer, at his own request he shouldered a gun. As a member of Company A, 16th Mississippi Infantry, Frauenthal distinguished himself at Bloody Acute Angle during the Battle of Spottsylvania Courthouse, Va., on May 12, 1864.

It was during this battle that Gen. Ulysses S. Grant wrote, "we will fight it out on this line if it takes all summer." Judge A.T. Watts, of Dallas, Tex., a member of Frauenthal's company, singled him out in a description of the battle as "a little Jew who, though insignificant, in battle had the heart of a lion. For several hours he stood at the immediate point of contact amid the most terrific hail of lead and cooly and deliberately loaded and fired without cringing." Watts said, "I now understand how it was that a handful of Jews could drive before them the hundred kings—they were all Fronthals." Frauenthal's name was variously spelled as Frankenthal, Fahrenthold, Fronthal, and Frontall. In Texas and Mississippi, after the Civil War, Confederates referred to a brave man as "a regular Fronthall," in admiration of Frauenthal's heroism.

After the war, Frauenthal settled in Conway, where he became a successful businessman, and was elected commander of the Conway Post of the United Confederate Veterans. A bachelor, Frauenthal later moved further north to Cleburne County.

Joe Frauenthal, Max's brother, and his wife, a non-Jewess, were the last of the family to live in the Frauenthal mansion, which is now owned by the Fansett family. Joe was president of the board of trustees of Arkansas State Teachers College, located in Conway, to which he made large contributions. His wife was also a patron of the college, and its music building, Ida Baridon Hall, is named for her.

The Frauenthal store, founded by Max and continued by Joe, went out of business in the 1950s after serving Faulkner County for more than 80 years. For many years the Frauenthal House was the social center for the town's young people. Joe Frauenthal bequeathed his collection of Arkansiana to Teachers College and Hendrix College, the latter also situated in Conway. Joe Frauenthal's name is on a plaque at the entrance to the Torreyson Library of the Teachers College.

EL DORADO
Temple Beth Israel, 712 Camp St.

FAYETTEVILLE
Hillel Club, University of Arkansas, 607 Stover Ave.

FELSENTHAL
Adolph Felsenthal's dream town, now a hamlet of 150 in Union County, was founded in the 1880s. Son of a Confederate veteran from Camden, Ark., and nephew of the celebrated Rabbi Bernhard Felsenthal of Chicago (see Illinois), Adolph Felsenthal planned the town as a metropolis of 150,000 when he learned that a large saw mill was to be built at the junction of two new railroad lines near the Ouachita River. He organized the Felsenthal Townsite Co. and bought up a large tract on which he established the town of Felsenthal. Ultimately, the mill was built two miles from Felsenthal and his plans never materialized. Felsenthal died in 1942.

FORT SMITH
Rosalie Tilles Home for Orphans, Tilles St., and Tilles Park and

Memorial Fountain are all named for members of the family of Andrew (Cap) Tilles, whose benefactions in Arkansas and St. Louis, where Tilles later settled, are estimated at $5 million.

United Hebrew Congregation-Tilles Memorial Temple, 126 N. 47th St., has an aluminum Menorah built into its outside wall.

GOLDMAN

J.D. Goldman and his brother, Isaac, are memorialized in this rice-growing town in Arkansas County. The Goldman brothers, who settled in-Jacksonport soon after the Civil War, and then moved to Pocahontas in Randolph County in 1872, made Goldman the headquarters of the early rice-growers. Until Stuttgart, five miles southwest of this town was founded, Goldman was one of the principal commercial centers of the rice country. J. D. Goldman was one of the original directors of the St. Louis Southwestern Railway Co., better known as the Cotton Belt. He was the donor in 1910 of the first building erected at the Arkansas Tuberculosis Sanitarium in Blytheville.

HEBER SPRINGS

Max Frauenthal (see above) founded this Cleburne County seat in the late 1870s and discovered the mineral springs from which this town takes its name. He bought several hundred acres of land here, including the medicinal springs, and established a town called Sugar Loaf. After erecting the first house, Frauenthal set aside a ten-acre plot, including the springs, for public use. He also donated lots on which the court house was built when the town became the county seat. Frauenthal named the town in honor of Heber Jones, son of the man from whom he had purchased the site.

HELENA

Temple Beth El, 406 Perry St.

HOT SPRINGS

Cong. Beth Jacob, 200 Quapaw St.

Cong. House of Israel, 300 Quapaw St.

Leo N. Levi Memorial National Arthritis Hospital, 300 Prospect Ave., was founded in 1913 by leaders of B'nai B'rith, among them the late Rabbi A.B. Rhine of Cong. House of Israel, as the country's only free, non-sectarian hospital for arthritic diseases. It is named for Leo N. Levi, an eminent Texas attorney from Galveston who was national president of B'nai B'rith. B'nai B'rith still helps support the hospital.

JONESBORO

Temple Israel, 203 W. Oak St.

LEVY

Max Levy is memorialized in the name of this town of 1,300 near Little Rock. Levy was an off-duty mecca for thousands of servicemen from Camp Joe Robinson during World Wars I and II. A merchant who settled in North Little Rock in 1888, Levy was president of the school board at the time of his death in 1916. Ernest L. Stanley, who founded the town in 1892, named it for Levy because the businessman had lent him the funds which made it possible for him to open a store.

LITTLE ROCK

Arkansas State Capitol, Wood Lane facing Capitol Ave., houses the State Supreme Court in whose courtroom hangs a portrait of Judge Samuel Frauenthal, who served on the Arkansas Supreme Court from 1909-1912. He was the son of Joe Frauenthal and nephew of Max Frauenthal (see above).

Cong. Agudath Achim, 7901 W. Capitol Ave., is the only active Orthodox congregation in Arkansas.

Jewish Welfare Agency, 945 Donaghey Bldg., Main at 7th Sts.

Pike Memorial Temple, Scott St., bet. 7th and 8th Sts., headquarters of the Masonic Grand Lodge of Arkansas, has in the Grand Masters Room a portrait of Jacob Trieber, who was Grand Master in 1906. Trieber, a German immigrant who first settled in St. Louis with his parents, came to Little Rock in 1872 when he was 19. He became active in Arkansas politics soon after being admitted to the bar. He became a leader of the Republican party and was a delegate to the Republican National Convention of 1888, 1892, and 1896. In the latter year he was an unsuccessful candidate for Congress. In 1897 President William McKinley appointed him U.S. Attorney for Eastern Arkansas. Three years later he was named U.S. District Court Judge for the same area. When Trieber was being considered for this post, he insisted that the President be told that the prospective judge would be the first Jew to hold such an office in the U.S. He remained on the Federal bench until his death in 1927.

Temple B'nai Israel, Rodney Parham Rd. and Rocky Valley, is the oldest Jewish congregation in the state.

Davis Woolf Goldstein Dermatological Library and Research Unit, in the Jeff Banks Student Union Building at the University of Arkansas Medical Center, is named for Dr. and Mrs. David W. Goldstein of Fort Smith. In active practice in Fort Smith for 52 years, Dr. Goldstein was president of the Arkansas State Board of Health.

McGHEE

Meier Chayim Temple, 410 N. 4th St.

NEWPORT

St. Paul's Episcopal Church, 3rd and Hazel Sts., erected in 1905, has the name of Aaron Hirsch listed on its cornerstone among the church founders. In the church itself are three Hirsch memorial windows, marked "Hirsch Memorial," "Hortense and Helene," and "Ralph and Carl." The windows were gifts of Mrs. Nettie Hirsch, whose husband was Aaron's nephew.

An immigrant born in France in 1829, Aaron Hirsch came to the U.S. in 1842. He landed in New Orleans where he lived until 1847. He peddled at Ridley on the Mississippi, and got along with the planters, even though he spoke only French and Yiddish. In the early 1850s he moved to Batesville, Ark. On the eve of the Civil War, Hirsch owned one of the largest general stores in northern Arkansas, operated the stagecoach between Batesville and Jacksonport, and had a governmental mail contract. During the Civil War, Hirsch raised a company of cavalry for the Confederacy. When Jacksonport refused to grant the Cairo and Fulton Railroad a right of way, the line by-passed the town and laid its tracks at Newport, a few miles down the river. Hirsch was one of the first merchants to move to Newport. When St. Paul's Episcopal Church was organized, Hirsch donated the site for the first building in 1879. This structure was torn down to make way for the present edifice on whose cornerstone Hirsch is memorialized. He later moved to St. Louis where his family became prominent in the Jewish community.

Newport was also the site of a short-lived Jewish agricultural colony, founded in the late 1880s for Jewish immigrants. Most of the colonists moved to St. Louis when the settlement was abandoned.

PINE BLUFF

Gabe Meyer Public School is named for a pioneer Jewish settler, who was a charter member of Temple Anshe Emeth and of the Arkansas Grand Lodge of Masons.

Temple Anshe Emeth, 40th and Hickory Sts., is the second oldest congregation in the state, having been founded in 1867.

TEXARKANA

(see state of Texas)

VAN BUREN

Cyrus Adler Memorial, a bronze plaque on the wall of the building housing the Van Buren Press Argus, faces the lot on which the now-razed building stood where Dr. Cyrus Adler was born in 1863. The plaque replaces a hand-made marker erected in 1941, a year after Adler's death, by the Mary Fuller Percival Chapter of the Daughters of the American Revolution. In a letter to Dr. Adler's niece, the regent of the DAR chapter explained that the rough wooden marker was the best it could do in view of its limited resources. The bronze marker was erected in 1968.

Dr. Adler was president and leader of a number of major institutions in American Jewish life—Jewish Theological Seminary of America, Dropsie University, National Jewish Welfare Board, American Jewish Committee , and American Jewish Historical Society. The marker indicates the great affection in which the Adler family was held nearly a century after they left Van Buren. Cyrus Adler was the third of Samuel Adler's children born in the house which stood until 1911. During the Civil War, the house was looted by Union troops who carried off the Adler's belongings in a hearse. Samuel Adler became friendly with the Union commander when they found a mutual interest in their Masonic affiliation. The Union officer gave the Adlers a pass which enabled them to get through the Union lines to Memphis and then to Philadelphia. On his 1911 visit, Dr. Adler disposed of his father's old timber tract which had been in the family for 60 years.

WEINER
Weiner, a German-Jewish immigrant who served as section foreman in charge of the track-laying of the St. Louis Southwestern Railroad, is memorialized by this Poinsett County town north of Waldenburg. The town that was settled in 1882 was named Weiner because the post office authorities were not familiar with the spelling of German names. Weiner's first name remains a mystery.

Florida

If Ponce de Leon was Florida's first tourist, then Moses Elias Levy, Jew from Morocco who came to Florida 305 years after de Leon, was Florida's first booster. It is unlikely that Levy knew that Florida's name had its origin in the fact that Ponce de Leon landed there during Easter, 1513, and accordingly called it "La Pascua Florida," or "the flowery Easter." But Levy did know that Florida had a great destiny, one in which he was to play a prominent role.

Levy was 18 when he migrated to the island of St. Thomas in the Virgin Islands in 1800, where he quickly made a fortune in lumber. His business frequently took him to Cuba, from which a Spanish governor ruled the uncharted domain of Florida. In 1816, Levy settled in Havana, where he became a government contractor, supplying Spanish troops. It was from the soldiers that he first learned of the vast forest and fertile soil of Florida. His first visit to Florida in 1818 persuaded him of its great potential. Shortly before Spain ceded Florida to the United States in 1819, Levy acquired some 60,000 acres in what are now St. Johns, Volusia and Alachua Counties in the northeastern part of the state. By 1820 he was promoting a fantastic plan for establishing a colony of European Jews in Florida. Levy visited New York, Philadelphia, and Charleston to press his idea on Jewish leaders, and appointed agents in Paris and London to recruit settlers.

It was in this connection that he prepared the earliest propaganda literature about Florida. "All accounts agree," one of his circulars read, "in extolling the fertility of its soil, salubrity of its air, sublimity of its scenery, abundant supply of cattle and stock of all kinds. . . ." Levy spent thousands of dollars on his project, bringing colonists from England and France at his own expense. He built homes, seeded virgin soil with fruit trees and with some of the first sugar cane imported to the United States, and cut roads through the wilderness. However, less than 50 people were settled on his land by 1823. Jews did not seem to have been attracted to Levy's proposed "Zion," although Achille Murat, Napoleon's nephew, who lived in Florida, called Levy a "Hebrew visionary," who wanted "to substitute the law of Moses for common law and the Prophets for statue law."

There is some evidence that Moses Levy was also interested in furthering reforms in Judaism. While so far as is known nothing came of his efforts to bring about religious changes, he may have had some influence upon the first Reform congregation in Charleston, South Carolina, in 1824.

Levy acquired American citizenship in 1823 in St. Augustine, and quickly became one of the most influential figures in the Florida Territory. His large landholdings, his active role in politics, his frequent contribution to the press under various pseudonyms, and his public religious controversies (one provoked a book published in England under the title of *Letters Addressed to the Jews, Particularly to Mr. Levy in Florida*) combined to make him a person of importance. His fame spread beyond Florida when he published a plan to abolish slavery, even though he himself used slave labor on his sugar plantation.

Two years before Levy became an American citizen, four others who from their names may have been Jews were naturalized in St. Augustine under the law granting citizenship to all who had lived in Florida at the time it came under American sovereignty. These four —Lewis Solomon, a watchmaker from England; Isaac Hendricks, a planter from South Carolina; George Levy, a planter from England; and M. Rodenberg, a grocer from Holland—may have preceded Levy to Florida.

In his first visit to the United States, Levy brought with him his youngest son, David, who was born in the West Indies in 1810. The younger Levy attended school in Norfolk, Virginia, where his father had placed him with Moses Myer (see Virginia), one of Virginia's leading citizens. David Levy first came to Florida in 1827 as manager of one of his father's plantations in St. Johns County. He later studied law and was admitted to the bar in St. Augustine in 1832.

Before long, David Levy was one of the best known men in Florida. He served as clerk of the Territorial Legislature, wrote the report of the conference between General Thompson, the American Indian agent, and the Seminole chiefs, including the famous Osceola, and was elected to the St. Johns County Legislative Council in 1836. The next year, Levy was sent to the Territorial Legislature where he championed the effort that led to statehood for Florida. He helped draft Florida's first constitution in 1838, and in 1841 was chosen Congressman-at-large from the Florida Territory, thus becoming the first Jew to sit in Congress. When Florida was admitted to the Union in 1845, largely through Levy's efforts, he was elected to the U.S. Senate, the first Jew to serve in that body.

Soon after he became a Senator, David Levy married the daughter of Charles A. Wickliffe, a former governor of Kentucky, who was Postmaster General under President Zachary Tayler. Simultaneously, Levy changed his name to David Levy Yulee by act of the Florida Legislature on January 12, 1846. Even before this, the elder Levy, who was always a professing Jew, had become estranged from his son. "The irritating subject of David Levy has become troublesome to me beyond measure," Moses Levy wrote in 1841. "The subject begins to make me unhappy indeed." While Yulee's political enemies, including ex-President John Quincy Adams, attacked him as "the alien Jew delegate," Yulee cut himself off from Jews, including his father, after 1845. He reared his children as Christians, and quietly encouraged the growth of a legend that his father was really not a Jew but a Moroccan prince named Yulee, who had assumed his wife's name for business purposes.

The Levys were not the first Jews in Florida. That distinction belongs to three merchants from Louisiana—Joseph de Palacios, Samuel Israel, and Alexander Solomons—who established businesses in Pensacola and owned property there soon after the British acquired West Florida in 1763. Isaac Montano, the first known Jewish resident in New Orleans, fled with his family to Pensacola in 1769 when Louisiana came under Spanish control. The first 19th century Jewish settler at Pensacola was Samuel Myers, member of a well-known family in Norforlk, Virginia, who practiced law there, served as an alderman, became deputy collector of customs, and held high rank in the Florida militia.

As early as the 1820s, Michael Lazarus, a businessman in Charleston, South Carolina, owned 156,000 acres of land just north of what is now Miami, in the direction of Daytona Beach. He had paid $1 an acre, which was very expensive for those days, but today it would be worth hundreds of millions of dollars. Lazarus, who was one of the founders of the Reformed Society of Israelites in Charleston in 1825, the first Reform congregation in the United States, sold half of his land in 1824 and the rest some years later. A number of Jews distinguished themselves in the Seminole Indian wars in Florida, among them Philip Diamond, Myer M. Cohen, and Abraham C. Myers. Cohen, who came from Charleston, South Carolina, where he had served in the State Legislature in 1836, and owned an "English and classical seminary," was a volunteer in the wars against the Indians. He was co-editor of a paper for the troops called *The Sunday Mor-*

ning Herald and Volunteer's Gazette, and later authored a book on the war and the blunders of the army commanders. Myers, who also came from South Carolina, was a West Point graduate, who was chief Army quartermaster in the Indian wars in Florida, 1836-1838 and 1841-1842. The town of Ft. Myers is named for him.

Colonel Leon Dyer of Baltimore and David Camden de Leon, an Army doctor from Camden, South Carolina, also served in the Florida Indian wars, as did Samuel Noah, one of the first Jewish graduates of West Point. Raphael Jacob Moses, whose ancestors had landed in Georgia in 1733, opened a store in Tallahassee in 1837, using merchandise salvaged from a fire that had destroyed his business in Charleston. Later, he worked for the first railroad built in Florida. When the railroad failed, he became a lawyer and practiced in Apalachicola before moving to Columbus, Georgia. In 1847 he was a delegate from Florida to the Democratic National Convention that nominated Lewis Cass for President.

A strong pro-slaver, Moses was one of the Southerners who withdrew from the convention when Cass refused to commit himself to the right of Southerners to carry slaves into the Northwest Territory. Emanual Judah, a popular actor in Virginia and Mobile, Alabama, in the late 1820s, built his own threatre in Apalachicola in 1839.

The first Jewish community in Florida was established in the early 1850s at Jacksonville, then the state's commercial metropolis and railroad center. The Jewish section of Jacksonville's oldest cemetery has gravestones dated 1857. Two Jews are known to have served with Florida troops during the Civil War. Gus Cohen fought with a Florida artillery battery, and Moses Daniel was in Company A of the 1st Regiment of Florida Infantry. Daniel died in a Union prision at Elmira, New York, and is buried in the Woodlawn Cemetery in that city.

In August, 1867, *The Occident* of Philadelphia, one of America's pioneer Jewish journals, reprinted a letter from a Jacksonville newspaper which had reported the organization in that city of "a society for the worship of the one and only true God—the God of Abraham, Isaac and Jacob—after the peculiar faith and manner of His ancient people, the Jews." This pioneer congregation in Florida disbanded in 1875, but was reorganized in 1882 as Congregation Ahavath Chesed. Frederick Delius, the noted British composer, was the organist of this congregation from 1882-1884. The oldest existing Jewish congregation in the state is Pensacola's Temple Beth El, founded in 1874.

In that year, the Hebrew Benevolent Society of Jacksonville published an appeal in the *Jewish Times* of New York asking for aid in helping "to relieve the suffering of many invalid visitors." The plea said that "anticipating the unusual influx of visitors to this famous winter resort during the coming season . . . this society is compelled to appeal to our Hebrew brethren in distant cities for funds." A similar appeal was published in 1892 in the *Jewish Messenger* of New York and the *American Israelite* of Cincinnati. Jacksonville was a popular winter resort until the extension of the railroad to Miami.

One of the founders of the Jacksonville congregation in 1867 was M.A. Dzialynski, who was mayor of the city from 1886-1894. Herman Goloski was mayor of Tampa from 1886-1894. Philip Water was a delegate to the constitutional convention of 1885 which wrote Florida's new constitution. Marcus Endel was grand master of the state's Grand Lodge of Masons in 1893. One of the leading citizens of Tampa and Polk County from 1895-1925 was Dr. Louis S. Oppenheimer. A native of Louisville, who had failed to make a living as a doctor in his native city and in Savannah, he learned from railroad officials that there were very few qualified doctors in Florida and a dearth of drug stores. He rode the Georgia Railroad's new line into northern Florida to its last stop, the rough frontier town of Barstow, where the discovery of huge phosphate deposits had made the place one of the busiest in Florida. In Barstow, Oppenheimer developed a large practice around 1890 and opened the only drug store in the area. Until 1897 he was one of Barstow's most influential citizens, having helped to create the local school system. In 1895 he was brought to Tampa by Henry Plant, the railroad builder who had just built the Tampa Bay Hotel at the southern terminus of his railroad. While developing a private practice, Oppenheimer became widely known as medical director of the railroad and the hotel's house doctor. His boosting of the health facilities at the hotel led the War Department to choose Tampa as the chief embarkation point for Cuba during the Spanish American War and to make the Tampa Bay Hotel military headquarters.

By the time the first intensive development of Florida began in the 1880s and 1890s there were small Jewish communities in Tampa, Key West, Jacksonville, Deland, Pensacola, and Ocala. In 1882 the Okeechobee Land and Improvement Co. undertook an unsuccessful effort to settle refugees from Czarist pogroms in an agricultural colony above the Everglades. The shift of the cigar industry from Cuba to Tampa, the opening of the North-South railroad, and the Spanish American War, in which five Jews from Florida served, started the first wave of migration from the North, including Jews.

The last part of the state to be settled was the now world-famous Greater Miami area. The first Jewish settlers came from Key West which had imposed a discriminatory tax on itinerant peddlers in the 1890s. Miami's expanding commercial life, stimulated by the extension of the railroad to Miami, attracted Jewish storekeepers from middle and upper Florida and from out of the state. Others who had seen military service at Key West, Tampa, and Miami during the Spanish American War, liked what they saw and stayed on.

So far as is known, the first Jewish resident of Miami was Samuel

Singer who came from Palm Beach in 1895 and sold dry goods from a shack on the south side of the Miami River. Isidor Cohen, a Russian Jew who came to Savannah from New York in 1891, moved to Fort Pierce in 1894 and to West Palm Beach a year later. He opened dry goods stores at both places. When Cohen heard that the railroad's southern terminus would be extended from West Palm Beach to the then little village of Miami, he moved there on February 6, 1896. By June 5, he was advertising his line of dry goods in the weekly *Miami Metropolis*. In December, Cohen noted in his diary that "Miami looks like a real town." Jake Scheidman, who became Cohen's partner in 1900, with stores in Miami and West Palm Beach, had operated his own store in Lemon City, three miles from Miami, where the railroad ended, even before Cohen arrived in Miami.

Other early arrivals in Miami were Jacob Schneider, Abe Safraneck, Julius N. Frank, Moe Hanes, M. Seligman, W. Wolfe, M. Bucholtz, N. Goldenberg, Charles and Morris Kanner, and David Singer. Miami's total population was barely 500 in 1896, and 25 were Jews. At the turn of the century the Jewish population fell to three, most of the settlers having been driven out by fire and yellow fever. It rose to 75 in 1913.

In its September 11, 1896 issue, the *Miami Metropolis* reported that "Rosh Hashanah began at sundown" and that "a Jewish organization was perfected Monday, with David Singer as president, and M. Bucholtz as secretary and treasurer." The membership of this pioneer association totaled 22. Until 1912 it was known as B'nai Zion when its name was changed to Congregation Beth David, which Cohen helped establish as the first in the Miami area. The first full-time rabbi was engaged by Beth David in 1925 when the hooded Ku Klux Klan still blew a whistle daily at 5 P.M. as a warning to blacks to get back to their section of the town. Cohen's widow, who died in 1971 at the age of 94, claimed that her eldest son, Eddie, who died in 1967, was the first Jewish boy born in Miami. Mrs. Cohen often told how the rabbi from Key West took three weeks to come by boat for Eddie's birth. For many years the rabbis from Key West and West Palm Beach visited Miami to care for the religious needs of the still tiny Jewish community. Today there are 46 synagogues of all denominations in the Greater Miami area, as well as many Jewish educational institutions.

Cohen, who was one of the signers of Miami's charter of incorporation and one of the organizers of Miami's Board of Trade, later renamed Miami Merchants Association, served several terms as president. As late as 1903, the association met in Cohen's store. Cohen was also a charter member of the first Masonic lodge and a member of the charter board that drew up the city manager form of government used by Miami for many years. Mrs. Cohen, known to two generations of Miamians as "Mama Cohen," was the founder and first president of Beth David's sisterhood. She was also a founder of the Jewish Home for the Aged and the local units of Hadassah and

National Council of Jewish Women. In 1921 the Beth David sisterhood was chartered as a section of the Council of Jewish Women and became involved in raising relief funds for East European Jews stranded in Cuba since the end of World War I. In May, 1939, the Council of Jewish Women and the year-old Greater Miami Jewish Federation sought to comfort the 900 German-Jewish refugees aboard the *SS St. Louis* who had been denied non-quota entry at Miami after they were turned away from Cuba.

During the frenzied real estate boom and wildcat speculation of the early 1920s many Jews made and lost millions in paper profits. However, the Jewish population of Miami began to increase between 1925 and 1930 despite the collapse of the boom and the devastating hurricane of 1926 that caused $100 million in damage. During this period many of the Jewish communal institutions that serve the Miami area were founded.

When the Miami area's Jewish population was first listed in the American Jewish Year Book for 1917, the figure was 175. Twenty-five years later it had climbed to 8,700. By 1954 it topped 60,000. A Jewish community census in 1972 reported that the Jewish population in Dade County (of which Miami and Miami Beach are the largest communities) numbered 187,000. At the end of 1977, it was estimated that there were between 200,000 and 250,000 Jews in Dade County. The 1972 study found that 31 percent of the Jews in Dade County were 65 years of age or older, that 85.3 percent were born outside of Dade County, and that almost half of them had moved to Dade County since 1960.

Statewide, the Jewish population showed similar striking growth. From 772 in 1877, it rose to 3,100 in 1907; 6,451 in 1917; 21,276 in 1937; over 80,000 in 1954; 112,000 in 1960; and over 310,000 in 1977. By then Florida had more Jews than any state except New York, California, Pennsylvania, New Jersey, and Illinois. In the decade 1965-1977 there was substantial Jewish population growth in Palm Beach County (Palm Beach, West Palm Beach, Lake Worth, Delray Beach, and Boca Raton); Broward County (Ft. Lauderdale, Hollywood, Hallandale, and Pompano Beach); Orlando; St. Petersburg; Sarasota; Daytona Beach; and Fort Pierce. There are also Jewish communities in the older areas of Jewish settlement—Tampa and Jacksonville—and smaller communities in Key West, Tallahassee, St. Augustine, and Gainesville, where the state university is located, and in or around the many retirement villages.

When Isidore Cohen arrived in Miami in 1896, there was only one house in Miami Beach, and as late as 1911 the Beach was little more than a snake-infested mangrove swamp and palmetto thicket.

A decade later it was still a sleepy little village of 641 residents with no idea that some day the city would have a permanent population of 85,000, 85 percent of them Jewish, who would play host to 8,000,000 visitors a year.

In 1917 there was still only a bare handful of Jews in Miami Beach, and none lived above Lincoln Road. One of these was the pioneer Weiss family, who owned the Beach's first restaurant at the south end of the peninsula, the forerunner of Jesse Weiss' Joe's Stone Crab Restaurant. Jesse Weiss was the first pupil enrolled in Miami Beach's first public school. Jewish high school students regularly encountered anti-Semitism among students and teachers at Miami Beach High School. The first Jew to address a graduating class of Miami Beach High School was Rabbi Kalman Zwitman of Miami's Temple Israel, in the late 1920s. In 1926, Malvina Weiss, then a high school student and now Mrs. Seymour Liebman, mother of Judaica scholar Charles Liebman, and wife of historian Seymour Liebman, started the first Jewish Sunday school on the Beach in a vacant lot across the street from her home at Collins Avenue and 2nd Street.

The first Jewish congregation in Miami Beach, Congregation Beth Jacob, was chartered in 1927. The first recorded Jewish High Holy Day services on the Beach were held on the roof of the David Court Apartments in 1926. The devastating earthquake of that year struck during the Kol Nidre services. Damage and destruction were so immense that no Yom Kippur morning service was held. The Beach was cut off from the mainland for four days and it was impossible to get to a synagogue in Miami. When ground was broken for Beth Jacob's first synagogue in 1928, the master of ceremonies was Harry Richman, the well-known nightclub entertainer. Temple Emanuel was founded in 1940 as the Miami Beach Jewish Center, and Temple Beth Sholom was founded two years later.

Miami Beach, more Jewish than New York, often reminds Israelis of Tel Aviv in its ethnicity and climate. There are ten synagogues, a Hebrew academy, and several day schools. Hardly a day passes without some kind of Jewish function—cultural or fundraising. A large proportion of the estimated 300 Jewish organizations in the Greater Miami area are located in Miami Beach. Most of the national Jewish organizations hold fundraising events in Miami Beach, Hollywood, and Palm Beach during the tourist season when their most generous donors are vacationing there. On Friday nights during the tourist season there are long lines outside Temple Emanuel and Temple Beth Sholom, seeking admittance to worship services.

The 375 hotels and 3,000 apartment buildings are mostly Jewish-owned and tenanted almost entirely by Jews. Twenty of the hotels, with 2,425 rooms, are kosher and the city has a full-time inspector to see that *kashrut* is not violated. Seven of the city's mayors have been Jewish.

Miami Beach was not always like that. The earliest hotels were restricted to white gentiles. A few Jews were accepted but they were friends of Carl Fisher—the Beach's chief developer in its early years. Among them were Irving Berlin and Julius Fleischmann, the yeast king, who dropped dead while playing polo on one of Fisher's six polo fields. The first Jewish hotels were the Sea Breeze and Nemo, both built within two blocks of Beth

Jacob's first synagogue. Until the 1930s real estate brokers were reluctant to sell property to Jews who began moving to Miami Beach in considerable numbers during this period, even though almost every beach front hotel was barred to Jews. By World War II, however, Miami Beach had become an almost all-Jewish winter resort and the Jews had become the dominant group in the city.

During World War II, the Air Force requisitioned most of the hotels south of 23rd Street and converted them into barracks housing personnel undergoing officer training. Synagogues became servicemen's centers and the National Jewish Welfare Board had a major assignment operating USO clubs. At the end of the war there were some 16,000 permanent Jewish residents in Miami Beach, most of them engaged in resort business, local services, or the professions.

The first big tourist boom began after the war when Miami Beach became a major winter resort for well-to-do Jews from the North, Middle West and Canada. The introduction of air package tours opened Miami Beach to the mass travel market and brought increasing numbers of Jews, first as tourists and then as residents. A building boom stimulated by national prosperity and greater mobility in the late 1960s made the availability of Florida vacation or retirement homes within reach of middle class families, and gave rise to a new wave of migration to Florida.

Among the 400,000 Cubans who began coming to the Miami area in 1959 to escape the Castro regime were several thousand Jews. Many of them brought means of their own and established new businesses in Miami and Miami Beach. They also opened medical and law practices once they were naturalized. Most of the Cuban Jewish expatriates did well in Florida after the early difficult years were behind them. The Cuban Jewish community created a number of its own institutions, including synagogues, community centers, cultural and benevolent societies, and have been generous supporters of the United Jewish Appeal and Israel Bonds.

There is only one Miami, but two Miami Beaches. One is comprised of the well-to-do and middle-class residents, permanent or temporary, of block after block of luxury hotels, motels, high-rise condominiums, and rental apartments along both sides of Collins Avenue, north of Lincoln Road, and of homeowners. The lower part of the city is the South Beach area, sometimes called "Bagel Beach" or the "other Miami Beach," because it is the site of the older and cheaper hotels and rooming houses where thousands of elderly Jews spend their twilight years. While many elderly, well-off retirees live in the luxury buildings, the Jewish aged in South Beach depend largely on Social Security checks or small pensions. Half of them live below or near the poverty line and some 500 Jewish South Beachers were on welfare at the end of 1977.

Nearly 90 percent of South Beach's estimated 40,000 elderly are Jews, many of whom are cut off from families and live empty and lonely lives. Haunted by the fear of spiraling rents and possible eviction to make room for new high-rise apartments when their owners sell the old buildings to developers, the elderly Jews worry that the business interests of Miami Beach would like to get rid of them because they spoil the image of the Beach.

Since 1972, the Greater Miami Jewish Federation has underwritten 25 percent of the cost of the South Beach Activities Center, housed in the Workmen's Circle Building on Washington Avenue. The Florida Department of Health and Rehabilitation Services picks up the rest of the cost. Administered by the South Florida Jewish Community Centers and open seven days a week, the Center is deep in the heart of the poverty area and only a block away from the city's only low-income public housing project. The senior citizens jam the center which gives them access to newspapers, arts and crafts classes, hobby programs, music, field trips, lectures, and companionship. The free kosher meals served five days a week at the center and at five other locations in South Beach are coordinated by the Jewish Vocational Service Bureau. Besides the year-round aged residents, other Jewish senior citizens come to Miami Beach by the thousands during the winter for cheap vacations in the older kosher hotels which no longer attract monied tourists. They also live in rundowm boarding houses and eat at the many kosher restaurants in the area.

Over the years, the Anti-Defamation League of B'nai B'rith made great gains in forcing the elimination of "no Jews wanted" signs and other types of discriminatory practices in the Miami area and southern Florida. During the White Citizens Council's attacks on Jewish institutions in the South as part of the war against civil rights, dynamite blasts seriously damaged the religious school of Congregation Beth El in Miami and of the Jewish Center in Jacksonville. Nevertheless, Miami and Miami Beach were the first places in Florida to eliminate overt racism. Miami Beach became a bastion of political liberalism. The Jewish population supported civil liberties causes and backed political candidates regarded as liberal and pro-Israel. During the 1974 Senatorial election, opponents of Senator Richard Stone used the phrase "Miami Beach crowd" to win votes in the rural counties.

Florida's older beach communities on both east and west Coasts had long barred Jews from desirable areas but merchants and professionals who took up residence in those communities succeeded in breaking down many of the anti-Semitic barriers by the end of the 1950s. Palm Beach, long notorious for the "No Jews Allowed" practices at its exclusive hotels and clubs, welcomed Jewish merchants as early as the 1880s, but the first congregation was not formed until 1963. The once *Judenrein* Breakers Hotel is now the scene of UJA dinners, Israel Bond banquets, and Hadassah luncheons.

The Jewish community around Cape Canaveral, where "lox" means liquid oxygen used as a rocket fuel, grew up in the 1950s when a once reptile-infested swampland became the launching pad for space and moon exploration. Thriving Jewish settlements developed at Satellite Beach, Merritt Island, Cocoa, Banana River, and Eau Gallie where the tens of thousands of Cape Canaveral civilian scientists, technicians, and supporting personnel lived, including many Jews. The Brevard Brotherhood serving Jewish military and civilian personnel developed into Temple Israel at Merritt Island and Temple Beth Shalom at Satellite Beach. Jacob A. Brodsky, a retired Air Force officer, was one of the first settlers at Cocoa Beach adjacent to Cape Canaveral before the space program began.

Despite its numerical and economic preponderance until 1964, when the state legislature was reappointed on a one-vote, one-man basis, southeastern Florida (Greater Miami) had little or no political power. It was wielded by north Florida. The first Jew to win election to public office on a county-wide basis in Dade County (Greater Miami) was Milton Weiss, who was elected to the County School Board in 1940.

All of the major cities have had one or more Jewish mayors: M.A. Dzialynski, Jacksonville, 1888-1896; Herman Goloski, Tampa, 1886-1894; Sam A. Wahnish, Tallahassee, 1939-1941; Gene Berkowitz, Tallahassee, 1968; Adolph Greenhut, Pensacola, 1913-1915; his son, Irving Greenhut, Pensacola, 1965; Max L. Baer, Pensacola, 1937; and Abe Aronovitz, Miami, 1953-1955. Other Jewish mayors were: Bernard Rubin, Fort Pierce, 1956; Morris Silverman, Florida City, 1936; Max Wyner, Kelsey City, 1920-1922; William Friedman, Dade City, 1926; Jerome Weiner, Dade City, 1966; Morris Rabinowitz, Graceville, 1961; David Cohen, Sarasota; and Louis Nathan, Miami Shores, 1930. Miami Beach has had at least seven Jewish mayors: Mitchell Wolfson, 1943; Marcie Liberman, 1947; Harold Turk, 1949; Harold Shapiro, 1953; Kenneth Oka, 1961; Jay Dermer; and Harold Rosen, 1973.

Two Jews have served on Florida's Supreme Court: Judge Philip Goldman, a native of Miami, whose grandfather, Louis Fine, was one of the founders of Miami's Beth David Congregation, was appointed in 1962. Judge Raymond G. Nathan, also from Miami, was appointed in 1974. Richard E. Gerstein was elected to his fifth four-year term as Dade County District Attorney in 1972. Robert Rust of Palm Beach was appointed U.S. Attorney for the Southern District of Florida in 1969. In Miami Beach, where signs once warned Jews and dogs to keep away, a New York-born Chief of Police, Rocky Pomerance, and his successor, Larry Cotzin, maintain law and order. Sidney Aronovitz of Miami, was named a U.S. District Court Judge in 1976.

In 1974 three Jews, all from the Miami area, battled for the Democratic senatorial nomination: Burton Young, a former president of the Florida Bar Association; Joel Kuperberg, executive director of the In-

ternal Improvement Fund, whose family was one of the early Miami settlers; and Richard Stone, who won the nomination and the election despite
some subtle anti-Semitic smears. Stone was the first Jew from the South
elected to the Senate by popular vote. His three predecessors—David Levy
Yulee, Florida, 1845-1851 and 1855-1861; Judah P. Benjamin, Lousiana,
1852-1861; and Benjamin Jonas, Louisiana, 1879-1885, were chosen by their
state legislatures. Popular election of United States senators began only in
1913. Stone had been Secretary of State in the same administration in
which Robert L. Shevin, another Miamian, served as Attorney-General.

Among other well-known Jewish Floridians was Ernest Maas, one of
the founders of Tampa University, who was named Tampa's outstanding
citizen. Mitchel Wolfson, a much-decorated World War II officer, was one
of the prime movers behind the formation of a metro-type government for
Miami and 25 other Dade County municipalities. He was one of the founders of Miami-Dade Junior College, and operator of theatres, radio, and TV
stations and tourist enterprises. Wolfson grew up in Key West where his
father went into business in 1888. Israeli-born Zev Bufman brought live
theatre to Florida and founded the Coconut Grove Playhouse, the Park
Playhouse in Ft. Lauderdale, and the Royal Poinciana Playhouse in Palm
Beach. Mrs. Sydney L. Weintraub, who was chairman-emeritus of the
Miami Museum of Science, persuaded the Dade County Commission to
build the museum which she headed for many years. She was named the
county's outstanding citizen. Mrs. Weintraub is descended from a family
that settled in Miami in 1896. Sidney Levin, executive vice-president and
general manager of Miami radio station WKAT, was named president of
the Greater Miami Chamber of Commerce in 1974. Harold David (Hank)
Meyer, who came to Florida as a boy seeking a cure for his hay fever, became known as "the miracle man of Miami Beach" because of his phen-
omenal success in publicizing and promoting the city. He was the first Jew
to be elected to Florida's Hall of Fame. Morris Lapidus, Miami Beach's top
architect, designed many of the newer multi-million dollar Miami Beach
hotels. Hal Cohen succeeded Meyer as the resort's chief promoter.

In early 1977, Florida counted 110 synagogues in 50 cities and towns,
Jewish federations in 15 communities, Jewish Community Centers in seven
communities, and Hillel Foundations at the University of Florida, University of Miami, and Florida State University.

The unique life style in the hundreds of condominiums that have
sprung up in southern Florida has given rise to a new kind of synagogue
whose members are made up of retired couples, widows, and widowers, few
of whom had synagogue affiliations before they came to Florida. These new-
comers have created synagogues in the condominium social hall, an apartment, a vacant store, or even in a nearby temple. Few of them have either a
rabbi or a cantor. There were some 40 such synagogues with a total mem-

bership of over 10,000 early in 1977 and another 30,000 who are prospective members.

* * * * *

ALTAMONTE SPRINGS

Cong. Beth Am, P.O.B. 4733.

Heritage, Central Florida Jewish News, 711 E. Altamonte Dr.

BAY HARBOR ISLAND

Town of Broad Causeway which links 125th St. in North Miami to 96th St. in Miami Beach, was founded by Shepard Broad, nationally known house builder and communal leader.

BELLE GLADE

Beth Torah Cong., First Federal Savings & Loan Association of Del Ray Beach Bldg., 200 E. Palm.

Temple Beth Sholom, N.W. Ave. G.

BOCA RATON

B'nai Torah Cong., 3650 N.E. 4th Ave.

Boca Raton Hebrew Cong., 2 S.W. 12th Ave. (Moravian Church) is where the congregation worships, but its office is at 455 N.W. 35th St.

BRADENTOWN

Temple Beth El, 2209 75 Street, W., is the first synagogue in Manatee County.

CAPE CORAL

Lee County Jewish Center, 915 S.E. 47th Terr.

Temple Beth El, 2721 Del Prado Pkwy.

CEDAR KEY

David Levy Yulee Plaque marks the site where the Florida Railroad Co. line, the first cross-state railroad organized in 1853 by David Levy Yulee, reached Cedar Key, now a small fishing village, in 1861.

CLEARWATER

Cong. Beth Shalom, 2177 Coachman Ave., N.E.

Cong. Sons of Jacob, 1230 Brookside Dr.

COCOA BEACH

Temple Israel of Brevard County, 15 Poinsetta Dr.

CORAL GABLES

Temple Judea, 5500 Granada Blvd., has a three-foot sculptured head of Moses on a marble base in the lobby above the inner entrance to the sanctuary.

Temple Zamora, 44 Zamora Ave.

University of Miami

● Maurice Gusman Concert Hall at University of Miami, adjacent to the music school complex, off San Amaro Dr., bet. the Ring Theatre and Charles Gautier Hall, was a gift from a one-time immigrant, who arrived in the U.S. as a penniless 14-year old boy from Russia in 1899. The hall houses a 700-seat auditorium and the offices of the School of Music.

● Hillel Foundation, 1100 Miller Dr.

● Joe and Emily Lowe Art Museum, was founded by a New Jersey ice cream manufacturer. Mr. and Mrs. Howard Garfinkle contributed $2,300,000 for the museum's expansion.

● Mailman Center for Child Development, 1601 N.W. 12th Ave., named for Abraham and Joseph Mailman, Florida financiers and philanthropists, who contributed over $1 million toward the center as a tribute to Abraham's grandaugther, a handicapped youngster.

● Baron de Hirsch Meyer Buildings of School of Law, constitute a complex of five buildings given to the University by one of its late trustees: the four-story faculty and administrative office building, the library building, a two-story classroom building, a one-story student lounge, and a four-story structure containing faculty offices, seminar rooms, and a student activities area.

● Rosenstiel School of Marine and Atmospheric Science, a 3-story building on Virginia Key between Miami and Key Biscayne, is named for Lewis S. Rosenstiel, New York liquor manufacturer, who gave the institution $12 million. The Rosenstiel School is part of the University's marine and ocean science complex.

● Arnold Volpe Memorial Building, memorializes the Russian-born Jewish conductor and composer who founded the University's symphony orchestra in 1926. The building was a gift of Mr. and Mrs. Albert Pick of Miami Beach, who also established the Albert Pick Music Library, adjacent to the Volpe Building. The Handleman Institute of Recorded Music, one of the buildings of the University's music school, was endowed by Mr. and Mrs. Joseph Handleman of Detroit.

CORAL SPRINGS

Temple Beth Orr, 2151 Riverside Dr.

DAYTONA BEACH

Art Museum for the Blind, a collection of sculpture which the blind can "see" by their sense of touch, and the Braille explanatory description attached to each piece, was founded in 1958 by Henry Saltzman and adopted as a project of the local B'nai B'rith lodge.

Temple Beth El, 507 5th at Wild Olive Ave.

Temple Israel of Daytona, 1400 S. Peninsula Dr.

DEERFIELD BEACH

Jewish Center-Temple Beth Israel, Century Village E.

DELAND

Temple Israel of Deland, 1001 E. New York Ave., is a quaint small blue and white building that serves about 40 families and seats 100.

DELRAY BEACH

Delray Hebrew Cong., meets at the Methodist Fellowship Hall, 342 N. Swinton Ave., but is erecting its own building on Atlantic Ave.

DELTONA

Temple Shalom, Providence and Elkham Blvds. (in the United Church of Deltona).

ELLENTON

Judah P. Benjamin Memorial, a state of Florida shrine to the Confederate statesman (see Louisiana), is on the Manatee River. Built in the 1840s as the mansion of Maj. Robert Gamble, the house was bought in 1926 by the Judah P. Benjamin Chapter of the United Daughters of the Confederacy, which deeded it to the state of Florida. The state has restored the house and grounds and preserves them as a historical monument. In May, 1865, when Benjamin was fleeing Union pursuers, he was hidden in the Gamble mansion while arrangements were being made for his escape from the country. Disguised first as a Frenchman and then as a farmer, Benjamin spent most of his time on the upstairs veranda of the mansion, scanning the Manatee River with a spyglass for Union gunboats which were hunting for him. When Union troops made a surprise raid on the Gamble estate, Benjamin barely had time to escape through the kitchen into a thicket of scrub palmetto in the rear. After this narrow escape, Benjamin moved to the secluded home of another Confederate sympathizer until he could be taken overland to Sarasota. There he boarded a sloop for Cuba and then sailed for England, where the former Confederate Secretary of War and Secretary of State carved out a second career as a leading member of the English bar.

FORT LAUDERDALE

International Swimming Hall of Fame, 1 Hall of Fame Dr., has a 12-foot high panel featuring, among other stars of swimming, diving, and water polo, Mark Spitz, who set a new Olympic record in 1972 when he won seven gold medals. Spitz is also included in a display on the second floor of the Hall of Fame.

Jewish Federation, 2999 N.W. 3rd Ave.

Jewish Student Organization at Broward Community College, 707 N. Federal Highway.

Shomer Shabbat Village, 6400 N.W. 64th Ave., is a private condominium with a synagogue. There are Shabbat elevators which stop at every floor so that Sabbath observers need not push the buttons.

Tamarac Jewish Center, 9106 N.W. 57th St.

Temple Emanu-El, 3245 W. Oakland Park Blvd. (Lauderdale Lakes).

Young Israel of Hollywood, The Oaks, 4111 Stirling Rd.

FORT MYERS

Col. Abraham Charles Myers, quartermaster for Florida troops at an Army fort built in 1839 during the Seminole Indian War, is memorialized by this Lee County, Gulf Coast town that grew up around the fort. Originally known as Fort Harvie, the name was changed to Fort Myers in 1859. A relative of Moses Cohen, the first rabbi in Charleston, S.C., Myers was an 1830 graduate of the U.S. Military Academy. He served with Federal troops in Indian wars from 1836-1842 and was with Generals Zachary Taylor and Winfield Scott in the Mexican War. During the Civil War, Myers was the first Confederate quartermaster.

FORT PIERCE

Temple Beth El, 302 N. 23rd St.

GAINESVILLE

B'nai Israel Jewish Center, 3115 N.W. 16th St.

Florida State Museum, 1st and 2nd floors of 10-story Seagle Bldg., on University Ave., six blocks south of the University of Florida campus, has among its portraits of noted Floridians, one of David Levy Yulee, first Jew to sit on Congress.

University of Florida

● Hillel Foundation, 16 N.W. 18th St.

● National Journalism Hall of Fame, School of Journalism and Communications, honors, among others, Adolph S. Ochs, publisher of *The New York Times*, and Joseph Pulitzer.

● Shepard Broad Center for Jewish Studies, is named for one of the University's greatest benefactor's. Shepard Broad, builder, banker, and Jewish communal leader of Miami Beach gave the institution property worth in excess of $1.4 million which was later sold to finance the building of the Center. The Mishkin Collection of 50,000 books, pamphlets, and journals, all related to Jewish history, acquired by the University from the family of Rabbi Leonard Mishkin, is to be housed in the Broad Educational Center.

GULFPORT
Jewish Center, 1854 54th St.

HALLANDALE
Jewish Center, 416 N.E. 8th Ave.

HIALEAH
Temple Israel, South Tropical Trail.
Temple Tifereth Jacob, 951 E. 4th Ave.

HOLLYWOOD
Hollywood Outreach Program of Jewish Community Centers of South Florida, 2838 Hollywood Blvd.
Jewish Family Service, 2838 Hollywood Blvd.
Jewish Federation of South Broward, 2838 Hollywood Blvd.
Temple Beth Ahm, 310 S.W. 62nd Ave.
Temple Beth El, 1351 S. 14th Ave.
Temple Beth Shalom, 4601 Arthur St.
Temple Sinai, 1201 Johnson St., has in front of its building a six-foot, seven-inch white marble sculpture entitled *The Masada.*
Temple Solel, 5100 Sheridan St.

HOMESTEAD
Homestead Jewish Centre, 183 N.E. 8th St.

HOMOSASSA SPRINGS
Yulee Park, one mile outside of this Citrus County Gulf Coast town, is a state historical shrine honoring the memory of David Levy Yulee. Maintained by the County Federation of Women's Clubs, the park has a plaque memorializing Yulee, and contains the remains of a large sugar plantation and mill once owned by him but destroyed by Union troops during the Civil War. Tourists heading for St. Petersburg via State Highway 19 go within a few miles of the park, which was the site of one of the last battles of the Civil War. The plaque's inscription reads: "1810—David Levy Yulee— 1886. This tablet marks the ruins of the sugar mill constructed by David Levy Yulee in 1851. The plantation covered approximately 100 acres. It is the property of Citrus County Federation of Women's Clubs. It was presented from the then owner, Mr. Claude Root, in 1923, and preserved as a historic monument. This tablet was presented by Mr. H. Maddox, of

Archer, Florida, and erected Oct. 26, 1950."
Maddox was a descendant of Yulee. The sugar mill was located on
Yulee's 10,000 acre estate called "Marguerita," one of the show places of
pre-Civil War Florida. Until 1864, the Yulee mill produced sugar for the
Confederate Army, but in that year the Union Forces captured the estate
and destroyed the mill. When Yulee died in 1886, the *Washington Post*
described him as the Senator from Florida "who was better known than the
state he represented," while the *Florida Times-Union* credited him with
having had "probably a larger influence upon the character and development of the state . . . than any other man."

JACKSONVILLE
Cong. Beth Shalom (see Mandarin).
Etz Chaim Synagogue, 5864 University Blvd., W.
Florida Hall of Fame, in the headquarters building of the Florida State
Chamber of Commerce, 8057 Expressway, included only one Jew in 1977 —
Hank Meyer, whose publicity efforts were largely responsible for the de-
velopment of Miami Beach as a resort center. A portrait of Meyer hangs in
the Hall.
Jacksonville Hebrew Academy, 5864 University Blvd., W.
Jacksonville University preserves the small wooden shack at Solarno
Grove, near Jacksonville, where the famed British composer, Frederick
Delius, wrote most of his music while earning part of his livelihood as or-
ganist at Cong. Ahavath Chesed. Philip Emanuel, a prominent British Jew,
close friend of Delius, and a trustee of his estate, received an honorary de-
gree from Jacksonville University in 1962 in recognition of his role in the re-
moval and restoration of the shack. Hillel Foundation at the University,
Box 27.
Jewish Center Synagogue, 10101 San Jose Blvd.
Jewish Community Council, 5846 Mt. Carmel Terr.
Jewish Family and Children's Service, 1415 LaSalle St.
Levy Memorial Building, Adams and Hogan Sts., which houses the
Levy Wolf clothing and specialty store founded in 1927, has on the main
floor a bronze plaque stating that Della M. Levy, widow of Benjamin S.
Levy, one of the store's founders, bequeathed the building to the Levy
Memorial Fund which annually received a guaranteed rent from the store
owners which is divided equally among eight general and Jewish charities
each year.
Mt. Carmel Gardens, 5864 University Blvd., is a community-
sponsored apartment house for the elderly.
River Garden Hebrew Home for the Aged, 1800 Stockton St.
Southern Jewish Weekly, 1838 Evergreen.
Temple of Cong. Ahavath Chesed, 8727 San Jose Blvd.

Samuel W. Wolfson High School, 7000 Powers Ave., is named for a philanthropist who gave the Duval County School Board a large contribution. Wolfson's portrait hangs in the school library.

KENNETH CITY
Kenneth Colen, son of Sidney Colen who founded this incorporated town of 3,000 in 1957 as a residential community near St. Petersburg, is the namesake of the town.

KEY WEST
Audubon House, Whitehead and Green Sts., named for the famed naturalist who worked here in 1832, was saved from destruction by Col. Mitchell Wolfson, a Key West native, who bought the building when it was known as Geiger House, in 1960, and at his own expense restored and converted it into a museum owned by the city.
Cong. B'nai Zion, 750 Umted St.

LAKELAND
Temple Emanuel, 730 Lake Hollingsworth Dr.

LAKE WORTH
Temple Beth Sholom, 315 North A St.

LAKE YALE
This lake was originally known as Lake Yulee, named for David Levy Yulee.

LAUDERDALE LAKES
Masada, 4202 N. State Rd., is an art and gift gallery featuring Israeli imports.

LECANTO
Beverly Hills Jewish Center (Cong. Beth Sholom), in the Civic Center, was a gift from Sam Kellner, wealthy builder of the Beverly Hills retirement community, 11 miles north of Homosassa Springs in Citrus County. He also donated sites for churches, built a hospital, and maintains in a community bank a special account from which residents may borrow short-term amounts, interest-free. He also operates a free bus service to nearby communities for residents who do not drive. A plaque in the synagogue honors Kellner for his "humanitarian efforts."

LEHIGH ACRES
Temple Emanu-El, Joel Blvd.

LEVY COUNTY

David Levy Yulee is memorialized by this central West Coast county. Although Levy changed his name to Yulee after his election to the Senate, the state's geographers retained his original name when they planned new counties. Levy County adjoins Alachua County, in which Yulee's father owned large tracts. Yulee was the first Jew to serve in the Senate. Because of his strong pro-slavery views, he was known as the "Florida fire eater." As early as 1840, he urged secession unless the North agreed to a constitutional amendment that would protect the South. Two months before the South seceded, Yulee was one of a number of Southern senators who helped plan the Confederate States of America in whose Congress he served.

He was the first member of the Senate to announce the secession of one of the Southern states. After the Civil War, he was arrested and confined in a Federal prison for five years. Yulee and Jefferson P. Davis were the last two Confederate leaders to be pardoned. After his release, he returned to Florida to rebuild the East-West Railroad he had organized in the 1850s, during the interim between his two terms in the Senate, and in the reconstruction of the state he and his father had helped build.

LEVY LAKE

Moses Elias Levy, Senator Yulee's father, is memorialized by the name of this popular fishing spot in Alachua County. The lake is part of the area where Levy tried to establish a Jewish colony in the 1820s.

LONGWOOD

Cong. Beth Am, P.O. Box 969.

MAITLAND

Jewish Community Center of Central Florida, 851 N. Maitland Ave.
Jewish Federation of Greater Orlando, 851 N. Maitland Ave.

MANATEE

Jewish Community Organization.

MANDARIN

Cong. Beth Shalom, 4072 Sunbeam Rd.

MARGATE

Margate Jewish Center.

MERRITT ISLAND

Brevard County Jewish Community Council.
Temple Israel of Brevard County, P.O. Box 592.

MIAMI

Agudath Achim Cong., 19255 N.E. 3rd Ave.

Ahavat Sholom Cong., 995 S.W. 67th Ave.

American-Israeli Religious Store, 1357 Washington Ave.

Anshe Emes Cong., 2553 S.W. 19th Ave.

Abe Aronovitz Villas, 430 S.W. 5th St., is a public housing facility for the aged that memorializes the late mayor of Miami. The adjacent Stanley and Martha Myers Senior Citizens Center, a public day center for the aged, is named for Stanley Myers, first president of the Greater Miami Jewish Federation and chairman of Miami's first Community Chest campaign, and his wife, a former chairman of the Jewish Family and Children's Service.

Beth David Cong., 2625 S.W. 3rd Ave., is the oldest congregation in Greater Miami area.

Beth David Cong., South, 7500 S.W. 12th Ave.

B'nai Israel and Greater Miami Youth Synagogue, 9600 Sunset Dr. (South Miami).

Central Agency for Jewish Education, 4200 Biscayne Blvd., has an extensive Jewish research library and stamp collection.

Cong. Bet Breira, 10755 S.W. 112th St.

Cong. B'nai Raphael, 1401 N.W. 183rd St.

Conservative Cong. of Kendale Lakes, 8900 S.W. 107 Ave.

Dade County Art Museum, 3251 S. Miami Ave., had among its Italian gardens and fountains, a large statue of Moses.

Florida Senior Parent Services, 6330 S.W. 118th St., provides advice and counseling to the elderly residents of the area. Their services often cover written reports to relatives on the general welfare of the senior citizen, information on adult activities, reduced rates on transportation and food, and general counseling with urgent problems which may arise.

Greater Miami Jewish Foundation, 4200 Biscayne Blvd., has a three-story high window wall of mirrored glass. The building also houses the Central Agency for Jewish Education and the regional offices of many national Jewish organizations. The entire cost of the building was met by a group of 100 men and women, each of whom contributed $10,000.

Maurice Gusman Philharmonic Hall, Flagler St., in downtown Miami, the home of the Miami Philharmonic Orchestra, is named for the Jewish philanthropist, who spent $4 million to rescue the venerable Olympic Theatre from being razed, and converted it into an all-purpose theatre.

Hillel Community Day School, 191st St. and N.E. 25th Ave.

Hillel Foundation, Florida International University, Tamiami Trail.

Hillel Jewish Student Organization, Miami-Dade Community College (North Campus), 10815 N.W. 27th Ave.

Hillel Jewish Student Organization, Miami-Dade Community College (South Campus), 1100 Miller Dr., Coral Gables.

Interfaith Chapel, Miami International Airport, is co-sponsored by the Rabbinical Association of Greater Miami and their Catholic and Protestant counterparts.

Israelite Center Temple, 3175 S.W. 25th St.

Israel South Temple, 9025 Sunset Dr.

Jewish Family and Children's Service, 1790 S.W. 27th Ave.

Jewish Floridian, 120 N.E. 6th St.

Jewish Historical Society of South Florida, 4200 Biscayne Blvd.

Jewish Vocational Service, 318 N.W. 25th St.

Martyrs Memorial, a granite monument at the main parkway entrance to Lakeside Memorial park, N.W. 25th St. and 103rd Ave., was erected in 1960 in memory of the 6,000,000 Jewish victims of the Nazi Holocaust.

Baron de Hirsch Meyer Community Building, 395 N.W. 1st St., which houses the Greater Miami United Fund and 13 of its agencies, was a gift of the late Baron de Hirsch Meyer.

Miami Jewish Home and Hospital for the Aged (Douglas Gardens), 151 N.E. 52nd St.

Anna Brenner Meyers Hall of Medical Center of Miami-Dade Community College, 950 N.W. 20th Ave., honors the lady who served on the board of the college from 1953-1971 and during her membership urged the establishment of a community college in Dade County.

National Hebrew-Israel Gift Shop, 949 Washington Ave.

Rephun's Bookstore, 417 Washington Ave.

Rosichan Park, 56th and 57th Sts. and N.W. 24th and 25th Aves., memorializes the late Claire Rosichan, whose husband, Arthur, was for many years executive director of the Greater Miami Jewish Federation. She was an ardent advocate of greater public park and recreational facilities.

Samu-El Temple, 8900 S.W. 107th Ave.

Shalom Judaica Shop, 18190 W. Dixie Highway.

Fred Shaw Memorial Plaza, at Miami-Dade Community College South, located between the Gibson Health Center and the Trammell Learning Resources Center, memorializes the college's late dean and director of its humanities division.

South Dade Hebrew Academy, 11801 S.W. 74th Ave.

Temple Adath Jeshurun, 1025 N.E. Miami Gardens Dr.

Temple Beth Am, 5950 N. Kendall Dr., has in its foyer a hand-made needlepoint tapestry, which depicts the story of the Prophet Nathan and David and Bathsheba. Seventeen members of the temple's sisterhood worked more than a year on the nine panel tapestry.

Temple Beth Tov, 6438 S.W. 8th St.

Temple Israel, 137 N.W. 19th St., has a prize-winning chapel and a Biblical garden planted with trees and shrubs mentioned in the Bible. The Nathan and Sophie Gumenick Chapel won the merit award of the National Conference on Religious Architecture for its unique 11 three-dimensional sculptured windows set into the sculptured cement walls. The windows depict the role and place of the Jewish people in history. The street fronting the temple has a scenic mall linking the various buildings of the temple complex. The temple also maintains the Sidney and Zenia Meyer Religious Retreat Center at 25001 S.W. 17th Ave.

Temple Israel South, formerly Temple Beth Tikva, which uses the Cross of Glory Church at Sunset Dr. and 92nd Ave. for worship purposes, is an integral part of Temple Israel.

Temple Or Olom, 8755 S.W. 16th Ave., has a stained glass facade depicting the 12 Tribes of Israel in their Biblical symbolism.

Temple Tifereth Israel, 6500 N. Miami Ave.

Temple Zion, 8000 Miller Rd.

Mitchell Wolfson Plaza, an offstreet parking area, is named for the chairman of the Miami Offstreet Parking Board, one of the city's leading civic figures.

Young Israel of Greater Miami, 990 N.E. 71st St.

MIAMI BEACH

Agudas Achim Nusach Sefard Cong., 707 5th Ave.

Agudath Israel Cong. 7801 Carlyle Pl.

American Israeli Religious Articles Store, 1357 Washington Ave.

Bass Museum of Art, 2100 Collins Ave., contains the multi-million dollar art collection of Mr. and Mrs. John Bass, which they donated to the city.

Beth El Cong., 2400 Pine Tree Dr.

Beth Israel Cong., 770 40th St., has a memorial monument to the 6,000,000 victims of the Nazi Holocaust in front of the synagogue.

Beth Jacob Cong., 311 Washington Ave.

Beth Solomon Temple, 1031 Lincoln Rd.

Beth Tfilah Cong., 935 Euclid Ave.

Beth Torah Cong., 1051 Interama Blvd.

Beth Yoseph Chaim Cong., 848 Meridian Ave.

B'nai B'rith Senior Housing Apartments, 6th St. and Collins Ave., and 11th St. and Collins Ave.

Broad Causeway, the main highway linking the mainland of Dade County with Miami Beach, was built by and named for Shepard Broad, attorney and civic leader, who was voted North Dade County's outstanding citizen in 1950. A bronze plaque with Broad's portrait in bas-relief is affixed to the causeway entrance.

Chabad House of Lubavitcher Movement, 1401 Alton Ave.

Cinema Theatre, Washington Ave. and 13th St., features Yiddish-American vaudeville at matinee and evening performances daily except Friday from mid-Dec. to mid-April.

Jacob S. Cohen Community Synagogue, 1532 Washington Ave.

Cong. Beth Jacob, 301 Washington Ave.

Cong. Etz Chaim, 1554 Washington Ave.

Cong. Ohr Hachaim, 317 E. 47th St.

Cuban Hebrew Cong., 1242 Washington Ave.

Cuban Sephardic Hebrew Cong., 715 Washington Ave.

Leroy D. Feinberg Elementary School, 1420 Washington Ave., one of the oldest schools in Miami Beach, was renamed in 1967 in memory of its brilliant young principal.

Golden Coast Synagogue, 5445 Collins Ave.

Golden Grill, (Saxony Hotel), is a kosher restaurant.

Greater Miami Hebrew Academy, 2400 Pine Tree Rd., has on the outside of its Louis Merwitzer Building, a multi-colored wall mural measuring more than 100 feet. Known as *The Saga of the Jewish People, Past, Present, and Future*, the painting traces the history of Judaism and mankind from Creation to the Messianic Era. The building also houses the Baumrid Art Center.

Hadassah Center for winter residents, mezzanine floor of Moulin Rouge Hotel, 41st St. and Indian Creek.

Hamifgash—The Meeting Place—a young people's coffee house, at Arthur Godfrey Rd. and Chase Ave., (entrance from the alleyway on Chase Ave., south of Temple Beth Sholom), is open every Friday evening from 9 p.m. to 1 a.m. The free coffee house features folk singing, Israeli folk dancing, food, and entertainment by visiting personalities. It is sponsored by the American Jewish Congress, Temple Beth Shalom, and student groups.

Hebrew Educational Alliance of Greater Miami, 2838 Prairie Ave.

Hebrew Home for Aged, 320 Collins Ave.

Israel Cultural Center, 2200 Park Ave., sponsored by the Greater Miami districts of the Zionist Organization of America.

Jewish Cultural Center, 429 Lenox Ave.

Jewish Vocational Service Nutrition Program, 920 Alton Rd., is the headquarters for the city-wide project which provides free kosher meals five days a week to the elderly Jewish poor at five different locations. Administered by the Jewish Vocational Service, the project is sponsored by the Greater Miami Jewish Federation and the United Fund of Dade County, with funding from the Federal government and the State of Florida Division on Aging.

Kneseth Israel Cong., 1415 Euclid Ave.

Landow Yeshiva, 1140 Alton Rd., has a Torah Ark with 17 pictures of the Holocaust on one side and dancing Chasidim on the other. The inscription reads, "those who plant in sorrow will reap in joy." The center panel, which opens to hold the Torah Scroll, is modeled after the panels in the Ark of an old and historic synagogue in Cracow, Poland, which was destroyed by the Nazis. The Torah Scroll in the Ark was carried by the family of William G. Mechanic to every community in which they had lived over several generations.

Lehrman Day School, 727 77th St.

Henry Levy Park, 71st St. and Bay Drive, honors the memory of one of the city's pioneer developers who donated the streets, park, and fountain in the Normandy Isle area.

Henry Liebman Sq., 41st St. and Pine Tree Dr., memorializes the late director of the Miami Beach Citizens Service Bureau. The square, which includes flower gardens and a fountain, is marked by a stone monument to which is affixed a bronze plaque describing Liebman as "a beloved and dedicated public servant."

Lubavitch Cong., 1120 Collins Ave.

Magen David Cong., 9348 Harding Ave.

Mount Sinai Hospital and Medical Center, 4300 Alton Rd., is a $100 million complex.

Alexander Muss Park, 44th St. and Chase Ave., a children's playground and recreation area named for the Miami Beach developer, was established through a gift from Muss' family.

National Conference of Synagogue Youth Drop-in-Centers, 711 40th St., Skylake Synagogue, 18151 N.E. 19th Ave. (North Miami Beach), and in Sunset Park, S.W. Miami.

National Hebrew-Israeli Gift Center, 949 Washington Ave.

North Bay Jewish Center, 1720 St. Causeway.

North Bay Village Jewish Center, 7800 Hispaniola Ave.

Ohev Shalom Cong., 7055 Bonita Dr.

Senior Citizens Housing Apartments are being built by the Jewish Federation Housing, Inc. of Greater Miami Jewish Federation at the southeast corner of West Ave. and 8th St., and on Collins Ave., between 9th and 10th Sts.

Sephardic Jewish Center, 645 Collins Ave.

South Beach Activities Center of Jewish Community Centers of South Florida, 25 Washington Ave., is a recreational center for aged Jews in Miami Beach, sponsored by the Greater Miami Jewish Federation and the State of Florida Division of Aging. The center has a sizeable Judaica library, including many books in Yiddish. It is also one of the stations of the Jewish Vocational Service kosher meal program. Washington Ave., from Lincoln Rd. South to 4th St., the main street of the elderly Jewish community of Miami Beach, is also a collection of shops selling ceremonial objects, kosher butchers, old-fashioned Jewish bakeries, and food shops.

Spinoza Outdoor Forum and the Liberal Club of Flamingo Park both meet in Flamingo Park, 12th and Meridian Aves., to conduct weekly lectures and discussions, listen to concerts, and view art exhibits sponsored by various Jewish groups. At the Liberal Club, the old arguments between the Jewish "left" and "right" still persist. At the Spinoza Outdoor Forum the *Jewish Daily Forward* is read aloud with comments. On Saturday afternoons men learned in Hebrew reread the *sedra* of the week and comment on it.

Talmudic College of Florida, 4014 Chase Ave.

Temple Beth Am, 5950 S.W. 88th St.

Temple Beth Raphael, 1545 Jefferson Ave.

Temple Beth Sholom, 4144 Chase Ave. at 41st St. (Arthur Godfrey Rd.), has a unique domed chapel which resembles an inflated tent, mounted on 12 arched doorways adorned with miniature Stars of David. The temple also houses the Lowe-Levinson Art Gallery. Forty feet above the temple's roof is the antenna of the "ham" radio station operated by the synagogue's youth group. The station has been in touch with Jews in more than 100 different countries. Visitors are advised to obtain tickets of admission in advance for Friday evening services. On the exterior eastern wall of the auditorium of the Temple's School of Living Judaism, there is a ceramic wall depicting the history of the Jewish people and their life in America.

Temple Beth Solomon, 1031 Lincoln Rd.

Temple Emanuel, 1701 Washington Ave., has a fine museum. During the winter tourist season, there is usually standing room only at Friday evening services. Visitors are advised to obtain tickets of admission in advance.

Temple Menorah, 620 75th St.

Temple Ner Tamid, 80th St. and Tatum Pkwy.

Wolfson Park, in Pier Park, is named for Col. Mitchell Wolfson, who was elected mayor of Miami Beach in 1943 but entered the Army before he completed his two-year term. He had previously served in the city council from 1939-1943.

Workmen's Circle Center, 25 Washington Ave.

MINERAL SPRINGS

Grossman Hammock State Park, a camping and recreation site on Lake Chekiba, 35 miles southeast of downtown Miami, is named for Mark L. Grossman of Coral Gables, who donated the area to the State of Florida.

MIRAMAR

Temple Israel, 6920 S.W. 35th St.

NORTH BAY VILLAGE
Jewish Center, 1729 79th St. Causeway.

NORTH MIAMI
Aventura Jewish Center, 2972 Aventura Blvd.

Beth Moshe Cong., 2225 N.E. 121st St.

B'nai Sephardim of Greater Miami, 20 N.W. 146th St.

Temple Sinai of North Dade, 18801 N.E. 22nd Ave., has a sanctuary designed like the tent sanctuary of the ancient Israelites.

NORTH MIAMI BEACH
Adath Yeshurun Temple, 1025 N.E. Miami Gardens Dr.

Agudath Achim Cong., 19225 N.E. 3rd Ave.

Beth Torah Cong., 1051 N. Miami Beach Blvd.

B'nai Raphael Cong., 1401 N.W. 183rd St.

Cong. Etz Chaim, the "gay" synagogue of the Miami area, holds Friday evening services in the Aljaman Art Clinic, 157 N.E. 166th St.

Farband Labor Zionist Center, 780 N.E. 183rd St.

Hillel Community Day School (next door to Jewish Community Center, see below).

North Dade Branch of YM-YWHA, 20400 N.E. 24th Ave.

Michael-Ann Russell Jewish Community Center, 18900 N.E. 25th Ave., is the main building of the Jewish Community Centers of South Florida. It occupies a 15-acre river-front site. Additional buildings are planned in the Sky Lake area in North Dade, bordering the Oleta River, and in the Kendall area of South Dade.

Sephardic Jewish Center, 571 N.E. 171st St.

Sinai Temple of North Dade, 8801 N.E. 22nd Ave.

Skylake Orthodox Synagogue, 1850 N.E. 183rd St.

Temple Israel of Greater Miami, Kendall Branch, 9900 N. Kendall Dr.

Young Israel of Greater Miami, 900 N.E. 171st St.

OAKLAND PARK
Jewish Federation of North Broward, 3905 N. Anderson Ave.

OCALA
One of Florida's oldest Jewish cemeteries, dating from the 1880s, is north of this town.

ORLANDO
Central Florida Jewish Community Council (see Maitland).

Cong. Beth Am, P.O. Box 4773, Winter Park, (services at Summit Plaza, see Sanford).

Cong. Liberal Judaism, 928 Malone Dr.

Cong. Ohev Shalom, 5015 Goddard Ave.

Disney World, serves kosher food in the Polynesian Village Hotel (Coral Isle Coffee Shop and Papeete Bay Veranda Buffet) and in the Contemporary Resort Hotel (Pueblo Room, Terrace Buffet, and Top of the World Buffet). Check for Friday evening services at the Royal Inn, in Lake Buena Vista, which is on Disney World property, a ten minute ride from the main gate entrance.

Hillel Foundation, Florida Technological University, care of Cong. Ohev Shalom (see above).

Kinneret Apartments, 515 S. Delaney Ave., a high-rise apartment house for Jewish retirees, sponsored by the Central Florida Jewish Community Council.

Stars Hall of Fame, 6825 Starway Dr., contains world famous entertainers, including many Jewish stars.

Temple Israel, 4917 Eli St.

PALM BEACH

Irving S. Strouse Theatre Collection, in the Blomeyer Library of Palm Beach Atlantic College, 1101 S. Olive Ave., contains more than 1,000 volumes covering all aspects of the theatre, including plays, movies, musical comedy, biographies, music, ballet, and humor. The collection was presented by Irving Strouse, a well-known theatrical press agent and producer.

Temple Emauel, 180 N. Country Rd., is the first Jewish congregation in this affluent town where Jews were formerly excluded from the exclusive hotels and clubs.

PALM COAST

Temple Beth Shalom, P.O. Box 557. (Services at Palm Coast Yacht Club.)

PALM SPRINGS

B'nai Jacob Temple, Faith United Presbyterian Church.

PEMBROKE PINES

Temple in the Pines, 1900 University Dr.

PENSACOLA

Cong. B'nai Israel, 1909 N. 9th Ave.

Federated Jewish Charities, 1320 E. Lee St.

Temple Beth El, 800 N. Palofax St.

PLANTATION
Plantation Jewish Cong., 400 S. Nob Hill Rd.
Reconstructionist Synagogue, 7473 N.W. 4th St.

POMPANO BEACH
Margate Jewish Center, 6101 N.W. 9th St.
Temple Sholom, 132 S.E. 11th Ave.

PORT RICHEY
Jewish Community Center of West Paseo, 1718 Kennedy Dr.

PORT ST. JOE
Constitution Monument, in a tiny park just outside of this town, lists the name of David Levy, along with the other members of the 1838 constitutional convention. They framed Florida's first constitution and petitioned for admittance to the Union. The granite monument stands on the approximate spot occupied by the building where the convention was held.

RIVIERA BEACH
Museum of American Comedy honors America's famous stage, film, radio, and TV comedians, among them Jack Benny, Ed Wynn, Bert Lahr, George Allen, Milton Berle, Fannie Brice, and many other Jewish comics.

ROYAL PALM BEACH
Jewish Congregation, New Covenant Community Church, Royal Palm Beach Blvd.

ST. AUGUSTINE
Cong. Sons of Israel, 163 Cordova St.

ST. PETERSBURG
Cong. B'nai Israel, 301 59th St., N.
Jewish Federation of Pinellas County, 8167 Elbow Lane N.
Temple Beth El, 400 Pasadena Ave., S.
Temple Hillel, 8195 38th St.

SANFORD
Cong. Beth Am of Orlando has purchased an old church here which was an abandoned synagogue, and is converting it to a synagogue in Winter Park.

SARASOTA
Benjamin Monument, in the town's civic center, is a simple granite shaft with an inscription identifying this location as the place Judah P.

Benjamin, Secretary of State of the Confederacy, escaped to Cuba on June 23, 1865, avoiding capture by the Union Army.
Cong. Beth Sholom, 1050 S. Tuttle Ave.
Jewish Family Service Agency, 307 S. Orange Ave.
Sarasota Jewish Community Council, 1900 Main Bldg.
Temple Emanu-El, 151 S. McIntosh Rd.

SATELLITE BEACH
Temple Beth Sholom, N.E. 3rd St.

SOUTH MIAMI
South Dade Hebrew Academy, 11801 S.W. 74th Ave.

SUNRISE
Mogan David Cong., 9348 Harding Ave.
Temple Beth Israel, 7100 W. Oakland Park Blvd.

TALLAHASSEE
Florida State University has in its display of rare books, a Torah Scroll more than 250 years old that was rescued from a burning synagogue in Nazi Germany. The last part of the Torah was so mutilated by the Nazis that another complete Torah Scroll was added to the original to complete it. Hillel Foundation, Department of Religion.

David Sholtz portrait in the governor's office of the State Capitol memorializes the Brooklyn-born Jew who was the first Northerner elected governor of Florida. Sholtz, who was not associated with the Jewish community, settled in Daytona Beach in 1915 where his father was one of the early real estate developers. After serving in the Legislature and as a county judge, Sholtz became president of the Florida State Chamber of Commerce. He was elected governor in 1933 and served one four-year term. While governor, Sholtz was elected grand exalted ruler of the Order of Elks. He died in 1953 at the age of 63.
Temple Israel, P.O. Box 3342.

TAMPA
Chabad Lubavitcher Student House, 3625 College Park Circle.
Cong. Beth Israel, 2111 Swann Ave., is planning to move to North Tampa.
Cong. Schaarai Zedek, 3303 Swann Ave.
Hillel Foundation at South Florida University, 13448 Village Circle, #182.
Hillel School, 2713 Bayshore Blvd.
Israel Room in the University of Tampa (room 243, 2nd floor of main classroom and administrative building), is decorated in Israel's national

colors. On the paneled walls are engravings of prominent Israeli leaders, a copy of the Israel Declaration of Independence, and a map of Israel. There are also Israeli-made artifacts and a collection of books on Hebrew and Israeli culture and history. The room, which is also used as a classroom, was decorated by the Tampa Jewish Community.

Jewish Association of North Tampa.

Jewish Community Center, 2808 Horatio St.

Jewish Community Council, 2808 Horatio St.

Temple Rodeph Sholom, 2713 Bayshore Blvd.

WEST PALM BEACH

Jewish Community Center, 2415 Okeechobee Blvd.

Jewish Federation of Palm Beach County, 2415 Okeechobee Blvd.

Jewish Floridian of Palm Beach, 2415 Okeechobee Blvd.

Temple Anshei Sholom, foot of Grove St., adjacent to Hastings section of Century Village. About 70 percent of the 15,000 people who live in Century Village, a retirement community, are Jewish. A Yiddish Culture Group has a membership of over 1,000. There is also an active B'nai B'rith lodge and a Hebrew Club.

Temple Beth El, 2815 N. Flagler Dr.

Temple Israel, 1901 N. Flagler Dr.

WEST PASCO

West Pasco Jewish Center.

WINTER PARK

Cong. Beth Am, P.O.B. 4733.

Cong. Beth El, 2111 Swann Ave., is planning a new building in North Tampa.

Jewish Association of North Tampa.

Jewish Student Organization, Rollins College, 928 Malone Dr., Orlando.

YULEE

David Levy Yulee, Jewish-born politician and leader of the Confederacy, is memorialized in this town of about 1,000 on the northeast Florida-Georgia boundary. Yulee once owned a sugar plantation here.

Georgia

Georgia was the only one of the original 13 colonies in which Jewish settlement occurred in the same year the colony was first organized. Last of the original 13 colonies to be settled, Georgia was founded by James Oglethorpe, a member of Parliament, who sought a place where imprisoned English debtors and harrassed Protestants in Germany might start life anew. The charter for the colony, issued on June 20, 1732, granted liberty of conscience to all except Catholics. Nothing was said about propagating the Christian religion, as was the case in the other colonies, as Rabbi Abram V. Goodman points out in *American Overture: Jewish Rights in Colonial Times*. The 20 trustees of the colony organized as a philanthropic corporation, conducted a campaign to raise funds among well-to-do Englishmen and encouraged migration among prospective colonists. The trustees also commissioned many people sympathetic to the colonization plan to solicit funds. Among those so authorized were three leaders of London's Sephardic Jewish community—Anthony da Costa, Alvaro Lopez Suasso, and Francis Salvador, Jr., whose grandson of the same name was destined to be the first Jew to die in the colonies' struggle for independence from Britain.

This trio, however, was more interested in solving the problem of the growing number of destitute German and Polish Jews who had arrived in London and were draining the charity funds of the Sephardic community. The Sephardim resented the presence of the Ashkenazim and were eager to

95

arrange for their departure from England. With this in mind, the Jewish solicitors asked the trustees whether Jews might also go to Georgia if their expenses were paid and the trustees did not have to assume any responsibility.

In January, 1733, the trustees decided that no Jews could be sent to Georgia and revoked their fundraising authorization. This latter action was due to the fact that the trustees had heard that the Jewish collectors planned to use their collections to ship Jews to Georgia. The rumor was true. Some time in January, 1733, 43 Jews were smuggled out of England bound for Georgia. Oglethorpe had sailed on November 17, 1732, on the frigate *Ann* with over 100 prospective colonists, debtors who had been in British jails, and Lutheran peasants known as Salzburgers who had been driven off their land in Germany by a Catholic archbishop. Oglethorpe founded Savannah on February 21, 1733, shortly after he arrived with the first Christian settlers.

The exact date when the first 43 Jews arrived is not known, but it was within a few weeks after the founding of Savannah. A second group of 40 Jews arrived July 11, 1733. These were mostly Sephardim of Portuguese origin who had been forced to leave their homeland by the Inquisition. Arriving with them was one Jew of Ashkenazic origin, Benjamin Sheftall; Dr. Samuel Nunez, who is said to have been a physician at the royal court in Lisbon, Portugal; Abraham deLyon, an expert in viniculture; and Abraham Minis. Sheftall and Minis founded families well-known in American Jewish history. DeLyon planted Georgia's first vineyard where he raised grapes "as big as a man's thumb." Nunez' medical skill halted an epidemic that threatened to wipe out the settlers who had come with Oglethorpe. Minis, whose son Philip, born July 7, 1734, is said to have been the first white child born in Georgia, brought with him a Torah Scroll, an Ark, and circumcision instruments.

When the trustees learned that Dr. Nunez had stemmed the epidemic, they were pleased and wrote to Oglethorpe saying "no doubt you have given him some gratuity," but expressed the hope that "you have taken some other method of rewarding him than in granting lands." On December 22, 1733, long after the Jews had arrived in Georgia, the colony's trustees in London demanded that the Jewish leaders in London return their commission to raise funds. The latter clung to their authority and ignored the trustees' demand that the London Jews recall their coreligionists from Georgia. The London Jews returned their commission on January 19, 1734, after the trustees had written Oglethorpe for a report on the Jewish settlement. The request reached Georgia after Oglethorpe had sailed for England. In his report to the trustees he must have spoken favorably of the Jewish colonists because they never again took any hostile step against the Jews. One of the trustees, however, remained adamant and warned that Georgia "will soon become a Jewish colony" unless the Jews were deported. The 83 Jewish passengers who arrived in 1733 constituted more than 20 percent of the total 400 inhabitants at the end of 1733.

In awarding land grants to the first settlers, Oglethorpe did not discriminate against the Jews. The Protestant Salzburgers welcomed the German Jews because both groups spoke German. John Wesley, the founder of Methodism, who visited Georgia, reported in his journal that "I began learning Spanish in order to converse with my Jewish parishioners, some of whom seem nearer the mind that was in Christ than many of those who called him Lord." This would seem to indicate that some of the Sephardim, who also spoke Portuguese, were attending Protestant worship services.

The Ashkenazim and Sephardim did not get along with each other. Reverend John Bolzius, pastor of the Salzburgers, said that one Ashkenazic Jew complained to him in 1738 that the Sephardim "persecuted the German Jews so much that no Christian would persecute another like that." Bolzius also reported in that same year that the Jews were holding services in "a wretched little shack" in Savannah. Actually services were held as early as 1733. Benjamin Sheftall's account of the coming of the Sephardim stated that a house was rented on Market Street and "divine service was regularly performed for years." This would indicate that Mickve Israel Congregation was founded in July, 1733. Except for an interval between 1740 and 1750 when many colonists, Christians and Jews, left Georgia, the congregation had been in continuous existence ever since.

In 1733, Oglethorpe had given the Jews a lot for burial purposes in the common burial ground in Savannah but the Colonial legislature turned down a request to confirm this grant in 1762. In 1773, Benjamin Sheftall's son Mordecai, who was already the leader of the Jewish community, contributed several acres for a cemetery and synagogue. The congregation began to meet in Sheftall's home in 1774. It was years later, however, before a synagogue was established, owing to the serious division between the Sephardim and Ashkenazim and Georgia's general lack of interest in religion. The first church of any denomination in Savannah was not established until 20 years after the first settlement. Bolzius wrote that he was shocked by the way the English hobnobbed with the Jews on Sunday. "They drink, play, walk and pursue all worldly amusements with the Jews," he said. "Indeed, they desecrate Sunday with the Jews, which no Jew whatever would do on his Sabbath to please the Christians."

In 1786 another reorganization of the congregation occurred, with Philip Minis as president and Emanuel de la Motta as *hazzan*. On November 30, 1790, the congregation was officially incorporated. A synagogue was finally built largely through the efforts of Dr. Jacob de la Motta, who served as an army surgeon in the War of 1812. It was consecrated in July, 1820. Destroyed by fire in 1829, it was rebuilt. The present synagogue was built in 1877 by a church architect in perfect 14th century Gothic style.

In 1738 when the colonists drew up a protest against the management of the trustees' agent and of the conduct of Oglethorpe himself, neither widows nor orphans nor Jews were allowed to sign. "Jews applied for liberty to sign with us," one leader of the protest wrote, "but we did not think it proper to join then in any of our measures." Bolzius, however, wrote that Jews "enjoy all privileges the same as other colonists." He even noted that they had permission "to carry muskets, like the others, in military style." Dr. Nunez was appointed physician to the colonists and deLyon was given a loan by the trustees to carry on his viniculture experiments.

Poor economic conditions in Georgia precipitated a wave of migration to South Carolina and Virginia in 1739 and 1740. So many Jews left with the others that an exaggerated report reached England that every Jew had departed. Under the royal charter that replaced the trustees' rule in 1752, religious liberty was extended to all but papists, but when the Church of England became the established church of Georgia in 1758, all Georgians, including Jews, were taxed to support it. Joseph Ottolenghi, an Italian Jew who had once been a *shochet* and who became a Christian in London, was sent to Georgia in 1751 by the trustees to supervise the silk industry there. In 1761 he was elected to the Colonial Assembly where he authorized the act that made the Anglican Church the established religion. Although there were religious tests for office holders, they may have been waived for Jews since Daniel Nunez, son of the doctor, and his cousin, Moses Nunez, had been made officers of the port of Savannah in 1765 and 1768. James Lucena, another descendant of the Sephardic pioneers, was a justice of the peace in the parish of Christ Church in 1773.

At the outbreak of the American Revolution there were some 40 Jewish families in Georgia. Mordecai Sheftall, who with his sons and brothers, owned a tannery, grist mill, and ranch, was the chairman in 1775 of the Savannah parochial committee (which resembled the committees of safety in the other colonies) and saw to the enforcement of the blockade against British goods. In 1777 he was named commissioner of general purchases and issues to the Georgia Militia. His son, Sheftall Sheftall, who was then only 16, was made assistant to the deputy commissary general of Continental troops in Georgia. Later he was named commissary general. David Sarzedas was an officer of the militia, as was Lt. Abraham Seixas, whose brother Gershom was the *hazzan* of the Shearith Israel Congregation in New York. William and James Minis served in the Georgia infantry and their father, Philip, was paymaster of Virginia and North Carolina troops on duty in Georgia. Levi Sheftall, another son of Mordecai, served as guide to Count D'Estang's French fleet during an unsuccessful attempt to capture Savannah from the British. Mordecai and Sheftall Sheftall were captured when the British first took Savannah. The former was regarded as "a very great rebel" and the Tory governor warned the British commander "to guard him carefully." They were exchanged in 1779 but were recaptured when a French naval force failed to capture Savannah. They were paroled again in 1780. While they were in prison, Mordecai's wife was compelled to do menial labor for Brisith officers. Levi Sheftall, who had given the French admiral poor advice as to where to attack the British, was unjustly branded a Tory when the assault was beaten off. When the patriots regained control of Georgia in 1781, Levi was banished and his property was confiscated.

By 1790, however, the Sheftalls and the rest of the Jewish community of Savannah had recovered from the upheavals of the Revolution. There were then only 15 Jewish families in Savannah, and Mordecai was their leader, according to Professor David T. Morgan in the *American Jewish Historical Quarterly*. In 1790, Mordecai led the effort to obtain a state charter for Mickve Israel Congregation. Mordecai and his sons were officers of the congregation when it was reorganized in 1786. It was this congregation which sent a famous letter to George Washington on his becoming President. In 1796, Mordecai was elected to the state legislature. One of his colleagues was David Emanuel, later to become governor. Early Jewish historians claimed Emanuel was a Jew but no proof of this has been found. Mordecai's election to the legislature occurred at a time when a Christian oath of office was still required but it is doubtful that he ever took such an oath. In 1789 Georgia removed all religious discrimination.

During a threatened Indian uprising on the Georgia-Florida border after the Revolution, Lieutenant Benjamin Sheftall commanded a militia company. Moses Sheftall, another son of Mordecai, became a prominent physician, and was twice elected to the legislature and later served as a county judge. Levi Isaac deLyon, Isaac Minis, and Moses Mordecai Myers, were also elected to the legislature in the early 1800s.

In the War of 1812, Abraham Massias led a company of 60 riflemen that fought off a British attempt to invade Georgia by sea. Others who served were Isaac Minis, of Savannah, in the artillery; Jacob Cohen in the militia; and Midshipman Abraham de Leon in the navy.

As late as 1826 there were fewer than 400 Jews in the entire state. There were then only two Jewish communities, the oldest in Savannah, and a new one founded in Augusta in 1825. Other pre-Civil War Jewish settlements were established in Atlanta (1845), Macon (1850), and Columbus (1854). The best known Jewish Georgian before the Civil War was Raphael J. Moses, a native of South Carolina, and a direct descendant of Dr. Samuel Nunez. A fifth generation American, who had practiced the law in Florida, he served in the South Carolina militia in 1832 when that state prepared to fight the Federal Government over the nullification of tariff acts. When Apalachicola, Florida, went into an economic decline, Moses moved his law practice to Columbus, Georgia, where he quickly became one of the state's leading lawyers. An ardent secessionist, Moses opposed compromise with the North. A fiery orator, he ranked with Robert A. Toombs, Howell Cobb, and Alexander H. Stephens, later vice-president of the Confederate States of America.

Though over military age when the Civil War began, he sought combat duty but had to reluctantly accept a quartermaster assignment, rising to chief commissary of the Army of Tennessee. He often ate at the same mess table with General Robert E. Lee who asked his assistance in relieving the food shortages which had developed in 1865. He was later named Confederate commissary of Georgia. Three of his sons served in the war; one was killed in action and one was wounded. To Moses fell the duty of receiving and carrying out the last order issued by the Confederacy. As Georgia commissary, he held gold bullion boxes set aside for the benefit of returning soldiers, but the disintegrating Confederate government was unable to distribute the gold. Though attempts were made to seize the bullion, Moses was able to reach Augusta with the treasure intact. There he turned it over to a Union general who agreed to use it to feed discharged soldiers and to care for Confederate wounded at an Augusta military hospital.

After the war, Moses returned to Columbus and resumed his law practice. During the Reconstruction period he served in the Georgia legislature where he became a leader of the lower house. In 1878, the 64-year old war veteran sought a nomination for Congress, but he was opposed by anti-Semitic politicians. To one of these, W.O. Toggle, who had assailed Moses' candidacy and taunted him with being a Jew, Moses replied with a now famous letter published in the *Columbus Daily Times* of August 29, 1878. This statement of pride in his Jewishness was later widely reprinted.

When Moses died in 1893 at the age of 81, the Jewish population of the state was just under 3,000 with well-established communities in Rome (1871), Albany (1875), Athens (1870), West Point (1859), and the older communities of Augusta, Macon, Columbus, Savannah, and Atlanta.

Post-Civil War Jewish settlement in Georgia occurred when the state was seeking foreign settlers, according to an article in the *American Jewish Historical Quarterly* by Steven Hertzberg. The war had devastated the state and the emancipation of the slaves had left the South with an inadequate and unreliable labor force. Railroad builders, industrialists, and planters eagerly supported the recruiting of new immigrants. In 1869, Samuel Weil, a German-born Jew from Atlanta, was named commissioner of immigration and was sent to Germany to recruit prospective settlers. The first postwar influx of Jews was mostly peddlers and small businessmen who spread out to all corners of the state. In 1875, the Atlanta *Daily Herald* said "we congratulate ourselves because nothing is so indicative of a city's prosperity as to see an influx of Jews who come with the intention of living with you, and specially as they buy property and build among you, because they are thrifty people who never fail to build up a town they settle in; and again because they make good citizens, pay their obligations promptly, never refuse to pay their taxes and are law-abiding."

Atlanta was a prime example of what the newspaper meant. There were Jews in Atlanta before there was a place by that name. The first Jews arrived in Marthasville, later renamed Atlanta, in the 1840s. In 1845 Henry Levi and Joseph Haas opened a general merchandising store in Marthasville after they learned that the railroad would establish its terminus there. The Haas establishment was the town's biggest business by the time it became known as Atlanta. Jacob Haas arrived in 1847 and his daughter Caroline is said to have been the first female white child born in Atlanta, according to Janice Rothchild in an article in the *American Jewish Historical Quarterly*. Aaron Haas married a sister of Morris Rich, whose struggling clothing store opened in 1867, became Rich's, the city's leading department store and one of the largest merchandising enterprises in the South.

Up to the Civil War there were probably not more than a dozen Jewish families in Atlanta. All but one were German immigrants, and, except for one watchmaker, all were shopkeepers or clerks in retail stores. Though there were few Atlanta Jews of military age when the war began, Aaron Haas became a blockade runner and David Mayer was a supply officer on the staff of Governor Joseph E. Brown. Some of the recent arrivals tried to remain aloof from the conflict or left the South. Jacob Lazar Straus, who had been a member of the Sanhedrin convened by Napoleon in 1806, settled in Talbotton in 1854 with his wife and three sons, Oscar, Nathan, and Isidor Straus. The latter was about to enter West Point when the war broke out. He joined a Talbotton company of volunteers which disbanded because it lacked equipment. In 1863 Isidor Straus went to London as secretary to an agent of the Confederacy who was buying ships to be converted into blockade runners.

David Mayer, who had practiced dentistry in Washington, Georgia, before coming to Atlanta in 1847, saved the city's new Masonic Hall from destruction when General William T. Sherman ordered Atlanta burned to the ground. Aware that Sherman was a Mason, Mayer placed a sign containing the letter "G" on the doorposts of his house and the Masonic Hall. It worked because those two buildings were among the very few left untouched. At the risk of his life Mayer protected hidden stores of cotton in Atlanta from looters after the war ended. Dr. Aaron Alexander, whose grandfather had fought in the Revolution, settled in Atlanta in 1850. His son resigned and appointment to West Point to fight for the South. Dr. Alexander brought the first load of ice to Atlanta and is said to have opened the first drugstore in Atlanta that had a soda fountain.

One Atlanta Jew who left for the duration of the war was David Steinheimer, an outspoken opponent of slavery. In some Georgia towns such as Talbotton, Milledgeville, and Thomasville, Jews were charged with "unpatriotic conduct" (trading with the North) during the war. In Thomasville a public meeting was called to consider the "unpatriotic conduct" of Jewish merchants, who were denounced and barred from entering the village, while those already living there were banished.

By 1875 there were perhaps 400 Jews in Atlanta and 2,300 in the rest of the state. One of Atlanta's leading citizens after the war was David Mayer, who became known as the father of public education in the city while serving on the Board of Education from 1872-1890. Aaron was the city's pro-tem mayor in 1875. Other Atlanta Jews who held appointive or elective office between 1874 and 1911 were Aaron Elsas, mayor pro-tem; Joseph Hirsch, Max Kutz, Aaron Haas, and Aaron Elsas, members of the city council; and Samuel Weil and Henry Alexander, members of the state legislature. Hirsch was also mayor pro-tem.

Another prominent citizen was Joseph Jacobs, son of Gabriel Jacobs, who had settled in Augusta in 1859, later moved to the village of Jefferson, 20 miles from Athens, and served four years in a Georgia infantry regiment during the war. Joseph Jacobs, who grew up in Jefferson, the home of Dr. Crawford Long, pioneer in the use of ether as an anesthetic, was apprenticed to Long after he was graduated from the University of Georgia and the Philadelphia College of Pharmacy. Later, Jacobs began making his own pharmaceuticals which he peddled through northern Georgia before opening a pharmacy in Atlanta in 1884. One of his good friends was Asa Candler, who also owned a pharmacy a few blocks from Jacobs' establishment. Jacobs and several partners had somehow acquired a one-third interest in the original Coca Cola formula, but traded the stock to Candler in exchange for the latter's agreement to close his drugstore. Jacobs was the first to open branch drugstores in the state and his Atlanta store was the first to sell Coca Cola.

The mass exodus of East European Jews brought only a handful of Yiddish-speaking Jews to Atlanta. In 1880 there was only one in the city, but by 1910 there were 1,283, including some 800 sent there through the Industrial Removal Office in Galveston, out of a total Jewish population in the city of 2,118. This was about half of all the Jews in the entire state. It was during this time that the Georgia Immigration Association was urging that immigrants be limited to the "best and highest" type, meaning those from Northern Europe, and the Georgia Federation of Labor warned against "flooding . . . Georgia with a population composed of the scum of Europe." Among these "undesirable" immigrants were the East European Jews who in 1910 constituted the largest foreign-born group in the city, with a small community of Levantine Jews from Turkey, Rhodes, and Greece.

Jewish religious services were first held in Atlanta in 1852 in the home of Adolph Brady. That same year the eminent Rabbi Isaac Leeser of Philadelphia tried to persuade some of the members of the Gemilath Chesed, a charitable society believed to be the first Jewish organization in Atlanta to form a congregation. All data about the history of the Jewish community before the Civil War was destroyed when General Sherman's forces burned the city. In 1867, when Rabbi Leeser was in Atlanta to officiate at a wedding—the marriage of Abraham and Emilie Rosenfeld on January 1, 1867—he again urged the formation of a congregation. The wedding party became the charter members. Most of them were young immigrants who had arrived in America just prior to the Civil War and found on their travels as peddlers that Atlanta would be a good place to settle down. Two Torah Scrolls were borrowed from the well-established congregations in Savannah and Augusta. The religious school was housed in a one-room bachelor quarters of Aaron Haas. The first rabbi was David Burgheim, who was called from Nashville, Tennessee. Its name was the Hebrew Benevolent Congregation, but since the turn of the century it has been known as The Temple. The first synagogue was dedicated in 1877. The officiating rabbi was Dr. Edward Benjamin Browne, The Temple's fourth spiritual leader, and the great-grandfather of Mrs. Janet Rothschild (now Mrs. David Blumberg), widow of The Temple's late rabbi, Jacob Rothschild. In 1895, when the congregation joined the Reform movement, it named as its rabbi the 23-year old David Marx, who had been ordained the year before.

Marx was to become a very respected figure in Atlanta. He took the initiative in organizing some of the city's major Jewish institutions, among them the YMHA, the National Council of Jewish Women, the Federation of Jewish Charities, and the Jewish Educational Alliance. During the 50 years that he was the congregation's rabbi, he represented Atlanta Jewry at countless interfaith meetings and in important civic groups and events. In 1906 he was a member of the committee to investigate the Atlanta race riot. During the Spanish-American War he ministered to Jewish soldiers stationed near Atlanta. Marx represented the city in greeting Presidents William McKinley, Theodore Roosevelt, and William Taft on their visits there. In 1917 the mayor named him director of all civilian relief efforts after the great fire of that year.

Rabbi Marx also appeared before the state legislature and the Atlanta board of education to arrange for Jewish pupils to be excused from school on religious holidays. He fought against the teaching of *The Merchant of Venice* in the schools and against school Bible reading. He was also a pioneer advocate of racial amity and civil rights for blacks. Under Marx's rabbinate, The Temple pioneered in caring for the needs of Jewish prisoners at the Atlanta Federal penitentiary. Like most of his congregation, Marx was a vigorous opponent of Zionism.

Atlanta's second congregation, Ahavath Achim, was founded in 1887 by Orthodox immigrants from Eastern Europe. Shearith Israel, a second Orthodox congregation, was established in 1904. It was this congregation that brought to Atlanta Rabbi Tobias Geffen, the city's first resident Orthodox rabbi, in 1910. He served for 60 years in the same pulpit. Rabbi Harry Epstein occupied Ahavath Achim's pulpit for 40 years. In total, Rabbis Marx, Geffen, and Epstein served 145 years in Atlanta's synagogues. Anshe S'fard and Beth Jacob were founded after Shearith Israel. The Sephardic community established Or Hahayiam in 1910 and Ahavath Sholom soon after. In 1914, they merged into Or V'Shalom.

In 1913, Atlanta's Jews, and in fact Jews throughout the state, found themselves traumatized by the horror of the Leo Frank case. On April 26, 1913, Mary Phagan, a 14-year old employee at Leo Frank's pencil factory, was found murdered. Frank, who had come to Atlanta from New York, was arrested, tried, and convicted of the crime on the flimsiest of evidence. The trial became the forum for a violent campaign of anti-Semitism led by Tom Watson, a Populist demogogue. Before the jury brought in its verdict, the presiding judge requested the prisoner and his counsel to be absent when the verdict was announced to avoid violence and a possible lynching in the event of an acquittal. Outside the courtroom a hostile mob of 2,000 waited for the verdict. Frank was sentenced to be hanged.

A long fight in the courts followed the sentencing. The case reached the United States Supreme Court which, with Justices Holmes and Hughes dissenting, held that the absence of the prisoner by agreement with his counsel when the jury brought in the verdict had not been a violation of Frank's constitutional rights. A nationwide campaign to win a new trial for Frank followed. Jews and non-Jews alike were aroused by the biased verdict. A huge mass meeting was held in Chicago. Members of Congress and governors of other states wrote to the Georgia State Board of Pardons on Frank's behalf. All of this activity outside the state enraged many Georgians who saw it as a reflection on their courts and themselves. After the Board of Pardons refused to interfere, Governor John M. Slaton commuted Frank's sentence to life imprisonment. Outraged Georgians called for Slaton's impeachment. In prison, Frank was stabbed in the throat by a fellow prisoner and nearly died of his wound. On the night of August 16, 1915, a mob broke into the State Prison Farm and carried Frank to Marietta, 125 miles away, where Mary Phagan had been born and where she was buried, and hanged him from a tree. The prosecutor of the case against Frank was elected governor of Georgia in 1916. Years later, Frank was exonerated of the crime which had been committed by an employee of his.

Rabbi Marx, who had visited Frank regularly at the Milledgeville prison, had received threats against his life because of his defense of Frank, a member of The Temple and president of the Atlanta B'nai B'rith lodge. After the lynching, Rabbi Marx was smuggled aboard the train that carried Frank's body to New York for burial. At the peril of his own life, Rabbi

Marx accompanied Mrs. Frank to New York where he officiated at the funeral.

After the lynching, scores of Jewish women and children from Atlanta and other Georgia cities were sent to visit friends and relatives in Birmingham, Charleston, Memphis, and New Orleans. Jewish businessmen throughout the state were threatened by the Knights of Mary Phagan, whose members circulated handbills reading: "Buy your clothing from Americans, Don't give your money to a Jewish Sodomite." In Marietta, Jewish merchants were warned to close up by June 25, 1915 "or else stand by the consequences." Two months after Frank's murder, the Knights of the Ku Klux Klan was organized at Stone Mountain, just outside Atlanta. By 1924, the KKK was a major national political force and Atlanta was the headquarters of the "invisible empire." The Klan and the Frank tragedy made Atlanta Jews adopt a policy of silence and non-involvement in controversial issues. For 30 years after the lynching of Frank, Atlanta's Jews and its leaders for the most part contented themselves with being "good Americans of the Jewish persuasion." The Frank case also contributed to the slow growth of the Jewish population in Georgia. In 1912 there were 16,051 Jews in the state. By 1917 it had grown to 22,414. In the next two decades, however, there was a slight decline, with the 1937 figure reaching 23,781. Of these Atlanta accounted for 12,000. Other communities were Savannah (3,900), Macon (850), Columbus (735), Albany (290), Thomasville (125), Brunswick (84), and Athens (90). There were also 70 other places each with 35 or less Jews.

When Rabbi Jacob Rothschild succeeded Rabbi Marx at The Temple in 1946, the attitude of the Jewish community began to change. A World War II Army chaplain for four years, Rothschild quickly became a vigorous exponent of racial equality at a time when Jews, like other whites in the South, accepted in silence "separate but equal" schools for blacks, separate rest rooms and water fountains, and segregation in buses. Only a few Jews spoke out against segregation and when they did they were often in danger of losing their jobs. A number of Southern synagogues had fired rabbis for speaking on civil rights and others were chastised by their congregations for "mixing the pulpit with politics."

In his own pulpit Rothschild spoke on civil rights and preached on this theme in both Jewish and Christian pulpits throughout the South. After the historic Supreme Court decision of 1954 outlawing "separate but equal" schools, some Georgians sought to circumvent the High Court's integration ruling through a state constitutional amendment. Rothschild led his congregation in opposition to it. In 1957 he helped write a "ministers manifesto" in which 80 Atlanta clergymen called for support of the Supreme Court's decision. Rothschild, however, did not sign the statement because he believed its effectiveness depended on its strong basis in

Christian theology. On the Saturday after the manifesto appeared in the press, he delivered a powerful sermon entitled "80 Who Dared: A Salute to My Christian Colleagues." Atlanta's two daily papers published the full sermon.

In 1958, the hatred against which Rothschild preached made him the target of the racist White Citizens Council and the KKK. On October 12, 1958, The Temple was blasted by 50 sticks of dynamite after the rabbi had received personal threats of violence. On the Friday evening after the bombing, a patched up sanctuary was filled to overflowing as Rothschild preached on "And None Shall Be Afraid." This single act of devastation, he said, "had lifted the curtain of fear and decent men are at last convinced that there can be no retreat from their ideals." After the bombing had been denounced by President Dwight D. Eisenhower, Atlanta Mayor William Hartsfeld took the lead in mobilizing communitywide support to raise funds for restoring The Temple.

At times dramatically, but more often quietly, Rothschild provided much of the leadership and initiative for Atlanta's striving toward civil rights and racial harmony. After Dr. Martin Luther King, Jr.'s assassination, Atlanta's clergymen chose Rothschild to deliver the address at a special memorial service. When Rothschild died, Mrs. Martin Luther King, Jr. called the rabbi "a champion for interracial brotherhood and an uncompromising advocate of social justice." Dr. King's widow acclaimed Rothschild as "an influential supporter" of her husband, and the *Atlanta Constitution* recalled that "he had guts when it took guts to have guts."

Morris Abram as a young Atlanta lawyer began the legal challenge to Georgia's county unit system of voting that made one white voter in a small rural county equal to thousands of blacks in Fulton County (Atlanta). Abram carried the fight to the Supreme Court where after ten years he won a landmark decision. The *Gainsville Times*, edited by Sylvan Meyer, was one of the few Georgia newspapers to endorse the 1954 Supreme Court decision on school segregation.

Although there were very few Jews in public office in Atlanta and other parts of the state between 1900 and 1930, the tradition of public service and communal leadership ran deep. As early as 1847, the firm of Haas and Levi was mentioned as having subscribed to a fund for a community Christian Sunday school. This same tradition animated Rabbis Marx and Rothschild. The first Jew elected to statewide office was Lyon Levy, who was state treasurer in 1826. Between 1830 and 1897 eleven Jews were elected to the state legislature. Savannah, Albany, Rome, Jessup, Fitzgerald, Carrollton, Alma, and Gulf Breeze have all had Jewish mayors, Savannah having had two. In recent years there have been Jews elected to the state legislature from various parts of the state. One of the leaders of the legislature, the late Charles Bloch of Macon, was a strong segregationist and political ally of Senator Richard Russell, whom he nominated for President at the 1948 Democratic National Convention and then led the walk-out when the convention adopted a strong civil rights plank. The late Major John S. Cohen, Atlanta newspaper publisher, who served in the United States Senate in the late 1920s, was of Jewish origin.

In 1965 Sam Massell, Jr., was elected vice-mayor of Atlanta despite an anti-Semitic undercurrent. Four years later he was elected mayor on the same ticket with a black vice-mayor, who defeated him for reelection in 1973. In 1974 Elliott Levitas was elected to Congress from an Atlanta district. H. Sol Clark, an active synagogue member and a former vice-president of the Savannah Jewish Council, was appointed to the State Court of Appeals in 1971. In the same year, Charles Harris, a merchant in the rural community of Ocilla was named to the State Board of Regents. Although the number of Jews in the small towns of Georgia has been shrinking, those who remain are highly regarded. A case in point is the Her-.a.. family of Dublin. Henry Hermann was postmaster in 1909; his son Elias was mayor of the neighboring town of Eastman; Dr. Jefferson Davis Hermann was mayor of Dublin in 1909 and 1910; and his brother Solomon succeeded him. In Waycross, however, the Jews were so alarmed by the active role of Northern Jews in the civil rights movement, that the B'nai B'rith lodge withdrew from the national organization in the 1950s.

Mayor Massell's uncle, Ben Massell, who made a fortune in the building business, built more than 1,000 buildings in downtown Atlanta and is credited with having changed the face of the city and set it on the road to becoming the leading metropolis of the South. Of him it was said, "Sherman burnt Atlanta and Ben Massell built it back." Harold Hirsch, one of the city's leading civic figures in the 1930s and 1940s, had been a football star of the University of Georgia. One of the state's most prominent lawyers, he was a university trustee, director of the Coca Cola Co., president of The Temple, and a leader in the Municipal Opera Association, the Atlanta Art Association, and the Stone Mountain Memorial Association. John Portman, a noted architect, was a major force in reshaping Atlanta's skyline.

The state's leading department store, Rich's, is as much an Atlanta institution as Scarlett O'Hara. Richard Rich, the founder's grandson, was long the city's number one good citizen. When Atlanta had to pay its school teachers in scrip during the Depression, Rich's exchanged it for money. When the Winecoff Hotel burned in 1946 with the loss of 119 lives, Rich's handed out free clothing to the survivors. Richard Rich helped build the Atlanta Stadium that lured big league baseball and football to the city. He served as chairman of the Metropolitan Atlanta Rapid Transit Authority that is building a subway. He also headed the group that built the city's famed cultural center.

In 1977, Georgia had a Jewish population of 27,700, and of this number

18,000 resided in the metropolitan Atlanta area. The second largest Jewish community was in Savannah (3,000). Augusta and Columbus were the only other places with more than 1,000 Jews. There were two cities with more than 500 Jews (Macon—785 and Albany—525) and 11 places with 100 or more Jews. There were one or more synagogues in 18 towns and cities. Several Atlanta Jews were part of the advisor groups to Jimmy Carter during the 1976 Presidential campaign. Two of them received key White House appointments: Robert Lipshutz, who was treasurer of the Carter campaign, is now counsel to the President; and Stuart Eizenstat, who headed the issues unit in the campaign, is the President's advisor on domestic issues.

* * * * *

ALBANY

Temple B'nai Israel, Oglethorpe and Jefferson Sts. In 1915 there was an attempt to establish a Jewish agricultural colony near here. Samuel Brown, the city's leading citizen, was elected mayor in 1901.

ANDERSONVILLE

Among the more than 12,000 gravestones marking the burial sites of Union prisoners of war held in the infamous Confederate prison camp are a good number of Jewish soldiers. Now a national historic site, the Andersonville Cemetery is being developed as a memorial to soldiers who have been prisoners of war during American conflicts.

ATHENS

Cong. Children of Israel, 1155 S. Milledge Ave.

University of Georgia

• Hillel Foundation in the rear of Cong. Children of Israel, is housed in the Stern Community House, named for Myer and Rachel Stern. In the lobby is a portrait of the late Hyman Jacobs of Atlanta, a B'nai B'rith leader who had a key role in raising the funds for the building.

• Harold Hirsch Hall, the main building of the School of Law, one of the best known structures at the University, is named for the late Harold Hirsch of Atlanta, one of the law school's most distinguished alumni. Hirsch's legal victories set major precedents in fair trade and trade-mark law. For a number of years he was chief attorney for the Coca Cola Co., winning many legal battles in defense of its trademark. When the building was dedicated in 1932—seven years before Hirsch died—he was described as "Georgia's most loyal living alumnus." He was also a founder and first chairman of the Atlanta Jewish Welfare Fund. Hirsch's portrait hangs in Hirsch Hall.

• Simon Michael II Memorial Clinic was erected in 1946 by Cecile and Max Michael in memory of their son who was killed in the Battle of Rapido River, Italy, in 1944. Lieutenant Michael was an alumnus of the university.

ATLANTA

Bureau of Jewish Education, 1753 Peachtree Rd., N.E.

Cong. Ahavath Achim, 600 Peachtree Battle Ave., N.W.

Cong. Anshi Sfard, 1324 N. Highland Ave., N.W.

Cong. Beth Jacob, 1855 La Vista Rd., N.E., has a circular sanctuary, symbolizing the eternity of Judaism, and a sunken bimah. The exterior of the synagogue appears at a distance as two hands clasped and raised in eternal supplication.

Cong. Etzchaim, (see Dunwoody).

Cong. Or VeSholom, 1681 Druid Mills Rd., N.E., a Sephardic congregation, has a stone wall around its Torah Ark, built to resemble the Western Wall in Jerusalem. A photo portrait of its former rabbi, Joseph Cohen, hangs in the library.

Cong. Shearith Israel, 1180 University Dr., N.E.

Council House, 793 Piedmont Ave., N.E., headquarters of local section of Council of Jewish Women.

Cyclorama, in Grant Park, a special building housing a graphic description of the Battle of Atlanta during the Civil War, has among its portraits and other historical exhibits a painting of Judah P. Benjamin, Secretary of State and Secretary of War in the Confederate States of America. The painting was added in 1954 as a gift of the American Jewish Tercentenary Committee of the Atlanta Jewish Community Council and the Georgia Department of the Jewish War Veterans.

East Atlanta Jewish Community, congregation in formation, meets at St. Michael's and All Angels Church, 6780 S. Memorial Dr.

Emory University

• Hall of Bishops, has a 10 by 33 foot painting, *Samson Slaying the Philistines.*

• Hillel-Federation House, 1531 Clifton Rd., N.E., in the Alumni Memorial University Center, serves Hillel Foundations at Emory University, Georgia Institute of Technology, Georgia State University, and Oglethorpe University.

• Rich Memorial Building, N. Decatur Rd., which houses the School of Business Administration, is named for Morris, Emanuel, and Daniel Rich, founders of Rich's, Atlanta's leading department store. In the Asa G. Candler Library, in the same building, there is a famous coin collection that includes a Maccabean Hebrew shekel.

• Goodfriend Collection of Holocaust Literature, University Library, 1364 Clifton Rd., N.E., was established by Ahavath Achim Synagogue in honor of its cantor, Isaac Goodfriend.

Feldman Bust, in the hall of Georgia State University, honors A. L. Feldman, former president of Atlanta Federation of Jewish Social Studies, a high school dropout who took night classes at the then little-known university and was honored as its oldest alumnus.

Georgia State Archives, 330 Capitol Ave., S.E., preserves the Sheftall papers in the M.A. Levy Collection. The Sheftall papers are historical documents dealing with the commercial, military, and religious activities of this famous Georgia Jewish family during the Revolutionary War. The archives also have microfilm records pertaining to the Jews of Georgia and Jewish migration to the state in the late 19th century.

Georgia State University's Urban Life Conference Center, has a VIP room dedicated to Max Cuba, an alumnus and prominent civic leader.

Daniel Guggenheim School of Aeronautics at Georgia Institute of Technology, N.W. cor. North Ave. and Cherry St., was a gift of the Daniel Guggenheim Fund.

Jewish Children's Service, 1430 W. Peachtree St., N.E., a regional foster care service for the entire South, is an outgrowth of the old Atlanta Hebrew Orphan Asylum.

Jewish Community Center, 1745 Peachtree Rd., N.E., has a mosaic floor by Perli Pelzig, who helped restore the Beth Alpha Synagogue. The work of Israel's famous mosaicist, the floor is a representation of seven Biblical fruit. Jewish Community Center Branch Building, Zaban Park, is being erected here.

Jewish Family and Children's Bureau, 1753 Peachtree Rd., N.W.

Jewish Home, 3150 Howell Mill Rd., N.W. The Jewish Home Tower, is a high rise apartment house for the elderly, sponsored by the Jewish Home.

Jewish Welfare Federation, 1753 Peachtree Rd., N.E.

Kriegshaber Memorial Library for the Blind, once housed in its own building, is now a part of the Library for the Blind, 1050 Murphy Ave., S.W. Victor E. Kriegshaber, who was president of the Atlanta Chamber of Commerce in 1916, established the library in 1922. The Kriegshaber collection includes thousands of Braille books and recordings.

Lubavitcher Chabad Center, 1471B Willow Lake Dr.

Ben Massell Dental Clinic of the Jewish Welfare Federation, 317 Pryor St., a free clinic for Atlanta's needy, is named for the late Ben Massell, who donated the clinic. An uncle of Sam Massell, Atlanta's mayor from 1969-1973, Ben Massell was the father of Atlanta'a modern skyline. He was also a prominent leader of the Jewish community, having served as president of the Jewish Welfare Fund.

Memorial Arts Center, Peachtree St. and 15th St., a memorial to the 122 friends of the arts, mostly Atlantans, who died in a plane crash at Orly

Field near Paris, June 3, 1962, was built by the Atlanta Arts Alliance, a coalition of the High Museum of Art, Atlanta School of Art, the Symphony Guild, and the Atlanta Municipal Theatre. The key figure in creating the alliance and raising $13 million for the concrete structure, was Richard H. Rich, head of Rich's department store. The memorial plaque lists among the 122 names those of Mr. and Mrs. Reuben Crimm, Mr. and Mrs. Arnold Kaye, Mr. and Mrs. Saul Gerson, Mr. and Mrs. Sidney Stein and daughter, Joan, and Mr. and Mrs. Lon Patz.

Memorial to the Six Million, 1173 Cascade Ave., S.W., in the Jewish section of Greenwood Cemetery, is a starkly majestic stone tombstone, topped by six huge candlesticks, honoring the memory of the victims of the Nazi Holocaust. A small casket containing the ashes of some of the unknown martyrs who died at Auschwitz is interred at the foot of the monument.

Miniature Statue of Liberty, on the grounds of the Georgia State Capitol, has affixed to it a plaque containing the text of Emma Lazarus' sonnet which is on the original Statue in the New York Harbor. The plaque was a gift of the Georgia State Association of B'nai B'rith.

Southern Israelite, 188-15th St., N.W.

Albert Steiner Cancer Clinic, Butler and Armstrong Sts., S.E., is the tumor clinic of Grady Memorial Hospital, the city's charitable hospital. Steiner, owner of a large brewery and an official of The Temple, angered because he was not chosen president of The Temple, withdrew his support of all Jewish causes, leaving his estate to Grady Hospital for the establishment of the clinic.

Temple Sinai, 5645 Dupree Dr., N.W.

The Temple, 1589 Peachtree Rd., N.W. is the city's oldest congregation. The educational wing is named for Rabbi David Marx, the congregation's spiritual leader from 1895-1946. In 1958 the building was badly damaged by a dynamite blast, an act of revenge because of the active role in the civil rights movement of its then rabbi, Jacob Rothschild. Atlantans of all faiths contributed toward its rebuilding. The ground plan for the main sanctuary is that of the Tabernacle in King Solomon's Temple. The Helen Massell Chapel is designed in the shape of a tent, with sand-colored carpeting to reinforce the effect.

Urban Memorial Forest, Rtes. I-85, I-75, and I-20 hub interchange, between the stadium and the State Capitol on Memorial Drive, includes 1,500 trees planted by the Jewish National Fund, in cooperation with the city of Atlanta and the state of Georgia. In exchange, the JNF, which has planted 130 million trees in Israel, planted 1,500 more in the Atlanta section of the American Bicentennial Park in Israel.

Yeshiva High School, 1787 La Vista Rd., N.E.

AUGUSTA

Cong. Adas Yeshurun, 935 Johns Rd.
Cong. Children of Israel, 3005 Walton Way Extension.
Federation of Jewish Charities, P.O. 3251 Hill Sta.
Interfaith Little Chapel, University Hospital, was erected in 1954 by David Rubenstein in memory of his only son, Adolph Jerome, who died in 1931.
Jewish Community Center, Sibley Rd.

BAINBRIDGE

Temple Beth El, Broad St.

BRUNSWICK

Temple Beth Tefilloh, 1326 Egmont St.

CLARKSTON

Cong. Beth Shalom, P.O. Box 298, serving east Atlanta suburbs, holds Friday evening services at Rehoboth Elementary School, Lawrenceville Hwy., Clarkston.

CLEVELAND

Camp Barney Medientz of Atlanta Jewish Community Center.
Coleman Camp Institute of Union of American Hebrew Congregations. The camp library is a memorial to the late Rabbi Jacob Rothschild of The Temple in Atlanta.

COLUMBUS

Cong. Shearith Israel, 2550 Wynton Rd., the second oldest congregation in the state, traces its origins to the Jewish Society, founded in 1854.
Esquiline Hill Cemetery, in Bennings Hills outside of Fort Benning, was established by Raphael J. Moses in 1849 as the private burial ground of the well-known Moses family of Georgia. Lawyer, statesman, and orator, Moses was a loyal Jew who sought to preserve the memory of his distinguished Sephardic ancestors by changing the names of two of his three sons in 1856 to Israel Moses Nunez and Alfred Moses Luria. The third son was named Raphael J. Moses, Jr. Moses and his three sons all served in the Confederate Army. Albert was killed in action. Resting on a pillar of marble that stands over his grave is the shell that killed him. Following the war, the elder Moses resumed his law practice and was elected to the Georgia legislature in 1866. In the course of his political career, an opponent, W.A. Toggle, referred sneeringly to Moses as "a Jew." Moses answered Toggle in a now-famous letter that was printed in the *Columbus Daily Times* of August 29, 1878. Excerpts from that letter follow:

"At West Point and in my absence, during your Con-

gressional campaign, you sought for me a term of reproach, and from your well-defined vocabulary selected the epithet of JEW.

"*Had I served you to the extent of my ability in your recent political aspirations and your over-burdened heart had sought relief in some exhibition of unmeasured gratitude; had you a wealth of gifts and selected from your abundance your richest offering to lay at my feet, you could not have honored me more gratefully than by proclaiming me a Jew. I am proud of my lineage and my race; in you severest censure you can not name an act of my life which dishonors either, or which would mar the character of a Christian gentleman. I feel it an honor to be one of a race whom persecution can not crush; whom prejudice has in vain endeavored to subdue; who, despite the powers of man and the combined governors of the world, protected by the hand of Deity have burst the temporal bonds with which prejudice would have bound them, and after nineteen centuries of persecution still survive as a nation, and assert their manhood and intelligence, and give proof of 'the Divinity that stirs within them' by having become a great factor in the government of mankind.*

"*Would you honor me? Call me a Jew. Would you place in unenviable prominence your own un-Christian prejudice and bigotry? Call me a Jew . . . Your narrow and benighted mind, pandering to the prejudices of your auditory, has attempted to taunt me by calling me a Jew—one of that peculiar people at whose altars, according to the teachings of your theological masters, God chose that His son should worship. Strike out the nationality of Judea, and you would seek in vain for Christ and his apostles. Strike out of sacred history the teachings of the Jews, and you would be as ignorant of God and the soul's immortal mission as you are of the duties and amenities of social life.*

"*. . . While I thank you for the opportunity which you have given me to rebuke your prejudice, confined to a limited number distinguished for their bigotry and sectarian feelings—of which you are a fit examplar—I pity you for having been cast in a mould impervious to the manly and liberal sentiments which distinguished the nineteenth century.*"

The cemetery remains private and is not open to the public. Several generations of the Moses family are buried there.

Jewish Welfare Federation, P.O. Box 1303.

Temple Israel, 1617 Wildwood Ave.

DALTON
Temple Beth El, Valley Dr.

DUNWOODY
Cong. Etz Chaim, P.O. Box 28904 (phone: 404-394-6727), serves a suburban area north of Atlanta, including the urban area of Marietta. Friday evening services are held at Mt. Zion United Methodist Church, 1779 Johnson Ferry Rd., Dunwoody.

Mitzvah House Creations, 5631 Trowbridge Way, is a needlework design studio which creates original artifacts used in celebrating Jewish festive events.

EMANUEL COUNTY
David Emanuel, governor of Georgia in 1801, for whom this county is named, was described by some writers as a Jew, but there is no proof of this.

FITZGERALD
Hebrew Congregation, 615 S. Sherman St., is an old Northern Methodist Church building converted into a synagogue in 1941. Fitzgerald was settled by Northern soldiers after the Civil War. One of the founders of the congregation, the late Martin Gottlieb, set up a trust fund in his will, the income of which provides a bright Christmas for the city's 700 to 800 children each year in perpetuity.

JEWTOWN
This village on St. Simon Island in Glynn County grew up around a store owned by a Jewish merchant during the Reconstruction era, and was given its name by blacks who worked at the sawmill on the nearby Hamilton plantation.

LA GRANGE
Cong. Beth El, c/o Isaac Struletz, 200 Springfield Dr.

MACON
Cong. Sherah Israel, 611 First St.

Grand Masonic Lodge of Georgia, 811 Mulberry St., has a large portrait of Max Meyerhardt, who was Grand Master from 1900-1907.

Masonic Home of Georgia, 1417 Nottingham Dr., is a monument to Max Meyerhardt, prominent attorney, Mason, and civic leader, during whose administration as Grand Master of the Grand Lodge of Masons of Georgia the home was built and opened. He was chairman of the Home's board of trustees from 1921-1923. Meyerhardt's name and the dates he served as Grand Master are inscribed on the granite cornerstone of the building.

Temple Beth Israel, 892 Cherry St.

ROCKEDUNDY ISLAND
Sheftalls Island was the original name of this island located between Generals and Wolff Islands in Altamaha Sound, having been named after the well-known Sheftall family.

ROME
Max Meyerhardt portrait hangs in the Masonic Lodge Hall, 4th and Broad Sts. Meyerhardt who became a member of Cherokee Lodge in 1880, was for many years a judge of the City Court.

Rodeph Sholom Cong., 406 East First St.

SAVANNAH
Cohen St. is named for a Jewish pioneer in Savannah.

Cong. Agudath Achim, 9 Lee Blvd.

Cong. B'nai B'rith Jacob, 5444 Abercorn St., has four murals, two on either side of the Ark, painted over wood panels to represent the huge granite blocks of the Western Wall in Jerusalem. This is the state's third oldest congregation, having been founded in 1864, some say by the local B'nai B'rith lodge, which was chartered in 1860.

Jewish Community Council, 5111 Abercorn St.

Jewish Educational Alliance (community center), 5111 Abercorn St. The Raymond Rosen Memorial Outdoor Recreational Area memorializes the late president of the JEA and the Savannah Jewish Council.

Mickve Israel Cong., 20 Gordon St., is the oldest congregation now practicing Reform Judaism, the oldest in Georgia, and the third oldest in the U.S. It was founded in July, 1733, five months after the establishment of the colony of Georgia, and was incorporated in 1790. The congregation built its first synagogue in 1820. The present sanctuary, consecrated in 1878, was designed from the plans of a church architect in purest 14th century Gothic. Levi Sheftall was president of the congregation when it sent a congratulatory message to George Washington on his becoming President. Washington replied as follows:

> *"I thank you with great sincerity for your congratulations on my appointment to the office which I have the honor to hold by the unanimous choice of my fellow-citizens, and especially for the expressions you are pleased to use in testifying to the confidence that is reposed in me by your congregation.*
>
> *"As the delay which has naturally intervened between my election and your address has afforded an opportunity for appreciating the merits of the Federal Government and for communicating your sentiments of its administration, I have rather to express my satisfaction than regret at a circumstance which*

demostrates (upon experiment) your attachment to the former as well as approbation of the latter.

"I rejoice that a spirit of liberality and philanthropy is much more prevalent than it formerly was among the enlightened nations of the earth, and that your brethren will benefit thereby in proportion as it shall become more extensive; happily the people of the United States of America have in many instances exhibited examples worthy of imitation, the salutary influence of which will doubtless extend much further if gratefully enjoying those blessings of peace which (under the favor of heaven) have been attained by fortitude in war, they shall conduct themselves with reverence to the Deity and charity toward their fellow-creatures.

"May the same wonder-working Deity, who long since delivering the Hebrews from the Egyptian oppressors, planted them in the promised land, whose providential agency has lately been conspicuous in establishing these United States as an independent nation, still continue to water them with the dews of heaven and to make the inhabitants of every denomination participate in the temporal and spiritual blessings of that people whose God is Jehovah."

G. Washington

Minis Street is named for members of the well-known Minis family who first arrived in Georgia in 1733.

Old Jewish Cemetery, adjacent to the abandoned railroad station which was razed to make way for a new highway, is the plot donated to the Jewish community in 1773 by Mordecai Sheftall. It remained in use until 1850 and is now a historic landmark.

Savannah Hebrew Day School, 5111 Abercorn St.

Sheftall Burial Ground, the corner of Cohen and Spruce Sts., is a small Jewish cemetery dedicated in 1773 by Levi Sheftall, half brother of Mordecai Sheftall, as a family burial ground. It is two blocks away from the Old Jewish Cemetery.

Sheftall House, now part of the Savannah Historical Area, at 321 East York St., is a frame building erected in 1810 by a member of the Sheftall family at 245 Jefferson St. It was moved intact from its original site.

Synagogue Marker, N.E. cor. Liberty and Whitaker Sts., is a bronze plaque embedded in the pavement that marks the site of the first synagogue built in Georgia. It was erected in 1820 by Mickve Israel Congregation.

TALBOTTON

Straus-Levert Memorial Hall, a town community center, occupies a building which dates from the 1850s when Talbotton was a cultural center for Georgia's young men and women. Talbotton was the early home of Lazarus Straus, founder of the Straus family of merchants, diplomats, and communal leaders. His grandson, Ralph I. Straus, was responsible for the preservation and restoration of the building in 1940. The structure once housed Levert College and later the Collingswood Academy for Boys. From 1919-1926 it was a county high school. When a new school was built, the old building was scheduled for demolition when the Straus family stepped in to preserve the structure for the community's benefit.

THOMASVILLE
Cong. B'nai Israel, 210 S. Crawford.

THOMSON
The grave of Abraham Simons, Jewish soldier of the American Revolution, is a short distance from the Old Augusta Road. Somewhat of an eccentric, Simons requested that he be buried in a standing position with his musket at his side so that he could shoot the Devil. The coffin was accordingly placed on end, which made it necessary to dig the grave twice the usual depth. Simons was described as "a Jew of strong, plain sense." His widow, Nancy Mills Simons, member of an aristocratic Christian family, remarried in 1827, three years after Simons' death. Her second husband was the Rev. Mercer, a well-known Baptist clergyman, who used the fortune accumulated by Simons to establish Mercer University, a Baptist institution in Macon. In 1911, Dr. H.R. Bernard, auditor of the mission board of the Georgia Baptist Church, in reviewing the history of Mercer University, said, "Mercer University is largely indebted to the skill and enterprise of a Jewish financier for much of the larger part of its life and power. A copious Providence this which founds a Christian college on Jewish cornerstones." Simons' grave is marked with a D.A.R. plaque. The grave is reached by taking a topsoil road, at the junction of State Highway 12 and State Highway 47, to Smyrna Church, then right to the Old Augusta Road one mile; proceeding right from the road 0.3 miles in the woods to the grave.

VALDOSTA
Temple Israel, 600 W. Park Ave.

VIDALIA
Cong. Beth Israel, Aimwell Rd.

WARM SPRINGS
Polio Hall of Fame displays in a quadrangle of the Warm Springs Foundation the busts of 17 men and women who played leading roles in the successful fight to control the disease. Among the 17 busts displayed are:

Dr. Jonas E. Salk, developer the polio vaccine; Dr. Albert Sabin, developer of the live virus polio vaccine; Dr. Joseph L. Melnick, who as a Yale University scientist studied polio incidence and immunity throughout the world; and Dr. Karl Landsteiner, Nobel Prize laureate who, in 1909, demonstrated that polio could be transmitted to an experimental animal. The Foundation, created in 1927 by Franklin D. Roosevelt six years after he was stricken with polio, is now a state institution that rehabilitates persons with spinal cord injuries, arthritis, birth defects, stroke and brain damage, and amputees.

WASHINGTON
Abraham Simon's Home (see above), once one of the showplaces of Wilkes County, is now the convent school of the Catholic Sisters of St. Joseph. The stately old house, six miles east of Washington, on the Augusta Road, was built by the Jewish Revolutionary War veteran in the early 1800s. Simons and his wife lived there and entertained lavishly in the house's famous ballroom. From this residence Simons conducted his extensive business affairs and it was his address when he was elected to the state legislature in 1804.

WAYCROSS
Waycross Hebrew Cong., 507 Elizabeth St.

WEST POINT
Temple Beth El, founded in 1859, was built on land once part of the garden of Herman Heymen, who settled here in 1854 together with Louis Merz. Heyman and Daniel Merz, who were rejected by the Confederate Army because of poor eyesight, owned a tannery where they made shoes for the Confederate troops. Heyman Pines, one of the town's neighborhoods, was once part of Heyman's property. The congregation also serves the Jews who live in Lanett, Alabama, across the Chattahoochee River. Rabbi David Marx of Atlanta came to West Point once a month to conduct services for many years.

YOUNG HARRIS
Walter H. Rich Memorial Building at Young Harris College, a school where rural boys and girls are taught home economics and vocational agricultural, was a gift of the Rich family of Atlanta.

Kentucky

Kentucky is a name which brings to mind the Cumberland Gap through which the pioneers headed west over the Appalachians; of Daniel Boone who blazed the Wilderness Trail; of Henry Clay, statesman and orator; of the famous Mammoth Cave; of bourbon whiskey; and of horse racing. A close look reveals reflections of Jews in all these images of Kentucky.

Before the name Kentucky appeared on any American map, Jewish merchants from Philadelphia and Lancaster, Pennsylvania, were engaged in far-reaching commercial and land ventures which helped open Kentucky, Indiana, Illinois, Ohio, and Tennessee to settlement. Michael and Barnard Gratz, David Franks, Joseph Simon, and Isaac and Nathan Levy were heavily involved in the affairs of the great land companies which before, during, and after the American Revolution acquired large tracts in what is now Kentucky and Illinois. In his fascinating study, *Early American Jewry*, Dr. Jacob R. Marcus traces the role of these enterprising Jewish businessmen in "the chain of events which linked the Mississippi Valley and the Atlantic Coast colonies."

Simon was a partner in a company which in 1763 advertised plans for a new city on the falls of Ohio, where Louisville now stands, and was also among the backers of the George Rogers Clark expedition which led to the founding of Louisville in 1778.

Daniel Boone was employed by Isaacs and Jacob I. Cohen of Virgina to survey Kentucky lands they had acquired through the purchase of land warrants. After one such assignment, in December, 1781, they gave the famous frontiersman an advance payment, and on the back of the receipt signed by Boone is an endorsement in Yiddish in Isaac's handwriting. In 1783, Isaacs and Cohen again commissioned Boone to locate lands for them, this time on the Licking River in Kentucky. In submitting his bill for £22, Boone wrote, "Send the money by the first opertunity. Mr. Samuel Grant, my sister's sun, will lyckly hand you this later. If so, he will be a good hand to send by, and I will be accountable for any money put into his hands, inless kild by the Indins." Copies of the correspondence relating to these transactions are on exhibit at the American Jewish Archives in Cincinnati.

None of the Jewish businessmen whose efforts helped pave the way for the colonization of Kentucky actually settled there. In fact, no one of unquestionable Jewish origin lived in Kentucky until the first decade of the 19th century, although Jewish ancestry has been attributed to some of the pioneer colonists. Among these were Colonel Nathaniel Hart, grandfather of Mrs. Henry Clay; Joseph and Jacob Sadowsky, who came to Kentucky in the late 1770s with German colonists from Virginia; and Isaiah Marks who owned 20,000 acres in Kentucky after the Revolution.

The romantic tale about the Jewishness of Hart—who together with Richard Henderson and members of the Transylvania Company acquired nearly all of Kentucky by treaty from the Cherokee Indians in 1775—grew out of a letter published in the *American Israelite* of May 24, 1900. The earliest Jewish writers on the history of the Ohio Valley Jewish communities rejected the idea that Hart was a Jew. The letter writer, however, claimed that when Dr. Bettman, a prominent Cincinnati Jewish physician, was called to attend a member of Henry Clay's family in the 1850s, Mrs. Clay showed the doctor a Hebrew Bible which she said belonged to her paternal grandfather (Hart), whom she described as a Jew. Yet, Colonel Hart is known to have belonged to a Protestant church in Kentucky.

Henry Clay's family became related to Jews in a later generation through Benjamin Gratz, youngest son of Michael Gratz, the Pennsylvania merchant and land speculator, and brother of the famous Rebecca Gratz. After serving in the War in 1812, Benjamin Gratz was graduated from the University of Pennsylvania in 1815 and admitted to the bar two years later. He was sent to Kentucky to look after the family's Kentucky land holdings, some of which were located around Lexington. Young Gratz settled there and in 1819 married Maria Gist, granddaughter of Christopher Gist who first surveyed and mapped Kentucky for the Ohio Company of Virginia. When Gratz first arrived in Kentucky he inquired of an earlier Jewish settler, a Mr. A. Solomon, who had settled in Harrodsburg in 1808, about the possibility of observing Jewish laws and rituals. Solomon is reported to have said "put your tefillin bag and your Shabbos in your tallis bag and forget about it."

Gratz and his wife became friendly with Henry Clay, the rising young politician and lawyer who had moved to Lexington from Virginia in 1797. Clay and Gratz served together as trustees of Lexington's Transylvania University and were associated in the business of manufacturing hemp. They also had close social ties even though Gratz attended occasional Jewish worship services in Lexington where he was jocularly called "the rabbi." Gratz was the organizer of a company that built a road from Lexington to Maysville and served as president of the Lexington & Ohio Railroad, the first west of the Alleghenies. He was also a founder of the Lexington Public Library and was the first president of the Kentucky Agricultural and Mechanical Association.

When Henry Clay died in 1852, Gratz was one of the 12 pallbearers at the funeral. The Gratz and Clay families were linked in marriage in 1873 when Benjamin's daughter, Anna, was married to Thomas Hart Clay, Henry Clay's grandson. Some of their descendants are still residents of Lexington. Benjamin Gratz's son, Joseph Shelby Gratz, (from his second wife, Anna Boswell Shelby), was the famous Confederate cavalry general. When Benjamin Gratz died in 1884, the faculty of the Kentucky State Agricultural and Mechanical College (now Kentucky State University), attended his funeral en masse in appreciation of the services he rendered in the promotion of higher education in Kentucky. In 1832, when Henry Clay was taken to task for referring to a man slurringly as "the Jew" during a debate in the United States Senate, he vigorously denied any anti-Semitic intent. "I judge men not exclusively by their Nation, religion &c. but by their individual conduct," he said. "I have always had the happiness to enjoy the friendship of many Jews; among them one of the Gratzes of Lexington (Benjamin), formerly of Philadelphia, stands in the most intimate and friendly relations to me."

The first settler in Kentucky who was probably a Jew was John I. Jacob, who came to Shepherdsville in 1802 and later settled in Louisville, where he became one of its leading citizens. He was the first president of the Bank of Kentucky, a member of the city council, and a founder of the local gas company and horsecar line. Married twice, both times to Christians, he was the father of 11 children, all of whom became well-known Kentuckians. Charles D. Jacob, mayor of Louisville from 1873-1890, was the father of Louisville's public park system. A daughter married Henry Clay's son , James. When the elder Jacob died in 1852, he was Louisville's wealthiest citizen and no longer a Jew.

In 1808, the Mr. Solomon who had advised Benjamin Gratz not to worry about "keeping Jewish," and reputedly related to Haym Salomon, the patriot of the American Revolution, came from Philadelphia and settled at Harrodsburg. When he was appointed cashier of the newly opened Kentucky branch of the Bank of the United States in 1816, he moved to Lexington, two years before young Gratz. Solomon, like Gratz, married a Christian, and like the offspring of Jacob, their descendants were lost to Judaism. Both, however, retained an interest in Jewish affairs. It is recorded that Gratz and Solomon both attended Jewish services whenever they were held in Lexington. Dr. Isaac Mayer Wise, who officiated at Gratz's funeral, used to tell his students at the Hebrew Union College, that there were only two Jews at the funeral service—the corpse and himself.

Phillip Strauss, a rabbinical student from Berlin, who, according to one story, was brought to Kentucky by Solomon about 1834 in the hope of stemming further intermarriage among the scattered Jews of the state, not only forgot all about being a rabbi, but also married a non-Jew. Two Hyman borthers arrived in Louisville in 1814 from Germany but, like so many pioneers Jewish settlers in frontier communities who "came singly, found no one to pray with, and . . . no one to mate with," intermarried.

The first member of a synagogue to settle in Kentucky was Abraham Jonas (see Illinois and Ohio), who came from Cincinnati in 1827 and settled at Williamstown. In Cincinnati he and his brother, Joseph, were among the founders of the Rockdale Temple (originally Kahal ha-Kodesh Bene Israel) in 1824, which was the first organized Jewish community undertaking beyond the Alleghenies. In a letter to the congregation in Charleston, South Carolina, asking for help in building a synagogue, the Cincinnati group noted that they had a cemetery "in which we have already interred four persons, who but for us would have lain among Christians. . . Two of the deceased persons were poor strangers, one of whom was brought to be interred from Louisville, a distance of nearly two hundred miles. . . "

During the 11 years that Abraham Jonas lived in Kentucky, he served three terms in the state legislature and once was narrowly defeated for speaker. He was also Grand Master of the State's Masonic Grand lodge and an ally of Abraham Lincoln in the organization of the Whig Party in Kentucky.

Louisville's first directory, published in 1831, listed three Levis, all of whom had already become Christians. The 1834 directory included a Jewish benevolent society and a number of Jewish individuals. By 1836, Louisville counted about a dozen Jewish families, some of Polish origin who had first settled in Charleston, South Carolina, and others from Germany. There had been an informal *minyan* in Louisville since 1834, as well as some private tutoring of children in Hebrew. The first recorded public Jewish worship services were held in Louisville in 1838. The *Kentucky House Journals* of February 18, 1834, record the approval by the legislature of a "bill to incorporate an Israelite Congregation in the land of the West at the city of Louisville." Abraham Jonas had introduced the bill six days earlier.

The state's first synagogue, Louisville's Temple Adath Israel, was not founded until 1842 and chartered the following year. Congregation Beth Israel, an Orthodox group, was chartered in 1851 as the "Polish House of Prayer" and reorganized as Beth Israel in 1856. It dedicated a synagogue in 1857 with the aid of Isaac Goldstein, a pioneer merchant, Hebrew scholar, and publisher.

In the next two decades Jewish merchants, moving southeast and southwest down the Ohio River, laid the foundations for the Jewish communities in Paducah, Owensboro, Ashland, Henderson, and Newport, while others went inland to Lexington and Frankfort. Some of these Jewish merchants and their sons helped develop Kentucky's distilleries, tobacco lands, and horse racing. By 1854 there were some 350 Jews in Louisville and that many more scattered around the state. In that year Moriah Lodge of B'nai B'rith was organized. Among the early presidents of Moriah Lodge were Rabbi Emil G. Hirsch, who was the spiritual leader of Temple Adath Israel from 1878 until 1880 when he was called to Sinai Temple in Chicago (see Illinois), and Lewis Dembitz.

Dembitz, the parents of Louis D. Brandeis, and the Flexners were among the Jews from Germany and Bohemia who settled in Louisville in the 1850s. Dembitz, Justice Brandeis' uncle and intellectual mentor (Brandeis changed his middle name from David to Dembitz in honor of his uncle), was one of the distinghished leaders of 19th century American Jewry, while the Flexners have been among the great American Jewish families.

Dembitz was one of Louisville's prominent lawyers who drafted the first American law providing for the use of the secret ballot in an American election. An early abolitionist, Dembitz helped establish the Republican party in Kentucky in 1856 and was one of the state's delegates to the Republican National Convention of 1860 which nominated Lincoln for President. Profoundly versed in Jewish lore, familiar with a dozen languages, including Hebrew and Arabic, he was known as "the Jewish scholar of the South." He was the author of *Jewish Services in the Synagogue and Home*, and translated some books of the Bible for the Jewish Publication Society of America. Dembitz served on the board of the Union of American Hebrew Congregations in the 1870s, but later became one of the organizers of the Union of Orthodox Jewish Congregations of America. He was also a founder of the American Federation of Zionists in 1897.

Brandeis, who was born in Louisville, was so devoted to the University of Louisville, the country's oldest municipally-operated college, where he studied as a youth, that his ashes and those of his wife, are buried on the front portico of the university's law school.

Moritz Flexner, founder of the famed family, came to Louisville in 1853 where he established a hat business which went bankrupt in the panic of 1873. "Our children will justify us," he repeatedly told his wife, with whom he raised seven sons and two daughters in Louisville. The oldest son, Jacob, was a physician, the first in Kentucky to receive tuberculin from Robert Koch, after its discovery. Jacob's daughter Jennie, headed the circulation department of the Louisville Public Library from 1912-1928 and later headed the children's department of the New York Public Library. Jennie's sister Hortense, was a well-known poet and professor of English at Bryn Mawr College.

Abraham Flexner, who briefly conducted "Mr. Flexner's School," a private school in Louisville, is known as the father of modern medical education. His 1908 book *The American College* created a stir in educational circles. He was awarded a grant from the Carnegie Foundation for the Advancement of Teaching to study medical education in the United States. His survey, undertaken in 1908 was based on visits to all of the 155 medical schools, and revolutionized American medical education. In 1913 he joined the Rockefeller-supported General Education Board of which he became general secretary in 1917. After he retired in 1929, he became the first director of the prestigious Institute for Advanced Learning at Princeton, New Jersey.

Simon Flexner, a bacteriologist and pathologist of world reputation, was a professor at Johns Hopkins University and the University of Pennsylvania from 1891-1903. In the latter year he became the first director of the Rockefeller Institute for Medical Research, now the Rockefeller University, a post he held for 32 years. He won international fame for his research and discoveries in infectious diseases, notably dysentery, infantile paralysis, and meningitis.

A third Flexner brother, Bernard, was a prominent attorney who was a member of the American Jewish delegation to the Versailles Peace Conference. Actively identified with the Joint Distribution Committee in its early years and a founder and president of the Palestine Economic Corporation, he was also one of the non-Zionist members of the Jewish Agency executive in 1929.

Horse racing and Kentucky have been synonymous with the blue grass state for more than a century and Churchill Downs, Louisville, is the horse racing capital where the Kentucky Derby is run. Two New England Jews— James Fried and Elias Norvin—are credited with having helped Colonel M. Lewis Clark—a Louisville sportsman and descendant of the American explorer, Lewis of Lewis and Clark—start the Kentucky Derby in 1875. The famed Colonel Matt Winn, who took over Churchill Downs in 1902 and glamorized it into the country's most exciting one-day sporting event, was encouraged to give up the tailoring business by competing Louisville Jews and become the impressario of the Kentucky Derby.

Quite a number of horses that won the Kentucky Derby were either trained or owned by Jews. Julien C. Cahn was both trainer and owner of

Typhoon II, the 1897 winner. Benjamin Bloch owned Morvich, the Derby king in 1922. Max J. Hirsch, one of the great trainers, conditioned Bold Venture, the 1936 winner, owned by Morton Schwartz, and Assault, the 1946 winner. John D. Hertz, the Chicago taxi tycoon, was twice a Derby winner, in 1928 with Reigh Count and in 1943 with Count Fleet. The late Colonel Harry F. Guggenheim saw his colors carried to victory by Dark Star in 1953. Herbert M. Wolf owned Lawrin, the 1938 winner, and Sol Rutchik trained Count Turf, the 1951 winner. Isaac Blumberg's Venetian Way was the Derby winner in 1960, and Jack Price's Carry Back led the field in 1961. Hirsch Jacobs trained many Derby winners. The 1978 winner was Affirmed, owned by the Wolfsons of Florida.

By 1877 there were 3,602 Jews living in Kentucky, the vast majority residing in Louisville. In 1907 the figure had grown to 10,000. This fell off to just under 5,000 in 1910, according to the *American Jewish Year Book*. There were then Jewish communities in Louisville, Paducah, Henderson, Ashland, Lexington, Newport, Owensboro, Covington, Shelbyville, and a scattering of Jews in 12 other towns and cities. The Jewish population increased to 13,362 in 1917 when all but 4,000 lived in Louisville. There was a further increase to 17,894 in 1937 but in 1960 the *American Jewish Year Book* listed the state's Jewish population at only 11,000; 8,500 Louisville; 1,200 in Lexington; 275 in Paducah; 140 in Henderson; 175 in Ashland; and 120 in Hopkinsville, In 1977 there was little change in these figures except in Louisville, up by 1,100.

The number of Jews who have held public office in Kentucky has not been large. Isidore Forst was president of the Louisville city council in 1903. Otto Cohen served on the council from 1906-1908. Samuel Rosenstein was city attorney of Frankfort from 1933-1937. Jewish mayors were: Abraham Wolf, Somerset (1921-1923); Isaac Ginsberg, Middlesboro (1933-1935); W.J. Hirschberg, Central City (1933-1935); Meyer Weil, Paducah (1871 and 1877); and David Aronberg, Ashland (1951-1955). Among the Jews elected to the state legislature was Morris Weintraub of Newport, who was first elected to the state senate in 1940 and then served 12 years in the lower house, including two years as speaker; Stanley B. Mayer was the first Jew elected to the state senate in 1933; and Leon Shaikun of Louisville, served seven terms in the senate of which he was the dean. Lee Simons was county clerk of Jefferson County (Louisville) and Lawrence Grauman was elected Jefferson County attorney in 1933. On the state-wide level Samuel Steinfeld of Louisville was elected to the Kentucky Court of Appeals in 1966; Edwin E. Schottenstein was chairman of the Commission on Higher Education of the Commonwealth of Kentucky; David Aronberg was president of the Kentucky Municipal League; Samuel M. Rosenstein was named a judge of the United States Customs Court; and Arthur Kling, chairman of the State Commission on Aging and one-time Socialist candidate for governor.

At the beginning of 1977 there were Jewish congregations in Ashland, Henderson, Hopkinsville, Lexington, Louisville, Owensboro, Paducah, and Hillel Foundations at the Universities of Kentucky and Louisville.

* * * * *

ASHLAND
Temple Agudath Achim, 2411 Montgomery Ave.

BARDSTOWN
St. Joseph's Cathedral, 310 W. Stephen Foster, has on each side of its exterior walls the Ten Commandments painted on boards which are fitted into five niches on each side.

BRANDENBURG
Col. Solomon Brandenburg is memorialized by this Meade County town. An early settler who fought in the War of 1812, Brandenburg is believed by some historians to have been a Jew. The site of Walnut Tavern which he operated is marked by a memorial plaque on Main St.

FLORENCE
The story of Felix Moses, the unlettered Jewish peddler who became the beloved friend of every family in Boone County in the years before the Civil War and who served three years with Morgan's Raiders in the Confederate Army, is still remembered in this little town near Covington. A pack peddler who came to Kentucky from Germany via New Orleans, Moses with his horse and wagon were a county institution. He enlisted at the outbreak of the war and became famous as the Morgan raider who hoisted the Confederate flag over the capital of Kentucky when the raiders briefly held Frankfort. Later, he was captured and imprisoned at Johnson's Island near Sandusky, Ohio. A member of Rabbi Isaac Meyer Wise's congregation in Cincinnati, Moses returned to Florence after the war and was hailed as a hero. The dramatic story of "Old Moses," as he was known, is told in John Uri Lloyd's novel, *Stringtown on the Pike.*

FORT KNOX
A memorial light in tribute to the Jews who perished in the Nazi Holocaust is in the Eleventh Avenue Chapel of Fort Knox. The light, which has six branches in mounting flames, symbolizing the 6,000,000 martyrs, is believed to be the first, if not the only, U.S. military installation having such a memorial.

FRANKFORT
Stephen Franks, an Indian trader who was killed by Indians in 1780 as

he and other settlers crossed the Kentucky River, and for whom the state's capital city is named, is said by some folklorists to have been a Jew. There have been attempts to identify this Franks with the famous Philadelphia and New York Jewish family of Colonial days.

GRATZ

The Gratz family of Pennsylvania is memorialized by this virtually deserted river town on the western bank of the Kentucky River. When Simon and Hyman Gratz took over the mercantile interests of their father, Michael, in the early 1800s, they made the town of Gratz an important shipping point. For half a century steamers for Louisville and Cincinnati stopped here to load and unload goods headed west and south from the Gratz warehouses in Philadelphia.

HENDERSON

Temple Adas Israel, Center and Alves St.

HOPKINSVILLE

Cong. Adath Israel, 6th and Liberty Sts., claims to be the smallest Jewish congregation in the country, with only 16 family members, five of whom live within a 35-mile radius in Greenville, Central City, and Russellville. Built in 1923, the synagogue is served by a student rabbi from the Hebrew Union College in Cincinnati. Small as it is, Adath Israel is well-known to thousands of Jews all over the country who were stationed at nearby Fort Campbell during World War II and the Korean War. The synagogue's basement was a JWB recreation center.

LEVI

This Owsley County town is named for one of the Levis who settled in Louisville in the early 1800s.

LEXINGTON

Cong. Chavy Zion, 120 W. Maxwell St.

Benjamin Gratz House, 231 N. Mill St., a notable example of late Georgian Colonial architecture, was for 60 years the home of Benjamin Gratz. Built in 1806, it was acquired by Gratz in 1824, and members of the Gratz family still own it and live in it. None of them are Jewish. Benjamin Gratz, brother of Rebecca Gratz (see Philadelphia) was one of the leading citizens of Lexington between 1820 and 1845. The entire area bounded by 2nd St., the Byway, 3rd St., and Bark Alley is known as the Gratz Park Historic District, a national historic shrine.

Hillel Foundation, University of Kentucky, Box 6B, University of Kentucky Station.

Lexington Theological Seminary, 631 S. Lime St., has in its library a

Torah Scroll given it on permanent loan by the Hebrew Union College-Jewish Institute of Religion in Cincinnati, the first ever presented by a Jewish theological school to a Christian seminary.

Julius Marks Elementary School, 3277 Pepper Hill Rd.

Julius Marks Home for the Aged, Georgetown Pike, honors a prominent civic leader who died in 1912.

LOUISVILLE

Albert S. Brandeis School, 925 S. 26th St., is named for a noted supporter of the city's public schools, who was related to Justice Brandeis.

Bureau of Jewish Education, 3600 Dutchmans Lane.

Community (newspaper), 702 Marion Taylor Bldg.

Cong. Anshei Sfard, 3700 Dutchmans Lane, next door to the Jewish Community Center, incorporated Cong. Agudath Achim. Their building at 1111 W. Jefferson fell victim to urban renewal.

Cong. Keneseth Israel, 2531 Taylorsville Rd., has 12 stained glass windows, each representing a phase of Jewish holidays and festivals. The congregation's original building, now a church, still stands at Floyd and Jacob Sts.

Eisenberg Museum of Egyptian and Near Eastern Antiquities, at the Southern Baptist Theological Seminary, 2825 Lexington Rd., was established by Jerome Eisenberg, a New York antiquarian, numismatist, and gallery owner, in honor of his parents. The collection includes archeological materials depicting everyday life in the Biblical period.

Four Courts, the Hebrew Home for the Aged, 2100 Millvale Rd.

Jefferson County Courthouse, W. Jefferson St., bet. S. 5th and 6th Sts., has on its entrance plaza a statue of Thomas Jefferson by Sir Moses Ezekiel, which was a gift of Isaac W. Bernheim.

Jewish Community Federation, 702 Marion E. Taylor Bldg.

Jewish Family Service of Nashville and Middle Tennessee, 3600 Dutchman Lane. The Elderly Residents Housing Complex is being erected by the Jewish Federation with the aid of a grant from the U.S. Department of Housing.

Jewish Hospital, 217 E. Chestnut St., now a cornerstone of the downtown Louisville Medical Center, was originally established at Floyd and Kentucky Sts. It was a gift of Isaac W. Bernheim.

Jewish Vocational Service, 702 Marion E. Taylor Bldg.

Kentucky Jewish Post and Opinion, 2004 Grinsted Dr.

Louisville Free Public Library, W. York St., bet. 3rd and 4th Sts., has on its front lawn a statue of Abraham Lincoln, a gift of Isaac W. Bernheim.

Louisville Jewish Day School, 3600 Dutchmans Lane.

Masonic Grand Lodge of Kentucky Headquarters has on one of its walls a portrait of Abraham Jonas, who was grand master of the Grand Lodge in the 1830s.

Temple Adath Israel-B'rith Sholom, being built at Brownsboro Rd. at Lime Kiln Lane, represents a merger of two congregations. Adath Israel, the oldest existing congregation in the state, was chartered in 1843, and B'rith Sholom, nearly a century ago. Until the temple is ready, services are held in the old B'rith Solom building at 1649 Cowling Ave.

University of Louisville

• Brandeis Avenue, a two-mile long thoroughfare from Shelby St. west to 4th St., in the south central part of the city, is named for Dr. Samuel Brandeis, an uncle of Louis D. Brandeis, who once owned extensive property in that area. The street is a traffic artery through the Belknap Campus of the University of Louisville.

• Brandeis Law Library, Law School, to which Justice Louis D. Brandeis left a fourth of his estate, and the library of the university, which he made the depository of his papers, letters, scrapbooks, and library, are monuments to his efforts and support. Brandeis also established eight departmental libraries at the university. These libraries cover World War I, classical literature, sociology, and economics, and are memorials to his brother Alfred. The Palestine-Judaica Library honors Brandeis' uncle, Lewis Dembitz. There are also Brandeis-created libraries on English and German literature, railroads, and music.

Before he was 40, Brandeis, who had left Louisville for St. Louis and later settled in Boston, had earned a fortune and a towering reputation as a lawyer for big business. The Homstead steel strike of 1892 converted him into a vigorous opponent of bigness and monopoly in business and industry and a champion of the little man. For 20 years he fought and won historic legal battles against the nation's corporate giants. The bitterness he engendered by his unremitting struggle against railroad monopolies, his untiring efforts to defend minimum wage and maximum hours legislation in the courts, and his successful organization of a state-run system of insurance in Massachusetts brought him the enmity of big business and corporation lawyers, but made him beloved by millions as "the people's attorney."

President Woodrow Wilson wanted to name Brandeis attorney general in 1913, but refrained from doing so in the face of the storm of disapproval of "the radical lawyer" from Boston. In 1916, the President nominated Brandeis to the Supreme Court, the first Jew so honored. This appointment touched off one of the bitterest political struggles of the time. Opposition to Brandeis was led by the organized bar and many leading Americans, among them former President William Taft. There was even some clandestine opposition from influential Jewish leaders. Amid anti-Semitic overtones, the Senate debated the nomination for five months and finally approved it by a vote of 47 to 22, with 27 Senators abstaining.

In the 26 years Brandeis served on the bench he became the symbol of economic and political liberalism. His judicial dissents helped pave the way for the New Deal of the Franklin D. Roosevelt administration. When he retired from the Court in 1939, at the age of 83, Brandeis had become one of the country's greatest jurists, having achieved rank with the memorable judges of American history.

Never an observant Jew, Brandeis had not concerned himself with Jewish matters until 1910 when his role as arbitrator in the clothing workers' strike brought him in contact for the first time with the Jewish masses. In 1912, he embraced Zionism. During World War I he headed the Provisional Zionist Committee and was the acknowledged leader of American Zionists. Brandeis played a part in the promulgation of the Balfour Declaration and was a decisive factor in laying the economic groundwork for large-scale colonization in Palestine. He was also a founder of the American Jewish Congress in 1916.

After 1921, he took no active role in Jewish affairs, but his advice, influence, and guidance were always sought and welcomed by leaders of American and world Jewry. In speeches and essays he outlined a basic philosophy for American Jewry which has become a classic: "To be good Americans, we must be better Jews, and to be better Jews, we must become Zionists . . . Let no American imagine that Zionism is inconsistent with patriotism."

The ashes of Louis Brandeis and his wife, are buried on the front portico. Date stones near the third column mark the graves. Brandeis was born in Louisville in 1856 and died in 1941.

• Ecumenical Center, Belknap Campus, is the home of the university's Hillel Foundation, the Catholic Newman Club, and the multi-denominational United Campus Ministry. The building has no entrance door. A series of arcs support three entrances extending from a center point. The unusual building was financed by the Jewish Community Federation and seven other religious denominations.

• Flexner Way, the 200 and 300 blocks of Madison St., which runs through Medical Center, honors Dr. Abraham Flexner, the Louisville-born educator. These same two blocks, from the turn of the century until shortly after World War II, were a solid phalanx of Jewish residences, perhaps the most concentrated area of Jewish population ever known in Louisville.

• Joseph Rauch Memorial Planetarium, Belknap Campus, honors the late Rabbi Joseph Rauch, for 44 years the spiritual leader of the Cong. Adath Israel, who was a trustee of the university for 13 years and president of the Free Public Library Board.

B.F. Washer Park, N.W. cor. 5th and Kentucky Sts., is named for attorney Ben F. Washer, who gave the playground to the city. Washer was also a benefactor of the Jewish Community Center.

MAMMOTH CAVE NATIONAL PARK
Mammoth Cave, one of the country's most popular tourist sites, was once known as Gratz Cave. The Gratz family owned this property from about 1810-1815. During the War of 1812 they used the nitrate deposits in the cave for the manufacture of gunpowder.

NEWPORT
Newport Hebrew Cong., 117 E. 5th St.

OTTENHEIM
Jacob Ottenheimer, a long-forgotten steamboat and railroad passenger agent, is memorialized by this village in Lincoln County which Ottenheimer established in 1885. The town was originally known as Ottenheimer. Jacob Ottenheimer's descendants include Mrs. Irving Silverman of East Hills, N.Y., and Richard Lederer of White Plains, N.Y. The coordinator of the Kentucky Place Name Survey reports that a Joseph Ottenheimer led German-Swiss immigrants to the area in the 1880s.

OWENSBORO
Temple Adath Israel, 429 Davies St., is the oldest existing house of worship in the city. Founded in 1862, the congregation is the second oldest in the state.

World War II Memorial, in Moreland Park, a monument to the war dead of Owensboro and Davies County, is in a sense also a memorial to Theodore Solinger and C. Robert Kaplan, local Jewish businessmen. In 1944, these two men compiled a record of war dead and anonymously erected a 30-foot obelisk in the courthouse square as a temporary memorial, with the intention of converting it into some permanent shrine after the war. When the war ended, a local and county group of ex-servicemen, looking for a project, proposed a war memorial. When they learned the identity of the sponsors of the temporary memorial, they obtained their permission to use their records and began a campaign for a permanent monument. Much of the money for the present monument was contributed by Kaplan, Solinger, and other Jewish citizens.

PADUCAH
Temple Israel, 330 Joe Clifton Dr., is the descendant of the Jewish community that suffered severely from the most sweeping anti-Jewish regulation in all American history—Gen. Ulysses S. Grant's infamous Order No. 11 of Dec. 17, 1862, ordering the expulsion of all Jews "as a class"

from the Department of Tennessee within 24 hours. This drastic decree was part of the Union Army's attempt to halt trading with the Confederacy and the resulting widespread profiteering. Dr. Bertram W. Korn, who gives a full account of this incident in his book *American Jewry and the Civil War*, wrote: "They still tell stories of the expulsion in Paducah, Ky.; of the hurried departure by riverboat up the Ohio to Cincinnati; of a baby almost left behind in the haste and confusion and tossed bodily into the boat; of two dying women permitted to remain behind in neighbors' care. Thirty men and their families were expelled from Paducah . . . "

Cesar Kaskel, a 30-year old Jewish merchant from Paducah, together with his brother, J.W. Kaskel, and D. Wolff, also of Paducah, took the lead in organizing a nationwide protest against Grant's order. First they sent a telegraph to President Lincoln against "this inhuman order, the carrying out of which would be the grossest violation of the Constitution and our rights as citizens under it, and would place us, besides a large number of other Jewish families of this town, as outlaws before the whole world." Kaskel and his two colleagues then hurried off to Washington to see Lincoln in person. En route, they wrote accounts of the expulsion for the press and the Jewish journals. Lincoln's reaction to their plea has been preserved in the following exchange:

LINCOLN: And so the children of Israel were driven from the happy land of Canaan?

KASKEL: Yes, and that is why we have come unto Father Abraham's bosom, asking protection.

LINCOLN: And this protection they shall have at once.

Lincoln quickly issued an order to Gen. Henry W. Halleck, general-in-chief of the army, and requested his visitors to deliver it at once. "You may leave for home at once if you wish," Halleck said, when he had read Lincoln's instructions directing him to telegraph orders canceling Grant's decree. "Before you reach there, Grant's order will have been revoked," Halleck said. The trio left for home that very night and were stunned on reaching Paducah to find that the revocation had not yet been issued. When the provost-marshal demanded of Kaskel: "By whose orders do you return?" Kaskel replied, "by order of the President of the United States." Order No. 11 was finally rescinded on Jan. 7, 1863, but it returned to haunt Grant when he ran for President in 1868. Many Jews campaigned against him by publicizing this anti-Semitic act.

In front of the circular-designed sanctuary of the temple, outside of which stands a tall Menorah, is a historic plaque of the Commonwealth of Kentucky giving a brief history of the congregation whose beginnings go back to the Chevra Yeshurun Burial Society, chartered in 1864.

SHEPHERDSVILLE

Bernheim Forest, a 10,000 acre area that was established as a public recreation site, about 35 miles south of Louisville, off Highway KY 245, was deeded to the public by the late Isaac W. Bernheim of Louisville. The forest, which includes a game refuge, is administered by a foundation endowed by Bernheim and charged with keeping the property in its natural state. There are no entrance fees to see its fire tower, 250-acre arboretum, nature trails, ecology station, and museum, or to use its picnic areas and four lakes for fishing.

Born in Germany in 1848, Bernheim came to Kentucky in 1868 as a penniless young man. Starting as a peddler, he made a fortune in the whiskey distillery business in Paducah. A founder of the Louisville YMHA—now the Jewish Community Center—he gave it its first building. He also founded the Louisville Jewish Hospital and provided the funds for the erection of the first library building at the Cincinnati campus of the Hebrew Union College-Jewish Institute of Religion, now the home of the American Jewish Archives. Bernheim was the donor of the statues of Kentucky's two most distinguished sons, Henry Clay and Ephraim McDowell, which are in the Great Rotunda of the Capitol in Washington. In his will, Bernheim provided that Bernheim Forest should be non-segregated.

Straus Gravestone, uncovered in 1974 in the dungeon-like basement of a 92-year old building at 724 W. Main St., marks the last resting place of Samuel Straus, who was born in 1828 and died in Jan. 18, 1864. The foot and headstones marking the grave are on the earth floor by a 6 by 6-foot niche in the stone and brick foundation of the building. Some Louisville historians theorized that the building was erected over an old Jewish cemetery where Civil War soldiers were buried. Others believe the building may have been erected around the grave inasmuch as Straus died 18 years before the building was completed in 1882.

Temple Adath Israel-B'rith Sholom, Brownsboro Rd. at Lime Kiln Lane, represents a merger of two congregations. Adath Israel, the oldest existing congregation in the state, was chartered in 1843, and B'rith Sholom, nearly a century ago.

Temple Shalom, 3600 Dutchman Lane, holds services in the Jewish Community Center.

Louisiana

Long before there were any Jews in Louisiana, French law, through the Black Code of 1724, excluded them by name from the entire territory and banned the practice of Judaism. There is no positive documentation that any Jew came to Louisiana during the early years of the colony, says Dr. Bertram W. Korn in his definitive work, *The Early Jews of New Orleans.* He also asserts categorically that such early immigrants to Louisiana as Jacob David, shoemaker; Romain David, tailor; Robert and Genevieve Jacob; and a soldier named Louis Salomon, all of whom arrived in 1719—a year after New Orleans was founded—and were regarded as Jews simply on the basis of their names, cannot be identified as Jews or Jewish converts to Christianity in any contemporary document. Dr. Korn also notes that there is no evidence that any of the early German colonists who settled in the area called "the German coast" were known to their fellows as Jews. The religion of almost every one of these early Germans is recorded, Dr. Korn points out, and none are identified in available lists or documents as Jews.

Dr. Korn also disposes of the argument that the ban on the residence of Jews in Louisiana under the Black Code should be regarded as presumptive evidence of the actual presence of Jews in the colony. Dr. Korn believes that a more likely explanation is that the text of the Code, drawn up in Paris, not Louisiana, was based on a prior document of 1685 issued before the French settlements on the Gulf Coast. This document ordered that "all Jews who may have established their residence" in Louisiana be driven out. Dr. Korn explains the seeming order to expel non-existent Jews is related to the church's concern for the conversion of the slaves. If Jews were denied the right to settle in Louisiana and if the practice of Judaism as a religion was outlawed, then there was no chance that slaves might be converted to Judaism by their Jewish masters. All of this is not to suggest, says Dr. Korn, that Jews would have been welcomed into the colony. He quotes from a document of the Company of the Indies urging the exclusion of Jews in 1717 because they would be politically unreliable and economically too aggressive. It was no accident, Dr. Korn observes, that Abraham Gradis and members of his family of Bordeaux Jews, who had established commercial branches in the French islands of the Caribbean and who in 1748 had organized the Society of Canada to promote commerce in French Canada, were unsuccessful with their proposal for a similar company to exploit commercial and agricultural opportunities in Louisiana.

There were individual Jews from the West Indies who did business in New Orleans in the 1740s and 1750s but none of them lived there. One of these was young David Dias Arias of Curacao, son-in-law of a rabbi and captain of the ship *Texel*. A British subject, Arias sailed his ship from Jamaica to New Orleans in March, 1759. The vessel was a so-called "parliamentaire," a British ship carrying French prisoners for repatriation under an international agreement characteristic of Colonial wars in the New World. Nominally an enemy vessel in French-controlled New Orleans, the *Texel* was allowed to carry cargo for sale in the prisoners' home port. Previous ships of that kind had been well received in New Orleans and their captains had profited from the trade because of the tight British blockade of France, on which Louisiana was totally dependent. The French governor and local French civilians were fighting for control of the colony, and the local officials seized the ship and its cargo. The governor promptly freed them and the power struggle soon involved Arias' Jewishness when the civilian officials complained to Paris that the governor was tolerating Jews in the colony, contrary to the Black Code. While the fight went on, Arias died. In their protest to Paris, the local officials had asserted that there were then six Jews in New Orleans.

The six have never been identified, but Dr. Korn has identified Isaac Rodriques Monsanto, a merchant from Curacao, and his partner, Manuel de Britto, also from Curacao, as the first documented Jews in New Orleans who established themselves there in 1758. They had brought with them Isaac Henriques Fastio, a Bordeaux-born Jew, who later established a business at Pointe Coupee, where he remained for nearly 50 years.

The presence of these Jews was illegal under the Black Code but under the French, no effort was made to interfere with their business activities. Isaac Monsanto traveled freely through the colony, sued and was sued in the courts, bought and sold property, and even acted as a translator for the Superior Court of Louisiana. He had dealings in many Louisiana settlements and became friendly with the French governor. On his behalf, Monsanto was one of the 29 Louisiana merchants who signed a statement on April 23, 1763 praising the governor's efforts to encourage the city's commerce during the Franco-British war.

In 1762, France and Spain signed a secret treaty under which France ceded Louisiana colony west of the Mississippi River to Spain to compensate her for the loss of Florida to the British in the general settlement ending the Seven Years War. The Spanish governors, stricter than their French predecessors, enforced the ban on foreign merchants and illegal trading. In 1769 the Spanish governor ordered 14 merchants "together with three Jews named Monsanto, Mets and Brito" to leave the colony. Korn says there is no document in which the governor ordered the expulsion of all foreign Protestant and Jewish merchants but this was the effect of his decree, which had economic rather than religious motives. Later, however, he did order the Jews to leave because "they are undesirable on account of the nature of their business and of the religion they profess." Isaac Fastio, the storekeeper at Pointe Coupee, was not disturbed.

Monsanto never actually left Louisiana colony but merely moved his base of operation to Manchac on the Mississippi River where it met the Iberville River. Once the Monsantos—Isaac and his brothers Manual, Jacob, and Benjamin—were driven out of New Orleans and lost their prominent position in its commerce, they were allowed to return quietly. All three sisters of the Monsantos married non-Jews. Benjamin, the youngest brother, who settled down at Natchez, married Clara la Mota, member of a Curacao Jewish family. The other brothers never married.

The Monsantos, the pioneer Jewish settlers in New Orleans as well as in Baton Rouge, Natchez, and Pointe Coupee,who "successfully tested and bested the French prohibition against Jewish colonists," were probably "the only Jews ever to be expelled from territory now part of the United States partly because they were Jews." There is considerable doubt about the Jewishness of Joseph Solis and his family, who came to New Orleans in 1771, and Antonio Mendez, who arrived in 1783. Both were credited with an important role in developing the sugar cane industry. When the United States acquired the Louisiana Territory from France in 1803, William C.C. Claiborne, the first American governor, appointed Mendez the United States commandant for a district "about six leagues below New Orleans" only to withdraw the appointment because of protests by the local residents with whom Mendez "is by no means a favorite." In his report of the incident to Secretary of State James Madison, Claiborne explained that Mendez "although a Catholic, is said to be of Jewish extraction" and this was one of the reasons why his neighbors objected to his appointment. In this same report, Claiborne noted he had subsequently named Mendez a justice of the peace for St. Bernard Parish. Obviously, Claiborne was worried that he might be charged with violating Article III of the treaty ceding Louisiana which provided that "the inhabitants of the ceded territory . . . shall be maintained and protected in the free enjoyment of their liberty, property and the religion which they profess." This article was intended to protect the largely Catholic population "of certain sections of Louisiana from any discrimination by the Protestant majority of the United States as a whole," Korn points out. The Federal Act of 1804, however, declared that ". . . no law shall be valid . . . which shall lay any person under restraint, burden or disability, on account of his religious opinions, professions, or worship; in all of which he shall be free to maintain his own, and not burdened for those of another." Thus if Mendez had been a practicing Jew, Claiborne "would not have been bound to revoke the appointment, let alone on the basis of a rumor that one of his ancestors was Jewish," Korn declared.

Korn found a record of a Jewess by the name of Sara Lopez Pardo who, in 1796 in Bordeaux, applied for a passport to leave for Louisiana with her two young children "in order to arrange her affairs in Louisiana." She described herself as a refugee from Saint Domingue in the French West Indies. Korn also turned up the application in Bordeaux of Daniel Lopes Dias for a passport for his son Abraham to travel to Louisiana to be near his family. In any event, Korn concludes that in Colonial Louisiana there "were Jews" but "there was no Judaism."

Judah Touro was the first known Jew to settle in New Orleans after 1800. He left Boston in 1801 and arrived in New Orleans just before it was ceded by Spain to France. He became well-to-do under American rule after 1803 as the agent for sale in New Orleans of merchandise shipped from New England or Europe. Touro, the son of Isaac Touro, the Dutch-born minister-cantor of the Newport, Rhode Island, Synagogue (see Newport, R.I.), was a broker acting for New England merchants, but he also dealt with New Orleans merchants, storekeepers, and plantation owners. He sold ice and was owner or part-owner of ocean-going cargo ships.

In New Orleans, Touro acquired a good deal of property, became interested in civic affairs, signed a petition in support of candidates for the Federal posts of port collector and inspector, served on a grand jury which denounced military excesses in the city, joined 140 other citizens in congratulating Governor Claiborne on his discovery of Aaron Burr's plot, and was elected to the board of the Bank of New Orleans. Badly wounded during the Battle of New Orleans in the War of 1812, his heroism was described by General Andrew Jackson in *Narrative of the Defense of New Orleans*. Touro, who is best known for his philanthropies, made his most dramatic contribution—a gift of $10,000 to help complete the Bunker Hill Monument in Boston—in 1839, and established the Touro Infirmary in

New Orleans two years before his death.

Those who settled in New Orleans from 1803 to 1815, the first period of American control, were pioneers comparable to the frontiersman in other states, and among these Korn has identified 15 Jews who established permanent residence in the city. The first of these was Benjamin Spritzer, who arrived in 1804 with a 17-year old partner, David G. Seixas. Young Seixas was a son of the Reverend Gershom Mendes Seixas, the patriot *hazzan* of Shearith Israel Synagogue in New York. Spritzer and Seixas dealt in drygoods, coffee, sugar, and liquors. Jacob Hart, who came to New Orleans in 1804 or early in 1805, also came from New York. In New Orleans he bought and sold ships and real estate, dealt in slaves, and had one of his schooners seized by Spanish officials in Mexico on the rumor that it was involved in a plot to invade Mexico. Hart was one of the sponsors of the fancy balls given by the young men of the city. He also had some dealings with the notorious pirate, Jean Lafitte, who operated on the Gulf Coast around 1810. Lafitte himself may have been of Jewish origin. He claimed to have been reared by his grandmother after his mother's death, that his grandfather had been killed by the Inquisition or had died in a Spanish dungeon. In Lafitte's autobiography he wrote that "my grandmother was of Spanish-Israelite descent" and that his maternal grandfather "was a free thinking Jew with neither Catholic faith nor traditional adherence to the Jewish synagogue."

Jacob Hart's brothers, David, Joseph, and Nathan, arrived in New Orleans between 1810 and 1819. His sister and her husband, Alexander Marks, arrived in 1840. Marks' granddaughter, Ida, became the wife of the celebrated Rabbi Max Heller and the granddaughter of the late Rabbi James G. Heller. Rabbi Max Heller, who served New Orleans' Temple Sinai from 1886-1927, was a member of the state board of education and a fighter for the abolition of the Louisiana State Lottery. He was also professor of Hebrew at Tulane University from 1912-1928.

Maurice Barnett, who turned up in Baton Rouge in 1806, was a Dutch Jew and the first Jewish immigrant to settle in Louisiana under the American flag. Samuel Hermann came to New Orleans before 1806 from Germany, and settled on the German Coast in St. John the Baptist Parish. Asher Nathan arrived in 1810. Hermann was a merchant banker who managed the affairs of other merchants and was involved in international transactions. He and his son, Samuel, Jr., contributed to the relief funds for the widows and orphans of the French Revolution of 1830, to the Charleston fire victims, and to survivors of a cholera epidemic. Young Hermann was elected steward of the New Orleans Jockey Club in 1837. Another son, Lucien, served on the Whig party's committee of correspondence. Samuel Kohn, who owned an inn at Bayou St. John in 1806, was a prominent banker, investor, and real estate promoter who was one of the city's wealthiest financiers when he died in 1853. His brother, Joachim, was a member of railroad, insurance company, and bank boards. Joachim's second son, Joseph Gustave, gave Tulane University a noted collection of 6,000 specimens of birds, fish, reptiles, mammals, insects, and plants. Joachim's third child, Amelie, married Armand Heine, a cousin of the poet Heinrich Heine. Armand Heine's niece, Marie Alice Heine, married Alberto, Prince of Monaco. All the Kohns became Catholics but Michel Heine remained a Jew.

Other early Jewish settlers were Ruben Levin Rochelle (1807); Hart Moses Shiff (1810), who was related to the family of Jacob H. Schiff, banker and philanthropist (see New York); Salomon DeJong (1808), a Dutch Jew who was one of the incorporators of the New Orleans Philharmonic Society; Alexander Phillips (1808), who had come from Philadelphia where he had served under General Anthony Wayne as a volunteer to put down the Whiskey Rebellion in western Pennsylvania in 1794; Asher Moses Nathan (1810); and Alexander Hart (1810), who later went into business at Baton Rouge. Hart later went to New York where in 1831 he became the cantor of Congregation B'nai Jeshurun, the second synagogue to be established in New York City. Phillips, who served three terms as an alderman in New Orleans from 1826-1828, was probably the first Jew to hold elective office in New Orleans. His brothers Isaac and Asher joined him in New Orleans in 1814 and 1819, respectively. Benjamin Levy, who arrived in 1811, was a pioneer stationer, bookseller, printer, and publisher. Son of a man who had taught Hebrew, English, and arithmetic in the day school of New York's Shearith Israel Congregation, Levy was a publisher of business publications for 40 years. Korn says he was probably the first Jewish printer-publisher in the United States.

Of the 15 Jews who became permanent residents of New Orleans between 1802 and 1815, seven remained bachelors, seven intermarried, and one, Manis Jacobs, married a Christian after his Jewish wife died. This high degree of intermarriage among the Jews of Louisiana, perhaps as high as 50 percent, continued into the 1850s. Eleven of the Jews who were in New Orleans between 1814-1815, served in the army under General Andrew Jackson at the Battle of New Orleans. Among them was Judah Touro, who was badly wounded while carrying ammunition for the Louisiana Militia and was saved from dying on the field when his friend Rezin Shepherd carried him off the field and took him to New Orleans for medical attention.

A mixed multitude of Jews were among the 30,000 whites who settled in New Orleans in the 1820s. Some were immigrants from Europe, many stayed only briefly and "then fanned out through the South and up the Mississippi," and quite a number were from cities in the North. These Jews, however, were still so few that Korn was able to identify and describe almost all of them. The 1820 census located only ten Jews in New Orleans but Korn identified one more. The 1822 New Orleans city directory listed seven more Jews but omitted some whose residence was confirmed by other sources. There were 25 Jews in the 1822 directory—merchants, brokers, commission agents, liquor dealers, owners of clothing and drygoods stores, a watchmaker, a hotel keeper, a bookseller, and a cigar maker.

Louisiana's Jews of the 1820s and 1830s were an interesting lot. David L. Kokernot, who was 12 when he arrived from Holland with his father, Levi Moses Kokernot in 1817, was apprenticed to a Mississippi River pilot for several years before he shipped out on ocean-going vessels. He was shipwrecked off Haiti, worked on a United States revenue cutter off the Texas coast, took part in the Battle of Anahuac and other campaigns of the Texas War of Independence, and then settled down in Texas as a storekeeper and rancher. When Kokernot's mother and brother arrived in New Orleans between 1817 and 1820, the Kokernots became the first Jewish family to settle in Louisiana as a household. Jacob Bodenheimer, who arrived in 1822, went to Moscow Landing in northern Louisiana in 1827, where he farmed, ran a store, and operated a ferry. His son became mayor of the town of South Highlands.

Daniel Goodman, a Hollander who landed in 1824, was the commissioner in New Orleans for the sale of stock in the Vidalia, Harrisonburg, and Alexandria Railroad. In 1837 he was chosen secretary of the young men's Howard Association, a society of rescue workers who rendered public service during the annual yellow fever and cholera epidemics. Edward Gottschalk, who came from London in 1823 and set up as a commission broker, married a wealthy non-Jewish refugee from Sainte-Domingue in 1828. Their first child, Louis Moreau Gottschalk, was the first great American-born composer-pianist.

Others who came to New Orleans in the 1820s were L. Daniel Warburg (1821), first of the celebrated German-Jewish family of bankers, scientists, and philanthropists to settle in the United States; Salomon Sacerdote, part owner of the Frascati Hotel in the suburb of Clouet, and his brother Simon, who operated a gambling house; Joseph LaSalle, an officer in the 2nd regiment of the Louisiana Militia in 1829, and clerk in the 4th Ward elections in New Orleans, 1828-1830; Dr. Michael Solomon (1823), a foot doctor; Dr. Gerson Adersbach (1826), a contract physician with the United States Army; Dr. G. Eichhorn (1828); Zachariah Levy Florance, a dentist; and Judah P. Benjamin (1828).

Organized Jewish life in Louisiana came late, half a century after the first permanent Jewish settler had arrived in New Orleans, and its organizer was Jacob S. Solis. Married into the prominent New York Hays family, Solis and his brother had opened a store in Wilmington, Delaware in 1815. Later he sought the poorly paid position of *shochet* at Philadelphia's Mikveh Israel Synagogue. When he came to New Orleans in 1827, he found no matzoth was available in the city, so he made his own.

The minutes of the first congregation list him as its founder in December, 1827, but the incorporation papers of the congregation, dated March 25, 1828, authorized six Jews listed by name "and all other white Israelites living in the city" to form the congregation and to engage in appropriate activity for 25 years. Solis was one of the six incorporators, who included Manis Jacobs. A native of Holland, he had come to New Orleans between 1809 and 1812 and engaged in a variety of mercantile enterprises. Jacobs manifested his open identification with Judaism by signing his name to commercial documents in English and using his Hebrew name, "Menachem," in Hebrew letters as a seal. Yet when his wife died, he took as his second bride, in 1826, a non-Jewish woman. The wedding, Korn points out, was probably the first of a Jew to a Christian in Louisiana not to be performed in a church. Korn speculates that since Jacobs would not submit to a Catholic ceremony, the marriage ceremony was performed by some other Jew or by Jacobs himself, since a rabbi is not required to take part in a Jewish marriage service. When Jacobs died in 1839, a newspaper obituary eulogized him as the "rabbi of the Hebrew Congregation of this city." Jacobs was the first president of the congregation which used the Sephardic ritual, probably on the insistence of Jacobs, who grew up in that ritual. So did many of the city's influential Jews, including Judah Touro.

In addition to the seven incorporators, the congregation's first by-laws listed the names of 27 members, 33 contributors, and 10 "honorable donors who are not Israelites."

Soon after the congregation was organized, the first documented Jewish wedding in New Orleans took place on February 26, 1828, when Daniel Goodman was married to Amelia Harris. Jacob Solis probably drafted the *ketubah* and Manis Jacobs probably officiated. Soon after, Solis and Jacobs bought a cemetery site in the suburb of Lafayette, now part of the city, and established the state's first Jewish burial ground at Jackson Avenue and Saratoga Street. The congregation adopted as its name Shanarai-Chasset, which over the years was variously written as Sharri Haset, Sharei Shisset, Shangarai Chasset, Shangarai Chased, and Shaarai Chesed, before it ultimately became known as Touro Synagogue.

Most of the wealthiest and most influential Jews in New Orleans neither joined the congregation, nor contributed to its support, with the exception of Touro and Edward Gottschalk, who made small contributions. Korn points out that these Jews had no interest in a synagogue or Jewish life because they had left the synagogue and the Jewish community behind when they came to New Orleans and found they could do without them. They also wanted to escape from the disabilities and restrictions that went with being a Jew. These were estranged Jews, but for the most part still Jews, Korn concludes. Some were buried with Christian rites and in Christian cemeteries, but not because they had become Christians but by decision of their families. Some of these alienated Jews gave support to Judaism elsewhere but not in New Orleans. Ruben Rochelle made an offering to Shearith Israel Synagogue in New York in 1819, and also made a contribution to the building fund of Philadelphia's Mickve Israel Synagogue. This congregation also received contributions from Asher Nathan, Samuel Hermann, Hart Shiff, and Touro, while Shiff sent money to B'nai Jeshurun in New York, and Sol Soher contirbuted to Shaaray Tefila in New York.

Touro made a token contribution to the congregation when Shanarai-Chasset was formed, but he refused to become a member. Prior to 1828 he had received requests for contributions from Shearith Israel in New York (1817), Mickve Israel in Philadelphia (1827), and Bene Israel in Cincinnati (1825), but the only request to which he responded was the one from Philadelphia. Not until 1847 did Touro take any genuine interest in Jewish life, according to Korn. Touro was actually more interested at the time in supporting Christian rather than Jewish religious institutions.

As early as 1816, Touro purchased a pew in Christ Church of the Episcopal Church, of which his friend Rezin Davis Shepherd was founder and warden. In 1822, when there were more than enough Jews in New Orleans to form a congregation, Touro bought the First Presbyterian Church (later Unitarian) for $20,000 so that the building would not be torn down and the land sold to pay the church's debts. This act and $2,500 from the sale of legal lottery tickets enabled the Reverend Theodore Clapp to stave off ruin. Touro was the legal owner of the church but charged no rent. He was probably the only American Jew who ever owned a church building. In 1840, Touro bought a house on Canal Street, where he lived until his death, but it was used as the rectory of Christ Church. In 1847 Touro traded a lot he owned at the corner of Canal and Dauphine for the old Christ Church sanctuary, which was converted into a synagogue for the second Jewish congregation, The Dispersed of Judah. Touro also bought $4,000 worth of bonds for the new St. Louis Cathedral, completed in 1851, about 10 percent of the total cost. That same year Touro bought a small Baptist chapel to aid the Reverend Clapp when his church burned down and other Protestant churches declined to come to his aid. Touro aided Presbyterians, Unitarians, Episcopalians, and Catholics.

New Orlean's first synagogue was a remodeled building at the corner of St. Louis and Franklin Streets, across from the St. Louis Cemetery. Efforts to build a synagogue came to naught for lack of funds. Manis Jacobs had tried vainly to borrow money from a wealthy Jew in New York since the wealthy Jews of New Orleans were not interested in a synagogue. In 1825, when the Jews of Cincinnati sought contributions for their synagogue building fund they said that "there is not a congregation within 500 miles of this city and we presume it is well known how easy of access we are to New Orleans, and we are well informed that had we a synagogue here, hundreds from that city, who now know and see nothing of their religion would frequently attend here during the holidays." The Cincinanti Jews were right about there being no synagogue in New Orleans at the time, but they were mistaken about "hundreds" of Jews in that city at that time.

Because of the numerous marriages among its founding members, as well as among other Jews in the city who were potential members, Sharar-ai-Chasset adopted by-laws providing that a "strange woman" (i.e. a non-Jewess), married to a Jew could be buried in a special section of the Jewish cemetery "after the Israelite custom." The by-laws also provided that "all children born of an Israelite, and not having abjured the religion of his father shall be entitled to burial." Members married to "strange" women could be buried next to their wives, but only in a special section. Jewish women married to "strange" men could be buried in the Jewish cemetery if they had not converted. The authors of the by-laws broke every Jewish law in formulating the regulations concerning "strange" wives and children of intermarriages. Yet, Korn notes, to have forbidden intermarried men from joining the congregation or contributing to it, would have been tantamount to rejecting a large proportion of the Jews in the city. It is worth noting that of all the Jews who married Christian women in Louisiana in those days, only one, Victor Souza, formally abandoned Judaism and adopted Christianity. All the others remained what they were, secularized Jews unaffiliated with the synagogue.

By the 1830s there were several hundred Jews in New Orleans. Among them were: Myer M. Cohen, who had run a private school in Charleston, South Carolina, came to the city in 1837. He opened a law office, served as the legal representative for the state of South Carolina, was the chief speaker at a rally to raise funds for victims of the great Charleston fire of 1838, and was a member of the administrative board of the University of Louisiana; Dr. Samuel Harby, son of Isaac Harby, the noted dramatist, educator, and pioneer of Reform Judaism in Charleston, was on the staff of the *New Orleans Bee* from 1838-1844 and later became one of its owners; and George Washington Harby, educator and social leader, owned a successful private school.

After the death of Jacob Solis, leadership of the congregation passed to Albert J. Marks, an actor by profession who made a living as the paid secretary of the congregation and its lay rabbi. He was also secretary of the Young Men's Philanthropic Association, founded in 1839 to cope with recurrent yellow fever epidemics. Marks often organized theatrical benefits for the association, wrote songs for fire companies, and served as a fireman, while at the same time he officiated at various religious events.

It was Isaac Leeser, the great religious leader of American Jewry, who spread his influence from Philadelphia to New Orleans through one of his disciples, Jacob Kursheedt. Kursheedt came to New Orleans from New York in 1840 after studying for the rabbinate. His Jewish commitment had been nourished by his mother, the daughter of the patriot minister, Gershom Mendes Seixas. In New Orleans Kursheedt was publisher and an editor of the *New Orleans Commercial Times*, active in the Whig party, and an early subscriber to Leeser's paper, *The Occident*, for which he solicited subscriptions in New Orleans. Kursheedt had joined the pioneer congregation soon after his arrival, and in 1841 was one of the 51 members who signed new by-laws which banned membership to any man who had intermarried and formalized the shift from the Sephardic to the Ashkenazic ritual, a change which had taken place in the 1830s. Kursheedt was the first secretary of the Hebrew Benevolent Society, organized in 1844, and helped found a new congregation which he called The Dispersed of Judah.

Dr. Korn suggests that the new congregation's name might have been adopted in the hope of securing Touro's cooperation. Touro would not help the older congregation which in 1843 had launched an appeal for a building fund and circulated it throughout the country, nor did he join the new congregation. He did, however, provide it with a synagogue by trading a desirable piece of property in exchange for the old Christ Church which was then remodeled into a synagogue. Isaac Leeser helped dedicate the synagogue in May, 1850, and to install its first rabbi, Moses N. Nathan. Touro did not attend this service but came to an earlier private service the same day at which he sealed a commemorative stone in the cornerstone. Following the dedication, Touro gave $500 to the University of Louisiana to endow an annual medal to a student who demonstrated proficiency in Hebrew.

Touro began attending synagogue regularly and in 1851 he built a school adjoining the synagogue. He was a regular contributor to synagogue funds, and a strict Sabbath observer. Shanarai-Chasset Congregation moved into a new building in 1845, and planned to erect a new synagogue. Rabbi James K. Gutheim came to the city as its spiritual leader. Gutheim, who was identified with New Orleans for 40 years, became rabbi of Dispersed of Judah in 1853, and officiated at Touro's funeral in 1854. Touro gave $5,000 to the older congregation when it was raising funds for its second synagogue and loaned it another $6,528, for which he held notes at the time of his death. A benevolent society founded in 1849 in what was then the suburb of Lafayette gave birth to a third congregation, Shaarei Tefila, in 1850.

Touro's funeral service in New Orleans drew the "largest assemblage of citizens we have ever beheld," wrote the *Bee*. "The funeral train was immense, almost every carriage in the city being filled." But even more astonishing was Touro's will which created nation-wide amazement among Jews and non-Jews, because of its gifts to many Christian welfare agencies in New Orleans and for the construction of a new almshouse. Institutions in

Boston and Newport were remembered. The Jews of New Orleans received
$108,000, including property for a Jewish hospital (Touro Infirmary);
$15,000 to local Jewish charities; aid to the dwindling Jewish community in
China; $60,000 for the relief of Jews in Palestine; and a total of $143,000 to
Jewish schools and congregations in Boston, Hartford, New Haven, New
York, Philadelphia, Baltimore, Richmond, Charleston, Savannah, Mo-
bile, Memphis, Louisville, Cincinnati, Cleveland, St. Louis, Buffalo, and
Albany.

In death Touro became "what he had never been nor ever wanted to be
in life, a local and national hero, a leader of men, a dignitary, a man of in-
spiring presence, an exemplary Jewish philanthropist," Korn writes.
Touro's will also brought "much renown to the Jewish community of New
Orleans, which had been notable only for the extent of its accommodation
to the environment and for its delay in establishing the foundations of
religious and communal continuity."

During the years immediately preceding the Civil War, "there was
probably less prejudice against Jews in New Orleans than in any other important city in the country," Korn says. He found all indications of a
"broad scale of acceptance of Jews by both the Creole and Yankee societies" of the city. The frequency of intermarriage was one measure of the
"welcome which was accorded them." Another was the fact that Jews were
elected to high office in Louisiana earlier than in any other state. At one
and the same time just before the outbreak of the Civil War, Judah P. Benjamin was in the United States Senate; his cousin Henry Hyams, was
lieutenant governor; and Dr. Edwin Warren Moise, who had already served
as state attorney general, was speaker of the state legislature. Hyams, who
also came from Charleston, settled in Donaldsonville as a bank cashier in
the 1830s. He presided over an anti-abolition rally there in 1835 and moved
to New Orleans in the 1840s. He was elected lieutenant-governor in 1859,
the first known Jew to hold that office in any state.

The widespread acceptance of Jews into almost "every nook and
cranny of social, political and cultural life"—in addition to the more obvious opportunities of the marketplace—explain why there was no negative
pressure upon the New Orleans Jews to create a congregation sooner than
they did, or to develop an intensive Jewish life, says Korn. "Their energies
were directed outward rather than inward." Many of the assimilated or intermarried Jews had business dealings with each other and were often
bound together by participation in each others' ceremonies of birth, marriage, and death. A noted exception to this type of Jewish identification was
Judah P. Benjamin. He had law clients and social friends who were Jews,
but he never took part in any Jewish religious or philanthropic activities.
Even in the United States Senate, when the question of discrimination
against American Jews by Switzerland was being debated, he remained
silent. He never acknowledged or replied to the vicious anti-Semitic attacks

to which he was subjected during the Civil War, in both the South and the North.

The formation of the Association for the Relief of Widows and Orphans in 1854, the first agency of its kind in the United States, provided many intermarried Jews with an opportunity to express concern for Jewish needs on a humanitarian rather than a religious level. Many of them contributed to the Association and a number left it bequests. Henry Hyams was one of its vice-presidents in 1855. The Association was an outgrwoth of Jewish participation in the Howard Society, founded in 1833 to help yellow fever victims. This society divided the city into districts, each with its own emergency station and pharmacy, and with members serving as volunteer nurses, helping all regardless of creed or color. Yellow fever epidemics were New Orleans' great scourge, taking thousands of lives in 1853, 1867, and 1878. In 1853, there were 7,849 burials, of which 137 were Jewish.

When the Hebrew Benevolent Society called a mass meeting of "the Israelites of the city" in 1854, it organized the Association for the Relief of Jewish Widows and Orphans. Chartered in 1855, it erected a home in 1856. By the end of the Civil War there were 50 children in the home from many parts of the South. In 1875 the southern region of the B'nai B'rith became a major sponsor of the home, which was closed in the 1940s. The Jewish Children's Regional Service is the home's direct descendant. In 1853, the Jews of New Orleans formed a Foreign Missions Society to help relieve the plight of the Jews abroad. It was this society that sponsored the ill-fated Jewish agricultural colony at Sicily Island in 1881.

In the pre-Civil War days, the early Jewish settlers and their sons were welcomed into the exclusive New Orleans clubs which today exclude persons of Jewish birth. Carl Kohn and his nephew Gustave were members of the Boston Club, as were Judah P. Benjamin, Isaac and Samuel Delgado, and Benjamin Franklin Jonas, later a United States Senator. Armand Heine was a founding member of the aristocratic Pickwick Club, of which Edward Barnett and Cohen M. Soria were presidents. Michael Heine owned the clubhouse of the Pickwick Club from 1884 to 1894. Carl Kohn's daughter, who was reared a Christian, married a Jew, Victor Meyer, whose brother Adolph was elected to Congress from Louisiana, 1891-1898. The first king of the famous New Orleans Mardi Gras carnival, which began in 1872, was Lewis Salomon, a cotton broker's clerk. He was said to be a descendant of Haym Salomon, the Revolutionary War patriot.

When the Union Army captured New Orleans in 1862, every citizen was required to take an oath of allegiance to the United States or be transported to Confederate territory. Rabbi James K. Gutheim of the Dispersed of Judah Congregation refused to take the oath and encouraged members of his congregation to do the same even though it meant losing homes, livelihoods, and personal belongings. An ardent supporter of the Confederacy, he denounced the oath as a false oath to God and a betrayal of the "cause of right and justice," which to him was the cause of the South. He left the city in May, 1863 for Mobile where the Jewish community welcomed him as a hero, but since that city already had a rabbi, he spent the war years as rabbi of the congregation in Montgomery, Alabama. He returned to New Orleans in 1865, but three years later accepted a call to New York's Temple Emanu-El. In 1872, however, he asked Emanu-El to release him so he could become rabbi of the newly-formed Temple Sinai in New Orleans.

In 1875 Gutheim joined Catholic and Protestant spokesmen in public declarations denying General Sherman's charge that the people of Louisiana were still rebellious against Federal authority. He was an active member of the Southern Historical Society and his wife was one of the founders of the Ladies Confederate Memorial Association of New Orleans. The Jews who remained in New Orleans during the Union occupation were subjected to the most violent anti-Semitic tirades. A reporter in the city seriously proposed the execution of all Jewish smugglers in a story reporting the arrest of three Jews allegedly caught on Lake Pontchartrain carrying "a large quantity of medicine for the rebels and also letters from 40 or 50 leading citizens of New Orleans to persons high in authority in the Confederate government." The writer said that "the Jews in New Orleans and all the South ought to be exterminated. They run the blockade and are always to be found at the bottom of every new villainy." Korn, in *American Jewry and the Civil War*, quotes a Cincinnati Jew returning North from Louisiana who told Rabbi Isaac Meyer Wise that "local editors and correspondents residing temporarily in New Orleans frequently ventilate their stupid prejudice against our race in revolting newspaper hoaxes and downright lies." When the *Jewish Messenger* of New York proclaimed its loyalty to the Union after secession began and called on its readers to stand by the flag, Southern readers denounced the editor, S.M. Isaacs. The congregation in Shreveport adopted a resolution denouncing Isaacs "as an enemy to our interest and welfare" and pledged its members to boycott the paper. At that time there was only one subscriber in Shreveport, and he was two years in arrears. Issachar Zacharie, a British-born Jewish physician and foot doctor, who became an intimate of President Lincoln during the war, went on a number of private missions for the President, including a couple to New Orleans where he interviewed local people in an effort to measure public opinion. Zacharie took pains, says Korn, to secure a generous hearing for Northern Jews caught in New Orleans at the outbreak of the war, and for New Orleans Jews who were ousted from the city when they refused to take a loyalty oath to the Union. In May, 1864, a group of New York Jews honored Zacharie for "his noble and fraternal efforts" in behalf of the Jews of New Orleans. Some 200 Jews from Louisiana served in the Confederate armed forces.

By the end of the Civil War, Jewish settlements had taken root in a number of cities outside of New Orleans, notably Alexandria (1854); Donaldsonville (1854); Plaquemine (1856); Baton Rouge (1858); Shreveport (1848); Morgan City (1859); and Monroe (1861). In the following decade Jewish settlements sprang up in Bastrop (1877); Opelousas (1877); and Natchitoches (1871). In 1881, the pioneer congregation, Shanarai Chasset (Gates of Mercy), merged with the second congregation, Dispersed of Judah, to create Touro Synagogue. Both early congregations had lost many members during the Civil War and the 1878 yellow fever epidemic. In 1875 the Orthodox Congregation Chevra Thilim was organized. The state's Jewish population was estimated to be 7,530 in 1877, with 5,000 of this figure accounted for by New Orleans. Two decades later there were 12,000 Jews in the state, 8,000 of them in New Orleans, where there were four different congregations. Outside of New Orleans there were synagogues in 15 different communities and Jewish residents in 60 others.

The move of Jewish population out of the state's small towns and into New Orleans and other cities began after 1910 and was reflected in the 1917 population figure. In that year there were 12,723 Jews in the state, and of these 8,000 were in New Orleans, 1,500 in Shreveport, 450 in Alexandria, 286 in Lake Charles, and about 2,000 in the rest of the state. A generation later 65 percent of the state's 16,100 Jews lived in New Orleans. There were 2,500 in Shreveport, 900 in Monroe, 875 in Baton Rouge, 500 in Alexandria, 210 in Lake Charles, and 200 in Crowley. In 1977 the Jewish population had increased to 17,340; of whom 10,500 were in New Orleans; 1,500 in Shreveport; 1,400 in Baton Rouge, the capital and seat of the state university; 600 in Lafayette; 450 in Alexandria; and 400 in Monroe. The remaining 2,500 lived in smaller towns and cities.

The Jewish community of New Orleans has grown in recent years in part from the attraction of the Tulane Medical School and in part from the city's increasing importance as a center of Latin American trade and commerce. The social status the community enjoyed in the ante-bellum and post-Civil War eras was different from what it became in the second and third quarters of the 20th century. Some prominent Jewish families leave New Orleans during the Mardi Gras carnival because they want to avoid embarrassment over being ignored when invitations are sent out for the balls of the socially prominent organizations, including some to which Jews belonged a generation or two ago. In 1969 one carnival organization brought Kirk Douglas, the Jewish film star, to the city to be its Rex for the carnival ball and as a result was shunned by other carnival groups. The following year a new carnival group composed of Jews and non-Jews was established. Some Jews participate in the lesser carnival organizations.

The unusually high level of integration into the larger community that Korn noted in the pre-Civil War era has continued. The late Rabbi Emil W.

Leipziger of Touro Synagogue was president of the Louisiana State Confederate of Charities in 1916. In 1925 he was the winner of the *New Orleans Times Picayune* annual trophy for "unselfish service" to the city. Five other Jews have won this trophy. The late Monte Lemann, one of the state's leading attorneys, served on President Hoover's commission to study prohibition enforcement. Mrs. Edgar Stern, a daughter of Julius Rosenwald, and her husband were among the city's most influential civic leaders.

In the political sphere there have been a number of prominent Jews. Jews who have served as mayors were: Arnold Bernstein, Shreveport (1918-1937); Ernest Bernstein, Shreveport (1906-1910); Lewis Arnheim, Vidalia (1869-1871); Samuel Levy, Shreveport (1873-1876); Meyer Lemann, Donaldsonville (1881); David Israel, Donaldsonville; and Samuel Klotz, Napoleonville (1939-1945). On the statewide level there have been two Jewish members of the United States Senate—Judah P. Benjamin (1853-1861) and Benjamin F. Jonas, (1879-1885). Max Dinkelspiel was justice of the State Court of Appeals (1919-1924). Emile Godchaux, a son of sugar king Leon Godchaux, served on the State Court of Appeals in the 1890s. Walter F. Marcus, Jr., was justice of the State Supreme Court from 1973 to date. Since 1966, Alvin R. Rubin had been a judge of the United States District Court for the Eastern District of Louisiana; he is now with the U.S. Court of Appeals. Charles Schwartz, Jr. and Morey L. Sear, also active members of Temple Sinai, were named judges of the Federal District Court in 1975. Abraham L. Shushan, president of the New Orleans Levee Board from 1929-1935, was a close political aide of Huey Long. Until Shushan was acquitted of charges of attempting to evade Federal income tax, the New Orleans airport was named for him. The late Seymour Weiss, a New Orleans hotelman and political ally of Huey Long, was the so-called "prime-minister" of the Long political machine in the 1920s and early 1930s and treasurer of the State Democratic Association.

After Long was assassinated in 1935, Weiss was part of a triumvirate of politicians that sought to revive the Long machine. Later Weiss served a 16-month prison term after his conviction of conspiracy to defraud the government of taxes owed by a corporation in which he was a principal stockholder. David B. Samuel presided over the Shreveport City Court from 1916-1931. In the 1960s, Sylvain Friedman was president pro-tem of the State Senate.

* * * * *

ALEXANDRIA
Cong. B'nai Israel, Vance at Hickory St.
Cong. Gemiluth Chassodim, 2021 Turner St.
Jewish Welfare Federation of Central Louisiana, 1261 Heyman Lane.

BATON ROUGE
Blondheim collection of 4,000 volumes on French dialects, linguistics, and literature, in the Louisiana State University Library, was acquired by the University in 1934. It also includes a good deal of French Hebraica, as well as rare dictionaries, periodicals, and reprints. Dr. David S. Blondheim, who was a professor of Romance languages at Johns Hopkins University, 1917-1934, and prior to that at the University of Illinois, took a leave of absence during World War I to join the staff of the National Jewish Welfare Board as its educational and program consultant. He served both in this country and abroad.

Hillel Foundation at Louisiana State University, 16420 University Station.

Jewish Welfare Federation, P.O. Box 15123; phone 275-9335.

Liberal Synagogue, 260 S. Acadia Thruway.

Judah Touro Sculpture, in a panel on the north side of the State Capitol Building, is one of the 22 carved heads of great men in Louisiana history.

BOGALUSA
Cong. Beth El, P.O. Box 1207.

BUNKIE
This town in Avoyelles Parish was built by Col. A.M. Haas and son, W.D. Haas. The colonel's youngest daughter Marcie, gave the town its name which was her father's nickname. Haas' descendants are no longer Jews.

DONALDSONVILLE
Bikur Cholim Cemetery, cor. St. Patrick and Marchand Dr., which dates from the 1850s, has many broken and fallen gravestones. The town had only four Jews residing there in 1976, and one of them, Gaston Hirsch, was trying to care for the burial ground with the aid of occasional contributions from relatives of those interred there. Cong. Bikur Cholim, whose members established the cemetery, was founded in the 1860s and a synagogue was erected in 1872. The congregation disbanded in the 1940s and the synagogue building on Railroad Ave. remained empty until an auto supply store bought the frame structure and put a modern store front on the building.

GEISMAR
Benjamin Geismar, a German immigrant from the town of Hofgeismar, who arrived in the U.S. in 1879 and found employment with a landsman, Abraham Heymann, who owned a store near New River Landing, is memorialized by this Ascension Parish town. In 1885 Geismar founded the firm of Picard and Geismar with his brother-in-law. The new firm

prospered in raising sugar cane, corn, and cotton. When the railroad from New Orleans to Memphis opened in 1889, the station established at the Geismar and Picard plantation was named Geismar and a town grew up around it.

KAPLAN

Abraham Kaplan, who in 1902 pioneered the development of the rice industry, is memorialized in this Vermillion Parish town he founded. Kaplan drained and developed thousands of acres of marsh land and built hundreds of miles of irrigation canals for watering rice fields. The town has many rice mills, including the Liberty Rice Mill with which the Kaplan family is associated. Kaplan gave the town its municipal library and swimming pool.

LAFAYETTE

Menachim Aveilim Cemetery, Lee and College Aves., has a statue of Andrew Mouton, a non-Jew who was governor of Louisiana from 1843-1846, and presided at the secession convention in 1861. In 1869, Mouton gave the Jews of Lafayette the ground for this cemetery and also the site on which the first Rodeph Sholem Temple was built.

Rodeph Sholom Temple, 603 Lee St.

LAKE CHARLES

Temple Sinai, 713 Hodges St.

MARKSVILLE

Marc Eliche, who came to Louisiana in 1820 from Alsace Lorraine, is memorialized in this town, the seat of Avoyelles Parish.

METAIRIE

Cong. Gates of Prayer, Richland and W. Esplanade, was the first synagogue to be established in the New Orleans suburbs when it dedicated its new synagogue in 1975. The congregation was founded in 1850.

Jewish Family and Children's service, suburban branch.

Tikvat Sholom Cong., 3737 W. Esplanade.

MONROE

Bernstein Park is named after the late Arnold Bernstein, mayor of the city for more than two decades.

Temple B'nai Israel, 2400 Orell Pl.

United Jewish Charities of Northwest Louisiana, 2400 Orell Pl.

MORGAN CITY

Cong. Shaarey Zedek, 708 3rd St.

NATCHITOCHES
Cong. B'nai Israel, 2nd St.

NEW IBERIA
Cong. Gates of Prayer, Charles and Weeks Sts.

NEW ORLEANS
Ray Abrams Elementary School, 6519 Virgilian St., is named for the first woman principal of an all-boys high school. Miss Abrams developed special programs to train young people for careers in the import-export field.

Marion Abramson School, 5552 Read Rd., is named for a prominent educator.

Judah P. Benjamin Elementary School, 4040 Eagle St.

Judah P. Benjamin Roll-Top Desk and an oil painting of the Confederate statesman are on exhibit in The Presbytere, an historic house on Jackson Sq., that is one of the eight buildings in the Old French Quarter which make up the Louisiana State Museum Complex. The Museum also owns a number of other portraits of Benjamin as well as artifacts from his latter years as a barrister in Great Britain. These include two wigs and a wig-case, a pair of gloves, a glove box and a glove stretcher, shoes, coat, vest, and tie.

The mahogany desk was purchased by *The Times Democrat* (now *The Times-Picayune*) after Benjamin fled the U.S., following Lee's surrender at Appomattox. There was a reward of $50,000 offered for Benjamin's capture alive because he had been Secretary of War and Secretary of State of the Confederate States of America. A native of Charleston, S.C., Benjamin came to New Orleans in 1828 and established himself as a brilliant lawyer and member of the State Senate. He was a member of the State Constitutional Convention of 1844-1845 and was a presidential elector in 1848. In 1853 he was elected to the U.S. Senate, the second Jew to serve in that office. He remained in the Senate until Louisiana seceded after which he was appointed first Attorney General of the Confederacy and then Secretary of War, and Secretary of State. President Franklin Pierce had offered him a seat on the U.S. Supreme Court. Known as "the brains of the Confederacy," Benjamin had no known Jewish affiliation. After the Confederacy surrendered, Benjamin escaped to England where he enjoyed a second career as a prominent member of the British bar. He is reported to have become a Catholic on his deathbed in Paris in 1884.

In his absence, his estate, Bellechase, and his other property were seized by the government. Bellechase, the pillared mansion on the west bank of the Mississippi, which was Benjamin's country home, was for many years one of the city's shrines, but it was destroyed by decay and neglect when the Daughters of the Confederacy and historical societies failed to rally the support needed to restore and maintain the mansion as a public museum. The roll-top desk was also sold at auction and bought by *The Times-Democrat*. For 105 years it was used in the newspaper office and then set aside and forgotten. In 1969, George W. Healy, editor of *The Times-Picayune*, gave the desk to the Louisiana State Museum. Near the desk·in The Presbytere there is a portrait of Benjamin.

Cabildo, Jackson Sq. in the Old French Quarter, the seat of the Spanish colonial government and now part of the Louisiana State Museum, displays on its second floor a portrait of Judah Touro.

Canal St., the city's main thoroughfare, was renamed Touro Ave. shortly after the eminent merchant and philanthropist died in 1854, when his friend and executor, Rezin Shepherd told the city council that he would give the city from $200,000 to $300,000 to embellish and improve Canal St. The name was later changed back to Canal St.

Chabad House of the Lubavitcher Movement, 7037 Freret St.,

Cohen Senior High School, 3520 Dryades, is named for Walter L. Cohen, a prominent civic leader who served on the board of education.

Commission on Jewish Education, 211 Camp St.,

Communal Hebrew School, 1631 Calhoun St., is a part of the Commission on Jewish Education, a division of the Jewish Welfare Federation.

Cong. Anshe Sfard, 2230 Carondelet St.

Cong. Beth Israel, 7000 Canal Blvd., has on its exterior wall a sculpture representing the Burning Bush, directly behind the Ark on the inside wall. The sculpture gives the impression of fire emanating from it. In front of the education wing is a huge free-standing Menorah.

Cong. Chevre Thilim, 4429 S. Claiborne Ave.

Cong. Gates of Prayer (see Metaire).

Conservative Congregation of New Orleans, 932 Napoleon Ave.

Delgado Art Museum, Lelong Ave., in City Park, the city's only art center, was established in 1910 by Isaac Delgado. When he was 14 years old, Delgado left his native Jamaica for New Orleans, where he got a job as a clerk. Later he became associated with his uncle in the sugar and molasses business. He rose to prominence in social and business life of the community. He was a charter member of the Louisiana Sugar Exchange, president of the Convalescent Home, and a member of many civic and communal boards. He also left funds for the Delgado Memorial of the Charity Hospital and the Delgado Trade School, now the municipal Delgado College at 615 City Park Ave. The museum also houses the Chapman H. Hyams Collection of statuary, and the Isaac M. Cline Collection of ancient bronzes.

Dispersed of Judah Cemetery, on the north side of upper Canal St., near City Park Ave., has a slab which bears an inscription to the effect that Judah Touro was buried here. Immediately after his death, Touro was interred in this cemetery, but later his remains were sent to Newport, R.I. for reburial,

First Jewish Cemetery, oldest in Louisiana, at Jackson Ave., and Saratoga St., dates from the 1820s. It is still intact and well-cared for, but has not been used since 1866.

First Unitarian Church, 1800 Jefferson Ave., is descended from the Baptist Church of the Rev. Theodore Clapp which was saved from having to close because of financial difficulties when Judah Touro acquired the church's mortgage and put its minister on his payroll.

Gumbel Vocational Training School, 5700 Loyola Ave., is a memorial to Mrs. Sophie Gumbel whose heirs gave the city $60,000 in 1912 to establish the school as part of the city's school system.

Hillel Foundation at Tulane University and Newcombe College, 912 Broadway.

Jewish Children's Regional Service, 5342 St. Charles Ave., is a direct descendant of the Association for Relief of Jewish Widows and Orphans, founded in 1854 and later know as the Jewish Children's Home. The agency now provides special services for Jewish children in seven southern states.

Jewish Community Center, 5342 St. Charles Ave., occupies the site where the old Jewish Children's Home once stood. In the Broverman Adult Lounge-Bernstein Memorial Library is a metal sculpture by John Clemmer entitled, *Pentateuch*, depicting the Five Books of Moses as they appear to reach out to touch the viewer from their background of the desert, the Exodus, and God's miracles.

Jewish Family and Children's Service, 107 Camp St.,

Jewish Federation of Greater New Orleans, 211 Camp St.,

Jewish Times, 211 Camp St.

Joseph Kohn, Jr. High School. 4001 N. Roman St., is named for a member of one of the city's pioneer Jewish families.

Lakeshore Day School, 7000 Canal Blvd.

Milton H. Latter Memorial Library, 5120 St. Charles Ave., a branch of the city's public library, is a memorial to Lt. Milton H. Latter, who was killed on Okinawa on April 25, 1945, while leading his platoon against a machine gun position. Latter was awarded the Bronze Star Medal and the Purple Heart. His parents, Mr. and Mrs. Harry Latter, gave the library to the city in 1948.

Norman Mayer Memorial Bldg., 211 Camp St., honors a prominent cotton broker and exporter, who bequeathed funds for the purchase of the building which houses the Community Chest, Jewish Welfare Federation, Catholic Charities, Family Service Society, and the Council of Social Agencies. Mayer also provided funds for the Gentilly Branch of the Public Library, 3000 Foy St., now known as the Mayer Gentilly Branch.

Adolph Meyer Elementary School, 2013 Gen. Meyer Ave., is named for Adolph Meyer, member of Congress from Louisiana from 1891-1908. He was a brigadier general in the Louisiana State National Guard.

Isidore Newman School, 1831 Jefferson Ave., the city's best private academic school, was founded in 1903 by Isidore Newman as a manual training school for residents of the Jewish Children's Home. It became a private school when the Home ceased operation in the 1940s.

Julius Rosenwald Elementary School, 6501 Berkley Dr., is named for the famed philanthropist and merchant.

Rosenwald Hall, on the campus of Dilliard University, 2601 Gentilly Blvd., is dedicated to the memory of Julius Rosenwald (see Illinois). A plaque in the entrance foyer reads: "Julius Rosenwald, Friend of Dilliard University, Humanitarian—World Citizen, Dedicated June 2, 1948."

Shakespeare Convalescent Home, 2621 Gen. Meyers Ave., was originally established through a bequest from Judah Touro and named for him and former Mayor Joseph Shakespeare. It is a home for chronically ill patients.

Edgar Stern Estate (Long Vue Gardens), one of the city's showplaces, was donated to the city by Mrs. Stern, a daughter of Julius Rosenwald. Tours are conducted by the Garden Study Club.

Temple Sinai, 6227 St. Charles Ave., has on the exterior wall of its Julian B. Feibelman Chapel two Tablets of the Ten Commandments taken from the old building on Carondelet St. In the chapel is an unusual tapestry whose central theme depicts symbolism from Jewish mystic literature. It is dedicated to Louis A. Weil. The Temple houses a major art collection, one of the largest in any synagogue, including over 60 works by contemporary artists. It was a gift of Jacob Weintraub in memory of his wife, Barbara.

Tikvat Sholom Cong., (see Metairie).

Touro Infirmary, 3500 Prytania St., is one of the largest hospitals in the South. In 1852 Judah Touro bought the Paulding estate for a hospital and put his friend, Dr. Joseph Bensadon, noted physician and surgeon in charge. It was largely through the efforts of Bensadon, who was a surgeon in the Confederate Army, that the Touro Infirmary gained wide recognition. A portrait of Touro hangs in the lobby. His porcupine quill, enclosed in a glass case, is attached to the portrait. Touro's oldest desk stands in the board room.

Touro Street, named for Judah Touro, runs from the junction of Royal and Kerlerec out to Lake Pontchartrain.

Touro Synagogue, 4238 St. Charles Ave., is the oldest synagogue in Louisiana, having been founded in 1828 as Cong. Shanarai Chasset. The state's second congregation, Dispersed of Judah, whose first building was dedicated in 1850, merged with the older congregation in 1881 to form Touro Synagogue. The altar in the present synagogue is the same one used in the old Dispersed of Judah synagogue.

Westbank Congregation, 3701 Behrman Place.

Willow Wood, the Home for the Jewish Aged, 3701 Behrman Place.

Samuel Zemurray, Jr., Gymnasium at Tulane University, 6823 St. Charles Ave., is a memorial to the son of the late Samuel Zemurray, "the banana king." Zemurray, Jr., was an Air Force major who was killed during World War II. The elder Zemurray rose from pushcart peddler to become the head of the United Fruit Co., with its half a million acres, 1,500 odd miles of railways, its Great White Fleet of 52 vessels, its Tropical Radio Telegraph, and the daily newspaper, *El Diario Commercial* in Honduras. In addition to running the world's biggest agricultural domain, Zemurray played a substantial role in state and national affairs. He fought the Huey B. Long machine from its beginning. At the request of President Franklin D. Roosevelt, who was his personal friend, he helped frame AAA industry codes, in World War II was advisor to the Board of Economic Warfare, and developed new sources of hemp, quinine, and rubber in Latin America. He gave millions to various philanthropic causes. To Tulane University he also gave a priceless collection of Mayan arts and letters for Central American Research.

OPELOUSAS

Temple Emanuel, 747 S. Main St.

RESERVE

Leon Godchaux, an Alsation Jew who settled in Louisiana in 1837, starting out as a peddler, is memorialized by this town and the Godchaux Sugar Refinery, which turns out 2,500,000 pounds of sugar per day. Driven away from a large plantation by its owners, who hated peddlers, Godchaux swore that one day he would be the largest landowner in St. John the Baptist Parish. He never forgot the insult of being chased out of a plantation and so, when he became a great merchant and industrialist, he kept his youthful pledge to *reserve* his lands against all interlopers and named the town that grew up around his sugar plantation Reserve. There is a Leon Godchaux Grammar School and a Leon Godchaux High School in Reserve. The Godchaux Sugar Refinery is now owned by eastern capital and Walter Godchaux is merely the general manager. Leon Godchaux's children became Catholics and the rose window on St. Peter's Church is a memorial to Edward Godchaux, Leon's son.

ROSA

Rosa Godchaux, member of a pioneer sugar-growing family, is memorialized in the name of this St. Landry Parish town. She was the third of the eight children of Leon Godchaux. When the Texas & Pacific Railroad opened a line through Big Cane, Godchaux gave the land on which the local depot was built. "Name it Rosa, for my daughter," he said, when the people of the area decided to name the place in his honor. Rosa Godchaux died in 1962 at the age of 90.

SHREVEPORT

Betty-Virginia Park, located in the city's most exclusive residential section, is named in part for Betty, daughter of Elias Goldstein, one of the park's donors.

Cong. Agudath Achim, 1707 Line Ave.

Jewish Federation and Family Services, 1021 Land Bldg.

Temple B'nai Zion, 175 Southfield Rd.

SICILY ISLAND

This Catahoula Parish town, 300 miles from New Orleans, was the site of an ill-fated Jewish agricultural colony established in 1881 on 450 acres by the Foreign Mission Society, a Jewish group in New Orleans. The colonists, all Russian Jews, were students, writers, artists, merchants, craftsmen, and peddlers, none of whom had ever farmed and few of whom were accustomed to manual labor. Their wives and children were temporarily housed in New Orleans until somewhat less primitive living conditions became available in the colony. Surrounded by deserted plantations, faced with failing crops, malaria, a shortage of drinking water, and a disastrous Mississippi River flood, the harried colonists left in despair in the spring of 1882, bringing to an end what had been called "The Experiment of the Cicily Island Colony."

Mississippi

A Jew by the name of Elias Stultheis was the director of the first organized colonization effort in what is now Mississippi, some time between 1718 and 1722. French historians of early Louisiana, of which Mississippi was a part, not only refer to *le Juif* (the Jew) Stultheis as the chief American agent of John Law's concessions in the lower Mississippi Valley, but indicate that some Jews were among the first colonists.

John Law, a Scots adventurer, financial speculator, and promoter, was the key figure in the fantastic Mississippi Bubble, which attempted to use imported settlers to exploit Louisiana's resources for the benefit of the French royal treasury. Law's Compagnie des Indes Occidentales, or Mississippi Company, as it was popularly called, was chartered in 1717 and given a virtual monopoly in Louisiana. In exchange, the company agreed to settle 6,000 white colonists and 3,000 slaves. In the hope of vast profits from Louisiana's wealth, the French government became involved in Law's schemes to such an extent that, when the Mississippi Bubble burst in 1720, the French monetary system was almost wrecked. Even England's economy was shaken by the feverish speculation in the shares of the Mississippi Company. Sampson Gideon, a Jewish broker of London, helped bolster British credit.

Law's financial manipulations brought ruin not only to investors but tragedy to the colonists who had been shipped to Mississippi. The first white settlement in the lower Mississippi Valley had been made at what is now Biloxi in 1699, as well as Natchez on the Mississippi. Although most of the settlers were military deserters, smugglers, and vagabonds who were punished by exile, there were a "certain number of people of standing" who were also deported, according to Baron Marc de Villiers du Terrage in his book, *History of the Establishment of New Orleans*. Since Villiers adds that information about these "people of standing" was systematically destroyed, there is the possibility that among them were Jews whom the French authorities were anxious to be rid of. Pierre Margry, in *French Discoveries and Settlements in the West and South of North America*, declares that the exiles numbered "more than 4,000 people, as many French as Germans and Jews."

The crash of Law's speculative empire left his Mississippi colonists stranded. Lacking supplies, funds, and leadership, many of them died of fever or were killed by hostile Indians. Stultheis' deputy, a man named Levens, led some of the helpless settlers south from the Arkansas River to New Orleans. Among the surviving colonists were two with familiar Jewish names, Simon Kuhn and Zweig.

If any of the Jews who came to Mississippi with Law's hapless deportees remained after 1724, they found themselves liable to expulsion under the Black Code of Louisiana which barred Jews from the colony. But just as some Jews defied the Black Code by settling in New Orleans and Mobile in the early 18th century, others ignored it in Natchez and Biloxi in the 1750s. When southern Mississippi became part of British West Florida in 1763, the British neither repealed nor enforced the Black Code, but they did forbid Jews to vote. This discrimination, however, didn't faze David Franks, Philadelphia merchant and purveyor to British troops in North America. He wrote to the British commander-in-chief, General Thomas Gage, on February 15, 1771, inquiring whether the firm of Levy & Franks should undertake to send supplies from their trading posts on the Illinois River to the British "troops stationed at the Natchese and Iberville on the Mississippy."

By the time the French regained control of the country around Natchez in 1781, some Jews were well-established there. Samuel S. Foreman of New Jersey, who visited Natchez in 1789, noted in his report that "in the village of Natchez there resided Monsier (sic) and Madam (sic) Mansante— Spanish Jews, I think, who were the most kind and hospitable of people." Foreman was referring to Benjamin Monsanto, whose brother, Isaac Rodriguez Monsanto, was one of the first three identifiable Jews to settle in New Orleans in 1758. In 1762, when Spain ceded Louisiana in a secret treaty with France, Jewish and British traders, among them Monsanto, were driven out of New Orleans. He returned later, but his younger brother, Benjamin, settled down in Natchez. Benjamin and his wife, a Jewish girl from Curacao, never hid their origin, but they lived as Catholics for more than 50 years although no evidence of conversion has ever been found.

Mississippi became American territory in 1798 and a state in 1817, by which time there were about 100 Jews living or doing business in the Gulf Coast towns and Natchez. In the generation after statehood, high cotton prices, cheap land, and the coming of the steamboat created a boom that brought a large influx of new settlers, including a considerable number of Jews. The Jews came in two waves—traveling north up the Mississippi from New Orleans to Natchez and Vicksburg, and south from Cincinnati and St. Louis to the inland river towns such as Greenville and Jackson. Most of the early Jewish arrivals were Germans from Alsace Lorraine and they had a command of both German and French. Many of them became peddlers and then branched out into country storekeepers and cotton brokers.

Traveling on foot, wagon, or via the steamboats that reached many of the inland plantations, the Jewish peddlers were a familiar feature of ante-bellum Mississippi life. At the outset, most of the peddlers lived in New Orleans where some of them may have received goods on credit from Judah Touro, the merchant prince whose vessels carried Mississippi cotton to the mills of New England. Eventually, some of the itinerant merchants opened stores and brought their families to Mississippi.

Not all of the early Jewish settlers were peddlers. Jewish professional men were also attracted to Mississippi. The eccentric Charles Lewis Levin, native South Carolinian who achieved notoriety by his leadership in the anti-alien and anti-Catholic Native American party of the 1840s (he was elected to Congress from Philadelphia in the 1840s), came to Mississippi in 1828 to teach school at Woodville. He was badly wounded in a duel in which his second was Jefferson P. Davis, the future president of the Confederacy. Dr. Joseph Hertz, who had settled at Nacogdoches, Texas, in 1832, practiced medicine at Natchez in 1835. Chapman Levy, another South Carolinian who had distinguished himself in his native state's legislature and in the War of 1812, practiced law in Mississippi in the early 1840s.

Natchez, the state's second oldest settlement, has the oldest Jewish community in continuous existence. There is a tradition that Jewish religious services were first held in Natchez about 1800, and perhaps even earlier. Tombstones bearing Jewish names and dated in the early 1800s are found in the city's oldest cemetery. An Orthodox congregation that went out of existence in 1910, and which never had a synagogue of its own, claimed to be the direct descendent of the group that began holding services at the turn of the 19th century. The Jewish cemetery in Natchez, the oldest in the state, dates from the 1840s. The oldest existing congregation in the state is B'nai Israel, established in Natchez in 1840. One year later, Anshe Chesed Congregation was organized in Vicksburg where Jews had lived since the 1830s.

Rodney, once an important river town, was settled by Jews in the 1820s. There are Jewish cemeteries in Biloxi and Woodville dating from the 1840s. Alsatian and German Jews who arrived in Columbus, on the Tombigbee River in 1836, founded Congregation Beth Israel in 1845. Before the Civil War, Jews had also established themselves in Chickasaw County (1836), Pontoto County (1840), Amite County (1848), Coffeeville (1850), Brookville (1852), Attala County (1852), Grand Gulf (1853), Summit (1856), Port Gibson (1858), Jackson (1858), Meridian (1855), and Marshall County (1857). E. Rubel and Co. of Corinth, was established in 1858 by Abe Rubel as a wholesale and retail dry goods store. During the Civil War, Rubel raised funds to outfit the first company of volunteers from Corinth that joined the Confederate Army.

The first synagogue in Mississippi was erected in Jackson in 1861, the year in which Congregation Beth Israel was formed. The frame structure, near the corner of South State and South Streets, was burned when Union troops captured Jackson in 1863. Beth Israel in Natchez built its first synagogue in 1867, and Vicksburg's Anshe Chesed followed a year later.

The wide dispersion of Jews in Mississippi prior to the Civil War is indicated by the fact that they enlisted in the Confederate Army from most of the towns in the state. In *The American Jew As Patriot, Soldier and Citizen*, Simon Wolf listed 158 Jewish soldiers from Mississippi in 37 different regiments. Later research has added 82 Jewish names to this list. Among the 158 were Max Frauenthal (see Arkansas), one of the Confederate heroes of the Battle of Spottsylvania Court House; and the four Jonas brothers, Charles, Julian, Benjamin, and Samuel, sons of Abraham Jonas of Quincy (see Illinois), Lincoln's political friend. A fifth brother, Edward, served with an Illinois regiment.

The Civil War gave Mississippi a permanent place in American Jewish history, for it was from Holly Springs, Mississippi that General Ulysses S. Grant issued the notorious Order No. 11, on December 17, 1862, expelling all Jews as a class from the Department of Tennessee, which included Mississippi. In *American Jewry and the Civil War,* Dr. Bertram W. Korn describes the general anarchy, chaos, bribery, and corruption that were responsible for the widespread profiteering by Northerners in Southern cotton which led to the most sweeping anti-Jewish regulation in all American history (see Paducah, Kentucky).

This libel, which attributed to the Jews all responsibility for the multimillion dollar contraband traffic, created a nationwide uproar.The Order itself was quickly repealed after a delegation of Jews from Kentucky had appealed to President Abraham Lincoln.Three Northern Jews, and the fiancee of one of them, reached Union lines at Oxford, Mississippi the day after Order No. 11 was issued. They had been trying to get out of the Confederacy ever since the war began. All three were arrested, their horse and buggy and luggage confiscated, and they were taken under guard to Cairo, Illinois. When they insisted on knowing why they were being mistreated, they were told: "Because you are Jews, and are neither a benefit to the Union or Confederacy." Several other Jews in Mississippi were caught in Holly Springs and had to go on foot to Memphis. Another was imprisoned for attempting to telegraph General Grant.

Former Mississippi governor and United States Senator Henry S. Foote, a member of the Confederate Congress during the Civil War, waged a violent campaign of anti-Semitism. He denounced Judah P. Benjamin, Secretary of War and Secretary of State of the Confederate States of America for allegedly protecting "Jewish profiteers who dominated the United States and who would own everything after the war." Foote was always threatening to expose Benjamin as the head of a "powerful Jewish conspiracy." When a Richmond paper, animated by Foote's propaganda, charged that a member of the Confederate Congress had accepted a bribe from three Southern Jews who wanted to go North, Foote demanded a full scale investigation, which was made and not a single substantiating fact was found.

The breakdown of the plantation system after the war transferred social status and economic power from the farms to the towns. The store usurped the prestige of the plantation, and brought about the growth of the towns. One effect of this development was a postwar influx of Jewish merchants and storekeepers. Just as the German and Alsatian Jews had spread through the river towns of Mississippi from 1830-1850, so later immigrants, many from Eastern Europe, moved into the Delta region between 1870 and 1890. As rural businessmen, plantation owners, mill operators, cotton brokers, and professional men, the Jews in postwar Mississippi became an important factor in the economic rebuilding of the state. The Grunfests settled in Cary around 1885 and started a business that is still run by grandsons in Mississippi, Arkansas, and Louisiana. Herman Dansker, who founded one of the oldest field seed firms in the Delta at the turn of the century, was one of Clarksdale's leading citizens for more than a generation. When he died in 1968, he had one of the largest funerals ever seen in the city.

Agricultural depression in the early 1890s led to the formation of the Whitecapping movement whose adherents espoused both anti-Semitism and anti-black violence. The Whitecaps used force to drive black field hands off lands owned by Jewish merchants and lumber companies. Because merchants could furnish farm tenants with goods from their stores, they had an advantage over non-Jewish farmers in inducing blacks to work for them, as William F. Holmes pointed out in the *American Jewish Historical Quarterly*. Merchants frequently did not closely supervise their black tenants, and white farmers resented the independence enjoyed by these former slaves. Since a substantial number of merchants in Mississippi's cotton-growing regions were Jews, "many victims of the merchant supply system—most of whom were white, Anglo-Saxon Protestants— came to believe themselves victims of a Jewish conspiracy." The secret White Cap clubs flourished in Lincoln, Amite, Franklin, Pike, Lawrence, Marion, and Copiah Counties.

The central White Cap club of Lawrence County complained that "pauperized Jews are imported here who use every damnable idea conceivable to obtain possession of our lands. . . The accursed Jews and others own two thirds of our land. . . Under no circumstances will the Negro be allowed to cultivate a Jew's or syndicate's land, unless such lands are bought and will be shortly paid for." One of the avowed aims of the White Cap societies was "to control Jew and Gentile land speculators, and, if necessary to force them to abandon our country and confiscate their lands for the benefit of the white farmers." During the 1892 fall elections, the White Caps began driving blacks from farms owned by Jewish merchants. Signs were posted on tenant houses warning the occupants to leave immediately: "This Jew place is not for sale or rent, but will be used hereafter as pasture."

Holmes cites H. Hiller, a Jewish merchant who had moved to Summit, in Pike County, in the mid-19th century and built a flourishing mercantile business, as a major target of the White Caps. His estate consisted of about 400 small farms, many acquired through mortgage foreclosures. From November, 1892 to January, 1893, the White Caps burned to the ground 27 tenant houses on Hiller's farms. As a result, the tenants abandoned his farms, causing heavy losses. His bill collectors were warned by White Cap night riders to return to Summit or he would "find himself food for buzzards." Hiller capitulated, sold his mercantile firm in 1893, and moved to New Orleans.

The Jewish population of Mississippi was never large. In 1877 it was estimated at 2,262. Thirty years later it had grown only to 3,300. Vicksburg was the largest community, with 717, followed by Natchez (575), Greenville (500), Lexington (450), Greenwood (125), and Jackson (115). In 1907 there were 20 Jewish congregations, 16 with their own synagogues. Between 1901 and 1907, the Industrial Removal Office settled 353 Jews in 45 different towns. Floods, yellow fever, tornadoes, fire, and the decline of the steamboat ruined many of the older river towns and caused a shift of Jewish population to the newer lumber, textile, and commercial centers.

It was in Mississippi that the late Dr. Joseph Goldberger of the United States Public Health Service discovered the cause and cure of pellagra, which was taking a heavy toll among poor blacks and whites throughout the South. Between 1914 and 1917, Goldberger conducted experiments among volunteers at Rankin Prison Farm and among adult volunteers in Sunflower County.

The chain store expansion into the small cities and towns of Mississippi, as in other Southern states, in the 1930s and 1940s led to the gradual disappearance of family-owned mercantile enterprises and the consequent decline of the Jewish population in many Mississippi towns. In 1937 the state's Jewish population numbered a little over 4,000, with more than half of the Jews living in six cities: Clarksdale (412); Greenville (450); Greenwood (300); Jackson (235); Vicksburg (378); and Meridian (350). Older communities were dying out. The larger cities, especially Jackson, attracted Jews because it is the home of the State University's medical, research, and development center, and the regional Veterans Administration hospital. Also, Jewish traveling salesmen in the lower Mississippi Valley made the state capital their home base. By 1960 the Jewish population of the state stabilized at 4,000. In 1977 it was only 4,165.

The civil rights struggle and the resulting turmoil impelled many Jews to leave Mississippi and deterred others from coming. In the late 1950s, when the White Citizens Councils sprang up to intimidate blacks from demanding their rights and to terrorize white sympathizers, Jewish merchants were frequently caught in the middle. Often they had no choice about whether to join the White Citizens Councils—it was join or go out of business. Some Jews joined willingly. There was even a pamphlet entitled *A Jewish View of Segregation* authored by a Mississippi rabbi which denied that the White Citizens Councils were anti-Semitic.

Two of Mississippi's rabbis were outspoken supporters of civil rights. Rabbi Charles Mantinband of B'nai Israel in Hattiesburg was one of the most forthright critics of the Ku Klux Klan and the White Citizens Councils. The former director of the Southern Regional Council, on whose board Rabbi Mantinband served for several years, said that "in Mississippi in the '50s, Rabbi Mantinband, publisher Hodding Carter II, and a Catholic bishop were the strongest voices in Mississippi for right. They represented three faiths and two professions . . . and each displayed tremendous courage." Rabbi and Mrs Mantinband defied the Citizens Councils by having the late Medgar Evers, assassinated black civil rights leader, as a guest at their home. On one occasion when a national foundation contributed $2,500 to Mantinband's temple in recognition of his sound approach in dealing with the race issue, his board members panicked, fearing if they accepted it, there would be reprisals by the White Citizens Councils. Only after Mantinband declared that if the money was rejected the congregation would lose not only the income, but also its rabbi, was it finally accepted. Rabbi Perry Nussbaum of Jackson, whose synagogue and home were both bombed in 1967 in reprisals for his outspoken stand on civil rights, was another potent religious influence in Mississippi in support of civil rights. Many rabbis from the North, as well as Jewish social workers, came to Mississippi as volunteers to help provide moral support for blacks in their fight for civil rights. Two Jewish youths from New York, Andrew Goodman and Michael Schwerner, and James E. Chaney, a black, who had gone to Mississippi in the summer of 1964 to help blacks register to vote, were kidnapped and murdered by the KKK and their bodies buried in the muddy bank of a country water dam.

Few Jews have held public office in Mississippi but many of them have risen to places of importance in the state's civic, cultural, and philanthropic life. In 1846 Moses Emanuel served in the state senate. From 1861-1878, Moses Ullman was a member of the Natchez city council, and Isaac Lowenberg was mayor of Natchez from 1882-1886. Other Jewish mayors were Jacob Alexander, Greenville; Simon Unger, Port Gibson (1891-1898); Jacob Cohen, Shaw (1892-1897); Eliaz Stockner, Lake Providence; Harry Appleman, Yazoo City (1954-1960); and Sam Rosenthal, Rolling Fork (1929-1969). Rosenthal served at $1 a year for his first year and in succeeding years was paid $35 a year, but at his request it was lowered to $28 during the Depression of the 1930s. Mrs. Gladys Ascher King was head of the State Board of Administration in the 1930s, heading up the agency that governs the state's charitable institutions. Bill Waller of Meridian served in the State Agricultural and the Industrial Board in the 1960s. When Richard Henry Kuh was appointed district attorney of New York in 1975 to fill a vacancy, it was reported that Mrs. Kuh was a native Mississippian Jew whose father, M.J. Dattel, was a cotton and soybean farmer and mayor of Rosedale. Rabbi Allan Schwartzman of Vicksburg's Temple Anshe Chesed, was elected to the Mississippi State Democratic convention in 1976 which chose the state's delegation to that year's Democratic National Convention. He was the only Jew at the state convention and was beaten out for a place on the state's national convention delegation by a black lawyer. Richard Marcus, a Vicksburg banker and synagogue president, served on the Vicksburg Port Commission. A well-known fact in the state is that the Roman Catholic bishop of Mississippi in the 1970s was the son of a Mississippi Jewish woman. Charles Kline, whose brother, a Russian immigrant, opened Kline's General Store in the Delta town of Anguila in the 1890s, was chairman of the Sharkey County Democratic party.

* * * * *

ABERDEEN

Joseph Herz Lodge of B'nai B'rith in this central Mississippi town, the only organized Jewish group here, has six members and was 105 years old in 1977. During the Yom Kippur War, the lodge raised funds for Israel, sold Israel bonds to the local banks, and convinced the local ministerial association to issue a public statement supporting Israel.

BAY ST. LOUIS

Sy Rosenthal Memorial Gym on the grounds of the Divine Word Seminary of the Catholic Society of the Divine Word, memorializes the late Sy Rosenthal, one-time outfielder with the Boston Red Sox baseball team of the American League, and his son Buddy, a member of the 1st Marine Division, who was killed during the American invasion of New Britain in 1943. The elder Rosenthal became a paraplegic confined to a wheel chair as the result of injuries suffered when the minesweeper on which he was serving was blown up by a German mine outside Le Havre, France, in 1944. For 25 years he was a patient in the Roxbury, Mass. VA hospital, where he spent hours every day easing the pain and sufferings of others regardless of race, creed, or color. In the gym, which is used for meetings, retreats, and ordination of priests, as well as for athletics, there hang portraits of Rosenthal and his son. Of the $120,000 cost of the gym, Rosenthal raised some $15,000 and contributed $5,000 himself. The gym was dedicated in 1966 with Rosenthal present. He died in 1969.

BILOXI

Cong. Beth Israel, Camelia and Southern Ave., sometimes known as the Gulf Coast Jewish Community Center, is the youngest Jewish congregation in the state, having been organized in 1958. It houses the local B'nai B'rith lodge, the Jewish Women's Club, and other Jewish organizations.

Jefferson Davis Shrine and Memorial Gardens, West Beach, the last residence of Jefferson Davis, president of the Confederate States of America, has two items of Jewish interest. On a wall opposite the museum entrance hangs a tattered Confederate battle flag, framed, with this descriptive paragraph: "The flag was made by the fiancee of Edwin J. Kursheedt, Miss Sarah Levy of Richmond, Va. It was carried by him throughout the war on the cannon of which he was in charge as a member of the Washington Artillery of New Orleans, La." Kursheedt was the son of Gershom Kursheedt who founded the second synagogue in New Orleans in 1845, and it later became part of the present Touro Synagogue.

Included in an exhibit of Confederate money are several reprints of a poem written by Major A.S. Jonas of Mississippi on the back of a Confederate note. The officer, having been paroled after the Civil War, was in Richmond arranging for transportation home when he met a young lady from the North, Miss Anna Bush. In conversation, she showed him some Confederate notes printed on one side only, which she was keeping as souvenirs. On an impulse, she handed Jonas one of the notes with the request that he inscribe a few autographed lines. The young major gallantly complied, and what he handed back were the lines of the poem, the text of which is included in the exhibit. The New York *Metropolitan Record* printed the poem which was officially acclaimed in 1907 when it enjoyed a place of prominence in the Historic Day program staged at the national convention of the United Daughters of the Confederacy in Norfolk, Va.

Jewish Cemetery, Reynoir and Elder Sts., dates from the early 1840s. It has not been in use for at least half a century. A city landmark, the cemetery was deeded to the congregation by the Hebrew Society of New Orleans (probably the Hebrew Benevolent Society) on August 25, 1853, "to be used as a burying ground until there shall be a synagogue in the town of Biloxi."

BROOKHAVEN

Cong. B'nai Sholom, Chickasaw and S. Church Sts.

CANTON

B'nai Israel Cong., Academy and Liberty Sts.

CLARKSDALE

Temple Beth Israel, 401 Catalpa St., once the largest congregation in the state, now has only 100 members, making it the third largest, after the congregations in Jackson and Greenville. The congregation's first synagogue, a one-story brick building erected at 69 Delta St., is now a private law office.

CLEVELAND

Adath Israel Cong., 201 S. Bolivar St.

COLUMBUS

Cong. B'nai Israel, 717 Second Ave., N., is a small octagonal brick building dedicated in 1961, on the same site as an earlier synagogue, founded in the 1870s. It had once been a Methodist church and during the Civil War served as a military hospital. The present building was acquired in 1907 and some bricks from the old building originally erected in 1845 were used in remodeling the church into a synagogue. The congregation also serves Jewish families from Starkville and Aberdeen.

GREENVILLE

Alexander St., one of the city's main thoroughfares, is named for Jacob Alexander who was the city's tax assessor in 1875 and later its mayor.

Goldstein St., in one of the city's finest residential sections, is named for Nathan Goldstein, a cotton factor and first president of the Hebrew Union Temple, who served from 1895 until his death in 1950. Mrs. Nathan Goldstein, 2nd, whose husband is Goldstein's grandson, was secretary-treasurer of the temple in 1974.

Hebrew Union Temple, 504 Main St., stands on the same site as the city's first synagogue, a wooden structure erected in the 1880s on land donated by the owner of the Blanton plantation—a non-Jew.

GREENWOOD

Cong. Ahavath Rayim, Market and George Sts.
Temple Beth Israel, 400 E. Adams St.

GRENADA

Ike Cohen Home, a historic house, 204 Cherry St., was built from material taken from a steamboat stranded by low water on the Yalobusha River in 1842.

HATTIESBURG

Cong. B'nai Israel, cor. Mamie St. and 12th Ave., serves a community of 125 people. Until the present brick structure was erected in 1946, the congregation worshipped in a white frame building on West Pine St. that had been built with building materials from the National Jewish Welfare Board's servicemen's hut erected for Jewish soldiers at nearby Camp Shelby during World War I.

JACKSON

Judah P. Benjamin Portrait is on permanent display in the Mississippi War Memorial Building, North State St. The oil painting of the man who served as Secretary of State, Secretary of War, and Attorney General of the Confederate States of America, was presented in 1903, at the invitation of the State Historical Department, by Jewish citizens of the state. The inscription under the portrait is a thumbnail biography of the eminent statesman, with his Jewish origin included.

Beth Israel Cong., 5315 Old Canton Rd., is the congregation that erected the state's first synagogue in 1861. It was destroyed during the Civil War when most of the city was sacked. The second synagogue, built in 1867, was destroyed by fire. The third was erected in 1875. The fourth building, dedicated in 1942, was badly damaged by a bomb in 1967, and two months later the home of Rabbi Perry Nussbaum, a strong advocate of civil rights for blacks, was also bombed.

Jewish Welfare Federation, 4135 N. Honeysuckle Lane.

Moses Holding the Ten Commandments is one of the figures on the facade of the Hinds County Courthouse, East Pascagoula St., bet. South Congress and South President Sts.

KAHNVILLE

Louis Kahn, a pioneer Amite County Jewish merchant, founded this town in the early 1850s. It has no listed inhabitants now, but it is still listed as a post office.

LAUREL

Knesseth Israel Cong., a one-story brick building erected in 1906 at 802

Fifth Ave., was demolished in 1970 when the once flourishing congregation dwindled to only three or four members. Salvagable material was contributed to churches and the plot was donated to the city for a playground.

LEXINGTON
Temple Beth El, 224 Court Sq.

LORMAN
Cohn Brothers Old County Store, 8 miles north of Fayette on US. 61, has been in continuous operation since 1875 when it was founded by Lehmann, Joseph, and Heiman Cohn. One of the country's oldest country general stores, Cohn Bros. retains the old name although no Cohns have been connected with the business since the 1930s.

MARKS
Leopold Marks, German-born Jewish merchant, planter, and legislator is memorialized by this Quitman County seat town he founded in the 1870s. Arriving in New York in 1868 at the age of 17, he peddled his way across the country and settled at Friar Point, Miss., in 1870. With his first earnings he acquired a small steamboat which plied the Coldwater River in the Delta area. In 1874 he opened a trading post where Marks now stands and built it into the biggest commercial enterprise in the area. Marks took such a leading role in organizing Quitman County that he was elected its first representative to the state legislature where he served from 1877-1885. He donated the right of way through his plantation to the Yazoo and Mississippi Valley Railroad, and also contributed ten acres. For many years he was levee commissioner for the Upper Yazoo District. In 1977, Marks had a population of 2,572.

MAYERSVILLE
David Mayer, for whom this seat of Issaquena County is named, bought the Mississippi hamlet known as Gipson's Landing in 1870. In 1875 he deeded part of his lands as a county seat, and the same year the town, which had been founded in 1830, was incorporated as Mayersville. Once a key shipping point for Sharkey and Issaquena Counties' cotton, it had only 450 people in 1977.

MERIDIAN
Arky Recreational Hall, 522 Russell Dr., a Salvation Army recreation center, was a gift of the children of Mr. and Mrs. Louis Arky, active leaders of the Jewish community. A plaque on the building memorializes the Arkys.

Beth El Cemetery, 19th St. and 5th Ave., where the oldest gravestone is dated 1869, has some unusual ornamentation on its gravestones. On one is an almost life-size statue of a young woman standing on a rock. Another is a marble bust of Marks Winner, who died in 1910. One man who died in 1898 has the initials I.O.B.B. standing for International Order of B'nai B'rith, and the organization's insignia, carved on his stone.

Camp Meridale of Meridian Area Girl Scouts, occupies a site donated by the late Joseph Meyer, a prominent industrialist, banker, and philanthropist, whose father, Jacob, settled in Meridian in the 1860s where Joseph was born in 1862. The elder Meyer had first settled in Kosciusco and Marion, Mississippi. Joseph Meyer gave or bequeathed funds to the churches of every denomination in Meridian, always insisting that his name not be mentioned. Regarded as one of the builders of the city, Meyer's name appears on the cornerstone of the Scottish Rite Masonic Cathedral and the tablet bearing the names of the original benefactors of the Carnegie Library. His sons and grandsons operate Meywebb Hosiery Mills, one of the largest manufacturers of unbranded men's hosiery in America.

Christ Lutheran Church, 4229 Highway 39 North, built in 1969, has two metal sculptures designed as the Hebrew words *Chesed* and *Sholom* permanently placed on its altar. When the new church was built, the then minister wanted something on the altar as a link with the Old Testament and he selected the two Hebrew words. When the church could only afford to pay for one of the sculptures, Cong. Beth Israel contributed the other.

Cong. Beth Israel, 5718 14th Pl., in the Broadmoor subdivision, occupies a complex of three buildings—a sanctuary, a school, and a house of fellowship, used as a social center. In 1952, this congregation created a nationwide stir by electing as its spiritual leader a woman, Mrs. William Ackerman, whose husband had been the congregation's rabbi from 1925-1952. Mrs. Ackerman served for three years as the unordained "rabbi" of the congregation, which was founded in 1869. In 1968 the congregation's religious school was virtually destroyed by a bomb explosion.

Cong. Ohel Jacob, 1300 25th Ave., is a small Orthodox congregation founded in 1884 having only a handful of members today.

Sammie Davidson Athletic Complex, on the road that bounds the Meridian Junior College on the west, and north of the Weems Mental Health Clinic, is named for one of the city's leading citizens who was born and raised in Meridian and who was the prime mover in the establishment of the complex which includes softball diamonds, tennis courts, playgrouunds, a football field, and a picnic area. Davidson is a former president of Cong. Beth Israel.

Greater Mississippi Life Building, cor. 22nd Ave. and 6th St., a 16-story structure that is the city's tallest building, was originally known as the Threefoot Building when it was first built. It was then named for the prominent Jewish Threefoot family which has been identified with the city almost from its inception in 1854. The name Threefoot is believed to be an Anglicization of the name Dreyfus, the French-Jewish form of the city of Treves from which the Dreyfus family no doubt originally came.

Highland Park, bet. 20th St. and State Blvd., a city-owned recreational area, was given to the city in 1906 by ten citizens, six of whom were Jews: I. Marks, H. M. and K. Threefoot, W. Rosenbaum, Levi Marks, and Sam Rothenberg. A plaque in the park lists the names of the donors.

I. Marks Monument, in Highland Park, was erected in 1906 to honor the prime mover in the establishment of the park. Marks was chairman of the board of commissioners that managed the park and was one of the city's leading businessmen and philanthropists. The inscription on the monument, a life-size bronze of Marks, reads: "I. Marks—Erected as a testimonial to his unselfish public services as president of the Park Commission. By his fellow citizens of Meridian."

Wechsler Junior High School, 1415 30th Ave., the first well-planned brick building in Mississippi built especially for blacks, is named for Rabbi Judah Wechsler, who was spiritual leader of Cong. Beth Israel between 1887 and 1893. He was 60 years old when he came to Meridian from St. Paul, Minn., and he became a leader in the struggle of the blacks for better education. He was reviled and laughed at when he proposed that a city bond issue include provision for this school. When the bond issue was authorized, he bought $1,000 worth from his meagre resources, and when the school was erected the blacks insisted that it be named for the rabbi.

NATCHEZ

Jewish Cemetery, on Cemetery Rd., a narrow walled-in strip of the city cemetery, is believed to be the oldest existing Jewish burial ground in Mississippi. It dates from about 1840.

Temple B'nai Israel, 606 Washington St., the oldest Jewish congregation in the state, was one of the founding members of the Union of American Hebrew Congregation in 1873.

PHILADELPHIA

Mount Zion Methodist Church, 12 miles east of here on a red clay country road, was dedicated in 1966 to the memory of three young men who were murdered near here in the cause of civil rights. The red brick church, whose congregation is all black, stands on the site where Michael Schwerner, Andrew Goodman, and James E. Chaney visited on June 21, 1964, only hours before they met their death at the hands of a lynch mob and were buried on the bank of a country water dam. A bronze plaque with a tribute to the trio—one a black from Mississippi and the other two, Jews from New York— is affixed to an inside wall of the church. It recalls how their "concern for others and more particularly those of this community led to their early martydom. Their death quickened men's conscience and more firmly established justice, liberty and brotherhood in our land." The Congress of Racial Equality (CORE), which had planned to erect a center in Meridian as a memorial to the three civil rights workers were unable to raise the necessary funds.

PORT GIBSON

Temple Gemulith Chessed, one of the oldest congregations in the South, having been founded in 1830, now holds services only on the High Holidays since its membership has dwindled to four families. The brick building is topped by a steeple and dome of Moorish design. The tiny congregation maintains the old Jewish cemetery here where there are tombstones with inscriptions dated in the 1840s.

STARKVILLE

Leveck Auditorium in the Animals Science Building of Mississippi State University, is named for Henry Leveck, a native Mississippian, who was associated with the university for 40 years when he retired in 1969. He taught in the university's animal husbandry department from 1925-1939 and on his return from World War II service with the 101st Airborne Division, he became director of the Mississippi Agricultural Experiment Station. Leveck was president of Temple B'nai Israel in Columbus.

TUPELO

Temple B'nai Israel, cor. Marshall and Hamblin Sts.

UNIVERSITY

Hillel Foundation, University of Mississippi, Box 508, School of Engineering.

UTICA

Henry S. Jacobs Camp for Living Judaism of the Union of American Hebrew Congregations.

VICKSBURG

Jewish Welfare Federation, 1210 Washington St.

Temple Anshe Chesed, 2414 Grove St., is the second oldest existing congregation in the state. Members of this congregation took an active part in the defense of the city when it was besieged by Union forces in 1863. Two Jewish survivors of the siege who died in 1938 and 1939, were accorded public funerals.

On the grounds of the synagogue is the grave of one of the congregation's rabbis who, for reasons unknown, committed suicide in 1936.

Vicksburg National Military Park has many Jewish names, both Union and Confederate, inscribed on the more than 200 monuments, historical tablets, markers, and memorials to the Union and Confederate troops who fought the decisive Battle of Vicksburg in 1863.

There is a small Jewish cemetery situated within the Military Park. It is claimed that the first Confederate trooper wounded when the Union forces moved down the Mississippi to begin the siege of Vicksburg was a Jew, Philip Sartorious, one of whose descendants still lives in Vicksburg.

WOODVILLE

Beth Israel Cemetery, on the outskirts of this old Mississippi river town, is all that remains of a once flourishing Jewish community. Still in use, the cemetery was consecrated in 1849 when two peddlers, Jacob Schwarz and Jacob Cohen, paid $50 for a small plot in which to bury a fellow peddler, Henry Brugance. Jewish services were held in Woodville as early as 1850, and in 1878 Cong. Beth Israel was founded. It went out of existence in 1910. Its abandoned synagogue was used as a public school and then as a theatre before it was destroyed by fire in the 1930s. Rabbi Henry Cohen, later to gain fame in Galveston (see Texas), was the congregation's rabbi from 1887-1888.

New Mexico

From the time a Marrano Jew was the Spanish governor, until the day a Jewish scientist directed the research experiments, construction, and explosion of the first atomic bomb, Jews have been identified with the history of New Mexico.

The earliest known Jews in what is now New Mexico were Marranos—descendants of the secret Jews who fled to the colonies of Spain and Portugal at the beginning of the 16th century to escape the Inquisition. A large number of them settled in Mexico (which included New Mexico until 1846), and it became one of the principal tasks of the Inquisition to detect and punish Jewish heresy. Through the next 75 years, some 900 persons suspected of being secret Jews were tried by the Inquisition in Mexico. A number were burned at the stake and hundreds more probably escaped detection.

Some of the Marranos from Mexico penetrated as far north as New Mexico, as cited in *Early American Jewry* by Dr. Jacob R. Marcus. One of these, Bernardo Lopez de Mendizabel, was governor of New Mexico from the 1650s to 1661. De Mendizabel fell afoul of the Inquisition, which had its own agent in New Mexico from 1625 on. A charge of Judaizing levied against the governor was based on the fact that he changed his linen on the eve of the Sabbath, after he had washed his feet. De Mendizabel later died in prison. Another Marrano, Luis de Carvajal y de la Cueva, who came to

Mexico in 1567, may have preceded de Mendizabel to New Mexico. In 1569, forty-one years after the Spaniards discovered New Mexico, Carvajal was authorized by Philip II of Spain to explore and govern the area extending from what is now Tampico, Mexico, as far north as San Antonio, Texas, on the east, and the Texas-New Mexico border near El Paso on the west.

Stray Jews who may have been in New Mexico before it became American territory left little evidence of their stay. One of these was Benjamin J. Latz, who served in the 1st Missouri Regiment under Colonel Alexander Doniphan in the Mexican War, later settled briefly in Santa Fe where he helped pacify the Jecarilla and Mescalero Indian Tribes in 1851. Latz served with New Mexican troops during the Civil War.

Jewish beginnings in modern New Mexico date from the arrival in 1846 of Solomon Jacob Spiegelberg, whose relatives and employees became the nucleus of the first Jewish settlement. Spiegelberg was born in 1826 in Westphalia, Germany. His father, Jacob of Nantzungen, was a commercial agent of Baron von Spiegelberg. When the Napoleon Code required all Jews to adopt a family name, Jacob took the surname of the Baron. Solomon Jacob was 16 when he sailed for America in 1842. After brief stays in New York, Philadelphia, and Baltimore, he headed west for Independence, Missouri, then the eastern terminus of the Oregon and Santa Fe Trails and the jumping-off point for west-bound colonists.

He reached Independence in May, 1846, just before the outbreak of the Mexican War. Spiegelberg joined the supply corps of Colonel Stephen W. Kearny who had been ordered to attack the rear of the Mexican army in New Mexico. He journeyed across the Rockies and the great prairies on the hazardous three-month trip to Santa Fe, which the Americans occupied in August. Within a month the young immigrant was on the road again with Colonel Alexander W. Doniphan's column which was marching south to aid in the conquest of Chihuahua. Spiegelberg was so well-liked by the officers, he was named sutler at Fort Marcy—the first American military post in New Mexico just outside Santa Fe.

Soon after, Spiegelberg established a wholesale and retail merchandise business in Santa Fe. The business prospered and he was soon able to bring his five brothers (Levi, Elias, Emanuel, Lehman, and Willi) over from Germany. All of them came via Leavenworth, Kansas, over the Santa Fe Trail in the 1850s. Through this same route the six brothers later brought wives from New York, Philadelphia, St. Louis, Kansas, and California. The Spiegelberg women were among the first white women in New Mexico.

In the 1850s and 1860s, the family brought to New Mexico additional relatives and a number of other young men who were engaged as clerks. These kinsmen and employees, as well as Jews who arrived on their own or as protégés of Benjamin Lowenstein, another pioneer, soon branched out for themselves. Lowenstein is said to have brought some 200 Jewish boys from Germany over a period of years and set them up in business in New Mexico and Arizona. Sigmund and Bernard Seligman, and their brother-in-law, Simon Nussbaum, all Spiegelberg cousins from Philadelphia, founded the Seligman Brothers Trading Company in 1850, and soon had branches throughout New Mexico Territory. Charles Ilfeld, who came to New Mexico as an assistant cook with a wagon train, found himself broke and stranded in Kansas, clerked for the Spiegelbergs and then established a network of trading posts in Las Vegas, Santa Fe, Taos, and Albuquerque, together with his brothers Bernard, Herman, and Noah, and a brother-in-law, Max Nordhaus. In the 1860s and early 1870s, other firms were launched by Abraham and Zadoc Staab; Nathan, Marcus, and Sam Eldot; Aaron, Louis, and William Zeckendorf; Emanuel, Joseph, and Nathan Eiseman; Carl Ballin; Jacob Amberg; the Ellsbergs; and the Barths. William Zeckendorf's grandson and namesake was the realtor who assembled the site on which the United Nations buildings were erected in New York.

Few New Mexican enterprises, with the exception of the railroads, bus lines, and airlines, are comparable today to the great trading companies founded by these pioneers in the days when the Santa Fe Trail was a busy road. Spiegelberg Bros. and the Staabs controlled the drygoods trade and their stores were general distributing points for merchandise until railroad junctions were established in 1879. Seligman Bros. loaded 83 wagons in Kansas City in one day, each carrying three tons for shipment across the plains. Until banks were opened, these Jewish mercantile houses not only sold and distributed goods, but served the Territory's banking needs. The merchants, among whom the Jews were most prominent, were New Mexico's first bankers. They not only accepted ranchers' cash for safe keeping but advanced trade credit against wool and cattle. When there was a shortage of hard money, the government permitted the Spiegelbergs to issue scrip which was legal tender throughout the region. The Seligmans were among the founders of the First National Bank, the state's pioneer banking institution, and the Spiegelbergs were the organizers of the Second National Bank.

The Jewish merchants and their employees rendered valuable help during the Civil War when New Mexico was invaded by Confederate forces from Texas. One of the invaders was David Camden deLeon, a surgeon in the Confederate Army, who settled in New Mexico after the war, practicing medicine there until 1872. Serving with Kit Carson's New Mexico Volunteers were Colonel Marcus Brunswick, Captain Louis Felsenthal, Major Arthur Morrison, and Captain Solomon Spiegelberg. The latter had crossed the plains in a mule train with his four small children. Emanuel Spiegelberg fought in the Battle of Glorietta, where the Union forces were defeated in 1862. Henry Lesinsky, who had settled in Albuquerque in 1859, was a government supply agent for Federal troops and later carried the mail through Indian country. The Staabs, Alex Gunsdorf, and the Zeckendorfs did much to allay sympathy for the Confederates by providing food, clothing, and even cash for the settlers. When the Confederates occupied Santa Fe and declared martial law, they impressed Willi Spiegelberg into service for guard duty. Mrs. Levi Spiegelberg, who had been forbidden to look out of the window during the occupation lest she be kidnapped, defied her husband's warning. Hearing a woman moaning outside the window, Mrs. Spiegelberg and her Indian maid slipped into the street and dragged a starving black woman into the yard of the Spiegelberg store and then back to the adobe house. The woman, who had been kidnapped from her master in Texas, was nursed back to health by the Spiegelbergs after they had bought her freedom. They did the same for several other blacks who had been forced to accompany Confederate soldiers.

The Spiegelberg wives all came overland in the 1860s and 1870s. Mrs. Levi Spiegelberg, who arrived as a bride of 17 in 1860, was the third American white woman in Santa Fe. Mrs. Willi Spiegelberg, last of the Spiegelberg wives to arrive, was the daughter of William Langerman, who had gone to California during the gold rush.

In the difficult days after the Civil War, when outlaws and Indians were terrorizing New Mexico, Jews again demonstrated their mettle. Morris Bernstein, a Spiegelberg clerk, in a posse that fought a pitched battle against Billy the Kid, was one of those killed. Another Spiegelberg employee, the colorful Sam Dittenhoefer, once had a face-to-face encounter with Billy the Kid and managed to outwit him. It was in the summer of 1877 when Dittenhoefer was on his way back from Chihuahua with 25,000 Mexican dollars. Knowing that he had to cover territory where Billy the Kid operated, Dittenhoefer had the silver packed in six large flour barrels, each with double heads and bottoms. The space was filled with flour and the coins wrapped in paper to keep them from jingling. Each barrel was marked "Mexican flour" and loaded in a wagon which Dittenhoefer rode as the sole guard. Passing through a narrow canyon, he encountered the outlaw. After some small talk, Billy the Kid struck one of the barrels with his gun butt, and said: "I've a good mind to help myself to a few pounds of this flour. I haven't had a slice of real home-baked bread since I was a boy." The Kid, however, did not press the issue and rode off.

Dittenhoefer was widely known as "Navajo Sam," and was one of the first white men to learn the Navajo language. He had lived on the Navajo Reservation and was a friend of the Indians. He had come to New Mexico in the 1860s from New York where his uncle, Judge Abram Dittenhoefer, had been a Lincoln Presidential elector in 1864. While many Indians were being cheated by the whites, "Navajo Sam" and the Eldot brothers at Taos earned their friendship by fair dealing. The six Bibo brothers, who were in business at Bernallilo, had an even closer relationship with the Indians. The Bibos had come to New Mexico in 1867 as employees of William Spiegelberg. Solomon Bibo married an Indian woman and raised his children as Jews. His bride was the daughter of an Indian chief from the pueblo of Acoma and was one of the first pupils at the Carlisle Indian School. Another Bibo married the sister of Albert Michelson, who was America's first Nobel Prize winner (see Maryland).

Between 1870 and 1900, when New Mexico was still largely frontier area (it was admitted to the Union as the 47th state in 1912), Jews had an extraordinarily large role in the life of the state. The Jews were freighters, retailers, wholesalers, sutlers, mail contracters, army fort suppliers, sheep herders, cattle ranchers, bankers, mining and railroad promoters, and builders of water works and irrigation systems. They grew hay and farmed other crops. They learned languages and won the confidence of the tribes.

One of the first New Mexican-trained lawyers was Louis Sulzbacher, a Spiegelberg clerk who was admitted to the bar at Las Vegas in the 1870s and then went on to greater fame as an attorney in Missouri and a Federal judge (see Oklahoma). Nathan Eldot was in the Territorial Legislature in the 1870s. Bernard Seligman, and Solomon, Willi, and Lehman Spiegelberg served as commissioners of Santa Fe County in the 1870s and 1880s. Willi declined President Grover Cleveland's offer of an appointment as Territorial governor. Columbus Moises, Jr., scion of a distinguished Jewish family from South Carolina, was elected city attorney of Las Vegas in 1874 and became Chief Justice of the Territorial Supreme Court in 1880.

When Las Vegas' post office consisted of two cigar boxes in Charles Ilfeld's store, its owner was the postmaster in Albuquerque and Adolph Seligman and Simon Nussbaum succeeded each other in the same office in Santa Fe. Henry N. Jaffa, who was one of Albuquerque's first merchants when he moved there in 1869, became the town's first mayor in 1885, five years before it was incorporated. Mike Mandell, an Alsatian, who arrived in Albuquerque in the 1870s, was mayor in 1890. Nathan Jaffa, a pioneer settler at Roswell, was mayor from 1882-1884. Later he was secretary and lieutenant governor of the Territory, and mayor of Santa Fe. He declined a nomination for governor. Charles Rosenwald and Ernest Meyer were members of the first Territorial Legislature. Herman Lindheim represented New Mexico Territory in Congress in the 1890s.

Bernard Seligman, who served in the lower house of the 25th Territorial Legislature and in the 28th Legislature as a senator, was chairman of the Santa Fe Board of Commissioners and Territorial Treasurer. His son, Arthur, born in Santa Fe, was a prominent banker and businessman, who served as mayor of Santa Fe from 1910-1912. He was a delegate to the 1916 and 1920 Democratic national conventions and was twice elected governor in 1930 and 1932.

Early New Mexicans ranchers included William Floersheim at Springer, Simon Herstein at Clayton, and Nathan Jaffa at Roswell. The accidental discovery of an artesian water source on Jaffa's property revealed an unlimited water supply in the Pecos Valley in the late 1880s. Jaffa was one of the organizers of the Pecos Valley Irrigation Company, which established an extensive irrigation system in 1889, thus paving the way for other irrigation and reclamation projects that made the valley a thriving agricultural center. Phoebus Freudenthal, a relative of the Freudenthals of Trinidad, Colorado (see Colorado), and Charles Rosenwald pioneered the copper deposits at Clifton and Cerillos. Freudenthal's son, Louis, was influential in the expansion of agriculture in the state. Philip Prager built a section of the Santa Fe Railroad, the first in New Mexico.

Kit Carson and General Lew Wallace, a Territorial governor, were frequent guests in the homes of the Jewish merchants. A Spiegelberg family tradition has it that when Wallace was writing his famous novel, *Ben Hur*, he used to read portions of it aloud in Willi Spiegelberg's living room. One of the first Catholic schools in the Territory was founded by Jewish businessmen in the 1870s when they contributed to the building of a school house in Santa Fe and presented it to a church school mission. Three of the Jews who enlisted in Theodore Roosevelt's Rough Riders (see Arizona), during the Spanish American War were from New Mexico. Samuel Goldberg, of Santa Fe, known as "Porkchop" in Troop F because he refused to eat non-kosher food, was wounded in the charge up San Juan Hill. Samuel M. Grier, a drygoods salesman from Albuquerque, won a decoration for bravery at San Juan. Hyman Lowitzki, also from Santa Fe, was in Troop E.

Lowitzki, whose father had worked for the Spiegelbergs, was a pupil in the Territory's first Jewish religious school which Mrs. Willi Spiegelberg began conducting in her parlor in the 1880s. Jewish religious life began in New Mexico not many years after the Spiegelbergs settled there. They invited their relatives and employees from all over the Territory to attend Rosh Hashanah and Yom Kippur services in Santa Fe. The first of these services is said to have been held in 1860 in the only two-story building in town, the adobe house of Mr. and Mrs. Levi Spiegelberg. Eighteen men and two women were in attendance. As more of the Spiegelberg wives arrived, they began dividing up the guests for holiday meals. Mrs. Willi Spiegelberg was fond of telling the story of the middle-aged German Jew en route to Santa Fe in the 1870s, who nonchalantly delayed a stagecoach crossing Indian country while he donned phylacteries and said his morning prayers at the side of the road.

The first Jewish organization in New Mexico was a B'nai B'rith lodge, founded in Albuquerque in 1882. Two years later there were enough Jews in Las Vegas to form Congregation Montefiore, named for Sir Moses Montefiore whose 100th birthday was being marked throughout the world in 1884. In 1886, Congregation Montefiore erected New Mexico's first synagogue.

Services had been held sporadically in Albuquerque since the 1870s. They were formalized by Albert Grunsfeld in 1886 when he organized Temple Albert, which was named in his honor. A synagogue was built in 1897. Services were first held in Roswell at the turn of the century and in Santa Fe in the early 1900s. In 1975 there were congregations in Albuquerque, Los Alamos, Lass Cruces, Las Vegas, Roswell, and Santa Fe. In the 1950s and 1960s the Jews in Los Alamos, Santa Fe, and Taos employed a circuit-riding rabbi. Rabbi David Max Eichhorn helped organize the Los Alamos congregation in 1946 while he was director of field operations of the JWB Commission on Jewish Chaplaincy. The first circuit-riding rabbi was Navy Chaplain Cerf Straus. Rabbi Solomon Starrels persuaded the Jewish scientists working at the Atomic Energy Laboratory in Los Alamos to organize a synagogue and establish a Hebrew school.

Los Alamos is the newest Jewish community in the state. It was here that the first atomic bomb was built—a scientific achievement in which a number of Jews were involved. The uranium boom of the 1950s brought a trickle of new Jewish residents. The popularity of New Mexico as a winter resort and as a year-round residence attracted additional Jews in the 1960s and 1970s.

The Jewish population has grown steadily from 108 in 1877 to 800 in 1907, 1,052 in 1927, 2,700 in 1960, and 6,245 in 1977. Albuquerque has been the largest Jewish community in the state since 1905 when it had 165 Jews. In 1977 it had over 4,500. There are smaller Jewish communities in Santa Fe, Roswell, Las Cruces, Las Vegas, Carlsbad, Taos, Tucumcaru, Gallup, Clovis, Bernallilo, Silver City, and a scattering of Jewish residents in some 35 other towns.

The tradition of Jews achieving the highest offices continued well into the 20th century. Harry S. Bowman was elected State Attorney General in 1921, and nine years later Arthur Seligman won the first of two terms as governor. Abe Zinn resigned as Chief Justice of the New Mexico Supreme Court in 1941 to serve as a lieutenant colonel in the United States Air Force. In 1959, Irwin S. Moise of Santa Rosa, who had served as chairman of the State Parole Board, was appointed to the State Supreme Court. Lewis Sutin, a native of Indiana, was serving on the State Court of Appeals in the 1970s. Professor Jack Kolbert of the University of New Mexico, who serves on the selection committee for the Nobel Prize in literature, was elected president of the Albuquerque City Council in 1974.

* * * * *

ALAMORGORDO

International Space Hall of Fame, adjacent to the Alamagordo branch of the State University of New Mexico, has a number of exhibits and displays that recall the important part played by Jewish scientists in the creation and testing of the first atomic bomb at Trinity. Among those honored is the late Dr. Louis A. Slotin, who was responsible for the delivery of the bomb from the laboratory at Los Alamos where it was assembled, to the Trinity test site. One of his most prized possessions was the receipt he received from the Army when he turned over the first bomb, representing the culmination of the $2 billion effort of the Manhattan Project—the code name for the atomic bomb project. Also honored is Dr. J. Robert Oppenheimer who was the director of the laboratory where the bomb was built.

ALBUQUERQUE

Albuquerque Gan (a Jewish pre-school and kindergarten) and Akiba Day School, 1100 Indian School Rd., N.E.

Sholem Aleichem Schule and Family Center, c/o Stan Rosenthal, 600 Louisianà, S.E.

Cong. B'nai Israel, 4401 Indian School Rd.

Havurath Hamidbar (Society of the Desert) is the name of a traditional Orthodox congregation which does not have its own synagogue, but meets for services every Friday night and Saturday morning, and on the holidays. Among its members are some Jewish faculty members from the University of New Mexico.

Hillel Foundation, University of New Mexico, 110 Amherst Dr., S.E.

Jewish Community Council, 600 Louisiana Blvd., S.E.

Temple Albert, 1007 Lead Ave., S.E., has on its outside walls a series of abstract renderings of the Creation, the enslavement of Israel in Egypt, and the Exodus, in a series of stories told in unusual designs in muted colors.

University of New Mexico, St. Joseph's Pl., N.W., has in the Zimmerman Library Archives the Flora Spiegelberg Collection of memoirs, letters, documents, and other material relating to the Spiegelberg family. The Spiegelbergs arrived in New Mexico in 1846.

BERNALLILO

Elsa Seligman Girl Scout Camp, 40 miles northwest of the city, was established through the generosity of Carl, Julius, and Siegfried Seligman, who owned a chain of trading posts in this part of the state.

BIBO

Nathan Bibo is memorialized in this Valencia County town. He was one of six Bibo brothers who were active in trading with the Navajo Indians around Bernallilo and at a number of army forts. In 1888, Solomon Bibo, who had learned the Keres language of the Indians of Acoma Pueblo and won their friendship by his fair dealings, was appointed governor or chief of the pueblo three years after he married the daughter of Chief Valle of the Acoma Tribe.

DEMING

County seat of Luna County, this town of 4,000 in the southwest corner of the state was founded in the late 1880s by Theodore Lindauer, a Jewish merchant, who brought his first goods in on horseback. Members of the Lindauer family still live here.

GRANTS

This Valencia County town was founded in 1880 by the grandfather of George Dannenbaum, who was mayor during the hectic uranium rush in the 1950s. The younger Dannenbaum, who never staked a claim, was editor of the *Uranium City News*.

Seligman Park, a children's playground located between the elementary and high school, was a gift of Siegfried, Carl, and Julius Seligman, who settled here in the 1880s, and then opened a chain of stores and trading posts where they sold the arts and crafts produced by the Indians.

ILFELD

Charles Ilfeld and his brothers, who once operated a busy trading post here in the 1860s, are recalled only by an abandoned building along the route of the Santa Fe Railroad. The name of Ilfeld, lettered on the false front of the crumbling structure, can still be seen.

LAS CRUCES

Temple Beth-El, 700 W. Parker Rd., was built largely through the generosity of Eugene J. Stern, merchant, farmer, and philanthropist, who settled in the Rio Grande valley in 1928 after selling his mercantile interests in Las Vegas. He established a loan fund for students at New Mexico State University, contributed to the building of every church in Las Cruces, underwrote the cost of building a clubhouse for the local unit of the Boys' Club of America, established the first Dona County Fair, and contributed $500,000 toward the construction of a Scottish Rite Masonic temple in the city.

LAS VEGAS

Temple Montefiore, 901 8th St., is the oldest congregation in the state, having been founded in 1884.

LEVY

This Morah County hamlet of 200 people on the northwest corner of the state, was named for an early merchant who ran a commissary for railroad workers during the construction of the first section of the Santa Fe

Railroad to reach New Mexico in 1879. The workers used to call the place "Levy's" and the settlement that grew up around it acquired the same name. Levy is largely a cattle loading zone for ranches near Las Vegas.

LOS ALAMOS

Los Alamos Jewish Center, 2400 Canyon Rd., serves one of the most unusual Jewish communities in the country. Composed mostly of scientists employed at the Atomic Energy Commission's Scientific Laboratory, and their families, with a sprinkling of merchants and professional men, the community was organized right after World War II as the Jewish Community Group when the whole town was still owned by the government. Rabbi David Max Eichhorn, then with the JWB Commission on Jewish Chaplaincy, had a hand in organizing the group. For a time a single rabbi served Los Alamos, Taos, and Santa Fe in a program initiated by Rabbi Solomon Starrels of Albuquerque.

Los Alamos Scientific Laboratory, where the first atomic bomb was built, is a monument to the late Dr. J. Robert Oppenheimer, who directed the laboratory and supervised the construction of the bomb. It was Oppenheimer, who used to vacation in New Mexico, who found the remote site where the laboratory was established in 1942 in the heart of New Mexico's prime year-round vacation land. Member of a prominent Philadelphia Jewish family related to the Rosenbachs, Binswangers, Egers, and Solis-Cohens, Oppenheimer was a professor of physics at the University of California in 1942 and already recognized as one of the top theoretical physicists in the world, when he was chosen to direct the laboratory where the bomb was to be assembled. He helped select the former Los Alamos Ranch School as the site and recruited the initial cadre of eminent scientists to build the biggest and most elaborate scientific establishment of all time under tight security. Secretary of War Henry Stimson's official report on the development of the bomb, published in July, 1945, credited Dr. Oppenheimer with "the implementation of atomic energy for military purposes," and called him the man whose "genius and leadership" brought success to the most sensational scientific undertaking of modern times. After he resigned as director of the laboratory, Dr. Oppenheimer devoted himself to a campaign for international atomic control. President Harry Truman appointed him to the seven-man board that drafted the Acheson-Lilienthal policy on the future of atomic energy. Oppenheimer was said to have been the author of that portion of the report proposing an international atomic development authority. In 1946, he was named director of the famed Institute for Advanced Study at Princeton, New Jersey.

As a member of Oppenheimer's staff, Dr. Louis A. Slotin, a 35-year old Canadian, son of Orthodox Jewish immigrants, was the first fatality of the atomic bomb building project. Slotin, who worked on the assembly of the bomb and delivered it to the army at the test site near Alamogordo, was scheduled to go to Tinian where the atomic bombs for Hiroshima and Nagasaki were assembled in the summer of 1945. However, his citizenship papers were late in arriving and he remained at Los Alamos awaiting security clearance needed for participation in the Tinian operation. On May 26, 1946, he was instructing his successor at the laboratory in the extremely delicate and complicated task of controlling the critical material in the atomic pile, when an accident touched off a plutonium reaction in the next room. Instantly, Slotin dashed into the room and pulled the material apart, halting the chain reaction. Although he knew this act would be fatal, his heroism saved the lives of seven other scientists in the room. He died nine days later and was posthumously awarded the first "martyr of science" medal.

In the city of Los Alamos which grew up around the laboratory there was for several years a Slotin Football Field named for the heroic scientist. It has since been incorporated into a park and Slotin's name is no longer associated with it.

Los Alamos Nuclear Museum displays replicas of the bombs which Oppenheimer and Slotin helped to create, letters from Albert Einstein in which he first suggested that an atomic reaction could be converted into a bomb, and letters from Oppenheimer. The receipt Slotin received for the first bomb is also on exhibit.

NEWMAN
This border hamlet on U.S. Highway 54, near the Texas line, was named for a Jewish real estate man from El Paso.

RIO RANCHO
Sholem Aleichem Schule and Family Center (office), 935 B Country Club Dr.

Rio Rancho Jewish Community Group (Phone: 898-8856).

ROSWELL
Cong. B'nai Israel, 8th and Washington Sts.

SANTA FE
Cathedral of St. Francis, opposite the post office, has inscribed over its main arch in easily visible letters the Hebrew word "Adonai." When Archbishop Lamy, hero of Willa Cather's novel, *Death Comes for the Archbishop*, began building the cathedral in 1869, the Spiegelbergs loaned the archbishop the money he needed. In appreciation he is said to have invited Solomon Jacob Spiegelberg to put one engraved stone in the cathedral. Another version is given in Father Angelico Chavez' booklet *The Cathedral*, as follows: "The Hebrew inscription of the Divine Name above the main

entrance has made old-timers relate that Archbishop Lamy had it done to honor his Jewish friends in Santa Fe, the Spiegelberg brothers in particular. The word Jehovah or Yahweh, placed in a triangle, has always been used by the church as a symbol of the Holy Trinity, and Jews do not believe in the Trinity. But it is a nice story." The cathedral stands on the site occupied by the first church and monastery erected in Santa Fe in 1622 by Benavides, the agent of the Inquisition. Archbishop Lamy used to send fruits and flowers from his own gardens to the Santa Fe Jews for Passover and Rosh Hashanah. When Lamy became archbishop in 1879, the citizens of Santa Fe celebrated the occasion at a dinner with Willi Spiegelberg as toastmaster.

Cong. Beth Shalom, 205 E. Barcelona Rd.

Dili Deli, tucked away in a downstairs corner of Santa Fe's 350-year old Plaza, is a kosher-style but not kosher faithful reproduction of a New York delicatessen store.

Palace of the Governors, north side of the Plaza, an adobe structure dating from 1610, houses in a narrow hallway east of the Mexican Room, a gallery displaying portraits of all the territorial and state governors who held office since 1846. Among the portraits is one of Arthur Seligman, governor from 1931-1933.

Spiegelberg House, 237 East Palace Ave., was built in 1888 of adobe on stone, for Flora and Willi Spiegelberg, pioneer settlers. It is now an historic landmark owned by Dr. and Mrs. Edward S. Cook.

State Capitol, on Galisto St. at Montezuma, has in the Secretary of State's office a portrait of Arthur Seligman, New Mexico's governor from 1931 until his death in 1933 in the first year of his second term. A native New Mexican of pioneer stock, Governor Seligman was the son of an eminent legislator and banker who came to New Mexico in the 1850s as an employee of the Spiegelbergs. Seligman was born in Santa Fe in 1873 and joined the family business in the 1890s. As mayor of Santa Fe from 1910-1912, he gave the city its first paved streets. From 1895-1920 he headed the Democratic Territorial and State Committees. In 1920 he was elected Democratic National Committeeman from New Mexico. Long before he became governor, he was a member of the State Irrigation Commission and the leading advocate of road, reclamation, and tourist projects.

Supreme Court Building, across from the Capitol, displays photographs of Abe Zinn, former chief justice of the Supreme Court; Columbus Moises, Jr., who was also chief justice; and has areas reserved for photos of Supreme Court Justice Irwin Moise and Court of Appeals Justice Lewis Sutin.

TAOS

Blumenschein Home, Ledoux St., former residence of Ernest Blumenschein, who was one of the two founders in 1898 of the world famous Taos art colony, is now a museum. A well-known painter who specialized in portraits, Blumenschein and another artist, Bert Philips, were driving a camp wagon on a sketching trip from Denver to Mexico when their wagon broke down near the Taos pueblo. During the three days needed for repairs, the painters became enamoured of the town and decided to stay. Other artists followed. The museum contains many of Blumenschein's works. He died in 1960 at the age of 86.

North Carolina

North Carolina was the only southern colony in which no Jewish community developed in pre-Revolutionary days. This was surprising because until 1729 North and South Carolina were a single colony governed by a common charter, yet, as Dr. Jacob R. Marcus points out, South Carolina "sheltered a flourishing Jewish community, while the other had none." There were no legal bars to Jewish settlement in North Carolina, but, like their Christian contemporaries, Jewish merchants and traders saw only limited economic opportunities there. An inadequate government, few good ports, not many towns or markets, and the danger of pirates made North Carolina unattractive to businessmen. The absence of full political and religious liberty played little or no part in the belated Jewish settlement in North Carolina.

As a matter of fact, the first constitution of the Carolinas explicitly welcomed Jewish settlers, but it was never formally adopted by any legislative body. *Fundamental Constitutions for the Goverment of Carolina* framed by John Locke, the eminent English philosopher in 1669 for the proprietors of Carolina, the vast area between Virginia and Florida that King Charles II gave to the noblemen who helped restore the monarchy, contained language specifically designed to appeal to Jewish colonists. Locke's charter promised religious and political freedom to all dissenters and non-conformists and mentioned by name Huguenots, Catholics,

Quakers, German sectarians, and Jews. The invitation could hardly have been meant for the Jews of England where they numbered barely 100 families in the 17th century, so it must have been intended for the Jews of the West Indies. The *Fundamental Constitutions,* proscribed atheism but promised "respect and protection for all religions" and contained guarantees against anyone being persecuted or molested because of his opinions in religion or his way of worship.

Few if any Jews took advantage of this invitation to settle in North Carolina. While Jewish immigrants to the New World in the late 17th and early 18th century preferred the safety of and opportunities in New York, Pennsylvania, and Rhode Island, only scattered Jews were found in the main North Carolina towns before 1776. They probably came from the British West Indian colony of Barbados and dealt in indigo which Jews had first introduced to America.

The first recorded Jew in North Carolina was Aaron Moses whose signature appeared as a witness to a will in 1740. A decade later one David David petitioned for and was granted 180 acres of land in New Hanover. In 1752 he was listed on a muster roll of the New Hanover County Militia. In 1750 Moses Mordecai, son of Jacob Mordecai of Philadelphia, became a country merchant in Warrenton, North Carolina, where he founded the first private school for girls in the South in 1809. One of Moses' sons, Alfred Mordecai, a West Point graduate, wrote the Army's first ordinance manual. Alfred Mordecai, Jr. distinguished himself during the Civil War and later commanded the Watervliet Arsenal. The next generation of Mordecais in North Carolina became Christians. One of them Samuel Mordecai, was dean of Trinity College (now Duke University) Law School. "Mr. Laney the Jew" was mentioned in Colonial records in 1750 and 1760 and periodically until 1784 in connection with various business matters.

Francis Salvador of South Carolina, the first Jew to die in the American Revolution (see South Carolina), also appears in North Carolina history. In a work entitled *Narrative of Colonel David Fanning, a Tory in the Revolutionary War, Giving an Account of his Adventures in North Carolina from 1775 to 1783,* mentions under the date of July, 1775, meeting "two Jews by the name of Silvedoor and Rapely," who "after making many speeches in favor of the rebellion . . . used all their efforts to delude the people." William Levy of Orange County is listed among 1768 petitioners to the royal governor setting forth grievances. Dr. Jacob Marcus cites the letters of Michael Levy of Edmonton whose communications referred to a friend by the name of Henry who Marcus identifies as Joel Henry, a German Jew from Fuerth, and father of Jacob Henry, later to be a member of the North Carolina State Legislature. North Carolina volunteers for George Washington's army included Aaron Cohen of Albemarle, whose daughter, Elizabeth, was the first to be buried in the Hebrew Cemetery in Charlotte. in 1859. There were also J. Nathan of Charlotte, Sigmund Freudenthal of

New Hanover, Will Solomon, Abraham Moses, Lazarus Solomon, Isaac Sampson, and Moses Stern, all probably Jews, who served in the 10th Regiment of North Carolina Infantry.

Under the religious establishment in North Carolina before 1776, "there was little room officially for the Jew as a religionist, although his presence as an individual might well be overlooked," Dr. Jacob Marcus states. The Church of England was the established church and Anglicans dominated all religious life. The state constitution adopted in 1776 (Article 34), forbade the establishment of "any religious church or denomination . . . in preference to any other" and provided that "all persons shall be at liberty to exercise their own mode of worship." In the state's bill of rights adopted the same year, it was acknowledged that freedom of religion was an inalienable right of man and provided that in the event of any contradiction between the bill of rights and the state constitution, the former took precedence.

Yet, Article 32 of that constitution provided "that no person who shall deny the being of God or the truth of the Protestant religion, or the divine authority of either the Old or New Testaments, or who shall hold religious principles incompatible with the freedom and safety of the state, shall be capable of holding any office or place of trust or profit in the civil department within this state." When the people of the state's Mecklenburg district sent delegates to the 1776 state constitutional convention, they were instructed to insist on the free and undisturbed exercise of religion "for all professing Christians." This emphasis on "Christians" was deliberate, according to Marcus, even though in that part of the state there probably were no Jews. Reverend David Caldwell, the Presbyterian clergyman who was chiefly responsible for the anti-Catholic and anti-Jewish clause in the state constitution, demanded during the North Carolina debate on the adoption of the Federal Constitution, that it be rejected because it contained no religious test for public office. Unless such a test was imposed, he feared that Jews and pagans would come to North Carolina and endanger its character. His bigoted view won little support and the Federal Constitution, which in Article VI specifically forbids a religious test for any Federal public office, was ratified by North Carolina together with the Federal Bill of Rights. When Article VI was being considered at the Federal Constitutional Convention in 1787, the vote in committee was 8 to 1 in favor, with the delegate from North Carolina voting nay.

An effort to change the North Carolina religious test clauses failed in the 1835 constitutional convention but the word "Protestant" was removed and replaced by "Christian," thus admitting the Catholics to full rights to hold any public office while still denying them to Jews. Not until 1868, during the Reconstruction period after the Civil War when North Carolina was amending its constitution to abolish slavery, were Jews finally fully enfranchised. The convention that put an end to the religious test clause included 13 blacks.

In 1809, the religious test clause became the subject of a great debate in the state legislature. It began when Jacob Henry, of Beaufort, Carteret County, who had been elected to the Legislature's lower house, the House of Commons, in 1808, won reelection in 1809. No one had challenged his right to the seat during his first term. Everyone was aware that he was a Jew, and as such did not subscribe to the "divine authority" of the New Testament, nor did he accept "the truth of the Protestant religion." At the beginning of the 1809 session of the legislature, Representative Mills of Rockingham County demanded that Henry be expelled from the House of Commons because he had not taken the oath of office on the New Testament and his election was invalid under Article 32 of the state constitution. During the debate on the motion to expel Henry, he delivered a now famous speech in defense of full religious liberty for all. After Henry had spoken, the House of Commons concurred in a recommendation that the resolution to unseat Henry be rejected and that he be allowed to serve. In its decision, the House of Commons interpreted the religious test clause in the constitution to mean that Jews and Catholics were permitted to hold legislative office but not executive or other positions.

Henry's speech, which some scholars claim was actually written by Chief Justice John L. Taylor, a Catholic, who might have feared that if a Jew lost his seat in the legislature, a Catholic judge might also be removed. In any event it ranks as an early and significant contribution in the struggle to realize in all the states some of the freedoms provided for by the United States Constitution. Henry's speech was published in a book called *The American Orator*, and it was cited during the fight over the "Jew Bill" in Maryland. Long after Jacob Henry had been allowed to keep his seat on what was tantamount to a technicality, North Carolina leaders who were Christians carried on a long struggle for the final elimination of the disability clause.

Henry began his dramatic address by speaking of his own faith: "The religion I profess inculcates every duty which man owes to his fellow men; it enjoins upon its votaries the practice of every virtue and the detestation of every vice; it teaches them to hope for the favor of heaven exactly in proportion as their lives are directed by just, honorable and beneficent maxims. This, gentlemen, is my creed. It was impressed on my infant mind; it has been the director of my youth, the monitor of my manhood, and will, I trust, be the consolation of my old age . . ."

He then went on to say that "I do not seek to make converts to my faith, whatever it may be esteemed in the eyes of my officious friend, nor do I exclude any man from my esteem or friendship because he and I differ in that respect. The same charity, therefore, is not unreasonable to expect, will be extended to myself because in all things that relate to the state and to the duties of civil life, I am bound by the same obligations with my fellow citizens. Nor does any man subscribe more sincerely than myself to the maxim, 'whatever ye would that men should do unto you, do ye so even unto them,' for such is the Law of the Prophets."

Henry's fellow legislators listened intently as he declared, "I certainly, Mr. Speaker, know not the design of the Declaration of Rights, made by the people of this state in the year 1776, if it was not to consecrate certain great and fundamental rights and principles which even the Constitution cannot impair . . . The language of the bill of rights is 'that all men have a natural and inalienable right to worship Almighty God according to the dictates of their consciences.' It is undoubtedly declared to be an inalienable right, and when it is declared to be an inalienable one by the people in their sovereign and original capacity, any attempt to alienate either by the constitution or by law, must be vain and fruitless . . . It is surely a question between a man and his Maker, and requires more than human attributes to pronounce which of the numerous sects prevailing in the world is most acceptable to the Deity. If a man fulfills the duties of that religion which his education or his conscience has pointed to him as the true one, no person, I hold, in this our land of liberty, has the right to arraign him at the bar of any inquisition . . . Nothing is more easily demonstrated than that conduct alone is the subject of human laws, and that man ought to suffer civil disqualification for what he does, and not for what he thinks."

North Carolina's earliest Jewish settlement developed at Wilmington, the state's leading seaport. Two early arrivals were Aaron Lazarus and Aaron Riviera, the latter a native of Charleston, South Carolina, who was one of the founders of the Wilmington and Weldon Railroad. Jacob Rodriquez Riviera, a relative of the Newport, Rhode Island, shipping magnate (see Rhode Island), was cashier of the Bank of Cape Fear. Around 1788 Abraham Isaacs was prominent in Wilmington Masonic circles. Jacob Levy, son-in-law of the Newport, Rhode Island, merchant prince, Aaron Lopez, died in Wilmington in 1827. By 1849 the city had some 20 Jews, and three years later they organized the True Brothers Society to acquire a cemetery. The first congregation in the state was organized in Wilmington in 1867 and it dedicated the state's first synagogue in 1876.

Jewish peddlers who came to North Carolina just before and soon after the Civil War became the founding fathers of the permanent Jewish settlements. Their bases of operation to which they returned on Friday in time to observe the Sabbath were way-stations at Wilmington, Albertville, and Yanceyville, where they stored small stocks of goods received from Baltimore wholesalers. Often the peddlers made the way-stations their permanent homes where they ultimately established stores. In the rural areas the Jewish peddlers dealt with blacks, Indians, and sharecroppers who made them welcome. The Cherokee Indians dubbed the Jewish peddlers "egg-eaters" because they avoided eating any meat while they were on the road. As Fundamentalist Protestants, the blacks, and poor whites saw in the Jewish peddler a living link to the Hebrews of the Bible and they loved to hear him read from the Bible.

In 1870, when there were between 250 and 300 Jews in the state, the most important Jewish settlement was in Statesville. The Wallace brothers, Isaac and David, who arrived in 1859 from Bamberg, South Carolina, sold supplies to the farmers, ran a small banking business, and a drug counter. They encouraged the farmers to bring their roots and herbs to the Wallace store and soon the brothers developed a crude drug business on a national scale which was a great help to farmers from five North Carolina counties for 75 years. Yanceyville was another town where an early Jewish settlement started by peddlers took root in the 1870s. Jacob Fels and his son, Samuel, were peddlers around Yanceyville. Joseph Fels founded the Fels-Naptha soap company and became a leading spokesman for the Single Tax movement. Congregation Emanuel was organized there in 1883. The name Silver is very common in Yancey County thanks to a Jewish immigrant peddler who settled there in 1854, married a local girl in 1861, who provided him with six children, all of whom were brought up as Christians according to a 1927 study by a Duke University sociologist. In 1858, 26 of the pre-war Jewish settlers vainly petitioned the state legislature for repeal of the office-holding restriction against which Jacob Henry had spoken so vehemently.

Fifty-two Jews from North Carolina fought with the Confederate forces during the Civil War, including six brothers from the Cohen family. The first Jew to die for the Confederacy is said to have been Albert Lurie Moses of Charlotte, killed in the Battle of Seven Pines in 1862. He had picked up a six-inch shell whose fuse was still burning after it had fallen into a gun pit and tossed it away, saving many lives, but losing his own. Abe Weil of Charlotte gave refuge in his home to Jefferson P. Davis, President of the Confederate States of America, when Union forces were hunting him. Frederick Rheinstein was a purchasing agent for the Confederacy in Wilmington. Lewis Leon was not yet 17 when he left his home on New York's Lower East Side in 1858 and headed South where he became a drygoods clerk in Charlotte. Even before North Carolina seceded from the Union, Leon volunteered to fight for the South, according to Morris Schappes in *A Documentary History of the Jews of the United States*. Leon served three and a half years, took part in many battles, and became a sharpshooter, according to his war diary. He mentions all the Jewish holidays, but gives no indication that he observed any of them. Leon refers to other Jews in North Carolina regiments and bitterly observes that after the war he "took the cursed oath" of allegiance to the United States of America. In Woodlawn

Cemetery, Elmira, New York (see New York), site of a Federal camp for Confederate prisoners of war, 18 Jews from North Carolina are buried.

A November 1875 issue of the *American Israelite* of Cincinnati reported that there were 25 Jewish families in Charlotte. In 1860, the following advertisement appeared in the *Hebrew Leader* of New York: "Wanted by Israelities of Wilmington, N.C., *hazzan, schochet,* and *mohel.*" By 1877, one-fourth of the state's 820 Jews lived in Wilmington, but there were also communities in Goldsboro, Raleigh, Tarboro, Charlotte, New Berne, and Greensboro. The most prominent Wilmington Jew in the 1870s-1880s was Solomon H. Fishblate, who was an alderman from 1872-1877 and mayor from 1878-1882.

Between the 1870s and 1890s, Jews also settled in New Berne (1881), Goldsboro (1878), Greensboro (1880), Tarboro (1874), Durham (1880), Raleigh (1870), and Winston-Salem (1890). By 1900 the state counted 6,000 Jews, nine towns with one or more Jewish institutions, and seven with Jewish congregations. Goldsboro (250), Durham (200), and Greensboro (150) were the largest Jewish communities.

One of the first Jewish settlers in Goldsboro was Herman Weil who arrived in 1858. After serving in the Confederate Army, he and his brother, Henry, opened H. Weil & Bros., a small general store that grew into one of the the state's leading department stores. Members of the Weil family were among the founders of the Congregation Oheb Sholom in 1883. One of the Weil women was a pioneer in the struggle against child labor in the textile mills. Henry Weil's daughter, Gertrude, an early woman's suffrage leader in the state, founded the North Carolina League of Women Voters. An early supporter of Jewish Palestine when Zionism was heresy among most Southern Jews, she was an outspoken advocate of socialism, too. Leslie Weil accepted appointment on local and state civic boards with the understanding that he would not be present at Friday night meetings. Mrs. Solomon Weil was the principal founder in 1921 of the North Carolina Association of Jewish Women. Sol Weil served as an alderman in Goldsboro from 1880-1896.

An even more important Jewish family is the Cones of Greensboro. Herman Cone, who came from Germany in 1854 and opened a country store at Jonesboro, Tennessee, added a small foundry during the Civil War and turned out bullets for the Confederate Army. In 1870 he and his sons, Moses and Monroe, established a wholesale grocery firm and a leather and cigar business in Baltimore. Later, another son, Caesar, joined the firm. Moses and Caesar Cone were salesmen for their father's groceries in the rural hamlets and small towns of the state during the 1870s. Passing through the rising mill towns of the state, they saw how fragmentized the new textile industry was. When their father went out of business, the Cone brothers settled in Greensboro and began persuading 38 mills to sell them their manufactured fabrics. They organized the Cone Export and Import Co,, which served both as banker and distributor for the mills. The Cones helped the mills create new finishing processes and promoted wider distribution of their output.

During the panic of 1893 the Cones were owed considerable sums of money by some mills who might have gone bankrupt except that the Cones encouraged them to buy what they needed and to pay when they could. When the Cones entered the textile field, few southern mills had any credit with New York banks and were turning out one product, a cheap gingham cloth. The Cones were the first to break away from the South's single product manufacture when they encouraged experimentation with different fabrics. They also introduced an orderly world-wide system of distribution and did much to encourage industrial development throughout the state. At one time the Cones were turning out 3 percent of the South's textile production.

All of the Cones were civic-minded people. They were among the first to establish welfare programs for their employees and were also among the leaders in signing union contracts. The villages that grew up around the Cone factories had better health and education facilities than other towns. Caesar Cone was a generous supporter of the North Carolina Tuberculosis Sanitarium and provided a YMCA building for blacks. Moses Cone left much of his estate for the building of a hospital in Greensboro. Herman Cone was president of the community chest. When the banks failed during the Depression, the Cones guaranteed all accounts in the textile branches of the banks. Claribel and Etta Cone, sisters of Herman and Caesar, were also prominent. Claribel earned a doctor's degree at Johns Hopkins University and served as a professor at the Baltimore Women's College. Etta was a noted modern art collector. She gave her collection to the Baltimore Museum of Art where it is housed in the Cone Wing. One Cone,Ben Cone, Jr., who had become an Episcopalian, converted back to Judaism after the State of Israel was established. It was a time when many of the old German-Jewish families of the South abandoned their anti-Zionist stance.

In some of the North Carolina towns, particularly Durham and Raleigh, the first East European Jewish settlers were cigarette makers imported from New York to work in the tobacco factories. Over 300 Jewish cigarette workers were brought to Durham in the early 1880s by William Duke & Son. Moses Gladstein, who had come to America at the age of 18, was only a year older when he led the first group of Jewish cigarette makers from New York to North Carolina. They were paid 70¢ per thousand for a 12-hour day. Duke's workers did not stay long because the first cigarette-making machines replaced them, despite a strike. The workers imported from New York were ready to go South because they were on strike against cigarette manufacturers in New York. J.M. Siegel of London had been hired by Duke to run his factory. When the jobs in the Carolina cigarette factories came to an end, most of the Jews returned to New York but some stayed on as peddlers or storekeepers in and around Durham and Raleigh. One of these was Moses Gladstein. Another was Isaac Evans who peddled around Fayetteville before opening a store there. The Nachmansons established a store at Dover where they did well doing business with the emloyees of a large lumber mill. Later they moved to Kinston, where 18 Jewish families had preceded them. They moved again to Durham to be near the universities. Isaac's son, Emanuel, had played basketball in college and set a record as a half-miler on the track team. The Nachmansons and Evanses were joined in marriage in 1928 when Emanuel Evans married Sarah Nachmanson. The latter's parents had been the leading Jews in Kinston where Mrs. Nachmanson founded the state's first Hadassah chapter and Eli Nachmanson opened the first movie house.

Emanuel Evans became Durham's leading citizen. In the 1940s, his store was the only place in town where blacks were welcome to eat or use the restroom in the downtown section. His United Dollar Store, that catered largely to blacks, was the first establishment where they could try on wearing apparel without having to buy it. From 1950-1962, Evans was mayor of Durham, serving during the turbulent early years of the civil rights struggle. A peacemaker in the community, he appointed the first black policemen and firemen and named blacks to municipal posts of authority. Evans established the South's first urban renewal authority and pioneered in creating an interracial human rights commission. The grandsons of some of the Jews who had been compelled to leave Durham when the cigarette-making machine was introduced came back to Durham as students and faculty at Duke University.

The late Moses Richter, who had come to Troy in 1908 from Russia to join his sister and her husband, became one of the country's leading peach growers and distributors. When he was 16 he went to New York to study to be an opera singer but when his brother-in-law opened a store in Mt. Gilead, Richter gave up his studies and settled in Mt. Gilead. While peddling and working in the store, he discovered that refrigerated railroad cars and trucks could get peaches to city markets before they could spoil. Although Mt. Gilead was in the heart of the peach-growing country, the fruit would spoil before reaching the markets in all but the biggest cities. Richter changed that. Over the years, he built an extensive business that embraced thousands of acres of peaches, apples, tobacco, cattle, and timber. In 1965, 10,000 people gathered in Mt. Gilead to honor him as the savior of the town where he had opened cotton mills to make women's garments and provide jobs for women while the men worked in the fields. This halted a mass exodus from town. Richter often recalled the Christian farmer's wife who kept reminding him of his duties to his family in Russia and to his religion while he was peddling. Gradually, other peddlers stopped at the same farm house, and soon dietary laws were looked after there. Breakfast biscuits were made without lard and eggs were kept away from the pigs. At his death in 1969, Richter was one of the country's leading independent peach growers and distributors, serving thousands of farmers and growers in North Carolina.

An immigrant of a different sort was David Ovinsky who came to Charlotte from Montreal in 1902. As he became wealthy in the wholesale grocery business, he changed his name to David Owens and his religion to Protestant, and became a patron of Protestant churches. The Charlotte municipal auditorium is named for him.

An immigrant's son who came South in the 1920s was Harry Golden, the northern Yankee whose wry and humorous *Carolina Israelite* revived personal journalism, punctured the pomposity of Southern politicians and racists, and made him a national figure. In his newspaper and on the platform, he crusaded for civil rights, winning nation-wide fame for his warmth and honesty and later for his books. In 1969, the University of North Carolina in Charlotte staged a Harry Golden Day in honor of the man who had put his adopted city on the contemporary literary map. Speaking and writing courageous opinions in a time of change when such views were looked upon with hositility in much of the South, Golden was honored for his unique contributions to journalism and human relations.

By the time Golden went to Charlotte, it was the home of the state's second largest Jewish community, accounting for 720 of the 8,262 Jews in the state. Asheville, with 950 Jews, was then the largest community. Other substantial communities were in Durham (360), Wilmington (330), Winston-Salem (315), Fayetteville (148), and Goldsboro (143). In 1950 Charlotte had become the largest Jewish community with 770 Jews, and Asheville had dropped to second place with 600, followed by Greensboro with 525, Durham with 360, Winston-Salem with 340, Raleigh with 350, and Wilmington with 303. Ten years later Charlotte had increased its Jewish population to 2,000 out of the state total of 10,300. In 1977 the state total was 11,000, with Charlotte having 3,000, slightly less than the Greensboro-High Point-Winston-Salem area with 2,700. A substantial number of towns had anywhere from 20 to 100 Jews and some 35 had ten or less.

The first state-wide Jewish organization was the North Carolina Association of Jewish Women, created to bring together the Jews in the scattered and isolated rural communities where a 1927 study by a Duke University sociologist had revealed that 53 percent of the state's Jews lived. Dividing the state into eight Jewish districts, the Association established religious schools in each of them and commenced conducting a traveling religious school institute and sponsoring a mobile Jewish library.

In 1955, the newly-established North Carolina Association of Jewish Men undertook the sponsorship of a circuit-riding rabbi who makes the round of 11 towns in a bus equipped as a small synagogue, including an eternal light, as well as an Ark and a small Judaica library. The circuit-riding project, the idea of I.D. Blumenthal of Charlotte, seeks to deepen the Jewish identity of those living in small communities who cannot afford their own rabbi, and to improve the relations with non-Jews through personal contact. The rabbi drives through the back roads of the state in a revival of the old days when ministers and judges rode the circuit on horseback or in buggies. He travels 1,000 miles a week to meet the religious needs of some 300 Jews dispersed among the towns and villages of eastern North Carolina.

In the first two years of the program several rabbis held the job, but gave up because of the rigorous schedule that requires the rabbi to drive over 200 miles a day to give an hour's bar mitzvah instruction to one child, and then drive 100 miles more to teach a class of six Jewish adults. The circuit-riding rabbi serves communities on a monthly, semi-monthly, weekly, and twice weekly basis, and many towns only periodically. The circuit includes Whiteville, Lumberton, Wallace, and Jacksonville, North Carolina, and Myrtle Beach, South Carolina. Of these, Wallace is the only town without a synagogue. Whiteville draws members from Blandensboro and Elizabethtown; Lumberton from Clarkton and St. Pauls; and Myrtle Beach from the nearby Air Force base and Conway. Passover, Sukkot, and Shavuot services are held in a different town each year. Once a year a full-page ad is taken in the local papers and signed by every Jew in each community, soliciting funds for the United Jewish Appeal. The importance of the circuit-riding rabbi is evident from the tiny number of Jews living in the towns he serves: Wallace—10, Jacksonville—3, Whiteville—8, Myrtle Beach—33, mostly retirees.

In the early months of World War I, Arthur Bluethenthal of Wilmington enlisted in the Lafayette Escadrille, a volunteer force of British and American aviators who flew for France from 1914-1917. Bluethenthal was killed in an air battle and Wilmington named its first airport for the Jewish flyer. Nearly 60 years later, the first major venture of black and white businessmen in the country was undertaken in Charlotte where two Jewish lawyers, Adam Stein and Jonathan Wallas, partners in a predominantly black law firm, became involved in East Independence Plaza, a black-white cooperative undertaking that erected the largest black-owned commercial building in the South.

In 1939, the Refugee Economic Corporation made a loan of $250,000 for an agricultural colony of Jewish and non-Jewish German refugees at Van Eden Farm, near Burgaw, 30 miles west of Wilmington. One Cuban Jewish refugee, Diego Grynspan, settled briefly in Charlotte before moving on to Miami. In 1974, Charlotte assumed responsibility for settling eight Russian Jewish refugees, one of whom translated the state's driver's manual into Russian.

In the mid-1970s, the state had 32 congregations, all but one of them housed in its own synagogue. In addition to Mayor Emanuel Evans of Durham and Mayor Fishblate of Wilmington, Monroe Evans, brother of Emanuel, was elected mayor of Fayetteville in 1965 and Ben Cone was chosen mayor of Greensboro; Leon Schneider was mayor of Gastonia; Stanley Seligson was a city court judge in Raleigh from 1939-1942; and Marshall Rauch of Gastonia, Arthur Goodman of Charlotte, and Newman Harris of Wilmington served in the state legislature.

* * * * *

ASHEVILLE

Cong. Beth Ha-Tephila, 43 N. Liberty St., has an interesting piece of sculpture entitled *The Exodus*, a gift of the neighboring St. Mark's Lutheran Church. The sculpture features robed figures, one from each of the 12 tribes of Israel, bearing the Ark of the Covenant on the long trek through the wilderness.

Cong. Beth Israel, 229 Murdock St.

Federated Jewish Charities, 236 Charlotte St.

Jewish Community Center, 236 Charlotte St.

Vance Memorial, a 7-foot hewn granite obelisk on the west side of Pack Square, memorializes Zebulon Vance, whose famous lecture on the Jews entitled *The Scattered Nation*, played a decisive role in ending the last civil disability of North Carolina's Jews in 1868. Vance was Governor of the state from 1862 to 1866, and U.S. Senator from 1879-1894. The monument was erected in 1923 and the dedication address was delivered by Dr. Stephen S. Wise. The Asheville B'nai B'rith lodge and the United Daughters of the Confederacy hold a patriotic service annually at the monument on May 13, Vance's brithday. In 1928, the B'nai B'rith lodge in Asheville erected a plaque in the yard of old Cavalry Church to Vance's memory. The plaque describes Vance as a "friend, patriot, philanthropist, scholar, orator, statesman, loyal friend of the Jewish people whom he honored in his classic lecture, 'The Scattered Nation'." Vance was friendly with the Jewish community of Statesville, his home town, before the Civil War. When Union cavalry came to take Vance prisoner after the war, a Jewish merchant, Samuel Wittkowsky, protested bitterly to the Union commander and personally drove Governor Vance to prison in Wittkowsky's buggy.

BEAUFORT

Jacob Henry's House, 229 Front St., is a two-story frame dwelling built by Henry (see above) between 1794-1802. Now marked as a national historical shrine, the building acquired its status because of Henry's eloquent speech in the North Carolina House of Commons in 1809 against religious discrimination.

BLOWING ROCK

Moses H. Cone Memorial Park, a 4,000 acre recreation area in the Stone Mountain section of Watauga County near the Tennessee line, was once the estate of Mr. and Mrs. Moses H. Cone of Greensboro. It was presented as a gift to the United States by Mrs. Cone's heirs. It is maintained by the National Park Service which receives an annual grant of $10,000 from the Cone estate. Mr. and Mrs. Cone are buried in one section of the park which is bisected by the Blue Ridge Parkway. Moses, Henry, and Caesar Cone were pioneers in the development of North Carolina's major textile-manufacturing area.

CHAPEL HILL

Judea Reform Cong., 203 W. Markham Ave.

Rosenau Hall, the North Carolina School of Public Health, on route 54, opposite the health sciences building, memorializes the founder of the school who was one of the pioneers in public health planning and service. Rosenau's name in large gold letters is on the front of the building. Rosenau memorabilia and much more about him and his work are available to researchers. Rosenau's portrait hangs in the library.

University of North Carolina

● Hillel Foundation, 210 W. Cameron Ave.

● Judge John J. Parker Collection, University Library, consists of briefs, documents, exhibits, and transcripts of the records of the Nuremberg War Crimes Trial of November, 1945-October 1946, at which Parker was one of the judges. The Parker Collection also includes a large number of papers on the Major Alfred Mordecai and Philip Phillips families, both prominent in the antebellum South.

● Tannenbaum Shakespeare Collection, consisting of more than 3,000 volumes collected by the late Dr. Samuel Tannenbaum, a noted Shakespeare authority and bibliographer, is housed in a special aircondi-tioned room. The collection was presented by Tannenbaum's widow and the university's alumni association. Tannenbaum had been a lecturer on Shakespeare at the university. His widow added a supplementary collection of 800 letters and other manuscript material which Tannenbaum had received from scores of contemporary Shakespearean scholars over half a century of study and correspondence. Tannebaum was a physician specializing in psychotherapy.

● Henry Weil Collection on Political and Social Sciences is also in the library. Henry Weil of Goldsboro was a trustee of the university.

CHARLOTTE

American Jewish Times-Outlook, 1400 W. Independence Blvd.

Judah P. Benjamin Memorial, a sidewalk marker on South Tryon St., a block from the city's main square, was erected in 1948 by Temple Beth El and Temple Israel as a memorial to Judah P. Benjamin, Confederate Secretary of State and Secretary of War, who found refuge here in the last days of the Civil War. The marker is on the site of the home of Abram Weil, a Jewish merchant, who played host to Benjamin from April 18 to 26, 1865 while the Union forces were hunting him. Weil was an early Jewish settler in that part of the state. The Weils of Charlotte are no longer Jews.

Charlotte Biblical Garden, in Eastover Park, Museum Drive at Museum Pl., is a public area containing plants, bushes, and vines that are native to Israel and that were mentioned in the Bible. Charlotte's synagogues have joined with local churches in maintaining the garden.

Harry's House, former residence of Harry Golden and office of his *Carolina Israelite*, is now part of the Central Piedmont Community College which maintains the building as a free community art center. A popular author, lecturer, and home-spun philosopher with an East Side background, Golden was a popular figure in North Carolina in the 1950s and 1960s. His books and lectures brought him national fame.

Hebrew Academy, 1006 Sardis Lane.

Hebrew Cemetery, McCall St. at Oaklawn Ave., an 11-acre plot, contains the last remains of Elizabeth Cohen, granddaughter of a Revolutionary War patriot, and a number of Confederate soldiers, among them Aaron Cohen, Lewis Leon, and Capt. J. Roessler. Also buried here is H. Van Straaton, a Dutch Jew who was brought to Mecklenburg County to paint portraits of children on one of the large cotton plantations. The Baruch plot contains the remains of Rowland Baruch, uncle of Bernard M. Baruch (see South Carolina), and two of his children. Aaron Cohen, a prominent goldsmith who came to Charlotte in 1824, made silver and gold plates bearing his signature—a Colonial hat in the center of a Star of David. Some of his plates are still in use by some of Charlotte's old families.

Jewish Community Center, 600 Sharon Amity Rd.

Jewish Federation of Charities, 4401 Colwich Rd.

Temple Beth El, 1727 Providence St.

Temple Beth Sholom, 1931 Selwyn Ave.

Temple Israel, 1014 Dilworth Rd.

CLEMMONS

I.D. and Madolyn Blumenthal Jewish Home of North Carolina honors a Charlotte couple who were the guiding spirits in the founding of the institution and raising funds to support it. Blumenthal, a Charlotte businessman and civic leader, is widely-known in the state for his communal and Jewish activities.

DURHAM

Cong. Beth El, Watts and Markham Ave.

Duke University

● American Musical Theatre Center was founded in 1977 by Richard Adler, Broadway producer and lyricist, with the university, to avoid the high cost of producing major musical dramas in New York.

● University Library has the papers of Emanuel J. Evans and his mother and father. Evans, a prominent merchant and civic leader was a six-term mayor of Durham and intimately involved in the city's civic, mercantile, and public affairs. The collection includes over 1,200 items of correspondence, speeches, scrapbooks, photographs, and original documents reflecting the story of the Evans family and to an extent, the story of the Jews of Durham.

● Hillel Foundation, 102 Campus Center.

Judea Reform Cong., 2115 Cornwallis Rd.

FAYETTEVILLE

Beth Israel Cong., 2204 Morganton Rd. Both the synagogue and the center are headquarters for off-base cultural, social, and religious programs for Jewish military personnel and their families stationed at nearby Ft. Bragg. One of the seven Fleischman brothers who owned clothing stores in almost every city of the state was for many years chairman of the local JWB Armed Forces and Veterans Service Committee.

FLETCHER

Robert Loveman Monument, in the yard of Old Calvary Episcopal Church, known as the "outdoor Westminster Abbey of the South," memorializes the eminent Southern Jewish poet. Born in Cleveland in 1864, Loveman spent most of his life in Dalton, Ga., where he became famous for his verses. Twenty-two of his poems are included in *Oglethorpe Book of Georgia Verse*. Loveman, who died in Hot Springs, Ark., in 1923, is memorialized in this Southern literary shrine. Much of his writing dealt with the postbellum South.

GASTONIA

Temple Emanuel, 320 South St.

GOLDSBORO

Herman Park is the gift of Henry and Solomon Weil in memory of their brother, Herman, who founded the firm of H. Weil and Bros. The park was presented in 1890 on the 25th anniversary of the firm. It is located between Ash, Beech, Herman (also named for Herman Weil), and Jackson Sts.

Lionel Weil portrait, in the Wayne County Memorial Community Building, cor. E. Walnut and Williams Sts., opposite the courthouse, memorializes one of the prime movers in the erection of the building as a Wayne

County memorial to its World War I dead. The building, of whose board of trustees Weil was chairman for many years, is the headquarters of the American Legion, Red Cross, Girl Scouts, Boy Scouts, community chest, and recreation council. Inserted in the wall beneath the portrait (which was given by Weil's children at the request of the trustees), is an inscribed bronze plaque: "Lionel Weil 1877-1948 Good citizen First chairman of the Wayne County Memorial Community Building 1925-1946 whose dream of and untiring efforts for a fitting World War I memorial made possible the erection of this building." Weil's mother, Sarah, is also memorialized in the building by a portrait and an inscription that cites her more than 30 years service as president of the Bureau of Social Service.

Temple Oheb Sholom, James and Oak Sts.

Mina Weil Park, in a predominantly black section, was established by Miss Gertrude Weil in memory of her mother.

Mr. and Mrs. Solomon Weil are memorialized in the public library building, 204 W. Chestnut St., which was formerly their home and was given to the city to be used as a library, together with the funds to permit its adaption for library purposes. A bronze plaque in the entrance hall memorializing the Weils reads: "Throughout their lives, their broad human sympathies were ever available to those who had need of them. To perpetuate that spirit, this, their home for fifty years, is given by their children to the City of Goldsboro for use as a public library and the enrichment of community life. August 5, 1929."

GREENSBORO

Moses H. Cone Memorial Hospital, 1200 N. Elm St., is the $20 million gift of the Cone family in honor of Moses H. Cone, founder of the Cone textile empire which changed the economic map of the state and contributed handsomely to welfare, education, and recreation. Cone and his brother, Caesar, began operating a mill in Greensboro about 1910. Today the Cone Mills and other property cover a good part of the city. The Negro YMCA, opened in 1940 before such agencies were desegregated, was a gift of Caesar Cone in honor of two of his black employees.

Cong. Beth David, 610 E. Lake Dr.

Jewish Federation, 414 N. Church St.

North Carolina Triad Jewish Federation, 414 Church St.

Rosenthal Gymnasium at Bennett College is named for Mrs. Weil's uncle, Jonathan Rosenthal.

Temple Emanuel, 713 N. Greene St.

Mina Weil Dormitory on the campus of the Women's College (Bennett College) of the University of North Carolina, is named for Mrs. Henry Weil, a lifelong patroness of the college and active leader in Jewish and civic affairs for 60 years, who died in 1940. The college's library in Pfeiffer

Science Hall is also named for her.

Wetherspoon Gallery of the University of North Carolina at Greensboro, Springgarden St., has on display the portrait of Herbert Falk, a former president of the gallery and now a member of its board of directors.

GREENVILLE
Hillel Foundation, East Carolina University, c/o Department of Foreign Languages.

HENDERSONVILLE
Cong. Agudas Israel, 415 Blythe St.

HICKORY
Hickory Jewish Center, 4th St. Dr. and 11th Ave., N.W.

HIGH POINT
Cong. B'nai Israel, 1207 Kensington Dr.
High Point Hebrew Cemetery has a modest memorial to Jewish war dead.
United Hebrew Charities, 1207 Kensington Dr.

JACKSONVILLE
Jacksonville Hebrew Cong., Wardola Dr., helps meet the religious and social needs of Jewish personnel at the Marine Corps' Camp Lejeune.

KINSTON
Temple Israel, Vernon and LaRoque Aves.

LITTLE SWITZERLAND
Wildacres, a 1,400-acre sylvan retreat on a woodland knoll 3,300 feet above sea level in the heart of the Blue Ridge Mountains, is the home of Jewish and interfaith conferences, retreats, seminars, workshops, and colloquia. It was founded by I.D. Blumenthal of Charlotte, who also fathered the state's circuit-riding rabbi program and sponsors the state's only Jewish paper, *The American Jewish Times-Outlook*. Wildacres, once owned by Thomas Dixon, author of *The Klansman*, has become widely-known not only for its breath-taking location but because of the hundreds of cultural and interfaith events that have been held here each summer for more than 30 years. Blumenthal, who became well-to-do through the manufacture of an auto radiator sealant, has used much of his wealth to underwrite Jewish educational projects in North Carolina. He was the first employer of Harry Golden when he came South after World War I.

LUMBERTON
Temple Beth-El, 1106 Water St., one of the congregations served by

the circuit-riding rabbi, has 27 members who live in Lumberton and six more who reside in outlying villages.

MONROE

Moses Cohen, who settled in North Carolina before the American Revolution, is one of the soldiers memorialized on the local Revolutionary War Monument.

MURPHY

The Field of Woods, a Biblical wonder of the 20th century in this Cherokee County town in the western part of the state, where North Carolina, Georgia, and Tennessee converge, has laid out on a mountainside in huge white stones, the Tablets of the Ten Commandments. Set in two rows, the Tablets are part of a project on the assembly grounds of the Church of God. Each letter is tall and the words can easily be read from a plane flying overhead.

NEW BERN

Temple B'nai Sholom, 233 Middle St.

RALEIGH

Beth Meyer Synagogue, 806 W. Johnson St., was founded in 1874 as the House of Jacob in a room of the house of Michael Grausman who settled in Raleigh in 1862. He made uniforms for the Confederate Army.

Governor's Mansion has in its main dining room a handsome chandelier that once adorned the home of a family named Horowitz in pre-Hitler Berlin. When the Horowitzes fled Germany, they left everything behind in their sumptuous mansion. After years of moving from place to place in South America, they settled permanently in Raleigh. Some years ago, the present owner of the former Horowitz house in Berlin, offered to sell them any of the furnishings. They chose the chandelier, a genuine work of art which they contributed to the State of North Carolina for use in the Governor's mansion. They also contributed an Oriental tapestry to the North Carolina Museum of Art.

Mordecai House, N.W. cor. Wake Forest Rd. and Walnut St., is named for Moses Mordecai, an early Jewish settler, whose descendants own and occupy it. General Lafayette was once a guest here.

North Carolina Museum of Art, intersection of I-40 and Blue Ridge Rd., has a complete collection of modern Jewish ceremonial art and pieces used to beautify the synagogue, especially Torah appurtenances. It was established as a state American Bicentennial project. Most of the pieces in the the collection were gifts of Dr. and Mrs. Abram Kanof. Also in the museum are Rembrandt's *Esther and Haman*, and the Kanof Collection of Israeli Gravures. Dr. Kanof, who developed a traveling Judaica collection at the State Museum, is the State Commissioner of Art and Religion.

Temple Beth Or, 5315 Creedmore Rd.

ROBBINS
Karl Robbins, a Jewish mill owner, is memorialized in the name of this townnwhich was formerly called Hemp.

ROCKY MOUNT
Temple Beth El, 838 Sunset Ave.

SALISBURY
Jewish sports writers and broadcasters are among those honored in the Sports Writers and Broadcasters Hall of Fame on the campus of Catawba College.
Temple Beth Israel, Brenner and Link Ave.

STATESVILLE
Cong. Emanuel, Kelly and West End Aves., was founded in 1883 when this town was one of the state's leading cities and its Jewish community was one of the most influential. Erected in 1890, the synagogue was closed for more than 30 years as the Jewish community dwindled. It was reopened in 1956 when the state's first circuit-riding rabbi began his rounds. Jewish merchants, among them Isaac and David Wallace who came here in 1859, were close friends of Zebulon Vance, Governor and U.S. Senator, and their friendship inspired his famous *The Scattered Nation* lecture. During Passover in 1865, Union troops raided the Wallace home in search of food and were disappointed when all they found was matzoth. When Vance's home in Statesville was surrounded by Union troops and he was arrested and ordered to Washington to stand trial for treason, Samuel Wittkowsky, a Jewish merchant of the town, drove him to Salisbury under the watchful eye of 200 Union cavalry men. After 1900, many Jewish families moved to the larger cities. In addition to the synagogue there is a B'nai B'rith lodge, a sisterhood, and a Hadassah chapter.

WALLACE
Hebrew Congregation uses the American Legion hall for services and activities during the periodic visits of the circuit-riding rabbi. The congregation's headquarters are c/o Michael Fox, Harrells St.

WELDON
Temple Emanu-El, 8th and Sycamore Sts., serves Jews from Roanoke Rapids, Enfield, Jackson, Scotland Neck, Emporia, and Lawrenceville in nearby Virginia.

WHITEVILLE
Cong. Beth Israel, Frink St.

WILMINGTON

Isaac Bear Memorial School, 1220 Market St., is a public school presented to New Hanover County in 1912 by Samuel Bear, Jr., as a memorial to his brother, Isaac. A plaque outside of the building notes that it was given "with the expressed wish that many children of Wilmington might, amid comfort and beautiful surroundings, find joy and happiness in the pursuit of learning."

Judah P. Benjamin Memorial, Green St., is a marker placed by the United Daughters of the Confederacy where Judah P. Benjamin went to school.

Cong. B'nai Israel, 2601 Chestnut St.

Site of the First Jewish House of Worship in North Carolina, 4th and Market Sts., is identified by a street marker placed in May, 1951 by the State Department of History and Archives. The inscription says: "Temple of Israel erected in 1875 First House of Worship built in North Carolina by Jews Congregation established in 1867."

Temple of Israel, 460 Alpine Dr., is the oldest Jewish congregation in the state, having been founded in 1867 and dedicated the state's first synagogue in 1876. The site is designated by the state as a historical landmark.

WILSON

Cong. Beth El, Kenan St. and Kincaid Ave.

WINSTON-SALEM

Cong. Beth Jacob, 1833 Academy St.
Cong. Emanuel, 201 Oakwood Dr.

YANCEYVILLE

Joseph and Samuel Fels, noted industrialists and philanthropists, were born here. Their father, Jacob, an immigrant peddler, opened a store here and his sons used it as a base for their peddling. Joseph founded the Fels-Naptha soap company and spent his fortune perpetuating Henry George's Single Tax philosophy. Samuel Fels gave Philadelphia its famous planetarium, which is part of the Franklin Institute.

Oklahoma

The singular origin of Oklahoma's first lawful white settlement of Americans in 1889, and the widespread illegal colonization that preceded it by many years, gave thousands of people, including a number of Jews, a rightful claim to having been among the state's founding fathers.

The first known Jewish association with Oklahoma—most of which was acquired by the United States through the Louisiana Purchase of 1803 —dates from the 1830s. Oklahoma was almost entirely unpopulated until 1834, when it was set aside as Indian Territory and reserved for the Cherokee, Choctaw, Chickasaw, Creek, and Seminole Tribes who had been moved en masse for "as long as grass grows and water runs." Whites were permitted to enter the Indian Territory only for trading purposes, but were forbidden to settle there. Among the early traders in the Indian Territory were the pioneer Jewish settlers in Arkansas near the Oklahoma border. Jacob, Hyman, and Louis Mitchell (see Arkansas), who had a general merchandising store at Fort Smith, Arkansas, were doing business with the tribes just after the Indians reached the Territory. Jonas and Samuel Adler, who established themselves at Van Buren, Arkansas, in the 1840s, also engaged in Indian trade. Jews who took the southern route to California in 1849, and halted at Fort Smith and Van Buren for supplies, passed through Oklahoma and a few of them may have stayed on to trade.

Jewish settlers, however, did not come to Oklahoma until after the

Civil War, arriving with the first Americans who began the illegal occupation of unassigned public lands and of territory to which the Indians held title. Like all the white intruders, the Jewish pioneers were a mixed lot. Among them were adventurers who married Indian women; traders and peddlers from Kansas, Missouri, Colorado, Arkansas, and Texas, who did business with the American soldiers at Forts Supply, Sill, Reno, and Gibson, all in Oklahoma, and with the Indian tribes. They were also stocktenders of the Texas cattle companies to whom the Indians leased grazing rights; agents, suppliers, and workers on the first railroads pushing across Oklahoma to link Texas and Kansas; and venturesome merchants whose stores were among the earliest in the towns along the borders of the Indian Territory.

There is no certainty as to the identity of the first Jewish settlers in Oklahoma, but a good candidate for this distinction is a Civil War veteran with the odd name of "Boggy" Johnson. In a paper, *The Story of Oklahoma Jewry*, Rabbi Joseph Levenson of Temple B'nai Israel, Oklahoma City, said that Johnson arrived in the Indian Territory after the Civil War and married a girl of the Chickasaw Tribe. Some prominent Oklahoma families count "Boggy" and his Indian bride among their ancestors. Sheriff Walter Colbert of Carter County told a similar story to the *Oklahoma Jewish Chronicle* in 1929.

Rabbi Levenson was of the opinion that Boggy Depot, an old town in Atoka County, was named for "Boggy" Johnson. It is more likely, however, that "Boggy" Johnson acquired his given name from some association with Boggy Depot, which was founded in 1837. The town's name comes from the Clear Boggy, Muddy Boggy, and North Boggy streams which the early French traders called *Vazzures*, from the French word *vaseux* for miry or muddy. An American trader, John Sibley, reported in 1805 that "we arrived at the mouth of the Vazzures or Boggy River." Depot was added to the name in 1837 when the Chickasaws were settled there and were paid government annuities at "the depot on the Boggy." The Post Office officially named the place Boggy Depot in 1849. After 1850, Boggy Depot became an important town at the junction of the Texas Road and a trail from Fort Smith to California. During the Civil War it was a military post and "Boggy" Johnson may have been stationed there. Since he married a Chickasaw girl, it is not unlikely that he met her while doing business with the Indians at Boggy Depot.

Another Jew identified with the early history of Oklahoma was Joseph Sondheimer. A boy of 12 when be emigrated from Bavaria in 1840, he lived briefly in Baltimore and then went west to St. Louis. During the Civil War Sondheimer became a military supplier to the Union forces and later opened stores in Memphis, Little Rock, and Hot Springs. When Texas cattlemen began driving their herds across the Indian lands in Oklahoma to the Kansas railheads, Sondheimer rode along the Chisholm, Western, and

Shawnee Trails, opening depots for the collection of furs, hides, and pecans. One of these depots was established at Muskogee in 1867, five years before the town was founded. Sondheimer, who married a Cherokee woman, became well-to-do marketing buffalo hides brought in by the Indians. In 1874, Sondheimer made Muskogee the headquarters of his enterprises. Joseph Sondheimer Sons is still one of Oklahoma's largest dealers in hides and pecans. Alex Sondheimer, Joseph's son, who settled in Muskogee in 1881, was the first court reporter in the Indian Territory.

The American Jewish Archives has data on one Adolph Kohn, a peddler and Indian trader, who was captured by the Apache Indians in 1870 while he was en route to the Indian Territory. For some reason, the Apaches spared his life and traded him to the Comanche Tribe with whom he rode the warpath for three years before they released him in 1873.

A number of Jews who had settled in northern Texas, around Gainsville, Jefferson, and Texarkana in the 1870s and 1880s, were among the builders of Ardmore, which grew up in 1872 around the station of the Missouri, Kansas, and Texas Railroad, the first to cross Oklahoma. Sam and David Daube came to Ardmore in the mid-1880s before the Atchison, Topeka, and Santa Fe reached the town. The Daubes were cotton brokers and merchants. Later they were active in the first oil discoveries. David served in the territorial legislature and played a part in preparing Oklahoma for statehood. Before 1887, Max Westheimer, Julius Kahn, and his wife Rebecca, the Bottowitzes, Zuckermans, and Munzesheimers were living in Ardmore. Kahn, whose confectionary shop on Main Street was for many years one of Ardmore's popular meeting places, organized the town's first band. Among the merchants licensed to trade in the Indian Territory before 1889 were Julius Haas and his brother-in-law, Sam Sondheimer of Atoka and Muskogee; Isaac Levy of Guthrie; the Laupheimers of Muskogee; Karney Friedman of Wagoner; and the firm of Byers and Levin of Checotah.

It was in Ardmore that Oklahoma's first Jewish community came into being through the efforts of the early Indian traders, aided probably by Jewish traveling salesmen and peddlers who made their headquarters in the increasingly important commercial center and railroad junction. Old-timers claimed there were periodic *minyanim* between 1887 and 1899, but the pioneer congregation, Temple Emeth, was not organized until 1899. A Jewish cemetery association was formed two years later.

The second phase of Jewish settlement began coincidentally with the historic "runs" that got under way in 1889. When the pressure of land hungry settlers, speculators, and farmers compelled the Federal government to open western Oklahoma to legal settlement, impatient thousands gathered at the Kansas and Texas borders to await the moment when they could freely cross and stake out a land claim. In the motley throng that raced into western Oklahoma at high noon, April 22, 1889, when a medley of bugle blasts and gunshots signaled that the land was open, was a fair sprinkling of Jews. On foot, on horseback, in covered wagons, and in wood-burning trains, they joined the wild scramble for desirable homestead sites, as this and the later runs to other parts of the Indian Territory marked the end of the last American frontier.

Like most of the '89ers, the vanguard of Jews headed for Gurthrie and Oklahoma City, which mushroomed into boom towns between noon and sunset. Among the very first to get there were David Wolff, Isaac Bree Levy, Isaac Jacobs, David Schonwald, H. L. Cohen, and S. E. Levi. The latter compiled Oklahoma City's first directory in 1889 in which he described himself as an "ad solicitor." Levy, one of the most prominent figures in Oklahoma's territorial days, was born in Chicago in 1859. At the age of 20, he was in business at Newton, Kansas. When Levy joined the rush to Oklahoma, he was a successful merchant at Kingman, Kansas.

David Schonwald, a Hungarian, participated in the run to Guthrie, and also in the later runs. Riding horseback and shirtless, he raced into the Cherokee Strip in 1893 after the area was purchased from the Indians. The following year, he made the run into the Kickapoo country. In 1901, he turned up at the opening of the Comanche, Kiowa, and Apache country to settlement. His first job was as a section hand on the Santa Fe. Later, he became a leading businessman in Ponca and Blackwell, and president of a gas and oil company and a bank in Blackwell. H. L. Cohen was a clothing merchant who came from Buffalo, New York. His son, Louis, later a leading citizen of Fort Smith, Arkansas, was an infant when his parents brought him to Guthrie. A younger brother, Ben, claimed to be the first Jewish male child born in Oklahoma.

Oklahoma City pioneers included Felix, Abe, and Victor Levy; Joseph Baum; Harry and Jim Gerson; Seymour Heyman; Max and Moses Herskowitz; Isaac Lowenstein; Samuel Epstein; and George Hyman. Epstein, who came by train from California, jumped off before the train reached the starting line for the "run," and staked a claim before the deadline. His drygoods store was established at a point that is now the heart of Oklahoma City. Lowenstein, a pioneer butcher, later opened one of the city's first vaudeville houses. His son, Morris, operated many theatres in various parts of the state. Hyman, who later built many of the huge government buildings in Washington, helped build the first temporary capital of the Indian Territory, after the Cherokee Strip was opened in 1893. Louis B. Epstein, who was raised in Denison, a lawless frontier town in Texas, also participated in the land rush to Oklahoma where he served as a circuit court judge during the troubled days when the Indian Territory was being settled.

Rosh Hashanah services were first held in Guthrie in 1889 and in Oklahoma City the following year. The Hebrew Cemetery Association was founded in Oklahoma City in 1902, a year before Temple Israel was organized. In 1900, a group of men began holding Orthodox services for the High Holidays on the second floor of the Grand Leader department store in Hartshorne. They had more than a *minyan* because worshippers came from Wilburton, Atoka, Caddo, Caney, Durant, Gowen, Lehigh, Coalgate, Haileyville, Alderson, Krens, and McAlester. These annual services continued to be held in Hartshorne until 1917 when the site of the services was switched to Atoka.

As Jews spread over the Indian and Oklahoma Territories, small settlements took root in most of the new towns. Jewish settlement began in Enid when Morris Gottschalk made the run to the Cherokee Strip. Morris Mayer came to Guthrie in 1889 and later homesteaded at Chandler where his wife was the first white woman. Jews first arrived in Tulsa in 1900, a year before the discovery of the state's first commercially important oil well. One of the Jewish pioneers there was Simon Jankowsky, who arrived in 1904 and built the town's first skyscraper.

Tulsa's first Jewish congregation, B'nai Emunah, dates from 1916, but Jewish services had been held there more or less regularly in private homes since 1906. Jake Katz, who settled in Stillwater in 1887, worked for his uncle, Eli Younger, who had opened a store there in 1889. Katz built up the business to a point where it expanded to 18 locations in the old Cherokee Strip. In Stillwater, Katz founded the mission for the poor, bought bonds to help the churches in town, headed the town council and the YMCA, and kept a strictly kosher house. Katz later brought scores of relatives to Oklahoma from Germany and many are still running the Katz stores. Robert Rubin, who runs the Katz store in Stillwater, is the godfather of the tiny Jewish community there of businessmen and lonely students at Oklahoma State University. Jacob Schweizer, who arrived with the 1889 homesteaders and settled at El Reno, was among the volunteers who joined Theodore Roosevelt's "Roughriders" in the Spanish American War.

By 1900, there were over 500 Jews in the two territories that later became Oklahoma. Ardmore, which had 50 Jews in 1890, counted twice that number in 1907 when there were congregations in Guthrie, Oklahoma City, and Ardmore. When Oklahoma became a state in 1907, its Jewish population had grown to more than 1,000, with the largest communities in Oklahoma City and Tulsa. Among the new arrivals were 145 immigrants from Eastern Europe settled in 22 different towns by the Industrial Removal Office between 1901 and 1907. From 1906-1916, Rabbi Joseph Blatt of Oklahoma City's Temple Israel was the only rabbi in the state.

From the very beginning of the Oklahoma and Indian Territories, Jews were prominent in public life. Isaac Bree Levy was elected to the first territorial legislature which created the first territorial government. Isaac Jacobs of Sequoyah County sat in the second legislature. One of Murray

County's representatives in the fourth territorial legislature was Charles B. Emanuel, who was elected to the first state legislature in 1907 from the town of Sulphur.

Leo Meyer, who first settled in Sayre in 1901 where he was elected mayor when his was the only Jewish family in town, became a cotton buyer and is believed to have purchased the first bale of cotton grown in Oklahoma. Later, as a resident of Ardmore, then the largest town in the Territory, he built the area's first cotton gin and with his brother-in-law, Ed Lewis, pioneered in raising broom cotton. A member of several territorial legislatures, Meyer and Isaac Levy participated in the convention that voted to united the Indian and Oklahoma Territories and seek admission to the Union as the 46th state. Meyer was elected secretary of this convention and led the successful fight for a single state. He also helped draft the state's first constitution. In 1907, Meyer moved to Guthrie when it was selected as the first capital. Meyer was appointed first Secretary of State, an office he held until 1910.

One of the first Federal judges in Oklahoma was Louis Sulzbacher. A German immigrant who had lived in New Mexico in the 1860s and 1870s, where he became a leading attorney, Sulzbacher was appointed Chief Justice of the Supreme Court of Puerto Rico in 1900. In 1905 he was named U.S. District Judge for the Western District of Oklahoma and Indian Territories. In that same year, Gus Paul, one of the founders of Oklahoma City's first synagogue, was elected city attorney of Oklahoma City. In the bitter struggle between Guthrie and Oklahoma City for designation as the permanent state capital, the Jews became the scapegoats. As Secretary of State, Leo Meyer had used his influence in favor of Oklahoma City. It was he who carried the state's great seal from Guthrie to Oklahoma City on the orders of the governor. Both he and Meyer were hanged in effigy by the angry residents of Guthrie. In 1910, the Guthrians restored to antiSemitism with a banner headline in the *Guthrie Daily Leader* proclaiming, "Shylocks of Oklahoma City Have State By the Throat." Another headline alleged that the "Levy Brothers, Jewish Landlords, Contribute $10,000 to the Capital Campaign." The *Leader* charged that there was "an unparalleled conspiracy on the part of Jews and Gentiles of a rotten town to loot the state." Rabbi Blatt, who used to circuit-ride around Oklahoma, took the initiative in protesting this campaign. In a daring action, he wrote to every voter in Guthrie, asking for fair play and warning against the use of religious bigotry in public affairs.

On the eve of World War I, there were about 2,500 Jews in the state, 1,000 in Oklahoma City, 500 in Tulsa, 225 in Muskogee, 150 in Ardmore, 125 in Chickasaw, 46 in McAlester, 37 in Lawton, and 35 in Guthrie. By 1950, Tulsa had caught and passed Oklahoma City as the largest Jewish community, the figures being 1,830 Jews in Tulsa to 1,600 in Oklahoma

City. By 1977, when Oklahoma's Jewish population reached 6,160, Tulsa was still the largest Jewish community, with 2,600, against 1,500 in Oklahoma City. There were also stable Jewish communities in Muskogee, Ponca City, Seminole, Ardmore, Norman, Enid, Lawton, and Guthrie.

Visitors to Tulsa and Oklahoma City are always surprised to learn what long distances many children travel from towns 40 and 50 miles away for religious school on Sunday morning and for Bar Mitzvah training. Because the Jews of the state are so widely dispersed outside of the two major cities, they have developed a tight sense of kinship and communal responsibility. The per capita average of donations to the United Jewish Appeal is one of the highest in the country, especially in Tulsa. Tulsa has such a reputation as a Zionist community that it was chosen as the place to launch the 1955 Israel Bond campaign.

One of the unlikely participants in the Oklahoma oil boom was the late Dr. Bernard Revel, founder and first president of Yeshiva University. After he married into the oil-rich Travis family of Marietta, Ohio, and Tulsa, he was torn between loyalty to his family and his concern for higher Jewish education. From 1912-1951, the bearded Talmudic scholar was part of the booming oil industry around Tulsa where he was one of the pioneers in the refining of natural gas. Revel left Tulsa in 1915 to accept the leadership of the newly merged Etz Chaim and Rabbi Isaac Eichanan Theological Seminaries, which became the nucleus of Yeshiva University. When the family oil business began to founder, Revel rushed back and forth between Tulsa oil wells and Yeshiva on New York's Lower East Side. By 1921, the need to put all his efforts into saving the family oil business from bankruptcy led him to resign his Yeshiva post, but ultimately, he severed his business ties with Oklahoma and remained in New York.

Among the leading figures in Oklahoma Jewry between the 1940s and 1970s were Gershon Fenster, Julius Livingston, Alfred Aaronson, and Maurice Sanditen. Fenster, who was the moving force behind much of Tulsa's Jewish communal efforts, worked for his brothers-in-law, the Sanditens, but he was happiest in his role as a Jewish teacher, scholar, builder of a notable Jewish art collection, and Zionist. Julius Livingston was involved in every important civic effort and a leader in many Jewish causes, national and overseas. Maurice Sanditen, who arrived in Tulsa from Lithuania with five dollars, built an immense tire and auto supply business with his brothers.

Alfred Aaronson, who built his own schul, was known as "Mr. Tulsa" because of his leadership in civic life. Once he contributed $10,000 to pay the cost of a special election that voted a $3 million bond issue to refinance the Gilcrease Museum which was on the verge of leaving the city because of indebtedness. Louis Fischl, who arrived in Ardmore in 1913, served in the State House of Representatives from 1929-1932 and in the State Senate

from 1932-1936. J. J. Aberson was three times mayor of Cordell and headed the Washita County Christmas seal campaign. Max Krouch of Tecum-
seh served as chairman of the State Excise Board under three governors.
Seymour Heyman was president of the Oklahoma City chamber of commerce and of the board of education. Harry Glasser of Oklahoma City was a
member of the State Senate from 1922-1924. Julian J. Rothman of Tulsa
served on the board of regents of Oklahoma State University from 1959-
1966 and was president in the latter year. Mrs. David Loeffler was elected
to the city council of Bristow in 1954, an office her father-in-law, Louis
Loeffler held from 1917-1924. Melvin Moran was elected mayor of Seminole
in 1975.

* * * * *

ARDMORE
Daube Public Swimming Pool, 3rd and F St., N.E., occupying an entire city block, is named for the late Sam Daube, one of the state's pioneer
cotton brokers. Daube's children donated the site where Daube's home and
part of his ranch once stood.
Jewish Federation, 23 B St., S.W.
Lake Murray State Park, largest in the state park system, was established in 1930 through the efforts of the late Louis Fischl, who represented
Ardmore in the lower and upper houses of the state legislature from 1929-
1936.
Temple Beth Emeth, 421 Stanley Blvd., is the oldest congregation in
the state, having been founded in 1899.

CARRIER
Solomon Carrier, the town's first merchant, is memorialized in this
northwest Garfield County village of 150 people, founded in 1897.

CHELSEA
Nathan and Mayme Levine, early settlers in this oldest oil town in the
state, are memorialized by a stained glass window in the Memorial Methodist Church to which the Levines donated chimes and other gifts.

CLAREMORE
Will Rogers Memorial, 10 blocks west of U.S. Highway 66, a shrine to
Oklahoma's most famous son, has on permanent exhibit a large bronze re-
plica of the official Will Rogers poem, *Howdy Folks*, written by David R.
Milsten, Tulsa Jewish lawyer and friend of the cowboy philosopher.
Milsten's poem, which describes the dedication of the memorial in 1938,
was voted the official poem commemorating Will Rogers by action of the
Memorial Board which erected the shrine, and by vote of the state legisla-
ture. Milsten also wrote the first biography of Rogers.

COHN

William Cohn, who operated a rock quarry from which the San Francisco Railroad bought material for track building and maintenance, is memorialized in this railroad switching and loading junction in Pushmataha County.

GOODMAN

Solomon F. Goodman, the first postmaster of this old southeastern Cotto County village, was memorialized in the town named for him in 1902.

LAWTON

Simpson Gun, a German 105 mm. artillery piece captured during World War I and now permanently emplaced at the summit of Signal Mountain in the western corner of Fort Sill, the Army's Field Artillery headquarters, is a joint memorial to Fort Sill's World War I dead and Morris Simpson, a pioneer Jewish settler. Affixed to a monumental stone in front of the gun is a bronze plaque with the inscription: "This stone was emplaced at the suggestion of Morris S. Simpson, an original settler of Lawton and a staunch friend of the Army." Two generations of artillery officers who trained at Fort Sill have regarded this memorial trophy affectionately as the Simpson Gun because Simpson and his wife adopted Fort Sill and its men as their special charges.

Simpson and his brother-in-law, Morris Israelson, both immigrants from Russia, arrived in Lawton on August 3, 1901, three days before the opening by lottery of the 3-million acre Kiowa-Comanche Indian reservation to white settlers. Barely 20 when he came to the U.S. in 1883, Simpson settled first in Marshall, Tex., with his brother-in-law. Later, he moved to Dallas. From there he and Israelson drove a covered wagon loaded with drygoods and house furnishings to the present site of Lawton, where they opened the town's first store in a tent. This establishment grew into the Lawton Mercantile Co., one of the largest stores in the southwest, but everyone called it "Simpson's." Before long, Simpson's house and store became headquarters for young and homesick officers who found the Simpsons friendly and sympathetic hosts. Long before there was a National Jewish Welfare Board or a USO, the Simpsons maintained what was tantamount to the first servicemen's recreation center in Oklahoma.

Simpson's scrupulous honesty and friendship in dealing with the Indians made him their idol. They found the Jewish trader's fair dealing and aid in time of need an extraordinary experience. Quanah Parker, last chief of the Comanches, who lived on the outskirts of Lawton for many years, named one of his sons for Simpson, "in honor of his good white friend." Simpson not only entertained the officers and men from nearby Fort Sill, but he was one of the prime movers in having the fort expanded and named the headquarters of the Field Artillery School. He was equally concerned with Cameron State School of Agriculture and in encouraging education for farm children. Lawton's economic development and its expansion into a major market for cotton were also Simpson's concerns. The Simpsons having no children of their own, raised orphans in their home. One such youngster, born in the Episcopalian faith, was given a Christian upbringing by the ardently Jewish Simpsons. For many years their home was a makeshift synagogue for Jews from Lawton and the surrounding towns. The Torah that Simpson brought with him to Lawton was said to have been the first to reach the Oklahoma Territory. It is now a prized possession of Fort Sill Chapel.

In 1929, when Simpson was dying of cancer, he made the suggestion that forever linked him with the Simpson Gun on Signal Mountain. He found that nowhere in Lawton or Fort Sill was there a memorial to the men from the fort who had died in World War I. Out of his suggestion for a memorial came the idea of imbedding the old German gun on Signal Mountain. The gun became known as the "Simpson Gun," a name given it by Brig. Gen. Dwight E. Aultman, commandant at Fort Sill when it was dedicated in 1929, two years before Simpson's death.

MUSKOGEE
Muskogee Orthodox Cong., 9th and Denver Sts.

Temple Beth Ahaba, 715 W. Okmulgee, has a stained glass window memorializing Joseph Sondheimer, one of the Oklahoma pioneers. The window was the gift of Sondheimer's son Samuel. Another son, Alexander, who became a Presbyterian, made a large cash contribution to the temple in memory of his father.

NORMAN
Hillel Foundation, University of Oklahoma, 494 Elm St., is housed in a building named for Julius Livingston, Tulsa oil man and civic leader.

Max Westheimer Flying Field, the airport for the University of Oklahoma and Norman's municipal airport, is named for a pioneer cattleman, rancher, and department store owner who settled in Ardmore in 1886. Originally established by his family after Westheimer's death in 1938, the field was opened in 1940. During World War II the Navy took over the field as a Naval Air Station. A plaque on the field records the Navy's use of the field, a gift of Westheimer's children, Doris Neustadt, Julien Westheimer, and his son-in-law, Walter Neustadt. During the Navy's tenure, the field was enlarged from the original 160 acres to nearly 1,500 acres. At the north campus of the university, there is a memorial gateway consisting of a 30-foot square structure on the left and a 42-foot high tower in the center, with stairways leading up to the tower. Max Westheimer's name is inscribed on the tower in 16-inch letters.

OKLAHOMA CITY

Cong. Emanuel, 900 N.W. 47th St., has a notable Menorah mural designed by the late A. Raymond Katz.

Heyman Street, which runs from 1400 S. Indiana Ave. to West Blvd., an area in a Federal housing project, is named for Seymour Heyman, one of the city's early merchants and civic leaders. Described as one of the city's builders, Heyman organized the city's social agency, and headed the Oklahoma City chamber of commerce and the board of education. He was known as "Mr. Oklahoma City."

Jewish Community Council, 1100 N. Dewey.

National Cowboy Hall of Fame and Western Heritage Center, on Persimmon Hill just outside the city, N.E. Expressway and Eastern, honors those identified with the development of the American West and the preservation of its traditions, among them Otto Mears, Colorado trail blazer, road and railroad builder, and Indian peacemaker in Colorado (see Colorado).

Oklahoma City YMCA, 5th and Robinson Sts., has three rooms which are memorials to three Jews—Mrs. Lillie Shoshone, Sophie Shonwald, and Capt. Edward Weiss.

Oklahoma Hall of Fame, Oklahoma Heritage House, 201 N.W. 14th St., includes three Jews—Rabbi Joseph Blatt, once the state's only rabbi; Alfred E. Aaronson of Tulsa; and Sylvan Goldman of Oklahoma City. Their photographs and a 220-word biographical sketch are contained in one of three large albums on view at the Heritage Center.

Southwest Jewish Chronicle, 324 N. Robinson St.

State Historical Society Building, Lincoln Blvd., south and east of Capitol, has in the State Archives long lists of Indians, many with pronouncedly Jewish surnames, indicating that some of the state's early businessmen were "squawmen" who fathered Indian children.

Temple B'nai Israel, 4901 N. Pennsylvania Ave.

PONCA CITY

Temple Emanuel, Highland and Poplar Aves.

SAMPSEL

Aaron D. Sampsel, first postmaster of this now abandoned hamlet in Cimarron County, was memorialized in its name. The Post Office was established in 1906 and closed in 1929.

SEMINOLE

Hebrew Center Cong., 402 Seminole Ave., serves in addition to Seminole, also Shawnee, Weoka, Prague, Konowa, Ada, and Norman. Jewish students from the University of Oklahoma at Norman make the 90-minute round trip drive every weekend to teach a Sunday school class. The congregation has a rabbi only for the High Holidays.

SOBOL

Harry Sobol, an early Jewish merchant in the nearby town of Ft. Towson, was namesake of this hamlet in extreme southeastern corner of Pushmataha County. Sobol had established a store at Ft. Towson, in Choctaw County, in 1907. When the residents of a nearby village wanted a Post Office, Sobol went to Washington to help get it. While there, he telegraphed and asked what to name the Post Office, and the return message said,"Call it Sobol." The Post Office was opened in 1911.

SPIRO

Abram Spiro, a prominent Arkansas merchant, is memorialized in this Leflore County town, just across the Arkansas border from Fort Smith. Spiro, who settled in Arkansas in the 1880s, came from Memphis and St. Louis. His daughter, Celia, married I. Nakdimen, Fort Smith banker and industrialist, who was one of the best known men in eastern Oklahoma at the turn of the century. When the Kansas City Southern Railroad was looking for a name for its station at its new Oklahoma Territory stop in 1895, Jim Brizzolara, Fort Smith postmaster, asked I. Isaacson of Fort Smith to suggest a name. Isaacson proposed Spiro. Spiro is a railroad point and marketing center for farm products. Spiro's son-in-law, Nakdimen, who was active in Fort Smith's United Hebrew Congregation, was so influential along the Arkansas-Oklahoma border that when Theodore Roosevelt was campaigning for President in 1912 as the Bull Moose candidate, Nakdimen was asked to introduce him at every whistle stop.

STILLWATER

Seretean Center for the Performing Arts, a $3,200,000 three-level building on the east side of the Oklahoma State University campus, Morrill and Knoblick Sts., is named for Martin B. Seretean, a 1949 alumnus of the university, whose $500,000 gift in 1969 speeded construction of the center. Seretean, who owned the Coronet Industries of Dalton, Ga., the fifth largest floor covering company in the country, merged with RCA in 1971, and became RCA's single largest stockholder.

TECUMSEH

Krouch Elementary School, 1000 block of West Park St., is a memorial to the late Julius Krouch, Max Krouch, and Erna Krouch, who were among the town's earliest settlers, having come here in 1894. Julius donated the land on which the school stands. In 1918 he moved to Oklahoma City where the youth center of Temple Israel is named for him.

TULSA

Boston Avenue Methodist Church, 1301 S. Boston Ave., has the original aluminum model of a pair of praying hands that are part of the church's architecture. The model was presented to the church in honor of Alfred Aaronson, one of Tulsa's best loved citizens and humanitarians, by the chief librarian of the Museum of Modern Art in New York who received it from the sculptor, Robert Garrison.

Cong. B'nai Emunah, 1719 S. Owasso Ave., has a large sculptured Menorah over its main entrance. The Gershon and Rebecca Fenster Gallery of Jewish Art, one of the country's largest public museums of Judaica, is an integral part of the congregation. The gallery began in 1949 when Rebecca Fenster donated a bronze Holy Ark by Boris Schatz in memory of her husband who had assembled a personal Jewish art collection which at the time of his death included works of more than 100 artists. Hundreds of pieces are displayed in the Fenster Gallery, which has a full-time curator and trained guides. One of the gallery's rarest items is a second century stone Chanukah Menorah excavated in Israel. In 1965 the gallery was endowed in the Fenster's memory by Mrs. Julius Sanditen, their daughter, and her husband.

Thomas Gilcrease Institute of American History, 2401 W. Newton St., which houses a remarkable collection of books, manuscripts, and documents dealing primarily with the American Indian and the Southwest frontier, was saved for Tulsa by Alfred Aaronson, the man called "Mr. Tulsa." As chairman of the "Save the Gilcrease Museum for Tulsa Committee," he was the prime mover in the passage of a $3 million bond issue that enabled the city to acquire the museum.

Jewish Community Council, 3314 E. 51st St.

Florence Nightingale Statue, on the campus of the Hillcrest School of Nursing, 1144 S. Troost, a life-size bust of the famed English nurse, is a gift of Julius Livingston, for more than a generation the city's leading Jewish communal figure. Unveiled in 1955, the bust is believed to be the only one of Miss Nightingale in the U.S.

Shalom Center, 71st and Lewis, is the community's Jewish center.

Herman P. Taubman Memorial Building, 1120 S. Utica, now called the Tulsa Psychiatric Clinic, a community clinic for mentally ill patients, was a gift of Herman Taubman, Jewish industrialist and communal figure.

Temple Israel, 2004 E. 22nd Pl., has two exterior 40-foot pylons covering the entire left side of the building, erected at a slight angle to represent the open pages of a book. On the pylons are representations of the Pillar of Fire by Night and the Pillar of Cloud by Day, which guided the Israelites through the desert. Superimposed on the pylons are the Ten Commandments. Between the pylons is a slender pattern of redwood and blue glass which form a continuous vertical design of Stars of David. The area between the street, the side of the pylons, and the path leading into the main vestibule has been converted into a small garden in which there is an 8-foot Menorah, which can be seen from all sides. The synagogue's Eternal Light, by Seymour Lipton, a four-foot high sculpture of nickel-silver and steel, is a highly modernistic and unusual-looking work.

Tulsa Public Library, 400 Civic Center, has the Aaronson Auditorium, named for Alfred Aaronson, who for many years guided the city-county library system. In the auditorium there is a plaque that reads: "Alfred Aaronson, without whose vision, wisdom, perserverance and continued untiring efforts the Tulsa City-County Library would not have been possible." He led the fight for passage of a $3,800,000 bond issue and a 1.9¢ levy to build and support the modern library system. Aaronson, a long-time member of the Tulsa Community Relations Commission, is honored annually by the Alfred E. Aaronson Lecture Series in the Arts and Humanities, administered by the Arts Council of Tulsa. The Diggs Collection of Americana in the Public Library was presented to the library in 1945 by the Tulsa Jewish Community Council. The 3,750 volumes, comprising the most valuable private library of Americana and Oklahoma history, was assembled by the late Judge B. Diggs, a Tulsa pioneer, and purchased from his widow by the Jewish Community Council at a cost of $10,000. Each volume has a specially designed bookplate containing a Menorah and the name of the Council.

Tulsa Recreation Center for the Physically Limited, 815 S. Utica, has the Livingston Lounge, named for Julius Livingston, oilman and communal leader. The center was the idea of Mrs. Charles Whitebook who persuaded the Tulsa section of the National Council of Jewish Women to establish what has now become a community agency funded by public support.

Tulsa University has a Judaica collection in its McFarlin Library that is maintained through an annual subvention by the Jewish Community Council.

VELMA

"Sholom Alechem Gasoline Plant," is painted on a large sign on Highway #7 (between Duncan and Ardmore), about a half mile before the Stephens-Carter County line. The sign is at the crest of a sharp rise in the road, about seven miles from the town of Velma in Stephens County. Many local residents believe the name of the plant is Indian in origin, but in fact it is of Hebrew origin.

During the Oklahoma oil fever in the early 1920s, the daily newspapers spurred the excitement by publishing a page of oil news every day. Ardmore, in the southern part of the state, was the center of this frenzy, and the editor of the *Daily Ardmoreite* was William Krohn. It was Krohn's custom, according to Walter Neustadt, Jr., a fourth generation Jewish resident of Ardmore, to greet people on the street with the expression, "Sholom Alechem." In due course, he educated people to respond with "Alechem Sholom." In addition to offering the traditional Hebrew greeting, Krohn organized a Sholom Alechem Society as an informal social group of men visiting and operating in and around Ardmore. It was customary then for people to come from all parts of the country to watch a well spew forth its first oil. The Ardmore Hotel was the gathering place for these oil enthusiasts and in the evenings, before an oil strike, Krohn was always at the hotel displaying Oklahoma hospitality.

Thus Krohn was responsible for the naming of the Sholom Alechem Oil Field. There are two versions as to how it happened. Louis Fischl, an Ardmore lawyer and state legislator, and Jerome Westheimer, a son of one of the part-owners of the original field, stated that Krohn named the discovery well "Sholom Alechem" in the *Daily Ardmoreite* in late 1923 or 1924. The name stuck. Usually an oil field assumed the name of the nearest town, but the initial well of this field was not adjacent to any municipality, so Krohn's title was accepted by the existing oil agencies. The second version, more plausible to many residents of the area, was told to Chaplain M. David Geffen (now rabbi of Cong. Beth Shalom, Wilmington, Delaware), by Walter Neustadt, Jr., a relative of one of the field's original owners. Neustadt described Krohn as a superb reporter who was extremely well-liked by the oilmen. On the night oil began to flow, Krohn was on the rig floor with the drillers and the observers. Because of his popularity among the entire oil fraternity, the well was named "Sholom Alechem." With the successful drilling of more wells in the area, the title Sholom Alechem was officially given to the entire field. The first well in the Sholom Alechem Oil Field was brought in December,1923, by the Humble Oil Co., on land partially owned by Max and Simon Westheimer and Sam and David Daube of Ardmore. The field is still productive, and Mobil, Pan-American, and Skelly all have wells there.

ZANGWILL

Israel Zangwill, the famed English Jewish writer, was honored in the name of this southwestern Garfield County village and Post Office which existed between 1897 and 1905.

South Carolina

There were Jews in what is now South Carolina more than thirty years before the area was cut off from North Carolina and made a separate crown colony in 1729. The first Jew of record in South Carolina was an employee of the British governor in 1695. When four Spanish-speaking Indians from Florida were captured by the British, they were brought to Charleston. In reporting the incident, the governor wrote "I had a Jew for an interpreter." Through his Jewish interpreter, the governor learned that the Indians were Christians and he ordered them released.

In 1665, the colony's second charter offered the Jews of the West Indies and Surinam religious, civil, and political privileges if they would settle in the Carolinas. The Fundamental Constitutions which the eminent British philosopher, John Locke, wrote for the Lord Proprietors of the Carolinas in 1669 granted religious toleration to the Jews and protected them from being assailed or libeled because of their religion. While the colony's assembly five times rejected Locke's constitution, the early settlers were tolerant of all Christian dissenters and of Jews as well. Locke's document stipulated that "heathens, Jues and other dissenters" would be entitled to the same rights as the followers of the dominant Anglican Church. It also provided that "no man shall be permitted to be a freeman of Carolina or to have any estate or habitation within it, that doth not acknowledge a God, and that God is publicly and solemnly to be worshipped." Thus only atheists were barred.

In 1697 the Colonial Assembly adopted a law aimed at improving the status of the large number of Huguenots who had settled in what is now South Carolina after 1685. The law declared that "all aliens, male and female, of what nation soever, which now are inhabitants of South Carolina" should have all the rights of anyone born of English parents. The measure also provided freedom of conscience to all Christians except Catholics but others were not to be interfered with in conducting religious services. Rabbi Abram V. Goodman notes in *American Overture,* that under the law, aliens, including Jews, were entitled to the full rights of British subjects in all respects but freedom of conscience if they applied by petition to the governor within three months after the act was adopted.

The act included a list of 64 men who had already petitioned the general assembly for the rights the law accorded. Of these, most were Huguenots, but four were Jews: Simon Vallentine, a merchant, who was the brother-in-law of Asser Levy of New York; Jacob Mears; Jacob Mendis; and Abraham Avilah. By the law of 1697 they had become naturalized British subjects. In his naturalization papers, still preserved in South Carolina, Vallentine was described as "an alien of ye Jewish Nation borne out of the Crown of England" who "hath taken his oath of allegiance to our Sovereign Lord William ye Third," Vallentine and Mears had both been in business in Jamaica but they left that West Indian island in 1692 after an earthquake that year and settled in Charleston. According to Dr. Jacob R. Marcus, of the American Jewish Archives, Vallentine was for a time a police commissioner in South Carolina, an honorary post. He was also the first Jew to own land in South Carolina, having acquired some property in 1699. In the year in which he was naturalized, Vallentine was denounced by one political faction as being an alleged go-between for the Colonial governor in a shady deal involving a payoff from a trader engaged in illegal business. Mordecai Nathan, whose name does not appear on the first naturalization list, was listed in a Charleston tax list in 1694, and may have been a Jew.

There seems to be some question as to whether even naturalized Jews had the right to vote in South Carolina in the early 1700s. In 1692, the Lords Proprietors vetoed a bill passed by the Colonial Assembly that extended the franchise to anyone who would swear that he was worth ten pounds, Rabbi Goodman says. In 1703, 150 inhabitants of Colleton County, all opponents of the Anglican party, protested to the Lords Proprietors that in the election of that year "Jews, strangers, sailors, servants, Negroes, & almost every French man in Craven and Berkley County came down to elect, & their votes were taken; & the persons by them voted for were returned by the sheriff, to the manifest wrong & prejudice of other candidates." This complaint seems to indicate that Jews were not entitled to vote but were used by the winners in the election to the detriment of the dissenters. It is hardly likely that blacks were permitted to vote in 18th century South Carolina.

A new naturalization law passed in 1704 required that a candidate for naturalization had to take an oath of allegiance to Queen Anne "on the Holy Evangelists or otherwise according to the form of his profession." The "otherwise" was the loophole which permitted Jews to vote. The new law, however, barred naturalized subjects from holding office in the Assembly, but permitted aliens to vote. In 1716 an attempt was made to limit the franchise and the right to sit in the Assembly only to Christians. This law, which the Lords Proprietors in London, repudiated would also have barred Jews from voting. A 1759 law which would have barred all but Protestants from holding office was vetoed by the Lords Proprietors, but the election law of 1721 giving the franchise only to "every free white man . . . professing the Christian religion" effectively barred Jews. In 1777, the South Carolina Assembly adopted a new constitution which excluded Jews from holding office, made Protestantism the established religion, excluded all but Protestants from membership in the Assembly and other high offices, and made only church bodies that believed in the Christian religion eligible for incorporation. All of these religious disabilities to which South Carolina's Jews were subject remained in effect until 1790 when a new constitution granted full religious equality and rights to all and extended complete civil rights to Catholics and Jews. General Christopher Gadsden, who with Charles Pinckney and Rawlin Lownds, fought for the new constitution, had learned Hebrew from Jewish fellow prisoners during their long imprisonment by the British in the Revolutionary War.

Since Jews were not restricted from engaging in any business or trade they wished, their numbers in South Carolina slowly increased. By the 1730s, Dr. Jacob Marcus cites a number of Jewish shipowners beginning to register their vessels in Charleston, and that Jewish merchants from New York and Newport discovered that Charleston was an excellent depot for distributing goods throughout the South. The activities of these merchants are traceable through their advertisements in the newspapers of that day.

By the early 1740s there were enough Jews in Charleston to hold worship services in private homes. In 1749, on the day after the High Holy Days, the arrival of discouraged Jewish settlers from Georgia gave impetus to the formation of South Carolina's first Jewish congregation, Beth Elohim Unveh Shallom (The House of God and Mansion of Peace). In 1764, the Coming Street Cemetery in Charleston, adjoining Isaac Da Costa's family burial ground, was acquired by the congregation. Between 1750 and 1757, Beth Elohim worshipped on Union Street, then on King Street, and later in Beresford Street. In 1780, Joseph Tobias gave the congregation a seven-year lease to his new house on Hasell Street in consideration of a "misheberach on every Yom Kippur night" during his lifetime. On this site, or very close to it, Beth Elohim has been worshipping ever since. Seven generations of Tobiases have been members of the congregation. The synagogue erected in 1794 was described by General Lafayette on a visit to the city as "spacious and elegant." Until it was destroyed by fire in 1838, Beth Elohim's synagogue was said to be the handsomest in America. This was one of the congregations that joined in felicitations to President George Washington, together with those in New York, Philadelphia, and Richmond. In 1784 the Hebrew Benevolent Society was founded, the earliest organization of its kind caring for the Jewish poor. In 1801, the Charleston Jews established the Hebrew Orphan Asylum, the first to place orphans in private homes.

Among the founders of Beth Elohim was Joseph Tobias who arrived in 1729 and was the first president of the congregation. He was not only a shopkeeper but an interpreter to British officials in their dealings with the Spanish in Florida. Another founder was Isaac Da Costa, who laid out the first Jewish cemetery as a family burial ground and turned it over to the congregation in 1764. In 1775 Da Costa tried to build a synagogue in Charleston but when he sought money for it from Congregation Shearith Israel in New York, he was turned down because the leaders of Shearith Israel felt that the Revolution was imminent. Da Costa served as *hazzan* of the congregation and Moses Cohen, a layman, served as "rabbi." A member of the Palmetto Society, Da Costa was a fervent patriot who believed that the colonies could survive economically without England.

One of his contemporaries was Moses Lindo, leader of the indigo industry, the second largest staple commodity of colonial South Carolina. He had been a merchant and broker in London and a member of the Royal Exchange, but left when Parliament revoked a bill that would have permitted the naturalization of British Jews. Lindo came to South Carolina in 1756, with his German Jewish clerk, Jonas Phillips, later a leader of the Philadelphia Jewish community. Lindo came to buy indigo and to send it back to his principals in London where he was a recognized expert, having testified on its value before a committee of Parliament. According to Dr. Marcus, Lindo encouraged the growth of indigo in South Carolina and improved its quality. He became a "prime channel for the flow of the dye stuff" from Charleston to Europe and was considered a one-man chamber of commerce for the promotion of indigo from South Carolina. The year he arrived indigo exports from South Carolina were valued at 350,000 pounds. After his efforts began to make themselves felt, annual indigo exports rose to over 1 million pounds. In 1762, 48 merchants and planters signed a petition to the governor urging Lindo's appointment as surveyor and inspector-general of indigo. In this unsalaried position, Lindo established standards of quality for indigo, judged the finished product, and encouraged its export.

Another founder of Beth Elohim was Joshua Hart, a successful merchant, who reached Charleston in 1762. One of his daughters, Richea, married Abraham Isaac Mendes Seixas of Georgia, son of Isaac Mendes

Seixas of Newport, Rhode Island. Abraham Seixas, too, was a well-known merchant who served as an officer with the American forces in Georgia and South Carolina.

In 1776 there were said to be only 68 Jews in Charleston, half of whom served with the American forces. A few cooperated with the British and later lost their property under South Carolina's confiscation act of 1783. There were 20 Jews from Charleston among the militia company of Captain Richard Lushington. One of them, Joseph Solomon, was killed in the Battle of Beaufort. David N. Cardozo distinguished himself in the attempt to recapture Savannah. Benjamin Nones, a radical-minded immigrant from France, made a name for himself during the siege of Charleston. Jacob de La Motta and Abraham Seixas were captains and Marks Lazarus was a sergeant-major. Ezekiel Levy, Jacob I. Cohen, and Solomon Aaron took part in the bitter South Carolina campaign. Nones and Isaac Da Costa were among the Jewish patriots ordered out of Charleston by the British after they had served with General Pulaski in the southern campaign. Mordecai Myers, who had been a merchant in Georgetown since the early 1770s, supplied General Francis Marion's American guerrillas who harassed the British in South Carolina and drove then out of Georgetown in 1781. Most of the Charleston Jews left the city during the British occupation and found refuge in Philadelphia where some of them became founders of that city's first congregation, Mikveh Israel.

The most celebrated Jewish figure in South Carolina in the early days of the American Revolution was Francis Salvador, sometimes called the "Jewish Paul Revere" because of his impassioned efforts to arouse the colonists to rebellion. Salvador, the nephew of the prominent English financier, Joseph Salvador, came to America in 1773 to manage family property in what is now Abbeville County. Born to wealth, reared in luxury, and well-traveled, he made friends with South Carolina's most prominent men of the day—Pinckney, Rutledge, and Drayton— and immediately enlisted in the cause of liberty. Impressed with his education, ability, and passionate dedication to the American cause, the leaders of the rebellion in South Carolina took him into their councils. He became a member of the first and second Provincial Assemblies which established the colony's independence. Whether he was elected—(under existing law he could not be elected unless he swore "on the holy evangelists") or appointed—Salvador was the first non-converted Jew in America to represent the people in a legislative body.

In 1776 Salvador was one of the two members of the State Assembly named to examine the new constitution after it had been engrossed and to compare it in word and meaning to the original draft. There is no indication that Salvador objected to the provision requiring the president of the Assembly to take an oath to "maintain and defend the laws of God, the Protestant religion and the liberties of America." This clause, though aimed at the Catholics, also affected the Jews.

When the British fleet attacked Charleston in 1776, Tory forces incited the Cherokee Indians to attack isolated settlements. Mounted on his horse, Salvador sped through the countryside, rousing the men of the plantations to action. While helping to defend the back country, Salvador's militia party was ambushed. He was killed and scalped on August 1, 1776, at the age of 29, near the present-day city of Clemson. Major Andrew Williamson, commander of the mounted troop in which Salvador served, included an account of his death in the official report of the battle, (see also: Charleston City Hall).

The influx of Jews from Georgia, North Carolina, and the West Indies made Charleston the largest Jewish community in the United States in 1800, with a reputed population of 500 Jews. A merchant writing in 1811 from Charleston said the Jewish population of the state was 1,000. There were also Jews in Columbia, Georgwtown, and Sumter before 1800. Abraham Cohen, son of Moses Cohen, Charleston's first "rabbi," settled in Georgetown before the Revolution. He and his brother helped supply the American guerrillas during the Revolution. A planter and secretary of the Winyah Indigo Society in 1798, Abraham Cohen was deputy postmaster of Georgetown from 1798-1800. Solomon Cohen was the town's tax collector and treasurer of the newly organized library society in 1798. The first Jewish lawyer admitted to practice in South Carolina was Moses Myers of Georgetown, who became a member of the bar in 1793 and later served as clerk of the court of general sessions.

Camden also had Jewish residents before the Revolution. Joseph Kershaw's will in 1788 left funds to the Jews of that town for a cemetery but the first congregation was not formed until 1880. Georgetown's first congregation dates from 1900. Jews settled in Columbia in 1786, soon after the Revolution. A congregation was organized in the 1830s but its synagogue was destroyed in the fire that leveled the city during General Sherman's occupation in 1865. The Female Auxiliary Jewish Society, founded in Columbia in 1823, had as its objective the colonization of Jews. The city had three Jewish mayors in the 19th century. The first Jew in Sumter, founded in 1798, was Mark Solomons, who came from Charleston sometime between 1815 and 1820. The Hebrew Cemetery was established in 1874 and the Sumter Hebrew Society dates from 1881.

At the beginning of the 19th century, Charleston was the cultural capital of America and the Jews were accepted in all levels of society. They belonged to yacht and literary clubs, edited newspapers, took sides in historic political debates, developed industry, held public office, were prominent in the professions, and served with distinction in the War of 1812, the Seminole Indian War, and the Mexican War.

Captain Abraham Seixas was a magistrate and warden of the Charleston workhouse in 1797. Myer Moses, a member of the South

Carolina Society for the Promotion of Domestic Arts and Manufactories in 1809, was elected to the state legislature in 1810 and served as commissioner of free schools in 1811. During the War of 1812 he was a major in the state militia. Lyon Levy was state treasurer in 1806 and again from 1817-1822.Dr. David Camden de Leon, an army surgeon in the Seminole Indian War and the Mexican War, resigned his commission to organize the medical department of the Confederate Army during the Civil War. Jacob de la Motta was secretary of the state medical society and of the Literary and Philosophical Society of South Carolina. Jacob Cardozo was a well-known journalist. Major Joshua Lazarus introduced illuminating gas to Charleston. Michael Lazarus opened up steamboat navigation on the Savannah River with a line between Augusta and Charleston. Solomon Solomons built the Northeastern Railroad, later merged with the Atlantic Coast Line. Dr. Elias Marks of Columbia founded the Columbia Female Academy in 1820 and later conducted the famous Barhamville School, a pioneer in higher education for women. Jacob Levy was secretary of the Charleston Riflemen during the War of 1812. Captain Isaac Cohen formed a company of volunteers to fight in the Seminole Indian War. David Camden de Leon, known as "the fighting doctor," was one of the heroes of the Mexican War. He was thanked by Congress on two occasions for his heroism in taking command of a company when all its officers were either killed or wounded and achieved a victory from almost certain defeat.

Colonel Chapman Levy, who represented Camden and Kershaw County in the state legislature from 1829-1833, was a well-known duelist. Judah P. Benjamin, later to serve as Secretary of State of the Confederate States of America and a United States Senator from Louisiana, went to Beth Elohim's religious school while his parents had a fruit shop in Charleston. When General Lafayette visited Charleston in 1825, the gold and silver plate used at the banquet tendered him was borrowed from Mordecai Cohen. Jacob Clavius Levy, an observant Jew whose father, Moses, came to Charleston after the Revolutionary period, became rich as a merchant. At the age of 90 in 1838, he rushed into the burning Beth Elohim synagogue to save the Torahs. Other pre-Civil War Jewish notables were Isaac Harby, dramatist, journalist, and literary critic; Abraham de Leon, eminent physician; Penina Moise, poetess and hymn writer; and Reverend Hartwig Cohen, cantor of Beth Elohim from 1812-1823, who was the great-grandfather of Bernard M. Baruch. In 1824, 47 members of Beth Elohim petitioned the synagogue elders to shorten the service, to pray in English rather than in Hebrew and Spanish, and to have a sermon in English. When the trustees rejected these requests, 12 of the dissenters organized "the Reformed Society of Israelites," the first Reform congregation in the United States.

Jews were actively involved in the fight over South Carolina's nullification of the 1828 and 1832 tariff acts which the state bitterly opposed because it favored free trade. Among the leaders of the State's Rights party were Myer M. Cohn, the party secretary; Myer Jacobs of Beaufort; Aaron Lopez of Winyaw; and Benjamin Hart of Lexington. Active in the Union party which opposed nullification were Franklin J. Moses; Nathan Hart; Chapman Levy; Abraham Moises; Jacob de la Motta; Joshua Lazarus; and M.C. Myers. At the 1832 convention which passed the ordinance of nullification, Phillip Cohen and Myer Jacobs voted in favor and Phillip Phillips, later a member of Congress from Alabama, and Chapman Levy voted against. So many Jews were active in both parties that 84 Jews signed a letter to the *Charleston Courier* in 1832 asserting that they did not wish to be represented as a sect in the nullification debate. Jacob Levy, who opposed nullification in the 1860s wrote an article (it remains to be published and is in the American Jewish Archives), titled *Vindiciae Judeaorum* (Vindication of Jewry), in which he suggested that England or France might want to reestablish the Jews in Palestine for purely political and strategic reasons.

In November, 1844, the Jews of Charleston protested vigorously against the governor's Thankgiving Day proclamation which referred to the United States as a Christian nation and called on Christian denominations to give thanks in the name of Jesus Christ. At a protest meeting on November 16, it was agreed to send a letter to the governor, which was signed by 100 leading Jewish citizens. In a belated reply, the governor refused to apologize and went even further by asserting that the United States was a Christian state in which non-Christians were merely tolerated.

So many Charleston Jews served in the Confederate forces during the Civil War that from 1862 until the end of the war, Beth Elohim suspended trustee meetings because it was impossible to obtain a quorum. In some families, every male member capable of bearing arms was in uniform. Of the 182 Charleston Jews who saw action, 25 were killed. Abraham C. Myers, a West Point graduate who served with General Zachary Taylor in the Mexican War, was commanding general of the Quartermaster Department at New Orleans when the Civil War began. He resigned his commission and became the Confederacy's first quartermaster general. Harassed by shortages and critical commanders, Myers was blamed for Confederate losses and he was removed by Jefferson Davis in 1863. David Camden de Leon resigned his United States Army commission to become the first surgeon general of the Confederate medical department. His elder brother, Edwin, a lawyer who had practiced in Washington where he edited a pro-slavery newspaper, became one of the chief propagandists of the Confederate States of America. In 1861 he ran the Union blockade to reach Europe as a special envoy to France and England. Before the war he had been United States consul general in Egypt.

Dr. Columbus Davega, a native of Charleston who had served with the Russian forces as a military doctor at the siege of Sebastopol in the Crimean War, was a surgeon in the 23rd regiment of the Confederate army. He operated a floating hospital attached to a floating battery. Moses Mordecai used some of his ships as blockade runners. In the 1870s he visited the battlefields where Confederate dead had been temporarily buried and brought back the remains and arranged for their interment in the South. At the outbreak of the war, Benjamin Mordecai gave $10,000 to South Carolina's war chest. He also organized a free market which fed hundreds of needy families whose breadwinners were at the front. Mordecai also invested most of his fortune in Confederate bonds.

Before the Civil War, Charleston Jews were exceedingly prominent in Masonry. In fact, Jewish Masons were responsible for Charleston becoming "the see city" of the Masonic Order. Isaac da Costa, a member of King Solomon's Lodge No. 1 since 1753, founded the Supreme Grand Lodge of Perfection in 1783. Abraham Alexander, Emanuel de la Motta, Isaac de Leibon, and Moses C. Levy helped organize the Supreme Council of the Scottish Rite of Freemansonry.

Dr. Simon Baruch, father of Bernard M. Baruch, served with distinction in the Civil War. He was 15 when he came to Camden from Germany and went to work in the store of Mannes Baum. Baum sent Baruch to the South Carolina Medical School in Charleston. When the war closed the school, he went to the Medical College of Virginia to complete his studies, after which he joined the 3rd South Carolina Battalion, taking part in the Second Battle of Manassas. Throughout the war he served in General Robert E. Lee's Army of Northern Virginia except when he was taken prisoner while tending the wounded in field hospitals. As a prisoner he helped the Union doctors. His essay on *Bayonet Wounds of the Chest*, written while he was a prisoner of war in Fort McHenry, is still the standard authority on the subject. He was captured again by the troops of General Sherman on his march to the sea. After the war Baruch made his way back to Camden on crutches where he practiced medicine for 15 years. During the Reconstruction period he joined General Nathan Forrest's Ku Klux Klan. In 1873 he was elected president of the South Carolina Medical Society. He moved to New York in 1881 where he became the first doctor to pre-operatively diagnose a case of ruptured appendix.

David Lopez, who built the present synagogue of Beth Elohim, invented a torpedo boat called the *David*, which damaged many Union warships in 1863. M.C. Mordecai's ship, the *Isabel*, was converted into a Confederate blockade runner. Major Edwin Moises, who opposed secession, nevertheless organized and equipped a cavalry company.

During the Reconstruction era Franklin J. Moses, son of Major Myer Moses, who had served in the state legislature from 1842-1862 and in the Confederate army, alienated many of his friends and Confederate associates by accepting an appointment as chief justice of the South Carolina

Supreme Court. When his son, Franklin J. Moses, Jr., whose mother was not Jewish and who was raised as a Christian, was elected governor in 1872, many of the Moses family in South Carolina and Georgia, whether related to him or not and who had all been Confederate patriots, changed their family name. Some of his second cousins adopted old South Carolina names such as Harby and De Leon. Justice Moses was a member of the Charleston Hebrew Benevolent Society before the Civil War, but Governor Moses had no Jewish associations. The Jewish community, however, was as outraged at his scandal-ridden administration as the rest of the state and was greatly relieved when he left office a bankrupt in 1875. Francis Lewis Cardozo of Charleston, a member of the South Carolina constitutional convention in 1868, and who later served as Secretary of State and State Treasurer, was a member of the same Jewish family to which the late United States Supreme Court Justice Benjamin N. Cardozo belonged. Francis Cardozo, however, was the son of a Charleston Jewish economist and a black woman.

Twelve years after the Civil War, half of the Jewish population of South Carolina numbering 1,415 lived in Charleston. There were also smaller Jewish communities in Sumter, Columbia, Darlington, Beaufort, Aiken, Florence, Georgetown and Orangeburg. By 1900 the Jewish population had risen to 2,500, with 1,500 in Charleston. Six cities had one or more Jewish institutions but only two boasted of year-round congregations. On the eve of World War II, the Jewish population had grown to 4,800. Charleston had 1,900, Columbia 281, and 77 smaller cities and towns accounted for 2,635. Thereafter the Jewish population continued to grow but slowly, reaching 6,851 in 1927, falling off to 3,780 in 1948, and then climbing again to 7,285 in 1970 and 7,485 in 1977. Charleston is still the largest Jewish community, with 3,100 Jews, followed by Columbia, the state capital, with 1,800, Greenville with 600, Sumter with 190, Florence with 370, Spartanburg with 225, Beaufort with 130, Orangeburg with 105, Aiken with 100, and Georgetown with 75. There are some 35 towns with from 10 to 50 Jews and 45 towns with ten or less Jews.

The second Jew elected to the South Carolina state legislature, Dr. Levi Myers from Georgetown and Charleston, was elected in 1796. Later he was appointed the state's apothecary-general and he was also a member of the Library Society of Georgetown, founded in 1799. Other Jews who served in the state legislature before the Civil War were: Myer Moses, 1810; Franklin Moses, 1810; Chapman Levy, 1812-1817; Solomon Cohen, 1831-1834; Myer Jacobs, 1833-1838; Mordecai Levy, 1834-1840; Moses C. Mordecai, 1845-1847 and 1855-1858   and Meir Hirsch, 1876.

Probably the most important Jew in South Carolina politics was Sol Blatt of Barnwell, whose father, Nathan, an immigrant from Russia, was a pack peddler based in Blackwell, beginning in 1893. Sol Blatt served in the state legislature for more than 40 years and retired as speaker of the lower house in 1973, after serving in that post for 36 years, longer than anyone else in any other state. Blatt, one of the state's most powerful political figures for a generation and a half, was a militant supporter of segregation policies. He married a Christian and his son, Sol Blatt, Jr., was appointed a United States District Court judge by President Richard Nixon in 1971.

August Kohn, a reporter on the *Charleston News and Courier* from 1889-1892, and later head of the paper's Columbia bureau, gained fame for his objective coverage of the state legislature. Son of a German-born Confederate veteran and a mother who headed a South Carolina unit of the United Daughters of the Confederacy in 1909, he was a strong opponent of lynching. His daughter, Mrs. Julian Hennig, was one of the founders of the Association of Southern Women for the Prevention of Lynching in 1930. Kohn was defeated for reelection to the board of trustees of the University of South Carolina in 1924 because the general assembly which conducted the election had 34 members of the Ku Klux Klan.

Josiah Morse, appointed professor of philosophy at the University of South Carolina in 1911, was an early advocate of civil rights for blacks. In 1912, he urged the University Race Commission, on which he served, to pressure colleges in the South to offer courses on race relations which he taught. In 1919, he toured Southern cities to rally support for the Commission on Interracial Cooperation which admitted black and white women in 1920.

Klyde Robinson, a former president of the Charleston Jewish Community Center, served as United States Attorney for South Carolina in the 1960s. Max Heller, who came to Greenville, South Carolina, as a penniless 19-year old refugee from Nazi-occupied Austria, was elected mayor of the state's largest city in 1971. Before his retirement in 1968, his shirt factory was a major economic force in the community and he was widely known as a progressive employer and civic leader. Other Jewish mayors were Sam Mass, Selma, 1887-1890; Dr. Oscar Alexander, Columbia, 1931-1937; Herman Mazursky, Barnwell, 1938-1970; Abraham Alexander, Columbia, 1897-1899; Mordecai H. de Leon, Columbia, 1833-1836; and Henry Lyons, 1850-1855. From 1925-1944, David Witcover headed the South Carolina State Fair. In 1969, while a third-year law student, Arnold Goodstein of Charleston was elected to the state legislature where he helped to create a labor-black coalition. Mrs. Anita Politzer of Charleston was one of the leaders of the suffrage movement and served as an officer of the National Women's party.

In 1975, the Charleston Jewish community fought to prevent the Arab-owned Coastal Shores, Inc., from winning a zoning variance that would enable it to build a $250 million residential and tourist complex on Kiawah Island, the city's last undeveloped barrier island. A company owned by Kuwait had acquired the island in 1974 for $17 million. While the Jewish community lost the zoning fight, it did succeed in persuading the county council to incorporate in the rezoning ordinance an injunction against any form of discrimination by the Arab owners or their American agents. The commitment made by the general manager of the Kiawah Beach Co., the American firm named by the Arabs to handle the project, to the chairman of the community relations committee of the Charleston Jewish Federation, reads as follows: "The Kiawah Beach Company, on behalf of the owners and developers of Kiawah Island, affirms a non-discriminatory policy as to race, color, creed, religion, sex, or national origin in all activities concerned with the development, business concerns, sales of property, facilities; and further, will abide with the letter and intent of the laws of South Carolina and the United States."

* * * * *

AIKEN
Cong. Adath Yeshurun, 900-B Greenville St., N.W.

ANDERSON
Temple B'nai Israel, Oakland Ave.

BARNWELL
Solomon Blatt Gymnasium is named for the Russian immigrant peddler's son who was speaker of the South Carolina House of Representatives from 1937-1947 and again from 1951-1973, when he retired, having enjoyed the longest tenure as speaker in any state legislative body in the U.S.

BEAUFORT
Cong. Beth Israel, Scott St.

CAMDEN
Camden Hospital was a gift of Bernard M. Baruch, noted financier and adviser to Presidents, in memory of his father, Dr. Simon Baruch. The hospital trustees wanted to name the institution for Dr. Baruch, but his son dissuaded them. A plaque in honor of Bernard M. Baruch's mother is in the nurses' home of the hospital.
Cong. Beth El.
Ivy Lodge, 1205 Broad St., is the birthplace of Bernard M. Baruch. Baruch's father, a surgeon in the Confederate army, is credited by the New York Academy of Science with the development of the appendectomy.

CHARLESTON
Addlestone Hebrew Academy, 182 Rutledge Ave.
Leon Banov Building of Charleston County Health Center, 10 Lockwood Dr., headquarters of the County Department of Health, memorializes Dr. Leon Banov, the county's first public health officer and head of

the County Health Department from 1921 until his retirement in 1961. A bronze plaque in the lobby includes a bas-relief of Banov and a brief biography. His portrait hangs in the center's library. Dr. Banov is said to have been responsible for the first pasteurization act in the world, enacted by the city of Charleston. He served as president of the Southern Medical Society and of the International Society of Medical Health Officers.

Brith Sholom Beth Israel Cong., 182 Rutledge Ave., is believed to be the oldest existing Orthodox synagogue in the South and one of the oldest in the country, having been organized in 1854.

Center Talk, Jewish Community Center, 1645 Millbrook Dr.

Charleston Hebrew Institute, 182 Rutledge Ave.

Coming Street Cemetery of Cong. Beth Elohim, 189 Coming St., the oldest Jewish cemetery in the South and the largest pre-Revolutionary Jewish burial ground, dates from 1762. Comprising some three quarters of an acre and surrounded by an old red brick wall, the cemetery is the last resting place of many of the notable Jews of the community which by the early 1800s was the largest, most cultured, and wealthiest Jewish community in America. There are some 600 tombstones in the cemetery, many of the older ones being flat slabs, some lying directly on the ground, but most rest on raised brick foundations. The oldest tombstone is that of Moses Cohen, a prominent merchant and "learned Jew" who served as Beth Elohim's first "rabbi." He died in 1762 when the cemetery was the private burial ground of Isaac Da Costa. Also buried here are the Rev. Hartwig Cohen, rabbi of Beth Elohim from 1818-1823, who was the maternal great-grandfather of Bernard M. Baruch, nine Revolutionary War veterans, five veterans of the War of 1812, and eight Confederate soldiers. The cemetery is said to be the only Jewish burial ground in the U.S. without a Star of David on any monument. In 1962, Bernard M. Baruch contributed $1,000 toward the restoration of this historic cemetery.

Cong. Kahal Kodosh Beth Elohim, 86-90 Hasell St., organized the day after Rosh Hashanah in 1749, is the oldest congregation in the state and one of the four or five oldest in the country. It was also the starting point, in 1824, of Reform Judaism in America. In the fire of 1838 that nearly wiped out all of Charleston, the synagogue was destroyed. In 1824, Isaac Harby, journalist, dramatist, literary critic, and Jewish teacher, led a group of 47 members who asked for shorter services and the use of English in the liturgy and sermon. When this was refused, Harby and his associates organized the Reformed Society of Israelites. Seventeen years later, while a new synagogue was under construction, another group petitioned the trustees for an organ in the synagogue. Although Rabbi Gustavus Poznanski supported the petition, the request was rejected by the board which was overruled by the membership. The "organ controversy," as it came to be known, caused a split in the congregation. Forty members withdrew, formed Congregation Shearith Israel, and erected their own synagogue. In 1866, however, this congregation disbanded and the members rejoined Beth Elohim. The present building, dedicated in March, 1843, was built by David Lopez. It is a model of Grecian Doric architecture. Over its doors is a marble tablet bearing the inscription of the *Shema* in Hebrew with an English translation. Remnants from the old synagogue include a wrought iron fence and gateway and the marble tablet with the *Shema*. Two murals are on the walls of the Bicentennial Tabernacle, dedicated in 1949, which serves as a religious school and social center. One mural is entitled *Founding of Beth Elohim, 1749*. The second mural is entitled *Patriots of Beth Elohim*. There are also two sculptures depicting Biblical prophets. Among the congregation's members were the parents of Judah P. Benjamin (see Louisiana). Judah himself attended the Hebrew Orphan Society's school for children of the poor. The parents of Bernard M. Baruch were also members.

In Beth Elohim's Archives Room is a permanent exhibit of materials dealing with the history of the Jews of Charleston since 1695. Among the items on exhibit are the original parchment grant of arms from the British Government, dated 1745, to the family of Francis Salvador; old minute books; rare documents; manuscripts; pictures; and other historic materials.

Lee C. Harby Memorial Tablet, in the old Exchange Building, at the foot of Broad St., was erected by the Daughters of the American Revolution in honor of the poet, author, historian, and educator who is credited with having written the official song of Texas. She was the niece of Isaac Harby, prime mover in the creation of the Reformed Society of Israelites.

Hebrew Institute, 182 Rutledge Ave.

Hillel Foundation, The Citadel, care of Brith Sholom Beth Israel Cong.

Holocaust Memorial, a plaque honoring the memory of the 6,000,000 Jews who died in the Nazi Holocaust, is in the garden of the Jewish Community Center, 1645 Millbrook Ave. It was erected by the Kalushiner Society.

Hunley Museum, 50 Broad St., a branch of the Charleston Museum, displays a replica of a torpedo boat called the *David*, which was invented by David Lopez, builder of Beth Elohim's synagogue. Armed with a single torpedo, the vessel severely damaged the USS *Ironsides* in the Charleston Harbor in 1863.

Jewish Community Center, 1645 Millbrook Ave.

Jewish Welfare Fund, 1645 Millbrook Ave.

Old Jewish Orphanage, 88 Broad St., founded in 1802 by the Hebrew Orphan Society, is a city landmark acquired by the society in 1833. Formerly the home of the First Bank of the U.S., the building dates from the Revolution. It was used as a temporary synagogue after the fire of 1838 destroyed Beth Elohim, as relief headquarters during the yellow fever epidemic of 1858, as a Jewish school, an orphan home, and a Federal court. In 1931 it was sold and became an office building. A plaque placed in the building by the Charleston Historical Commission notes the building's connection with the Hebrew Orphan Society. In 1951, the Hebrew Orphan Society and the Hebrew Benevolent Society, founded in 1784, merged into the Charleston Jewish Social Service, the community's case work agency.

Francis Salvador Marker, in City Hall Park, a bronze plaque mounted on a granite shaft in front of one of the east wall arches, not far from the monument to General Pierre Beauregard, memorializes Francis Salvador, probably the first Jew to die for American independence.

On the marker in City Hall Park are these words:
> Born an aristocrat, he became a democrat—An Englishman, he cast his lot with America; True to his ancient faith, he gave his life for new hopes of human liberty and understanding.

Synagogue Emanu-El, 78 Gordon St.

Unitarian Church, 4 Archdale St., has on one of its stained glass windows, the Hebrew words, Adonai Echod (the Lord is One).

CHESTER

Simmons Memorial, a large engraved stone in front of the Chester Courthouse was erected by non-Jews as a memorial to Jack Simmons, a childless Jewish merchant who loved children. Simmons was described as "a lovable character, friend to all." The stone is inscribed: "In memoriam Jack Simmons, 1926."

CLEMSON

Fort Rutledge, on the campus of Clemson Agricultural College, is sometimes referred to as Fort Salvador after Francis Salvador, the Jewish patriot of the Revolution.

COLUMBIA

Cong. Beth Sholom, 4536 Trenholm Rd.

Hebrew Benevolent Society Cemetery, cor. Gadsden and Richland Sts., has a plaque on the corner memorializing the society's origin in 1826. Jews first settled here in 1786 when the city became the state capital. The town's first synagogue was destroyed by fire when General Sherman bombarded the city in 1865.

Jewish Community Center, 4540 Trenholm Rd.

Jewish Welfare Federation, 4540 Trenholm Rd.

South Carolina Confederate Relic Room, 1430 Senate St., displays a photograph of Dr. Simon Baruch and of his field hospital on the Gettysburg battlefield which he surrendered on July 5, 1863.

State House, the Capitol of South Carolina, has hanging in the chamber of the House of Representatives portraits of four notable Southerners,

among them Solomon Blatt, Speaker of the House for more than 30 years, who was so powerful in state affairs, that he was known as "King Sol" to the legislators; and Bernard M. Baruch. A new state office building in Columbia will bear Blatt's name.
Tree of Life Temple, 2701 Heyward St.

University of South Carolina
● Belle W. Baruch Coastal Research Institute, is named for the eldest of Bernard M. Baruch's children, who established the Belle W. Baruch Foundation. The institute, founded in 1969 with the aid of a grant from the foundation, engages in research and teaching programs in marine science. Miss Baruch also gave the Institute Hobcaw Barony, the 17,500 acre estate bordering Winyah Bay, North Inlet, and the Atlantic Ocean, near Georgetown, which her father acquired in the early 1900s.
● Baruch Silver Collection, in the University Museum, World War Memorial Bldg., Bull and Senate Sts., a valuable collection of largely 18th century silver, was given to the University by Bernard M. Baruch's executrix in 1965. It includes a number of historic pieces as well as a Chinese filigree silver dish given to Baruch by Mme. Chiang Kai-shek, and a loving cup presented to Baruch in 1915 when he was head of the War Industries Board.
● Blatt Physical Education Center honors Solomon Blatt, an alumnus and trustee of the university who was one of its most zealous supporters in the state legislature.
● Rabbi David Gruber Collection, 7,200 volumes of Judaica in the University's library, was presented in 1971 by the sons of Rabbi David Gruber, who was rabbi of Columbia's Tree of Life Temple when he died in 1970.
● Hillel Foundation, University of South Carolina, 606 Security Federal Building.

DILLON
Cong. Ohav Shalom, 10th and Calhoun Sts.

FLORENCE
. Temple Beth Israel, 316 Park Ave.

GEORGETOWN
Hebrew Cemetery, cor. Duke and Broad Sts., is one of the oldest Jewish cemeteries in the country. Some gravestones ante-date the Declaration of Independence.
Harold Kaminski Home, 1003 Front St., which dates from 1760, is one of the city's most beautiful restored residences overlooking the Sampit River.
Temple Beth Elohim, Screven St.

GREENVILLE
Beth Israel Center, 425 Summit Dr.
Temple of Israel, 115 Buist Ave.

KINGTREE
Temple Beth-Or, 107 Hirsch St.

LEVY
A crossroads village in Jasper County, about seven miles from Hardeeville, is in the southeastern corner of the state. On local and state maps it is variously called Levys, Levy Station, and Levi. The Levy for whom the place is named appears to be unknown even to Professor Claude Henry Neuffer, editor of *Names in South Carolina*, and Mrs. Grace Fox Perry, author of *Moving Finger of Jasper*.

The place appears to have been named for a Levy family which owned a large general store located at a crossroads in Jasper County. In the early 1900s, a branch line of the Seaboard Railway passed the store and the place was then called Levy's Station. In the 1940s it became a post office called Levy, which was discontinued in the 1950s. On April 8, 1976, the United States Board on Geographic Names approved the name Levy for the same locality and it is listed on current South Carolina highway maps. The South Carolina State Planning Board reported the existence in 1943 of a place called Levy in Beaufort County, which adjoins Jasper County, but the Board of Geographic Names has been unable to locate this place.

It is possible that the places called Levy were named for a Union officer, Col. Simon Levy, who commanded a regiment at St. Helena Island, South Carolina. Both Simon Levy and his sons, Capt. Ferdinand Levy, Lt. Alfred Levy, and Sgt. Benjamin C. Levy all served in the Union forces. It is possible that a Union topographer named a place for the Levys after the fighting ceased.

MYRTLE BEACH
Temple Emanu-El, 65th St., N.

ORANGEBURG
Temple Sinai, 800 Ellis Ave., N.E.

ROCK HILL
Joslin Park, on Mt. Gallant Rd., Route 4, is a public recreational area on the Catawba River, with facilities for boating and swimming, named for Archie O. Joslin, a New England textile mill owner, who established the park. An oil painting of him hangs over the fireplace in the park's redwood center. Joslin was one of the leaders of the Rhode Island Jewish Federation in Providence.

Temple Beth El, 100 E. Main St.

SPARTANBURG
Cong. B'nai Israel, 145 Heywood St.

SUMMERVILLE
Saul Alexander Memorial Playground was established through bequests of Saul Alexander, Jewish merchant and philanthropist, who died in 1952. His $750,000 estate was bequesthed to Jewish and non-Jewish charities.

SUMTER
Cong. Sinai, 11 Church St., is an outgrowth of the Sumter Hebrew Benevolent Society, organized in 1881 by the founders of the Hebrew Cemetery Society, whose burial ground was acquired in 1874. Many of the founders and leaders of the congregation were prominent citizens who have had streets named for them: Moise Dr. for David deLeon Moise, father of Mrs. Herbert A. Rosefield; Marion Ave. for Marion Moise, granddaughter of Mrs. Rosefield; Harby Ave. for Horace Harby, Mrs. Rosefield's maternal grandfather; Levi St. for the Levi family; Barnett St. for B. J. Barnett; and Phelps St. for A. C. Phelps. The land on which the Sumter County Courthouse stands was formerly the site of the home of Mr. and Mrs. A. S. Solomons, who donated the courthouse site.

WALTERBORO
Temple Mount Sinai, Neyle St.

Tennessee

There were no white settlements within the present borders of Tennessee at the time Sir Alexander Cuming, a Scotsman, conceived a fantastic scheme for colonizing 300,000 Jewish families from Europe "as industrious honest subjects," in what is now eastern Tennessee. Between 1740 and 1750, a century before the state's first Jewish community was established, Cuming fathered the chimerical venture for transporting the equivalent of 1,000,000 Jews over a period of two decades to the wilderness area of western Virginia and North Carolina, now part of Tennessee.

In 1730, Cuming had explored the Cherokee lands in the back country of Virginia and North Carolina, winning the friendship of the Indians and prevailing upon them to sign a treaty with the British. This achievement, plus the fact that the royal house of Hanover was greatly indebted to him and his father, were the genesis of Cuming's visionary plan, which he proposed to finance by establishing banks in Colonial America. Cuming had in mind personal profit, the development of a vast and unknown region by British subjects, the repayment of some $400 million of the British national debt, and the ultimate conversion of Jews and Indians to Christianity. The quixotic project, which Cuming had also discussed with some eminent London Jews, was rejected by the government of George II.

Tennessee's earliest white settlers established themselves along the Wautega, Holston, Clinch, Nolichucky, and Cumberland Rivers, beginning in 1769, in the very region where Cuming had hoped to colonize European Jews. There were no known Jews among Tennessee's pioneers, who came mostly from Virginia and North Carolina. Individual Jews were in and out of Virginia and North Carolina during the 18th century, and some writers have expressed the belief that a few Jews may have been trading in Hawkins County along the Holston River, in northeastern Tennessee about 1778. One or two may even have penetrated as far west as the Tennessee River, in their dealings with the Indians after North Carolina and Virginia (both claimed Tennessee) made peace with the Cherokees.

Peddlers moving north from New Orleans and the river towns of Mississippi, south from St. Louis, and west from Cincinnati and Louisville in the late 1830s and early 1840s, together with scions of old established Jewish families in the South, were probably the first Jewish settlers in Tennessee. There were Jews in Memphis and Nashville before 1845. Settlement in Chattanooga dates from the 1850s. Joseph J. Andrews, who came from Charleston, South Carolina, in the 1840s, is credited with being the founder of the Memphis Jewish community, the first and largest in the state. Son-in-law of Haym Salomon, the Revolutionary War patriot, Andrews gave the Jewish residents of Memphis several acres on Bass Avenue for a cemetery in 1847. To administer this property, the Hebrew Benevolent Society was organized in 1850. The first buried in the cemetery was Andrews' brother, while Andrews' son, Joseph G., is believed to have been the first Jew born in Memphis. Under the auspices of the Hebrew Benevolent Society, religious services were conducted on the High Holy Days until Congregation B'nai Israel was formed in 1853. While B'nai Israel is the oldest existing congregation in Tennessee, it was not the first. A short-lived congregation founded in Bolivar preceded it in 1851.

A hall in a building on Front Street was B'nai Israel's first house of worship. A $2,000 bequest from Judah Touro of New Orleans (see Louisiana), in 1854 was invested in a lot, and four years later the former Farmers and Mechanics Bank Building on Main and Exchange Streets was dedicated as the first synagogue in Tennessee. The Reverend Jacob J. Peres, who came to Memphis in 1858, was the first reader, *schochet*, and teacher. After ending his ministry at B'nai Israel in 1860, Peres taught in a secular school from whose halls a whole class marched off to join the Confederacy in 1861. The school was maintained by B'nai Israel from 1863-1868. Peres was the founder of Congregation Beth El Emeth in 1864, an offshoot of B'nai Israel with which it was reunited in 1882 (another Beth Emeth was formed in 1916), and was president of the Memphis board of education in 1866. Years later, his son, Israel, held the same office.

The same act of the legislature that incorporated Memphis' B'nai Israel in 1854 also chartered Nashville's first congregation, Khal Kodesh Magen David. A Hebrew Benevolent Society had been founded in Nashville a year earlier. In 1862, a second Nashville congregation, B'nai

Jeshurun, was organized. Both groups barely survived the Civil War, and in 1868 they were merged with Khal Kodesh Chavai Sholom, sometimes called the Vine Street Temple. When its first temple was dedicated in 1874, former President Andrew Johnson was one of the speakers.

There were a number of Jewish families listed in Knoxville's first directory published in1859 when the town had 3,000 people, but the community had no corporate existence until the close of the Civil War. When the bodies of two Knoxville Jewish boys—Joseph Schwab and Isaac Stern —who died fighting in the Confederate Army, were brought home for burial, the Jewish residents acquired a cemetery plot and organized the Hebrew Benevolent Society in 1864. For several years the society conducted religious services in the basement of a vinegar store, with the worshipers sitting on vinegar barrels. In 1877 the society changed its name to Temple Beth El. Its first synagogue was not dedicated until 1914. Jewish settlement in Chattanooga dates from 1858. A Hebrew Benevolent Society organized in 1866 later became Mizpah Congregation.

One of the leaders of Knoxville's Hebrew Benevolent Society was Julius Ochs, father of Adolph S. Ochs. Julius Ochs was a cultured youth of 18, fluent in six languages, including Hebrew, when he arrived from Germany in 1845, and immediately volunteered for service in the Mexican War. After teaching school and dabbling in business in Mississippi and Kentucky, he settled in Cincinnati with his bride, the former Bertha Levy of Nashville. Mrs. Ochs, too, was a woman of excellent education. Her family, which was related to Achille Fould, minister of finance in the government of Napoleon III, had fled Germany after the revolution of 1848.

The Civil War found Julius and Bertha Ochs with divided loyalties, as was the case throughout Tennessee, a border state. Mr. Ochs. whose brother was in the Confederate Army, was a strong Confederate sympathizer. Julius Ochs enlisted in the 52nd Ohio Infantry and was a captain at the end of the war. In 1865, Captain Ochs took his family to Knoxville, where he opened a drapery shop. More of a scholar than a businessman, Ochs reluctantly permitted his eldest son, Adolph, to go to work at the age of eleven, and even more reluctantly permitted an advertisement in the *Knoxville Register*, "To the Ladies of Knoxville and Vicinity—Mrs. Bertha Ochs and Miss Fannie Levy will give lessons in embroidery, needlework and all other kinds of ladies' fancy work; sewing, fine-stitching, etc. Having been educated in one of the best academies of Europe, they feel confident that they will give general satisfaction. Their method is simple and easy. Terms will be liberal. Apply to Mrs. Ochs, Cumberland St., near the corner of Market."

Almost from the day he settled in Knoxville, Captain Ochs served as the lay reader of the Jewish Congregation. Virtually bankrupted by the Southern panic of 1867, he was successively an insurance salesman, justice of the peace, United States commissioner, and manager of a German theatre. From 1868-1875, he served as judge of the Bridge County Court, probably the first Jew to hold public office in the state. Ochs was delegate from Tennessee to the 1872 Liberal Republican convention that nominated Horace Greeley for President. When Ochs moved to Chattanooga in 1878, after his son Adolph became publisher of the *Chattanooga Times*, the only Jewish organization in the city was the Hebrew Benevolent Society. For ten years Julius Ochs was the lay reader at all services conducted by the Society, which became the Congregation Mizpah in 1881.

With less than a decade of existence behind them at the beginning of the Civil War, the Jewish communities of Tennessee found themselves the principal victims of the utterly ineffective efforts of the Federal government to shut off the illicit commercial traffic with the Confederacy. Because of its strategic location, Memphis was the focal point of this trade in which public officials, army officers, and civilian speculators made fortunes selling vast quantities of goods to the South in exchange for the cotton the Union blockade kept from being exported to Europe.

On November 9, 1862, five months after the Union forces captured Memphis and proclaimed martial law, General Ulysses S. Grant sent orders from LaGrange, Tennessee, to Major General Stephen A. Hurlbut at Jackson, Tennessee, to "refuse all permits to come South of Jackson for the present. The Israelites especially should be kept out." The following day Grant instructed General Webster at Jackson to "give orders to all the conductors on the road that no Jews are to be permitted to travel on the railroad southward from any point. They may go North and be encouraged in it; but they are such an intolerable nuisance that the department must be purged of them."

These instructions paved the way for Grant's notorious Order No. 11 decreeing the expulsion of all Jews from the military Department of Tennessee, which included northern Mississippi, and all territory in Kentucky and Mississippi west of the Tennessee River (see Kentucky and Mississippi for the effects of this order and Jewish reaction to it). Some Jews undoubtedly violated the regulations and engaged in smuggling, but their role in the lucrative but forbidden traffic was minor. Those known to be engaged in it were bitterly and publicly denounced by the rabbis and other Jewish leaders. At the very time Grant's order was issued, hundreds of Jews in both the Union and Confederate armies were on active duty in the area from which Jews were to be expelled. Moreover, of the approximately 2,000 Jews then residing in Tennessee, some 40 were fighting with Tennessee regiments on both sides of the conflict. Of these, seven were killed in action, two died in prison, and three were wounded.

A number of Memphis Jews who were arrested and imprisoned for alleged violations of the regulations were, as Dr. Bertram W. Korn shows in *American Jewry and the Civil War*, victims of prejudice. General Hurlbut's Order No. 162, issued in Memphis on November 30, 1863, prohibited

15 clothing stores "reported to have stocks of military clothing on hand, and not having the necessary authority to trade in same from these headquarters," from selling these stocks and ordered them to send their merchandise north of the lines of the Department of Tennessee. All 15 stores were owned by Jews, but two non-Jewish stores were not included in the prohibition. Since "only Jews" and not all traders were "banished," and in view of the fact that "cotton traders as a group were never expelled," Korn concludes that the Jews were the scapegoats while "the other traders and speculators, civilian and military, stood to profit."

Jewish resentment against the "most sweeping anti-Jewish regulation in all American history," was directed largely at the military and lower political echelons. When Lincoln was assassinated, expressions of grief among the Jews of Tennessee were profound, for they remembered how promptly he had rescinded Grant's order. Both Memphis congregations joined with other denominations in a joint memorial service in the city park, and the entire membership of the Memphis lodge of B'nai B'rith marched in the funeral procession.

When General Grant ran for President in 1868, Jewish feeling against him was still strong in Tennessee. In Memphis, the largest city in the area affected by Order No. 11, this sentiment expressed itself in the form of an unprecedented public mass meeting at which the Jewish community, under rabbinical leadership, adopted resolutions assailing Grant "as a man unfit for the high position to which he aspires, and incapable of administering the laws to all classes with impartiality and without prejudice." Pledging all those present to "use every honorable means," to defeat Grant, and urging other Jewish communities throughout the country to follow suit (only Nashville did), the meeting was probably the first and only time in which a Jewish community as a whole took such action in an American Presidential election.

The Ku Klux Klan of Reconstruction days was founded in Tennessee in 1865. One of the victims of Klan violence against carpetbaggers was S.A. Bierfield, a young Russian Jew who owned a dry goods store at Franklin, about 50 miles from Pulaski, where the KKK was born. Bierfield was an active Republican known for his friendly attitude to the emancipated blacks, one of whom he employed as a clerk. One night in 1868, masked horsemen broke into Bierfield's house, dragged him into the street, and prepared to hang him. The young Jew managed to escape, taking refuge in a livery stable, but the Klansmen caught him and he was shot.

Before, during, and after the Civil War, Jews also settled in some of the state's smaller towns and cities. Jacob Felsenthal opened a general store in Brownsville in 1848 and Meyer Sternberger settled there in 1865, three years before the formation of Congregation Adas Israel. After the war Jews began settling in Clarksville, Jackson, and Columbia. Jacob J. Noah, who had been a lawyer, politician, and landowner in St. Paul, Minnesota, 12 years before the Civil War, came to Tennessee after the war as a carpet-bagger, serving as one of the state's special attorneys-general.

Although some of the fiercest battles of the Civil War had been fought on the soil of Tennessee, it made a faster recovery than any other of the seceding states. Consequently, the cities, particularly Memphis, enjoyed a postwar boom that brought large numbers of businessmen, cotton traders, and professionals, among them Jews, from the East and other parts of the war-ravaged South. By 1877, Tennessee was estimated to have 4,000 Jews and nine congregations. So many young Jews were in business as storekeepers or peddlers in the small towns of Tennessee in the 1870s and 1880s that the Jewish young ladies of Memphis held open house for them during the High Holy Days when they came to the city. Hattie Schwarzenberg, Birdie Hesse, and Mattie Goldsmith all advertised in the *Memphis Avalanche* that they "will tomorrow receive at their home."

The series of postwar plagues, climaxed by the yellow fever epidemic of 1878 that took thousands of lives, temporarily drove many Jews out of Memphis. Among those who died in the epidemic was the rabbi of Memphis' Beth El Emeth Congregation, Ferdinand I. Sarner, the first rabbi to serve as a regimental chaplain in the American army. Sarner had enlisted in 1863 with the 54th New York Volunteer Infantry, and was wounded at Gettysburg. He became rabbi of Beth El Emeth in 1872.

An inscription found on a stone excavated in 1885 from a burial mound in Bat Creek, Morganton, Tennessee, was described 85 years later by a Brandeis University professor as evidence that Hebrews fleeing the Romans, discovered America 1,000 years before Columbus. The stone, which is now in the Smithsonian Institution in Washington, D.C., was not recognized for what it is because when it was photographed and published by the Smithsonian Institution in 1894, it was printed upside down and its significance went unnoticed. Professor Cyrus H. Gordon, professor of Mediterranean Studies at Brandeis, said in 1970 that a professor at the Museum of Arts in Columbus, Georgia, sent him a photograph of the inscription which Gordon deciphered as being in the writing of Canaan. There are five letters in the inscription, the fifth of which, Gordon says, corresponds to the style of writing found on Hebrew coins of the Roman period. Gordon translated the inscription as reading "for the land of Judah." According to Gordon, "the archeological circumstances of the discovery rule out any chance of fraud or forgery and the inscription attests to a migration of Jews . . . probably to escape the disastrous Jewish defeats in 70 and 135 C.E."

A new community grew up in Obion County in the northwest tip of the state when Jewish peddlers and storekeepers settled in Union City during an industrial boom the area enjoyed between the late 1880s and 1900. A second Jewish influx occurred in the 1950s when a number of Jews opened shirt and shoe factories in the area and other Jews followed as plant managers, engineers, doctors, lawyers, and optometrists. The area's only Jewish institution, the Jewish Center in Union City, was founded in 1959.

By 1900, there were 15,000 Jews in Tennessee, nearly half of them in Memphis, which has never lost its place as the state's largest Jewish community. On the eve of World War I the Jewish population had increased to 14,000. In 1927 it reached 22,632 and a decade later it had climbed to 25,811. In 1937 Memphis had 13,350 Jews, followed by Nashville with 4,200, Chattanooga with 3,800, and Knoxville with 1,700. In the 1950s, there was a falling off in the Jewish population, Memphis dropping to 8,000 in 1954, Nashville to 2,700, Chattanooga to 2,500, and Knoxville to 800. In 1977 the state's total Jewish population was 17,610. In that year Memphis had 9,000 Jews; Nashville 3,700; Chattanooga, 2,250; Knoxville, 1,250, Johnson City, 210; Oak Ridge, 240; and Jackson, 120.

In 1916 the Hebrew Farmers Association of Chicago established the short-lived Jewish colony near Nashville. Rabbi William H. Fineshriber of Memphis' Temple Israel was one of the state's leading public figures from 1911-1924 when he left for Philadelphia. He was the first man in Tennessee to publicly plead for women's suffrage and was a vigorous foe of lynching. A sermon of his denouncing a lynching in 1917 created widespread attention, some praise as well as criticism. In the 1920s, Rabbi Fineshriber warred on the post-World War I Ku Klux Klan in sermons and addresses outside his pulpit. He also aligned himself in opposition to those who opposed the teaching of evolution in the public schools.

Rabbi William Silverman, when he was rabbi of Nashville's Temple Sholom, registered vigorous opposition to a Tennessee legislative probe of school textbooks during the McCarthy witch-hunting era. He led the way in the creation of the Nashville Community Relations Council to promote the orderly and peaceful process of school integration. When mob violence led to school bombing, Rabbi Silverman warned the Jewish community not to be deluded into believing it would escape the abuse of the hatemongers by remaining morally quiescent. On March 16, 1958, the Jewish Community Center was bombed by the "Confederate underground." For six months the rabbi carried a gun and armed guards were stationed at his house after threats on his life.

Rabbi James Wax of Memphis' Temple Israel walked side by side with black ministers at the head of a procession of 150 black and white, Catholic, Protestant, and Jewish clergy to City Hall to urge the mayor to settle the garbage strike that had brought the Reverend Dr. Martin Luther King, Jr. to Memphis and to his death by an assassin's bullet. The first university chair in Jewish studies in the South was created at Vanderbilt University, Nashville, in the mid-1950s, and Rabbi Lou Silberman occupied it for nearly 20 years while also serving as director of the Hillel Foundation.

Jews elected or appointed to public office in Tennessee included three mayors—L.A. Gratz, mayor of North Knoxville in 1870; George

Washington Ochs-Oakes, brother of Adolph S. Ochs, mayor of Chattanooga, 1895-1899; and Joseph Wasserman, mayor of Chattanooga, 1900. Henry Loeb, who was mayor of Memphis when Dr. King was assassinated, was a Jew and had been a member of Temple Israel but converted and became a member of the Episcopal Church.

Among the Jews who have served in the state legislature were Ralph Davis, 1890-1894, and speaker in 1893; Joseph Hanauer, Democratic floor leader in the House of Representatives, 1918-1919; Fletcher Gans Cohn, Democratic floor leader, 1929-1933; William Bailey Rosenfeld, House of Representatives, 1917-1919; Leo Jacobs, House of Representatives, 1890; Abe Cohen, House of Representatives; Ben Cash, floor leader in the Senate, 1911; and Julian Straus, House of Representatives, 1913-1915. Other Jewish officeholders include A.D. Waldauer, Collector of Customs for Memphis; Mrs. Corinne Lieberman, chairman of the Nashville Board of Education; and Will Gerber, city attorney of Memphis. Jewish judges were Clarence Friedman of State Criminal Court; County Court Judge Charles Gilbert; Herman Sander, Davidson County Court; Hyman T. Kern, Knoxville Municipal Court; Chancery Court Judge Nathan Cohn; Sam Taubenblatt, Shelby County Court; Judge Ben Cash, Chattanooga; and S.L. Kopalk, Jr., who served as chairman of the Tennessee Republican Executive Committee. Lee J. Loventhal of Nashville was the founder of the Nashville Community Chest and served as trustee of Vanderbilt and Fisk Universities.

* * * * *

BLOUNTVILLE

Cong. B'nai Sholom, in the Mount Tucker addition of the city, on Blountville Highway, occupies a building that was formerly the main house of a plantation. The congregation serves the Jews of Kingsport, Johnson City, and Bristol, the latter being partly in Virginia. The stateline runs down the main street of Bristol. Until 1957, the synagogue was on the Virginia side of Bristol, on King Street. Following the move to Blountville, the congregation added the Armand Hecht Jewish Center, named for the chairman of the building fund committee who died while working on the project.

BRENTWOOD

The Observer, Culbertson Bldg., Wilson Pike Circle.

BROWNSVILLE

Cong. Adas Israel, Washington St.

CHATTANOOGA

Beth Shalom Synagogue, 20 Pisgah Ave., was bombed in 1976.
Cong. B'nai Zion, 534 Vine St.

Cong. Mizpah, cor. 923 McCallie Ave., (also known as the Julius and Bertha Ochs Memorial Temple) was a gift from Adolph S. Ochs, *The New York Times* publisher, as a memorial to his parents.

Hillel Foundation, University of Tennessee at Chattanooga, University Center.

Jewish Community Center, 5326 Lynnland Terr.

Jewish Welfare Federation, 5326 Lynnland Terr.

Adolph S. Ochs Observatory and Museum, in Lookout Mountain Park on the site of the Civil War battles of Chickamauga and Missionary Ridge, overlooks the city of Chattanooga, whose citizens erected the observatory and museum in honor of the city's leading citizen and the prime mover in most of its major civic enterprises. Located in a government reservation, the museum is maintained by the U.S. Park Service. It is an octangular-shaped building, 50 by 70 by 26 feet. The observatory enables visitors to view the breathtaking Great Smokies and Blue Ridge Mountains. The museum houses exhibits, documents, and material pertaining to the history of the area. Ochs was largely responsible for establishing and financing Lookout Mountain Park. The park is part of Chickamauga and Chattanooga National Military Park. One of the two main roads through the park is called Ochs Highway. A memorial marker to Ochs, who donated 3,000 acres of land for the park, stands at the junction of Ochs Highway and Fairland Road.

Over the fireplace in the museum's exhibit hall there is a bronze plaque with the inscription: "In memory of Adolph S. Ochs, journalist, philanthropist, statesman—whose vision, enterprise and generosity created the beautiful park on the sides of this mountain upon which this edifice stands, did so much for the community which lies in the valley below, and served so conspicuously the nation of which he was a distinguished citizen—his friends and neighbors who were honored by his comradeship and influenced by his ideals have dedicated this building."

Born in Cincinnati in 1858, Ochs began his newspaper career as a printer's devil on the *Knoxville Chronicle* in 1869, the successor to William "Parson" G. Brownlow's *Knoxville Whig*, a violently anti-Jewish paper of pre-Civil War days. By 1877, Ochs was managing editor of the *Knoxville Tribune*. That same year he went to Chattanooga to launch the *Daily Dispatch*. After merging this paper with the *Chattanooga Times*, Ochs made it one of the most influential publications in the post-bellum South. One of the organizers of the Southern Associated Press, Ochs was Chattanooga's leading citizen by 1890.

While in New York in 1896, to discuss an offer to become publisher of the *Daily Mercury*, Ochs learned that *The New York Times*, founded in 1851, was in financial difficulties. Invited to reorganize the company, he received a contract giving him control of the paper when he had put it on a paying basis. In 1899, Ochs became owner of the *Times*. Under his leadership it became the "outstanding triumph of modern journalism in any land," and Ochs won fame as the mastermind of the greatest organ of American public opinion. Because of its unrivaled and complete coverage of world news and its rigid separation of news from opinion, the *Times* is considered the most influential newspaper in the world.

Ochs, who married Effie Miriam Wise, daughter of Dr. Isaac Mayer Wise (see Ohio), was one of the prominent leaders of Reform Judaism. In 1925, he headed the Hebrew Union College endowment campaign for $5 million, toward which he contributed $500,000. He gave a similar sum to underwrite the monumental *Dictionary of American Biography*. The Adolph S. Ochs Chair in American Jewish History at the Cincinnati campus of Hebrew Union College-Jewish Institute of Religion, occupied since 1954 by Dr. Jacob R. Marcus, is a memorial to the eminent publisher. One of the Ochs' younger brothers, George Washington Oakes (he changed his name during World War I because he regarded Ochs as too German), was one of the two Jews who served as mayor of Chattanooga. Ochs-Oakes was the city's chief executive from 1895-1899 and he was succeeded by Joseph Wasserman. ▪

Moses and Garrison Siskin Memorial Foundation, 526 Vine St., is the overall name of a complex of three buildings erected and paid for by the Siskin Brothers of Chattanooga. To date, they have contributed nearly $4 million to the foundation in cash, real estate, construction equipment, and maintenance. The entire complex is a memorial to the Siskins' parents, Anna and Robert Siskin. The building at 526 Vine St., is a non-denominational chapel open to the public for prayer and meditation and used on special occasions for worship by Cong. B'nai Zion. In the chapel is the Harris Swift Museum of Religious and Ceremonial Arts and Library of Rare Books, collected from all over the world by the late Rabbi Harris Swift, in whose honor the museum is named. On permanent exhibit are unusual objects of religious art pertaining to all religions, and a unique collection of Bibles in many languages. Among the unusual artifacts is the smallest Torah in the world housed in a silver hand-chased Ark. The Torah is complete in every detail from the crown and *yad* to the breastplate and *rimmonim*. The writing is authentic Hebrew minutely inscribed on parchment. There is also a hand-chased ivory model of Jacob's dream, done in the Flemish tradition in 1750. The artifacts collection was originally owned by Rabbi Harris Swift, who was one of the leaders of the World War II Jewish resistance movement in Europe.

CLARKSVILLE

Harriet Cohn Guidance Center, 1300 Madison St., is a mental health center named for the late Mrs. Jessel Cohn, who together with her husband and children, were interested in the city's mental health program for many years. Over the fireplace in the waiting room of what was once the living room of the Cohns' mansion, is an oil portrait of Mrs. Cohn.

DAYTON

Scopes Trial Historic Marker lists the name of the late famed Jewish lawyer, Arthur Garfield Hays, who, together with Clarence Darrow, was defense counsel for John T. Scopes, a local teacher whose trial in 1925 was based on a charge of teaching evolution and contradicting the divine inspiration of the Bible. The trial made this town famous as the scene of the so-called "Monkey Trial," in which William Jennings Bryan was the attorney for the prosecution.

JACKSON

Cong. B'nai Israel, 32 Russell Rd.

KNOXVILLE

Arnstein Building, Market and Union Sts., is named for the late Max B. Arnstein, department store owner who, when he died in 1961 at the age of 102, was one of the most respected merchants in the South. As a young immigrant from Germany, he had first settled in Camden, S.C., where he opened a small store. Later he went into business with Harman Baruch, an uncle of Bernard Baruch. When he and Baruch missed a train connection for Birmingham, Ala., where they planned to open a store, they stayed the night in Knoxville, where Arnstein settled down and became one of the city's leading citizens. The Arnstein Building is occupied by the Tennessee Valley Authority.

Arnstein Jewish Community Center, 6800 Deane Hill Dr., is named for Max B. Arnstein and his wife, Lalla, who were among the Center's principal founders and among its chief benefactors. In the lobby of the Center is a bronze bas-relief plaque bearing the likeness of the late Milton Collins, the Center's executive director for 21 years.

Cong. Heska Amuna, 3811 Kingston Pike, S.W.

Gratz Street is named for Major Louis A. Gratz, a German Jew who served with Pennsylvania and Kentucky cavalry regiments during the Civil War. Studying law in leisure moments, he was admitted to the bar and opened an office in Knoxville after he was demobilized. Gratz became prominent in public affairs and acquired a considerable amount of property. He laid out the Gratz addition to North Knoxville of which he was elected the first mayor in 1889. Previous to this time he had twice been elected city attorney of Knoxville.

Jewish Welfare Fund, 6800 Deane Hill Dr.

Tennessee Valley Authority, popularly known as TVA, whose headquarters is in Knoxville, is the greatest development in large scale planning

in the U.S. and in some respects a monument to the vision, heart, and brain
of David Eli Lilienthal, one of America's great public servants. Lilienthal
was only 34 when President Franklin D. Roosevelt named him one of the
original triumvirate to build and operate TVA in 1933. He was chairman of
TVA from 1938-1946, when he became the first chairman of the Atomic
Energy Commission. In two decades, TVA transformed the economic and
social life of the Tennessee watershed and of 3,000,000 people. It created,
developed, and distributed electric power, provided flood control, improved navigation, developed industries, furthered forestation, and raised
the income level in the area by 75 percent. Without TVA the first atomic
bomb couldn't have been built at Oak Ridge. TVA helped during World
War II by providing the power for key industrial plants. As chairman of the
Atomic Energy Commission, Lilienthal was largely responsible for draft-
ing the Acheson-Lilienthal report which became the basis of American
atomic policy and Bernard M. Baruch's recommendation for United Nations' control of the atom bomb. When President Harry Truman created
the Atomic Energy Commission, Lilienthal was made chairman, serving
until 1950. Born in Morton, Ill., Lilienthal was a lawyer who went into public service. Before his appointment to TVA, he had been chairman of the
Wisconsin Public Service Commission.

University of Tennessee

● Max and Lalla Arnstein Collection, a permanent exhibit of etchings,
paintings, bronzes, miniatures, and other rare items collected by the Arn-
steins and bequeathed to the University.
● Hillel Foundation, P.O. Box 10173, Knoxville.
● Newspaper Hall of Fame, Communications and Extension Building,
has a plaque and citation, honoring among other Tennessee journalists,
Adolph S. Ochs, who published papers in Knoxville and Chattanooga, in
addition to *The New York Times*.

MEMPHIS

Belz Bais Midrash of Yeshiva, 5255 Meadowest Ave.
Beth Sholom Synagogue, 482 S. Mendenhall Rd.
B'nai B'rith Home and Hospital for the Aged, 31 N. Tucker St.
Buring Field, the baseball park on the south campus of the Memphis
State University, is named for Nat Buring, prominent local philanthropist
who also donated the land on which Anshei Sphard Beth Emeth Synagogue stands.
Cong. Anshei Sphard Beth El Emeth, 120 E. Yates Rd., N., is, through
a series of mergers, the oldest existing congregation in the state. When it
was founded in 1854 it was known as B'nai Israel. Out of schism in 1860
came Beth El Emeth. Anshei Sphard was founded in 1904, and in 1966 was

merged with Beth El Emeth.

Cong. Beth El, Millington Naval Air Station, is served by the Jewish naval chaplain.

Goldsmith Garden Center, in Audubon Park, was a gift to the city from the children of Jacob and Dora Goldsmith.

Goldsmith Library, in St. Agnes College, a Catholic institution, was presented in 1936 by the children of Jacob and Dora Goldsmith. The college is housed in the Goldsmith residence.

Baron Hirsch Congregation, 1740 Vollentine, located on a 13-acre site, named for Baron Maurice de Hirsch, the French Jewish industrialist who contributed tens of millions of dollars for the resettlement of Russian Jews in South America, the United States, and Canada, is said to have the largest sanctuary of any Orthodox synagogue in America.

Baron Hirsch Cong. East Educational Center, 5631 Shady Grove Rd., houses the synagogue's educational center and facilities for meeting, lectures, and religious classes.

Jewish Community Center, 6560 Poplar Ave., has on its grounds an 18-foot tall marble memorial to the victims of the Holocaust. Atop the memorial are six lamps—one for each million killed by the Nazis—that burn constantly. The monument was a gift from Paul Lewis of Dallas, Tex., who also designed, built, and contributed Holocaust memorials in Dallas, Houston, San Antonio, Brooklyn, N.Y., Long Beach, Ca., and Washington, D.C.

Jewish Federation, 6560 Poplar Ave.

Jewish Union House, 3624 Midland, houses the Hillel Foundations that serve Southwestern University, Memphis State University, University of Tennessee at Memphis, and Southern College of Optometry.

Leo Levy Memorial Wing, a new addition to the Jewish Community Center, 6560 Poplar Ave., houses the Jewish Welfare Fund, Jewish Social Service Agency, and the Jewish Community Relations Council. The building is named for the late Leo Levy, Memphis philanthropist.

Dr. Louis Levy Portrait in the lobby of the Memphis Eye, Ear and Nose and Throat Hospital, 1060 Madison Ave., honors the late physician who founded the hospital.

Memphis Hebrew Watchman, 227 Jefferson Ave.

Abe Plough Bust, in the lobby of the Memphis Area Chamber of Commerce, 42 S. 2nd St., memorializes the late philanthropist and pharmaceutical manufacturer whose generosity benefited the entire community. The bust is inscribed, "Godfearing, community leader, friend and philanthropist."

Temple Israel, 1376 E. Massey Rd.

Abe Waldauer Portrait, in the Memphis State University Law School, Central Ave., honors the prominent attorney and communal leader who was the founder of the law school.

NASHVILLE

Akiva School, 3600 West End Ave.

Cohen Memorial, on the campus of George Peabody College for Teachers, 21st Ave., S. and Edgehill Ave., houses the department of fine arts and a collection of art bequeathed by Mrs. George Etta Cohen. She gave the college the building as well as a valuable collection of paintings, porcelains, laces, tapestries, and antique furniture.

Cong. Ohabei Sholom, 5015 Harding Rd., has a mosaic mural in its foyer that depicts an unusual juxtaposition of the races of man, the *shofar*, the Menorah, and the fire of the Shekkinah. On the curved exterior facade there is a ten-foot high limestone sculpture based on a verse from Pirke Avot. In the inner brick wall of the temple garden is set the cornerstone from the congregation's old Vine St. temple, which was dedicated in 1875 at exercises in which President Andrew Johnson participated. "No one felt a deeper interest in the success" of the Jews and their temple than he did, the President said, expressing the hope that "it would ever remain a monument to the industry, prosperity and welfare of the Jewish citizens of Nashville." In 1861, when Johnson was a Senator from Tennessee, he attacked Jews. Johnson berated Senator David Yulee (see Florida) as "that contemptible little Jew," and referred to Judah P. Benjamin (see Louisiana) as "there's another Jew—that miserable Benjamin."

Cong. Sherith Israel, 3600 West End Ave.

George Gershwin Memorial Collection of Music and Musical Literature is part of the library of Fisk University, Jefferson St. and 17th Ave., N., the well-known black college. The collection was founded by Carl van Vechten and named for the beloved composer "to recall the fact that this American belonged to a minority group" and that "much of his best music was inspired by Negro rhythms." In the collection are autographed letters from musical greats such as Wagner, Meyerbeer, Kreisler, Gounod, and Patti; biographies of musical notables; operatic libretti; manuscripts; scores; programs; and photos.

Hillel Foundation, George Peabody and Vanderbilt Universities, 2410 Vanderbilt Place.

Jewish Community Center, 3500 West End Ave.

Jewish Federation of Nashville, 3500 West End Ave.

Joint University Library at Vanderbilt University, 21st Ave., S., has one of the largest collections of Judaica south of Cincinnati. It contains the Ismar Elbogen Library, named for the late scholar and historian, which was a gift of Mrs. Henry Teitelbaum of Nashville in memory of her husband; the Sandmel Collection, named for Rabbi Samuel Sandmel, the eminent Biblical scholar; the Leo L. Loventhal Collection, named for the founder of Nashville's Community Chest, prominent patron of education, and member of the board of trustees of Vanderbilt and Fisk Universities; and the Goodhart Philo Collection. The library is a joint venture of Vanderbilt University and Peabody and Scarritt Colleges.

Sam Levy Community Building, a public housing project, honors one of the original members of the board of commissioners of the Nashville Housing Authority, an office he held from 1939 until his death in 1947. Head of Sam Levy & Co., a wholesale shoe firm he founded in 1884, Levy was one of the city's most beloved citizens. His portrait hangs in the lobby of the building.

The Observer, (see Brentwood).

West End Synagogue, 3810 West End Ave.

OAK RIDGE

American Museum of Atomic Energy has a Hall of Fame where 15 scientists are recognized as having made especially important contributions in the field of atomic energy. Included in the 15 are Albert Einstein and Niels Bohr, the Danish Nobel Prize winner, whose mother was Ellen Adler, member of a prominent Jewish banking family. The Hall of Fame is in the form of an automated slide lecture.

Jewish Congregation of Oak Ridge, Madison Lane at Michigan Ave., was founded in 1943 by Jewish scientists, technicians, and other civilian personnel, as well as military personnel assigned to the synthetic city secretly set up by the government around the Clinton Engineer Works where the first atomic power pile was built. Soon after the personnel arrived at the secret war installation, Maj. William C. Bernstein, one of a group of Army medical officers from the University of Minnesota Medical School assigned to organize a clinic and hospital, took the initiative in developing a Jewish community. When the Army's Oak Ridge chapel was dedicated on the second night of Rosh Hashanah, 1943, Rabbi Jerome Mark of Knoxville's Beth El Temple came to conduct the first Jewish service. In October of that year, regular Friday evening services began, with religious appurtenances, prayer books, and a Torah provided by the National Jewish Welfare Board. A Sunday school was started in 1944. After World War II, the Jewish personnel at Oak Ridge built a small synagogue with their own hands, with young Ph.D.s spending their leisure time as bricklayers, carpenters, electricians, and plumbers. In 1959, the government gave up the Oak Ridge plant and the place became the incorporated city of Oak Ridge. In 1962, an addition to the synagogue was built. The first full-time rabbi of the congregation was Martin Kessler, who served from 1954-1957. Rabbi Kenneth Bromberg served from 1958 into the early 1960s.

TULLAHOMA

International Churchmen's Sports Hall of Fame, temporarily housed in the Tennessee Space Institute, periodically honors outstanding sports personalities who have also distinguished themselves through leadership in the work of their faith or through interfaith activities. As of 1975, the following Jews were included: Sandy Koufax, all-star pitcher of the Los Angeles Dodgers; David Blumberg, president of B'nai B'rith from 1971-1978; Edward Rosenblum, one-time executive director of the Greater Washington Jewish Community Center and a member of the U.S. Olympic Committee; and Scott Shulman, a tackle on the 1973 University of Maine football team.

UNION CITY
Jewish Center, 100 S. Home St.

Texas

The first European settlement of what is now Texas took place in 1718 when a group of five families led by the Carvajals, who were of Jewish descent, settled at the headwaters of the San Antonio River. The last Carvajals who were Jews were burned at the stake in Mexico City in the Spanish Inquisition's Grand Auto da Fe around 1590. The descendants of these settlers are still prominent in San Antonio, and they have been devoted Catholics for over 250 years. Professor Richard Santos of the Department of Ethnic Studies at Our Lady of the Lake College in San Antonio, who claims Marrano origin for himself, interviewed some old Texas families about their traditions of lighting candles Friday nights and preparing certain dishes and deduced that they had Marrano ancestors. These families were highly incensed at the accusation that they were not of pure "Spanish blood."

For a number of years, the Jewish Histo-Wall at the Institute of Texas Cultures, a permanent state exhibit in San Antonio, stated that the first Jew to enter Texas was Gaspar Castana de Sosa, a Portuguese adventurer and Marrano, who became governor of Neuvo Leon, Mexico, in 1590. He had led an expedition in 1590 through what is now the southwestern Texas —where the Pecos River enters the Rio Grande—en route to New Mexico, seeking the Seven Cities of Cibelo and their fabled gold. De Sosa was later tried and convicted by the Inquisition in Mexico City for leading an unauthorized expedition into what is now New Mexico.

Mrs. Perry Kallison, of San Antonio, a leading authority on Texas Jewish history, and Philip Hewitt, research associate of the Institute of Texas Cultures, sought diligently but vainly to prove that de Sosa was a Jew or at least a Marrano. They pursued every lead and original and secondary source to no avail. The only reference to de Sosa's having been of Jewish origin was found in Seymour Liebman's book, *The Jews in New Spain*, which states that de Sosa was purported to be the son of Jewish converts. The basis for this assertion is the fact that de Sosa was Portuguese and "Portuguese" was a synonym for "Jew" in colonial New Spain, and that he was tried by the Inquisition. His name has since been removed from the Jewish Histo-Wall.

The first North American Jew known to have been in Texas was Captain Samuel Noah, an 1807 graduate of West Point, who was serving with the United States Army in Florida and in the Gulf States. Discouraged by slow promotion and boring duty, Noah resigned his commisssion as first lieutenant and joined Augustine W. Magee, in the famous Gutierrez-Magee expedition against Spanish rule of Texas in 1812. Magee had been won over by Mexican rebels, headed by Bernardo Gutierrez de Lara. They formed the "Army of the North," put out a bulletin offering to pay all recruits $40 a month and a grant of one league of land in Texas as a reward at the conclusion of the rebellion. This army was also called the "Mexican Patriot Army" and the "Republican Army of the North" but it is best known as the Gutierrez-Magee Expedition. Commanded by Colonel Magee, an American citizen and a West Pointer (class of 1809), the army had many Anglo-Americans as well as Mexican citizens on its roster.

Noah met this army at the Brazos River, and marched with it to Fort Bahia, where it was besieged by a Spanish royalist force. The siege was raised and Noah was placed in command of the little army's rear guard, as it pursued the royalists westward towards San Antonio. The "patriots" had been reinforced, and on April 4, 1813, they engaged the Spanish forces in sharp combat near San Antonio, and three days later they entered San Antonio and forced the surrender of the city by the Spanish governor. However, the rebels were unable to hold the city. Noah escaped and made his way overland to Washington, D.C. soon after the War of 1812 began. He sought to regain his United States commission but was rejected.

The Galveston historian, J.O. Dyer, said that one Jao de la Porta, purportedly a Marrano Jew of Portuguese origin, was with the pirate Jean Lafitte when he established himself on the island that later became the city of Galveston. This unsupported claim is part of the legend that Lafitte himself was of Marrano descent.

The first written record of a Jew in Texas is a Spanish grant of "one league and one labor" of land in Fort Bend County to Samuel Isaacs in 1821. After Mexico won its independence from Spain in 1821, it contracted with American promoters to bring in settlers to colonize Texas, which had become a Mexican state. Moses Austin, a St. Louis banker, had secured permission from the Spanish authorities to settle 300 Anglo-American families in Texas. His son, Stephen, carried out the project in 1821. Isaacs was one of Austin's settlers. Later Isaacs received 300 acres of land in Polk County from the Republic of Texas for his services in the Texas War of Independence.

Nacogdoches, in the eastern part of the state, was the site of the first Jewish settlement in Texas in 1826. The first to arrive was Adolphus Sterne. A boy of 16 when he arrived in New Orleans in 1817, Sterne worked as a clerk, studied law, and became an active Mason. Fluent in French, Spanish, and German, he became a successful merchant soon after he came to Texas. In the earliest American insurrection against Mexico, the so-called Fredonian War, Sterne played a key role. The war began when Hayden and Benjamin Edwards, who had been given Mexican land grants around Nacogdoches, quarreled with Mexican officials and as a result lost their land titles. They rounded up a force of 15 men and captured Nacogdoches. Proclaiming Texas independent of Mexico, they established the Fredonian Republic. One of the more serious complaints against Mexican rule was the fact that only Catholics and converts to Catholicism could own land in Texas. The rebellion collapsed quickly when most of the American settlers refused to support Fredonia. One who did back the rebels was Adolphus Sterne who had been mayor of Nacogdoches and custodian of municipal funds. He had smuggled in from New Orleans arms and munitions hidden in bales of cotton and casks of tobacco consigned to his general store.

Sterne was arrested by the Mexicans, tried by a military court, and sentenced to be shot. Pending his execution, he was chained in an old building in Nacogdoches. Ultimately, he was freed when the Masonic lodge in Mexico interceded for him because he was a Mason and he was paroled on his promise never again to fight against Mexico. This pledge kept him from personal participation in the Texan War of Independence, but he personally raised and equipped a company of volunteers from Louisiana known as the New Orleans Greys. Dr. Joseph Hertz and his brother, Hyman, settled in Nacogdoches in 1832. When Abraham Labatt, one of the founders of the first Reform Jewish congregation in the United States (Charleston, South Carolina, 1824), came to Texas in 1831 he found two Jews in Velasco, south of Galveston on the Gulf of Mexico. They were Jacob Henry, who had come from England, and Jacob Lyons, who hailed from South Carolina. When Henry died, he left his fortune to the city of Velasco to build a hospital. Maurice Hertz, also an Englishman, had settled in Velasco in the 1820s.

Sterne, who had lived for a time in Tennessee, where he first met Sam Houston, became close friends with the future first president of the Republic of Texas. When Houston came to Texas he stayed for a time with Sterne whose solidly built house in Nacogdoches had served as a refuge for women and children during Indian raids. It was in Sterne's parlor that Houston was baptized and converted to Catholicism, with Sterne's wife acting as godmother. She had been Lutheran. There is no mention of Sterne as godfather and no evidence that Sterne converted. In his diary, which is preserved in the Texas State Archives, there is a notation dated October 6, 1840, that "tonight is erev Yom Kippur." In 1841 he helped raise funds for and supervised the construction of a Catholic church in Nacogdoches, but that same year he wrote in the diary that he had "dined at the house of Mr. de Young. He is a German Jew of the old reverend class." In the early years of the Texas Republic, Sterne was the postmaster of Nacogdoches and he served in both houses of the Texas Congress. He was a member of the Texas Senate when he died in 1852.

On the eve of the Texas Revolution against Mexico, there were probably only 100 Jews in Texas but many of them took an active part in the war that led to the establishment of the Republic of Texas in 1836. When Colonel William B. Travis stormed the Mexican port of entry at Anahuac on the Gulf of Mexico in 1832 and precipitated the first military engagement of the Texan Revolution, serving under him was Dr. I. Kokernot, a Dutch Jew who came to Texas in 1830 and settled in Gonzales. Kokernot also took part in the battle of Gonzales and in other campaigns.

When the Texans captured San Antonio in December, 1835, among those in the Texan forces was Dr. Moses Albert Levy, a native of Virginia, who received his M.D. from the University of Pennsylvania in 1832. On a visit to New Orleans, he joined the New Orleans Greys. He not only served as the regiment's surgeon-general but also fought bravely. After the capture of San Antonio, the regiment marched back to New Orleans, but Levy remained in Texas. He later became a surgeon on *The Independence*, a Texan warship captured by the Mexicans. Levy was taken prisoner but managed to escape. After the war he settled at Matagorda, where he practiced medicine until his death in a yellow fever epidemic in the 1840s. Levy served on the first Board of Medical Censors created by both houses of the Texas Congress in 1837.

Edward I. Johnson, member of a pioneer Jewish family in Cincinnati (see Ohio), joined a company of volunteers that came to Texas in October, 1835. He later enlisted with Captain Burr H. Duval's company and fought in the Battle of Goliad where he was among the 300 men in Colonel James W. Fannin, Jr.'s army who were executed by order of the Mexican General Santa Anna. Benjamin H. Mordecai, who also fought with Fannin, had his life spared by the Mexicans, only to be killed by Indians in 1840. A third Jew with Fannin, M.K. Moses, managed to escape the massacre. There were no Jews among the valiant defenders of the Alamo, who were wiped out after a bitter siege in 1836. In the Battle of San Jacinto, April 21, 1836, when the troops of General Sam Houston, shouting "Remember the

Alamo! Remember Goliad!" won a decisive victory over Santa Anna that led to Texas' independence, there were Jewish soldiers: Albert Emanuel, who had been one of the first to volunteer in the Texas Army; Lieutenant Kohn of the Texas Spy Company; Colonel Leon Dyer; surgeon Isaac Lyons; and Eugene Joseph Chimene, who settled in Houston in 1835. Dyer served as one of the guards over Santa Anna after he surrendered to Sam Houston.

Leon Dyer was also among a number of Texas Jews who served in the Mexican War. Others were Henry Wiener, who fought in the Battle of Buena Vista, and Henry Seeligson, a lieutenant in the Galveston Cadets, composed of young men 15 to 18 years of age, who helped repel a Mexican invasion of Galveston. Later he was praised by General Zachary Taylor for conspicuous service in Mexico. Seeligson's father,Michael, who arrived in Galveston in 1838, became one of the city's leading citizens. Seeligson and his sons, Henry and Lewis, worked untiringly for annexation of the Texas Republic to the United States. Michael Seeligson resigned as mayor in August, 1853, and moved to Goliad where he acquired 4,441 acres of land for ranching. He wrote to *The Occident*, a Philadelphia Jewish magazine, inviting Jews to come to his area and become landowners and engage in agriculture. He appealed to Jewish philanthropic organizations to buy some of his land for settlement of "persecuted Israelites" at $1 to $3 an acre. Seeligson's sons both married non-Jewish women and became Episcopalians. Michael Seeligson, who also operated a chain of small general stores with his sons in Galveston, Victoria, Goliad, and Indianola, died in 1867. He and his wife are buried side by side in the first Galveston Hebrew Cemetery. Michael de Young, a French Jew who settled in St. Augustine in the 1840s, furnished equipment to volunteers protecting Texas during the Mexican War.

Jacob de Cordova, a native of Jamaica, who was in New Orleans doing business with Texas when the Texas Revolution broke out, moved to Galveston in 1837, where he founded the state's first Odd Fellows lodge. In the 1840s he settled in Houston when it was hardly more than a cluster of shacks on a muddy road. De Cordova quickly became the town's leading merchant, helping to make it the most important trading center for the area east of the Brazos River. On a tour of the vast empty areas of Texas, he was deeply impressed with its immense potential. For five years he visited every corner of Texas, charting its resources, and then opened a settlement office in Houston to promote immigration to Texas. With his half-brother, Phineas, de Cordova published *De Cordova's Herald and Immigrant Guide* in Houston. They distributed the paper free at crossroads stores and county post offices throughout the South and Midwest. "Come to Texas" was the paper's message.

At the request of the governor, the de Cordovas moved their paper to Austin, the state capital, where the name was changed to the *Southwestern American*. Phineas ran the paper and also owned a land agency, while

Jacob remained in Houston, contributing articles. Jacob visited other states to promote immigration to Texas, authored a book entitled *Texas, Her Resources and Her Public Men*, a who's who and an encyclopedia on land laws, climate, railroads, cotton growing, and cattle and sheep raising. With two other men, Jacob de Cordova founded the town of Waco and served in the state legislature as a representative from Harris County (Houston). Until the Civil War, he was known as "Mr. Texas," and was praised as the man responsible for persuading thousands to settle in Texas.

Married to a Baptist, Jacob de Cordova helped his wife organize a Baptist church in Houston, and he headed a building fund drive for the church. His descendants in Houston have denied he was Jewish, claiming that he had converted to Protestantism. His biographer, James M. Day, found no evidence of his conversion. Neither did Mrs. Kallison who strongly doubts the claim by Rabbi Henry Cohen of Galveston that the first Jewish worship services in Houston were held in Jacob de Cordova's home in 1844. What is a matter of record, however, is that in 1846 he bought the plot that became Houston's first Jewish cemetery. He died in 1868 from pneumonia contracted while surveying the Brazos River in search of a suitable site for a textile factory to be powered by the river's flow.

Phineas de Cordova, a journalist, came to Galveston in 1848, stayed briefly, and moved to Houston where he joined his half-brother's enterprises. He was secretary of the 8th, 9th, and 10th state legislatures, served on the executive committee of the State Democratic Committee for six years, and edited the *Southwestern American* in Austin. During the Civil War, he served on the Texas State Military Board, which was responsible for protection of the Texas frontiers from Indians and for keeping Texans supplied with food and weapons. As early as 1852, Phineas de Cordova was serving on various committees to promote the construction of railroads in Texas. Under his sponsorship, a convention of delegates from eight counties developed a plan for bringing railroads to Texas and for financing them. In his newspaper he vigorously championed railroad building and urged support of a plan adopted by the state legislature for financial support. He was one of the founders of the first synagogue in Austin, Congregation Beth Israel, established in 1876, serving as vice president and later president.

Levy L. Laurens, a native of Charleston, South Carolina, who had worked for his uncle, Mordecai M. Noah's *New York Star*, was only 21 when he came to Houston to work on the *Telegraph*, then the city's only newspaper. He was also a reporter on the paper published by the Texas Congress before he was killed in a duel in 1837.

After Texas became an independent republic, its first president, Sam Houston, saw the need for more settlers and sought a colonization loan from a French bank headed by Henri Castro. After persuading Houston that Texas needed people more than money, he signed a five-year agreement to colonize a huge area of Texas west of San Antonio. Ultimately, he brought over from France 2,137 colonists between 1844 and 1847 who settled in the towns of Quihi, Vandenberg, D'hanis, and Castroville.

Although the first Jewish cemetery in the state was established in Houston in 1844 and the state's first congregation—Beth Israel—was organized in Houston in 1854, Galveston had the state's largest Jewish community until the 1880s. Among the earliest Jewish settlers in Galveston were Joseph and Rosanna Dyer Osterman who arrived in 1839 and established a general store. Michael Seeligson reached Galveston in 1838, and Samuel Maas was listed as a property owner there in 1841. Rosanna Osterman's brother, Isadore Dyer, arrived in the late 1840s. The first recorded Jewish death in Galveston in 1838 of H. Abrahams indicates that he had probably been the first Jewish settler. He was buried in a non-Jewish cemetery because the first Jewish cemetery was not established until 20 years later, at the urging of Rosanna Osterman. She and Isidore Dyer brought Rabbi M.N. Nathan from New Orleans for the consecration of the cemetery, making him probably the first ordained rabbi to officiate in Texas. In 1840 Michael Seeligson was elected an alderman and in 1853 he became mayor. First Jewish worship services in Galveston were held in Isadore Dyer's home. Congregation B'nai Israel, the state's second oldest congregation, was founded in 1868.

During the Civil War, the port of Galveston was so effectively blockaded by Union gunboats that the city was economically ruined. Most Jews joined the exodus from the city to the mainland, but Rosanna Osterman remained to nurse the wounded of both sides. When the Union forces captured the city she sent military information to the Confederates in Houston and her messages helped the Confederates retake the city in 1863. Mrs. Osterman, who was killed in a Mississippi River steamboat explosion in 1866, bequeathed $3,000 each to Jewish hospitals in New York, New Orleans, and Cincinnati, and left $5,000 to build a synagogue in Galveston and $2,500 for a synagogue in Houston. She also left the income from two buildings she owned in Galveston for the establishment and maintenance of a nonsectarian home for widows and orphans.

In 1866, it was reported that 21 out of 26 merchants in Galveston were Jewish. Two years later five out of seven retailers listed in the Galveston directory were Jews and three out of five drygoods dealers were Jews. Among the leading citizens in pre-and post-war Galveston were Moritz Kopperl, Harris Kempner, and Morris Lasker. Kopperl, who had been in business in Mississippi in the late 1840s, came to Galveston in 1857. One of the state's early railroad builders, he was president of the National Bank of Texas and served in the state legislature from 1876-1880. A Bosque County hamlet is named for him.

Kempner, who began his business career at Cold Springs, in San Jacinto County in 1858, served in the Confederate Army with Parson's Cavalry Brigade. He arrived in Galveston in 1868 where he established a wholesale grocery business. Later he became one of the largest cotton factors in the southwest, advancing credit against a cotton crop which when harvested was received by Kempner at a predetermined price and then sold abroad or to cotton mills in the North. One of the promoters of the Gulf, Colorado and Santa Fe Railroad, he was responsible for the line's consolidation with the Atchison, Topeka and Santa Fe. Kempner's son, Isaac, was mayor of Galveston from 1917-1919. The city's third Jewish mayor was Adrian Levy, who served from 1935-1939.

Morris Lasker, the younger brother of the German statesman, Eduoard Lasker, arrived in Texas in 1860, settling in Weatherford as a peddler and later as a clerk. He joined a band of Indian fighters, voted against secession, but joined the Confederate Army, serving with the 2nd Texas Cavalry in Louisiana, at the Sabine Pass, and in the capture of Galveston. He was one of more than 100 Texas Jews who fought with the Confederates. After the war he became a peddler again, settling in Galveston in 1872. By 1880 Lasker owned two banks, a milling business, and extensive real estate holdings. Bankrupted by the panic of 1893, he rebounded in 1895 and was elected to the state senate from Galveston. When he died in 1916 the city honored him by a five minute cessation of all activity. His son, Albert Lasker, was the noted advertising tycoon and chairman of the United States Shipping Administration under President Warren Harding. The widow of Albert Lasker founded the famed Lasker Awards for scientific achievement.

Another noted Galveston Jew was Abraham Cohen Labatt, a member of the board of aldermen from 1869-1877. Labatt, who had first come to Texas in 1831, and returned in 1837 in charge of a cargo of goods on a merchantman, settled permanently in Galveston after the Civil War, after having lived for some years in San Francisco where he was one of the founders of the first synagogue. Leo N. Levi, who was born in Victoria where his father settled in 1849 as a pioneer banker and merchant, began practicing law in Galveston in 1876. A tireless worker for civic betterment and for many years an unofficial lobbyist for Galveston's interests before the state legislature, he was elected president of Congregation B'nai Israel in 1887 and in this capacity brought Rabbi Henry Cohen to its pulpit in 1888. In 1900 Levi was elected national president of B'nai B'rith. He was the author of the Kishnev Petition for which thousands of signatures were obtained by B'nai B'rith after the Kishnev pogrom of 1903 in the hope that President Theodore Roosevelt would send it to the Czar urging him to end the outrages.

Rabbi Cohen soon became a familiar sight on Galveston's streets as he sped along on his bicycle, coattails flapping behind him. Each morning he scribbled the day's appointments on his starched shirt cuffs. The range of his activities was incredible. Rabbi Cohen found jobs for the unemployed, hospital beds for the sick, food for the hungry, train tickets for the stranded. In the 61 years that he served B'nai Israel, he helped thousands of poor, sick, and troubled people, Christians and Jews, and fought hard for causes he believed to be right. He was a militant advocate of prison reform, including vocational training and separation of first offenders from hardened criminals.

Cohen gained national recognition for his tireless efforts in the relief work following the disastrous Galveston flood of 1900. He was a member of the central relief committee that helped care for the flood's survivors, and took the first steps toward rebuilding the stricken city. The hurricane that caused the flood drove many Jews out of Galveston and they settled in Houston and Dallas. B'nai Israel's synagogue was one of the only five Galveston houses of worship not destroyed during the flood.

In 1907, Jacob H. Schiff underwrote the Jewish Immigrants Information Bureau with headquarters in Galveston in order to distribute Jewish immigrants from Europe to the smaller towns and cities of the South and West. The so-called Galveston movement, which sought to divert the immigrants from the big eastern cities, was directed by Rabbi Cohen. The immigrants were met at the pier by Rabbi Cohen, fed and housed in Galveston, and then sent on to communities in the South and West which had agreed to help resettle them and find employment. The B'nai B'rith played a major role in this program in which Schiff invested over half a million dollars and through which more than 10,000 persons were settled between 1907 and 1914, when World War I brought the project to an end. In 1914, at the request of Secretary of State William Jennings Bryan, Rabbi Cohen directed aid to American citizens driven out of Mexico by the revolution there. He was credited with having persuaded President Woodrow Wilson to sign the bill authorizing Jewish chaplains in the United States Navy.

Rabbi Cohen was an ecumenist long before the term had come into popular vogue. Among the many anecdotes told about Rabbi Cohen is the one concerning an immigrant from Russia who was ordered deported by the authorities for illegal entry. The man had gotten into trouble with the Russian authorities, and the rabbi believed if he were sent back, he would have to face execution. The rabbi went to Washington to plead his case where an official of the Department of Labor told him that he was sorry, but that it was a clear case of illegal entry and the Russsian would be deported. The rabbi then called on his Congressman requesting an appointment with the President. President Taft received the rabbi, but told him that the matter was under the jurisdiction of the Department of Labor. "I'm sorry this had to happen to you, Rabbi Cohen," the President said. "But allow me to say that I certainly admire the way you Jews help each other—traveling all the way up here from Galveston, Texas, when a member of your faith is in trouble."

"Member of my faith? This man is not a Jew," the rabbi said. "He's a Greek Orthodox Catholic." Taken aback, the President said, "you mean to say you traveled all the way up here at your own expense to help a Greek Catholic?" To which Rabbi Cohen replied, "he's in trouble. They're going to deport him on the next ship, and he'll face a firing squad when he gets back to Russia. He's a human being, Mr. President. A human life is at stake. That's the way I see it." President Taft then dictated a telegram to the chief inspector of the Immigration Service at Galveston: "Hold Lenchuk in Galveston and release in custody of Rabbi Cohen on his return."

Rabbi Cohen's associate in providing relief for the Galveston flood victims was I.H. Kempner, who not only helped bury the dead and supervise the rehabilitation of the city, but originated the commission form of municipal government for the city after the flood. Kempner was a member of the first city commission. Harris Kempner, grandson of the first Harris Kempner, was the patriarch of one of the city's three wealthiest families in the mid-1970s. The chief executive of the Kempner bank in the 1970s was Arthur Alpert, president of the Galveston Arts Council. The Hebrew Benevolent Society, founded in 1869 as the successor to an informal Jewish relief society organized in 1839 by Rosanna Osterman, is still in existence and charged with caring for the city's four Jewish cemeteries. Mrs. Osterman's original legacy was used for the burial of 40 members of the community who died in the yellow fever epidemic of 1868.

The first Jewish names officially identified with San Antonio were Samuel Noah, who was with the Mexican rebel force that captured San Antonio from the Spanish in 1813, and Moses Albert Levy, who took part in the capture of San Antonio from the Mexicans in 1835. Joseph Landa came to San Antonio in 1844 but settled in New Braunfels, which he helped to found in 1847. He acquired a grist and saw mill on the Comal River, which was operated by Comal River water power. For years the Landas were the only Jewish family in town. They worshipped in their home and observed all the Jewish holidays.

Landa's son, Harry, was one of the great benefactors of New Braunfels. After taking over the mills from his older brothers in 1887, he modernized them and induced the International and Great Northern Railroad to run a spur line to this town. In 1890, he established the Landa Electric Light and Power Co. which supplied power to the area. In 1929, Landa sold the mills, divided the property among his sisters and brothers, and moved to San Antonio where he and his wife became civic and social leaders. When his wife died, he donated the Landa mansion to the San Antonio Public Library.

Michael Konigheim, a leading cattleman and merchant, reached San Antonio around 1848. He left during the Civil War, but returned in 1865. Konigheim, who helped found the city of San Angelo, gave land for the establishment of churches there. Daniel and Anton Oppenheimer, who opened a store in Rusk in the early 1850s, founded the banking house of D. & A. Oppenheimer in 1858 in San Antonio. It is still the oldest private bank west of the Mississippi. The brothers served in the Confederate Army, and after the Civil War worked their way back to San Antonio, then the state's largest city, where they reopened their merchandising enterprise and their bank. For a time the bank was a sideline through which the Oppenheimers financed early cattle drives from Texas to the Kansas railheads. Their sons and grandsons continue to operate the bank. J.D. Oppenheimer was a leader of the Jewish community in the 1940s, and Dr. and Mrs. Frederick Oppenheimer (son of Daniel Oppenheimer) were noted art collectors who established the Oppenheimer wing at the Marion Koogler McNay Art Museum.

Mayer and Solomon Halff, who came to Texas in the 1850s and moved to San Antonio in 1864, expanded from storekeepers in Liberty to ranch owners. They once owned 6,000,000 acres of ranchland and were among the largest stock raisers in Texas in the 1870s. The Halffs were among the first to import Hereford cattle and were among the founders of the City National Bank and the Alamo National Bank.

Mrs. Anna Hertzberg, who came to San Antonio in 1882, was a talented musician who established the city's Tuesday Musical Club, which brought nationally known artists to the city. From 1911-1914 she was president of the Texas Federation of Women's Clubs. The first woman elected to the school board in 1915, she organized San Antonio's first night school. Her son, Harry, served in the state senate and gave the city the famous Hertzberg Circus Collection.

Jewish worship services in San Antonio were held over a store beginning in 1854. That same year, an informal religious school was organized in the Mayer home. The oldest cemetery dates from 1854, two years before the establishment of the Hebrew Benevolent Society. Temple Beth El, the city's first Jewish congregation, was organized in 1874.

In 1905, when Nat M. Washer was president of Temple Beth El, he was selected to make the city's presentation to President Theodore Roosevelt when he visited San Antonio. Washer later served as chairman of the state board of education. From 1918 to the 1940s, M.M. Harris was editor of the *San Antonio Express* and *San Antonio Evening News*. G.A.C. Halff headed radio station WOAI, the largest in the southwest in the 1940s. In 1976, Beth El's Rabbi David Jacobson was elected president of the National Conference of Social Welfare, the first rabbi to head this major body of social welfare leaders. He had previously served as president of the United Community Services of Texas, among whose founders were Rabbis George Fox of Ft. Worth, Henry Cohen of Galveston, Martin Zielonka of El Paso, and Rabbi Harvey Wessel of Waco.

The late Joseph Freeman, and his brother, Harry, were the founders of the famed San Antonio Livestock Show and beloved philanthropists of south Texas. The Joe Freeman Bexar County Coliseum, where the stock show is held, is named for Joe Freeman, who was largely instrumental in its erection while he was president of the San Antonio Chamber of Commerce. Perry Kallison, known throughout south Texas as "the Old Trader," has been broadcasting his farm and ranch program without a break for 40 years, making it the oldest consecutive radio program of its kind. What began as a commercial program advertising his business, became a public service program in which Kallison helped locate missing persons, announced benefit affairs, funerals, etc., and broadcast free advertisements for anyone seeking to sell an animal or a possession. Broadcast each weekday morning and played back by tape at noon, the program enabled him to promote soil and water conservation, the organization of the San Antonio Livestock Show, and the passage of the county bond issue that made possible the building of the city's coliseum. Since the days of World War I, the Jewish community of San Antonio has played an important part in providing for the religious, welfare, and social needs of Jewish military personnel stationed at army and air force bases in and around San Antonio.

Jewish settlement in El Paso dates from before the Civil War when the town was known as Franklin and was a trading station on the Chihuahua Trail leading from Santa Fe, New Mexico to Chihuahua, Mexico. Simon Hart built the first flour mill around El Paso and established its first industry. Solomon and Joseph Schutz, who arrived in 1860, established a store on the Chihuahua Trail. The Schutz brothers voted against secession but Hart voted for it. Until the 1940s there was a monument to Hart in the city. Solomon Schutz, who was named postmaster in the 1870s, later served as Federal collector of customs. He was elected mayor in 1881. When El Paso was incorporated in 1873, Samuel Schutz was one of two commissioners appointed by the state legislature to inaugurate the city government.

Adolph Krakauer, who came to El Paso in 1870 to work as a bookkeeper in the Schutz brothers store, later pioneered along the trading trails to Mexico. In 1889 he was elected mayor, but two months after his election he had to give up the office when it was discovered that he had not yet received his second citizenship papers and therefore was ineligible. Adolph Solomon, another early settler, was elected mayor pro tem in 1893 and the following year won a full term. Maurice Ullman founded the city's first volunteer fire department.

Ernst Kohlberg, who came to El Paso in 1875 on a steamship ticket purchased by Solomon Schutz, first worked in the Schutz enterprises. Later he and his brother Moritz founded the International Cigar Co., the first cigar factory in the southwest. Kohlberg also founded the Rio Grande Valley Bank and Trust Co., operated the St. Regis Hotel, and built the El Paso Electric Railway Co. In 1893 he was elected to the city council. Mrs. Kohlberg, founder of the state's first free kindergarten, organized the

Ladies Benevolent Association which in 1892 opened the city's first hospital. She was a member of the library board for 25 years and through her efforts the first library building was erected. Kohlberg, who was murdered by a drunken tenant in 1910, is the fictional character Ludwig Stern in Tom Lea's novel, *The Wonderful Country.*

Joseph Goodman, a Russian immigrant who arrived in El Paso in 1902 after earning a stake with a general store in Vado, New Mexico Territory, started a successful feed and grain business. He brought over from Lithuania 47 members of his family, all of whom settled in the El Paso area. One of them was I.B. Goodman, one of the leaders of the Jewish community in the 1940s and 1950s. Hyman Krupp, another Russian-born Jew, organized the Texon Oil and Land Co. in 1919 to finance a wildcat well on lands owned by the University of Texas in Reagan County. The oil strike there brought in millions of dollars to the permanent fund of the University of Texas system. The oil finds of Krupp's company launched the immense oil boom in west Texas. Samuel Freudenthal, who came to El Paso in 1884, was a prominent merchant who served on the city council, the school board, and the El Paso County Commission. He was one of the founders of the Mount Sinai Association in 1887 which was renamed Temple Mt. Sinai in 1899.

Just as many of the early Jewish settlers began as traders at the nearby military posts and with the Indians in the surrounding area, later Jewish residents came to El Paso while serving in the armed forces during World Wars I and II. They fell in love with the city and its climate and returned after the wars to settle down.

In the years following the Civil War, Jews began to settle in many areas of Texas. In the 1870s there was a sprinkling of Jewish cowboys in the cattle country. Isaac Levy dispensed rough justice, and Louis B. Epstein was the terror of outlaws in Grayson County while he was judge in the frontier town of Denison in the early 1880s. In some towns there were scattered Jews some years before the Civil War. Dan Doppelmayer, who reached Marshall in 1849, served in the Confederate army together with Leo and Emanuel Kahn, who settled in Tyler in the 1860s. Charles Weil and Max Lichtenstein arrived in Corpus Christi in 1860 and Ben Melaskey came to Austin that same year. Austin's first congregation was founded in his home in 1866. Charles Brachfeld, whose family settled in Henderson in 1872, practiced law there and was elected county judge in 1898. He served in the state senate from 1904-1908 and was elected judge of a five-county district court. Grandmaster of the Texas Grand Lodge of Odd Fellows, Brachfeld is memorialized in the Henderson lodge, which is named for him.

Among the other small towns and cities where Jews settled in the 1870s, and 1880s, were Brownsville (1870), Texarkana (1880), Jefferson (1862), Victoria (1885), Waco (1888), Palestine (1886), Beaumont (1894), Austin (1876), Corsicana (1898), Gainesville (1882), Greenville (1890),

Hempstead (1880), Marshall (1884), Mexia (1895), and Calvert (1873). In 1877, when there were only 3,300 Jews in Texas, Galveston, with 1,000, was the largest Jewish community, followed by Jefferson, a small town, with 461, and San Antonio with 302. By 1905, there were 27 cities and towns with one or more Jewish organizations and 24 congregations in 17 different communities. The total Jewish population was 15,000. This figure more than doubled to 31,000 in 1917 when Dallas, with 8,000 Jews, had become the largest community, followed by Houston with 5,000, San Antonio with 3,000, Fort Worth with 2,250, Waco with 1,500, Galveston with 1,100, Beaumont with 400, and Austin with 300. There were another 7,500 Jews dispersed in 286 small towns.

Between 1900 and 1917 many Jewish settlements either dwindled to a handful of residents or vanished entirely. Among such communities were those in Bonham, Brenham, Columbus, Ennis, Gainesville, Greenville, Halletsville, Hempstead, Jefferson, Luling, Mexia, Marlin, Navasota, Orange, Palestine, Terrell, and Calvert. Palestine, an Anderson County city that acquired its name from the belief of its early Protestant settlers that the area reminded them of the Holy Land, once had a synagogue and a flourishing Jewish community. Until the 1940s the six remaining Jews maintained Temple Beth Israel in a private home. Now all that remains of the original Jewish settlement is the Jewish cemetery.

Calvert, 60 miles south of Waco, which had a population of 10,000 until World War I, and was the hub and mercantile center for the cotton industry from 1850-1890, had 40 Jewish families as late as 1875. Half of the Jewish population died in the yellow fever epidemic of the 1870s. Until 1870 there were only five or six graves in the Jewish cemetery, but it filled during the epidemic and now contains 160 graves. Jewish names can still be seen on the windows of empty stores in the now deserted main part of the city. A Jew named Oscar built an opera house in Calvert in the 1860s and worship services were held in the opera house when Calvert had the largest Jewish community between Dallas and Houston. When the cotton business shifted to Waco and other cities, Calvert began to decline and its population fell below 2,000. The last Jewish resident was an eccentric member of the Oscar family. The town of Calvert cares for the Jewish cemetery with funds provided by an association of relatives of those buried there. The official history of Robertson County has many references to and photos of Calvert's Jewish citizens of the period from the late 1850s to the 1880s.

The oil discoveries before World War I transformed Texas and greatly increased its population, including hundreds of Jewish families from other parts of the country. The World War II military installations that dotted southwest Texas brought an additional Jewish influx that continued into the 1960s and 1970s as the commercial, industrial, shipping, livestock, natural gas, petro-chemical, space, and electronic industries created new growth in the state's small and large cities. In 1927 the state's Jewish population had increased to 46,648, with more than half of the Jews living in Houston (13,500) and Dallas (10,400). San Antonio was the third largest community (5,900), followed by Fort Worth with 2,400, El Paso with 2,250, Beaumont with 1,300, and Galveston with 1,200. By 1960 Dallas had a slight edge over Houston, 17,800 to 17,000. In 1977 Houston was the home of the largest Jewish community with a population of 26,000, trailed by Dallas with 20,000. San Antonio retained third place with 6,500 Jews, followed by El Paso with 4,500, Forth Worth with 2,850, Austin with 2,000, Amarillo with 1,245, Beaumont and Waco with 800 each, Corpus Christi with 1,030, and Galveston with 620. The entire state had 71,000 Jews in 1977.

Perhaps the first Jew to settle in Dallas was Alexander Simon, who arrived in 1858. An 1865 census listed H. Hirsch, A. Shirek, Sam Shirek, and Saul Shirek, all merchants. The French Archives of Israelites refers to shops on Dallas' Main Steet being closed for Rosh Hashanah in 1865. In 1872, when Dallas was still a dusty prairie town, 11 merchants organized the Hebrew Benevolent Society which became Congregation Emanu-El two years later. The first synagogue was dedicated in 1876 on the eve of Shavuoth near what is now Field and Commerce Streets, but services had been held as early as 1871, using a Torah borrowed from New Orleans. Congregation Shearith Israel was founded in 1884. There was an earlier congregation called Ahavas Shalom, established in 1882, but it no longer exists.

Early in 1857, young Isaac Sanger came to Texas to make his fortune, starting with a general store in McKinney. Oldest of ten children, he picked McKinney to open his store because Collins County then had more people than neighboring Dallas County. A younger brother, Lehman, arrived in 1859 and within a year Sanger Brothers had stores in Decatur, Weatherford, and McKinney. Both brothers enlisted in the Confederate army. After the war they were joined by Philip Sanger. In the next seven years the Sangers opened stores in Bryan, Calvert, Kosse, Groesbeck, and Corsicana. A fourth brother, Alex, arrived in 1872 to open the Dallas store and the following year Sam Sanger established the store in Waco. The Sanger stores were the first to adopt the one-price rule. By the mid-nineties Sanger Brothers were doing a million dollar business. In 1900, the Sangers supplied free bedding and clothing to the Galveston flood victims. Alex Sanger served as a Dallas alderman in 1873 and was a founder of the Dallas Chamber of Commerce and its president for many years. He was one of the originators of The Dallas Fair, which became the official State Fair of Texas, and served as its first president. From 1911-1917 he served on the Board of Regents of the University of Texas. The Sangers have long since closed the stores in the small towns and cities, but the Sanger-Harris stores in Dallas stand as a memorial to the mercantile success of five Jewish immigrant brothers.

The world-famous Neiman-Marcus store in Dallas is another success story of an immigrant Jewish family. When Herbert Marcus, Sr., opened the Neiman-Marcus store in 1907 with his sister, Carrie, and brother-in-law, A.L. Neiman, Sanger Brothers and A. Harris, also Jewish firms, dominated the southwestern merchandising area. Marcus worked for the Sangers in Dallas as a shoe salesman. The Neiman-Marcus store was the first in the southwest to carry an exclusive line of ladies clothes never before offered in the area and was successful in combining the aspects of a department store with those of a specialty shop. What began as a modest enterprise was built into a fashion empire founded on taste and flair. Stanley Marcus, who ran the Dallas store for 24 years as successor to his father, demonstrated a superior talent for merchandising, salesmanship, and promotion. Although the store is now owned by a merchandising conglomerate, a Marcus continues to direct it.

Fred Florence, son of Russian immigrants whose parents settled in Rusk in east Texas in 1892, began as a floor sweeper at 15 for the First National Bank of Rusk. After a brief stint as a teller, he became president of the State Bank at Alto when he was only 24. After serving in the Air Corps in World War I, he resumed his job as bank president. He was elected mayor of Alto in 1919, a year before he moved to Dallas. There he founded the Guaranty Bank and Trust Co., forerunner of the Republic National Bank of which he became president in 1929 when he was only 38. Florence headed the Texas Centennial Exposition in 1936 and the Pan American Exposition in 1939.

The Zale Foundation of Dallas is the creation of two young Jewish immigrants who remembered when they were poor and victims of discrimination. In 1924, Morris and William Zale founded the Zale Corporation in Wichita Falls. Today it is said to be the world's largest retail jewelry chain. The foundation has assets of $12 million and provides seed money for testing innovative ideas, supports remedial studies programs, and underwrites scholarships for Dallas blacks planning medical careers. In 1969 the Zale Foundation created the Dallas Communications Committee to seek peaceable solutions to conflicts between various community groups. It also supported a health program for Mexicans in San Antonio. Since 1973 the Zale Award has been a $25,000 annual prize to an American who has made a significant contribution to the betterment of mankind in his chosen field of endeavor.

Julius Schepps, who was called "the irreplaceable citizen" by a Dallas newspaper, gave funds and leadership to scores of philanthropic and civic causes in Dallas for half a century. He arrived in Dallas in 1901 and went to work in a bakery and as a newsboy. Later he headed a successful wholesale liquor business. Schepps was the leading factor in the building of the Dallas Home for Jewish Aged, headed the city's first interracial commission, and in 1954 was named Dallas's outstanding citizen. Irving Goldberg, son of immigrants who settled in Port Arthur, came to Dallas in 1932 to practice law. A leading civil rights champion and a leader of the Jewish community,

Goldberg received national prominence the day President John F. Kennedy was assassinated in Dallas in 1963. Before Vice-President Lyndon B. Johnson was sworn in as President, he telephoned his old friend Irving Goldberg for advice on who should administer the oath of office aboard the Presidential plane, Air Force I. Goldberg suggested Federal Judge Sarah Hughes. In 1966, President Johnson appointed Goldberg a judge of the 5th United States Circuit Court of Appeals.

Robert Strauss, a former synagogue president who became chairman of the Democratic National Committee in 1974, was a Dallas lawyer and radio station owner. Victor Hexter, president of the Dallas school board in 1907, served on the city council under the first city manager government in 1931. Sam Klein had been president of the Dallas city council in 1905. Sixty years later, Joe Golman was elected to the city council, and in 1966 was named deputy mayor pro tem. Isidore Lovenberg had been president of the Dallas school board in 1904 and again in 1917.

Jewish settlement in Houston dates from 1835, two years before the city was named, when Eugene Joseph Chimene arrived from New York. Henry Wiener came there before Texas won its independence in 1836. The first Jewish services were held in 1844, probably in the back of a store. Jacob de Cordova donated a plot for the city's first Jewish cemetery in 1846. Other early settlers were Gustav Gerson, Robert Cohen, Manheim Jacobs, Henry Fox, and Isaac Collman. Religious services were held occasionally before 1856 in de Cordova's home. In 1856 the early *minyan* became Congregation Beth Israel, Texas' first congregation. The congregation was formally organized in 1860 and the first minister was Z. Emmich, who doubled as *hazzan* and *shohet*. Beth Israel dedicated its first synagogue in 1870.

Jacob Taub, who came to Houston after the Civil War and opened a cigar store, was the father of Ben Taub, one of the city's leading real estate developers. He gave land for the University of Houston when it was organized in 1936, and donated millions for medical research, education, and hospitals. Simon and Tobias Sakowitz, who opened a small clothing store for seamen in Galveston in 1902, opened a Houston branch in 1910 which became the key unit in a chain of speciality shops bearing the Sakowitz name. Robert Sakowitz, who headed the company in the 1970s, was one of the city's leading citizens. David H. White, for many years editor and publisher of the *Jewish Herald Voice*, was one of the early advocates for civil rights when it was dangerous to advocate black equality. For many years White was known as the most prominent Jewish figure in Texas because of his leadership in Jewish and civic causes. In the 1940s, David Daume was one of Houston's leading citizens. He was an officer of the United Gas Corporation and vice-president of the Harris County Junior Chamber of Commerce. In the 1940s, Congregation Beth Israel was badly split when it temporarily adopted an anti-Zionist platform which led to the organization of a new Reform congregation.

In 1925, Mrs. Hattie L. Henenburg of Dallas was named a special justice of the Texas Supreme Court, the first Jewish woman in the United States appointed to this judicial office. Henry Dannenbaum of Houston was a District Court judge from 1915-1919, and president of the Houston school board from 1912-1914. Reuben Williams of Fort Worth, who was secretary to Governor O'Daniel, served as State Highway and State Insurance Commissioner in the 1940s. Bayard Friedman was the first Jew elected to the Fort Worth city council in 1962. Maurice Hirsch, Houston attorney, was a brigadier general in the United States Army's Judge Advocate branch during World War II. Isaac Dahlman established the Dahlman Dressed Beef Co. in Fort Worth in 1889 when he built the city's first packing plant, marking the beginning of a new era in the Texas livestock industry. Dr. Jacob Taubenhaus, a native of Palestine, became chief of the division of plant pathology and physiology at the Texas A & M University's agricultural experimental station in 1915. His research in cotton root rot and other plant diseases was of great value to American agriculture.

Many Texas cities have had Jewish mayors: A.M. Goldstein, Waco; A.A. Lichtenstein, Corpus Christi; Adlene Harrison, Dallas; Louis Kariel, Marshall; Sam Glosserman, Lockhart; Michael Seeligson, Adrian Levy, and Isaac H. Kempner, Galveston; Adolph Solomon and Samuel Schutz, El Paso; William Levy and Jake Levy, Sherman; Ben M. Jacobs, Luling; Louis Franklin, Laredo; Benjamin Kowalski, Brownsville; Samuel Schwartz, Eagle Pass; I.L. Goldberg and Ben Bloomingdale, Jefferson; Sol I. Berg, Ysleta; Morris Hoffman, Dublin; Harry Shapiro, Sam Saba, and Jeffrey Friedman, Austin; and Ruben Edelstein, Brownsville.

* * * * *

ABILENE
Temple Mizpah, 849 Chestnut St.

AMARILLO
Garden of Four Chaplains, part of a community cemetery, memorializes the four heroic World War II chaplains, including Rabbi Goode, who gave up their life preservers to soldiers when the troopship *Dorchester* was torpedoed in 1943.

Temple B'nai Israel, 4316 Albert St.

AUSTIN
Cong. Agudas Achim, 4300 Bull Creek Road, was dedicated Dec. 30, 1963, at exercises at which President Lyndon B. Johnson was the speaker. It was the President's first non-official address since he was sworn into office following the assassination of President Kennedy.

Henry Hirschfeld House and Cottage, 305 W. 9th St., is a national registered historic place.
Jewish Community Council, 8301 Balcones Dr.
Lubavitch Chabad House, 2101 Neuces St.
Temple Beth Israel, 3901 Shoal Creek Blvd.
Texas State Archives, Texas State Library, 1201 Brazos St., preserves the diary of Adolphus Sterne, one of the state's early Jewish pioneers who participated in the Fredonian War; the personal papers of Rabbi Henry Cohen of Galveston; and the correspondence of Jacob de Cordova.

University of Texas

● Hillel Foundation, 2105 San Antonio St.
● L.B.J. Library, the East Mall, has among the 31,000,000 documents that make up the Lyndon B. Johnson papers, the exchange of notes between Johnson and ranking officials of Israel and of the Soviet Union during the Six-Day War of 1967. Among the many gifts received during his years in the White House on display are a silver Menorah presented by the then Ashkenazic Chief Rabbi of Israel, Isser Unterman, in 1965 at a meeting in the White House. Also here are a silver-covered Jerusalem Bible and a number of rare volumes of Judaica presented in 1967 by the Jewish National Fund of America, and the America's Democracy Legacy Award which the President accepted in 1965 when he addressed the Anti-Defamation League of B'nai B'rith.
● University of Texas Tower, a 307-foot high building that houses the main library and administration offices, has inscribed on the upper south corner of its east side, in large gold leaf letters, the five successive alphabets from which our own is derived: Hebrew, Egyptian, Phoenician, Greek, and Roman. In the library are the Abraham J. Schechter Collection of Judaica, established in 1939 by the Kallah of Texas Rabbis in memory of its founder, Rabbi Schechter, and the Rabbi Henry Cohen Library of 7,000 volumes bequeathed to the university by the Galveston rabbi.
● The Humanities Research Center of the university has among its collections the Presidential campaign archives of Barry Goldwater, grandson of a Jewish peddler from Poland, who was the Republican candidate for President in 1964.

BAY CITY
Beth David Center, 3521 Seventh St.

BAYTOWN
Cong. Knesseth Israel, 100 W. Sterling.

BEAUMONT
Cong. Kol Israel, 3150 McFaddin St.
Jewish Federation, P.O. Box 1981.
Temple Emanuel, 1120 Broadway.

BELLAIRE
Cong. Brith Shalom, 4610 Bellaire Blvd.
Jewish Home for Aged, 6425 Chimney Rock Rd. A B'nai B'rith residential complex adjoins the home.

BRECKENRIDGE
Temple Beth Israel, 1317 Cypress St., (c/o Marvin Socal).

BROWNSVILLE
Temple Beth El, 825 W. St. Francis St.

BRUCEVILLE
Greene Family Camp for Living Judaism of the Southwest Council of the Union of American Hebrew Congregations is located here, 30 miles from Waco and 20 miles from Temple.

BRYAN
Temple Freda, the only synagogue near the Texas Agricultural and Mechanical College, at College Station, is named for Ethel Freda Kaczer, whose husband, Benjamin, was one of Bryan's leading citizens. Kaczer and Joe Gelber, another prominent Jewish citizen, built the synagogue as a memorial to Mrs. Kaczer on land donated by John W. English, a non-Jew.

CALVERT
Old Jewish Cemetery, seven blocks from the heart of this old and declining town, dates from the 1850s when a flourishing Jewish community developed here. The burial ground is surrounded by open country. The town cares for the cemetery with funds provided by relatives of those buried here.

CASTRO COUNTY
Henri Castro, the Jewish colonizer, is honored in the name of this county, located in the Texas Panhandle, south of Amarillo. It is one of only two counties in the country named for a Jew. The other is Levy County in Florida.

CASTROVILLE
Henri Castro, a French Jew, soldier, banker, diplomat, and colonizer, is memorialized in this town just south of San Antonio, on the west bank of the Medina River, which he founded in 1844. A veteran of Napoleon's

army, Castro emigrated to the U.S. in 1819, settling in Providence, R.I. When he became an American citizen he was appointed consul to the Kingdom of Naples. He returned to France in 1838 and went into the banking business. When Texas seceded from Mexico in 1836 and became an independent republic, President Sam Houston sought a loan from Castro's bank, but Castro persuaded Houston that Texas needed people more than money. In 1842 he signed a five-year agreement to colonize a vast area west of San Antonio. What are now Medina County and large parts of Frio, McMullen, Zavalla, Uvalde, Bexar, and Bandara Counties, were part of the lands granted to Castro, who became Texas' consul general in France. Though the Mexican War delayed settlement, he published maps, and distributed pamphlets about Texas in French and German in Alsace and the Rhenish provinces. Once hostilities ended, Castro mobilized a fleet of 26 ships to bring his newly recruited immigrants to Texas. By the end of 1847 he had settled some 2,100 farmers and fruit and vine-growers in the towns of Castroville, Quihi, Vandenberg, and D'hanis, all founded by Castro. He invested $150,000 of his own money in this colonization and never received a penny in return. The first town he established was named in his honor by unanimous vote of the colonists. In a town plaza, bounded by Florella, Lafayette, and Alamo Sts., stands a large granite slab that commemorates the founding of the town and Henri Castro. There is a large portrait of Castro on the monument and a list of the first settlers. In the 1970s, the town authorities wanted to name a street for Castro but were dissuaded lest it be construed that they were honoring Fidel Castro.

CLEAR LAKE CITY

Cong. Shaar Hashalom, El Camino Real and Buoy Rd., serves young Jewish families associated with the L.B. Johnson Spacecraft Center.

COLLEGE STATION

Hillel Foundation at Texas A & M University, 800 Jersey St., is known as the Fannie and Sablosky Hillel House in honor of a Dallas couple. In the college's library there is a memorial plaque to Dr. Jacob J. Taubenhaus, one-time state plant pathologist and head of the station's department of plant pathology and physiology from 1917 to his death in 1937. His wife, Esther, who was named director of the college's Hillel Foundation in 1936, was the first woman Hillel director. The college library also has a collection of Judaica established by Hillel and the Jewish Chautauqua Society. Dormitory 12 on the campus has a marker bearing the name of Joe Utay, Jewish civic leader of Dallas, who served on the college's board of trustees for many years. The dormitory was first called the Joe Utay House, but all dormitories are now numbered. In 1974, Utay was elected to the National Football Hall of Fame. In his student days he was a football star at Texas A & M.

CORPUS CHRISTI
Cong. B'nai Israel, 3434 Fort Worth St.
Jewish Community Council, 750 Everhart Rd.
Temple Beth El, 1315 Craig St.

CORSICANA
Cong. Agudas Achim, Park Ave. and 19th St.
Temple Beth El, 208 S. 15th St.

DALLAS
Akiba Academy, 6210 Churchwill Way.

American Red Cross, Dallas County Chapter, 2300 McKinney Ave., is housed in a building that memorializes Rose Titche Spencer, whose son gave the building to the Red Cross. A plaque in the lobby notes the gift of Edward Titche in 1943.

Cong. Agudas Achim, 5810 Forest Lane.

Cong. Beth Torah, Chapel of Preston Hills Church.

Cong. Shearith Israel, 9401 Douglas, has a sanctuary in the form of an equilateral triangle, with the Ark at one of the apexes of the triangle. The diagonal walls have sloping ceilings to focus attention on the Ark, which is in the form of the tablets of the Ten Commandments. Cong. Anshe Sphard, founded in 1906, merged with Shearith Israel in 1956. In the lobby of the synagogue is a memorial to the Six Million victims of the Holocaust, a gift of Paul Lewis. This is said to be the first Holocaust memorial erected in the U.S., having been dedicated in 1959. The memorial consists of a long marble wall in front of which are six lamps burning perpetually as a tribute to the Six Million "innocent victims of a madman's fury."

Dallas Jewish Archives, 7900 Northaven Rd., (Jewish Community Center), plans to build a library and exhibit hall.

Garden of Memories (The Lewis Park), a 24-foot high monument in a hexagon form, in the new park of the Dallas Jewish Community Center, was built by Mr. and Mrs. Paul Lewis, Dallas philanthropists. They donated this Holocaust monument to the memory of the 6,000,000 Jews who died in Nazi concentration camps. The Garden of Memories is located in the extended Center Park, 7900 Northaven Road. The monument contains a bronze structure entitled *The Last March*.

On the front portion of the structure is a brief inscription of the story of the Holocaust. One side has the number of Jews lost in each country and another, the names of the concentration camps. There are poems also inscribed which pertain to the tragic events. At the top of the monument are six perpetually burning lamps.

Mr. Lewis has dedicated Holocaust memorials in a number of other cities and established the first chair for the study of the Holocaust through a grant to Yeshiva University in New York City.

Home for the Jewish Aged, 2525 Centerville Rd. Adjoining the home is the Byer Square Apartment and Activity Center named for Mrs. Mabel Dyer.

Jewish Community Center, 7900 Northaven Rd., was formerly named for Julius Schepps—one of the country's leading citizens and businessmen. In 1948 he donated the entire proceeds of his business to the UJA. The center has a 10 foot permanent Menorah on its lawn. In the lobby is a three-dimensional bronze sculpture designed as a memorial to the Holocaust victims. It was a gift of Paul Lewis, Dallas philanthropist.

Jewish Family Service, 1416 Commerce St.

Jewish Vocational Counseling Services, 11300 N. Central Expressway.

Jewish Welfare Federation, 8616 Northwest Plaza.

Jerry Lewis Neuromuscular Disease Research Center, Baylor University School of Medicine, is named for the popular entertainer, who as national chairman of the Muscular Dystrophy Association has raised millions each year through his 24-hour Labor Day telethon for the MDA's research program.

Olla Podrida, 12205 Cold Rd., North Dallas, a shopping bazaar for artists, craftsmen, and collectors, which is part of the 275-acre office park known as Park Central, has at its front entrance part of one of the stained glass windows that once graced the old Temple Emanu-El at South Blvd. and Harwood St. The section of the old Temple Emanu-El window acquired from a dealer of architectural antiquities is the upper section of a larger panel, with the Stars of David in either corner.

Sanger Bros. complex, bounded by Elm, Lamar, Main, and Austin Sts., is a nationally registered historic site recalling the pioneer mercantile establishment of Isaac Sanger.

Southern Methodist University, 6005 Bishop Blvd., has in its Bridewell Library the Harrison Bible Collection, which comprises more than 350 Bibles in many languages, including Hebrew, dating back to the 13th century. In 1973, Dr. Menahem Schmelzer, librarian of the Jewish Theological Seminary of America, identified one item in the Bible collection as a Torah Scroll that once belonged to the now-vanished Chinese Jewish community which flourished at Kaifeng from the 12th to the early 19th centuries. The Bridewell Library also houses the Sadie and David Lefkowitz Collection of Judaica established by the sisterhood and brotherhood of Temple Emanu-El in honor of the 50th wedding anniversary of Rabbi and Mrs. David Lefkowitz, Sr. Also in the library is the Levi Olan Collection, established by friends of Rabbi Olan, a former rabbi of Temple Emanu-El. The Olan Collection profiles the development of the book as an art form. There is a Hillel Foundation at the university.

Temple Emanu-El, 8500 Hillcrest Rd., has a unique 90-foot high dome supported by curved walls of accoustical fins and hung with 47 tubular lights. The Ten Commandments hang on the brick Ark wall, inlaid with flecks of gold that form a giant Menorah.

Temple Shalom, Hillcrest and Alpha Rds:, has a *bimah* backed by a huge expanse of Mexican brick into which the curtain of the Ark is set like a jewel, evoking a distant memory of the desert. On a marble wall in a corridor is a combined memorial to the 6,000,000 victims of the Holocaust and to the people of Denmark who risked their lives to save Danish Jewry during World War II. One-third of the Menorah in the memorial is missing to symbolize the loss of one-third of the Jewish population of the world.

Texas Jewish Post, 1621 Main St.

Texas State Fair, in Fair Park, has a monument near the Park Ave. side that honors the three men who founded the fair in 1889. One of them was Alexander Sanger who served as the first president of the fair. Sanger St., running between Grand Ave. and the Santa Fe Railroad tracks, is named for Alexander Sanger, pioneer merchant and Jewish communal leader. The Alexander Sanger branch of the Dallas Public Library is also named for him.

Tifereth Israel Cong., 10909 Hillcrest Rad., has a huge tree of life sculpture on an outside brick wall.

Thanks-Giving Square, founded by an interfaith group of four businessmen, including Julius Schepps, in the heart of downtown Dallas, is a beautiful garden in the center of which is a 91-foot white marble shell designed in the form of a spiral.

United Fund of Metropolitan Dallas, 901 Ross Bldg., has a portrait of Julius Schepps, Dallas philanthropist, in its board room and a photo of him in the executive director's office. The portrait originally hung in the old Community Chest building on S. Akard St. which had been a gift from Schepps in 1944 and was named for him.

Zale Library at Bishop College, 3837 Simpson-Stuart Rd., was a gift of Morris Zale whose portrait hangs in the library.

EL PASO

Cong. B'nai Zion, 210 E. Cliff Dr.

Jewish Federation, 405 Mardi Gras.

Krakauer Memorial Bldg., 510 S. Oregon St., which houses the El Paso Family Welfare Association, was a gift of the Krakauer family, one of whose members, Abraham, was an alderman here in the 1880s.

Schutz Street is named for Solomon Schutz, one of the city's pioneer settlers and its mayor from 1880-1881.

Maurice Schwartz Memorial in the chapel of Old Fort Bliss, one of the city's landmarks, is a plaque erected in 1954 by the Fort Bliss 100th Anniversary Memorial Commission to honor its chairman and the man who sponsored a replica of the first Fort Bliss.

Temple Mount Sinai, 4403 N. Stanton, has a soaring tower-like peak set against the mountain and desert backdrop that recalls the Israelites' tents in the desert. The synagogue has a wedge-shaped parabolic arch in the sky which opens into a prayer hall in the desert and the mountains. The tower that dominates the viewer's attention as one beholds the synagogue from afar is symbolic of the rabbi's outstretched arms as he invokes the priestly blessing.

University of Texas, El Paso, Hillel Foundation, 6063 Bel Mar.

FORT WORTH

Brachman Hall, a student residence on the Worth Hills campus of Texas Christian University, is named for Solomon Brachman, a trustee of the university for more than 20 years, a prominent insurance and oil company executive, and Jewish civic leader.

Cong. Ahavath Sholom, 1600 W. Myrtle St. (in Overton Park area).

Cong. Beth El, 207 W. Broadway, has one wing named for Sadie and Dan Danciger.

Dan Danciger Jewish Community Center, 6801 Granbury Rd.

Hebrew Institute, 2308 Warner Rd.

Jewish Federation, 6801 Granbury Rd.

Kimball Art Museum, 1101 Will Rogers Rd., has, in its permanent collection, Rembrandt's painting, *Portrait of a Young Jew*. Painted in 1663, the work is a portrait of a young bearded man wearing a dark cloak and a *yarmulke*.

Dr. Louis J. Levy Hall, Fort Worth Children's Museum, 1501 Montgomery St. This hall is named for a prominent Jewish physician and communal worker.

Texas Jewish Post, 3120 S. Pecan St.

GALVESTON

Biblical Marker, inscribed with a quotation from Exodus 20.24, is imbedded in the concrete walk at 39th and Sea-wall Blvd., as a reminder of the "greatest Engineer of them all." It was created by a private citizen as a memorial to the victims of the Galveston tornado of 1900. The inscription reads: "In all places where I record my name I will come unto thee and I will bless thee. Hallowed be Thy Name."

Henry Cohen Community House, erected in 1928 by Temple B'nai Israel at 22nd and Avenue I, became a Masonic clubhouse in 1953 when the congregation's new building was dedicated. The inscription on the cornerstone which still remains reads: "Erected in honor of Dr. Henry Cohen's forty years service as rabbi in this community."

Cong. Beth Jacob, 2401 Avenue K.

Jewish Community Council and Welfare Association, P.O. Box 146, Galveston, 77558.

Kempner Park, 26th St. and Avenue O, was given to the city by Stanley Kempner as a memorial to his father, Isaac H. Kempner, one of Galveston's most distinguished citizens, who served as city treasurer in 1899 and as mayor from 1917-1919.

Lasker Home for Homeless Children, 1019 16th St., is named for its founder, Morris Lasker, philanthropist and one-time member of the state senate.

E.S. Levy & Co. Store, 2227 Central Plaza, has been designated as a landmark by the Texas State Historic Survey. One of the few retail establishments in the country owned and operated by the same family for over a century, the store was founded in 1877 by Abraham Levy.

Lovenberg Junior High School, 39th and T. Sts., honors the memory of Isidore Lovenberg, member of the school board for 39 years, and its president from 1904 until his death in 1917. His portrait hangs in the lobby.

Osterman Oleander Memorial, recalls the oleander brought from Jamaica in 1839 by Joseph Osterman, one of the earliest Jewish settlers in Texas, and planted on what is now the s.e. cor. of Rosenberg St. and Sealy. It is commemorated by a marker on the building of the Southern Union Gas Co. Osterman was killed in the Civil War. His wife, Rosanna, bequeathed her whole estate to Jewish and general philanthropies when she died in 1866.

Temple B'nai Israel-Henry Cohen Memorial, 3008 Avenue O, honors the late Rabbi Henry Cohen who served the temple for 61 years. A large Menorah is silhouetted on the brick entrance wall. Five huge Hebrew letters set out in brick on the south wall symbolize five of the Ten Commandments. Five other letters on the north wall symbolize the other five. In the front foyer are oil portraits of Rabbi and Mrs. Cohen.

GOLIAD

Memorial to Col. William J. Fannin and his men who were massacred on orders of Mexican General Santa Anna during the Texas War of Independence on March 27, 1836, is in Goliad State Park, on U.S. Highway 59, where the event took place. Fannin and his men are buried beneath the monument. One of those who died with Fannin was 21-year old Edward Johnson, a Jew from Cincinnati, a volunteer in the Texan army.

HARLINGEN

Temple Beth Israel, 1702 E. Jackson.

HEMPSTEAD

Sam Schwarz Training School is named for Sam Schwarz, a Confederate veteran. The school was founded by his son, Ben Schwarz, Jr., whose wife raised funds locally and obtained a grant from the Julius Rosenwald School. There is also a Schwarz High School and Schwarz Park in this town which once had a flourishing Jewish community.

HOUSTON

Cohen House, faculty house at Rice University, Cullen Blvd., was built in 1927 as a gift of George Cohen, philanthropist, in celebration of the 70th birthday of his parents, Mr. and Mrs. Robert I. Cohen.

Commission for Jewish Education, 5601 S. Braeswood.

Cong. Beth Am, 1431 Britmoore Rd.

Cong. Beth Israel, 5600 N. Braeswood, the oldest congregation in the state, having been founded in 1854, has in its front lobby 12 needlepoint artistic interpretations of Marc Chagall's 12 windows in the Hadassah chapel in Jerusalem. The needlepoints are a memorial to Trudy Levy.

Cong. Beth Yeshurun, 4525 Beechnut, has in the Berkman Chapel of the William S. Malev School for Religious Studies, (named for the congregation's late rabbi), carpeted tiers surrounding the Ark so that worshippers may sit informally as did the ancient Israelites when they praised God. Also in the chapel are needlepoint canvas recreations of 12 lithographs by Israel's noted painter, Reuven Rubin. The congregation also has a major museum of Judaica that includes the 150 pieces collected by Isaac Toubin, for many years executive vice-president of the American Association for Jewish Education. His collection was acquired for Beth Yeshurun by Mr. and Mrs. Louis Kaplan and Mr. and Mrs. Irvin Kaplan.

In the front hall is a large memorial to the Holocaust victims, a gift of Paul Lewis, who has given similar memorials to a number of other synagogues. Affixed to a brick wall on the interior is a marble plaque with a reproduction in reduced form of the sculpture in the Jewish Community Center of Dallas (see Dallas). Under the reproduction are the words "For These I Weep" from the Book of Lamentations, 1:16. Below are six lights burning eternally and a brief inscription.

Cong. Brith Shalom, 4610 Bellaire.

Cong. Emanu-El, 1500 Sunset Blvd., has in its lobby a three-figure statue entitled *The Bar Mitzvah*, a terra cotta sculpture that memorializes Jacob E. Lecher, a former vice-president of the congregation. In the Robert I. Kahn Gallery there is a Nierman tapestry and a piece by Alexander Liberman, *Sacred Precinct 11 (2)*, a gift in memory of Harry Allen by his wife, Mr. and Mrs. Sid Atlas, and Mr. and Mrs. Budd Allen.

Consulate of Israel, 1520 Texas Ave.

J.B. Goldberg Senior Citizens Housing Complex, based on a $2,300,000 award from H.U.D., is being erected at Fondren and Bankside, near the Jewish Community Center, by the Houston B'nai B'rith Lodge.

Hillel Foundation, University of Houston, 106-08 A.D. Bruce Religious Center.

Houston Congregation for Reform Judaism, 801 Bering Dr.

Jewish Community Center, 5601 S. Braeswood. There is a Memorial Area branch at 245 Town & Country.

Jewish Community Council, 5601 S. Braeswood.

Jewish Family Service, 4131 S. Braeswood.
Jewish Herald Voice, 4003 Bellaire Rd.
Jewish Home for the Aged, (see Bellaire)
Jewish Medical Research Institute, in the Research Building Compound of Baylor University. The entrance has a large Star of David.
Lubavitcher Chabad House, Fondren Rd. at Portal.
Rothko Chapel, Barnard and Yupon Sts., in the Institute of Religion and Human Development, a part of the Texas Medical Center, is named for the late American abstract artist, Mark Rothko. Designed as an ecumenical house of worship that gives equal consideration to all religions, the chapel displays 14 paintings by Rothko, who devoted three of the last years of his life to creating what has been described as a major project of 20th century religious art on the scale of the Matisse Chapel in France. In a reflecting pool in front of the chapel is a 20-foot upside down steel obelisk dedicated to the memory of Dr. Martin Luther King, Jr.
South Texas Hebrew Academy, 5435 S. Braeswood.
Ben Taub General Hospital, 1502 Taub Loop, is named for the prominent real estate developer and philanthropist.
United Orthodox Synagogues of Houston, 4221 S. Braeswood, has a glass sculpture by the noted artist Herman Perlman that is a memorial to the victims of the Holocaust. The sculpture depicts six towering candles and a dove flying over the symbolic Jewish remnants.
Pauline Sterne Wolff Memorial Home for Orphans and Widows, 1400 Hermann Dr., was established in 1931 with a bequest by Mrs. Pauline Sterne Wolff. Since most orphans and widows are cared for in foster homes, the home is now used for indigent and ill children of all faiths. Part of Mrs. Wolff's bequest was used to erect the old Home for the Jewish Aged.

JEFFERSON

Jefferson Playhouse, 211 W. Austin St., a landmark of this once booming steamboat town, is the old building of the Hebrew Sinai Cong., built in the 1870s. For many years the synagogue stood unused but was maintained by an endowment from an old Jewish family. Now a popular tourist attraction because of its historic homes, Jefferson draws thousands of visitors to the annual presentation in the playhouse of the town melodrama, "The Diamond Bess Murder Trial." The production reenacts the final trial in the 1877 murder of Anne Stone Moore Rothschild in Jefferson. The victim, known as Diamond Bess because of her jewels, was secretly married to Abe Rothschild, a dandy and scion of a Jewish diamond dealer in Cincinnati. Three days after they arrived in Jefferson, Diamond Bess disappeared and her body was found two weeks later in the woods outside the city. Seven years and three trials later, Rothschild was acquitted of the crime.

KEMPNER

Isaac H. Kempner, Galveston merchant and public official, is memorialized in this Lampasas County hamlet of less than 100 people.

KOPPERL

Moritz Kopperl, an early railroad builder, is memorialized in this Bosque County hamlet of 200 people.

LAREDO

Cong. Agudas Achim, 2100 Laredo St.
Temple B'nai Israel, c/o M.A. Mandel, P.O. Box 59.

LONGVIEW

Temple Emanuel, 209 Eden Dr., has a large Menorah built into the facade over the main entrance. The synagogue also serves the Jews of Kilgore, whose Beth Sholom Synagogue is no longer used.

LUBBOCK

Temple Shearith Israel, 1706 23rd St.

MC ALLEN

Temple Emanuel, 1410 Redwood.

MARSHALL

Leo N. Kahn Memorial Hospital, the city's general hospital, is named for Leo N. Kahn, who, with his brother, Emanuel, settled here in the early 1850s. Emanuel fought with the Confederates while Leo served in the Union army. Leo Kahn's heirs gave the city the funds to buy the ground on which the hospital stands.

Temple Moses Montefiore, 209 W. Burleson.

MESQUITE

Beth Israel Cong., 4805 Gus Thomasson Rd., is housed in a building donated by Paul Lewis, Dallas realtor and philanthropist, who has given many synagogue memorials to the 6,000,000 victims of the Holocaust.

MEXIA

"Uncle" Joe Nussbaum founded this Limestone County town in 1922 when he was in his 80s and a beloved patriarch. He was so well-liked by the residents of the town, including the Ku Klux Klan, that they often asked him to settle disputes rather than resort to legal means.

NACOGDOCHES

Stephen F. Austin State College has among its Bible collection one in which the name "Adolphus Sterne" is inscribed.

Hoya Memorial Library and Museum, 211 S. Lanana St., is the sturdy old house built in 1828 by Adolphus Sterne as a refuge for women and children during Indian raids. Sterne was one of the first settlers here. Sam Houston, the first president of the Republic of Texas, was a guest here on a number of occasions.

NEW BRAUNFELS

Landa Park, on the Comal River, off Landa St., is a memorial to Joseph and Helena Landa who settled here in 1847 and developed enterprises that included feed and flour mills, cotton gins, cotton seed oil mills, corn shellers, and power and ice plants. The only Jewish family in town, the Landas worshipped in their home and observed all the Jewish festivals. The park, once 150 acres of irrigated vegetable fields, was sold to the town by Harry Landa, the pioneer's son. The old Landa Victorian home on the Main Plaza was also given to the city for a city hall, but it has since been torn down to make room for a parking area.

PALESTINE

Old Jewish Cemetery is all that remains of a once-flourishing Jewish community. There was once a Temple Beth Israel in this city whose name has no connection with the Palestine of the Bible. It was founded and named by a group of "Predestinarian Regular Baptists." The synagogue has long since been sold to a church.

PORT ARTHUR

Temple Rodef Shalom, 3948 Procter.

RICHARDSON

Cong. Beth Torah, is housed in Community Lutheran Church, 810 Lookout.

Cong. Beth Tsiyon, 401 Canyon Creek.

SAN ANTONIO

Abe Street is named for a member of the family of Michael Konigheim, a prominent merchant and cattleman of the 1870s.

Agudas Achim Synagogue, 1201 Donaldson Ave.

Boy Scouts Home, 2519 Broadway, an armory and recreation headquarters, was a gift of Alexander Joske, civic leader and merchant, to the Boy Scout Council in memory of his son. The youth center has a plaque memorializing young Joske.

Cong. Rodfei Sholom, 115 East Laurel St.

David Street is named for the oldest son of Michael Konigheim.

Joe Freeman-Bexar County Coliseum, 3201 Houston, where the annual stock show is held, is named for the late Joe Freeman, one of the principal founders of the livestock show and rodeo. Freeman was chairman of the farm and ranch committee of the San Antonio Chamber of Commerce in the 1940s when he began to gather support for a coliseum to house a livestock show. Joe and his brother, Harry, grew up in San Antonio, engaging in various businesses from automobile sales to pecan shelling.

Golden Manor–Jewish Home for the Aged, 130 Spencer Lane.

Anna Hertzberg Hall of Music Memorial, cor. N. St., St. Mary's St., and Alpine Dr., honors the memory of Mrs. Eli Hertzberg, notable patron of music, art, and literature, and mother of Harry Hertzberg. Owned by the city, the hall was built by public subscription.

Harry Hertzberg Circus Collection, housed in two rooms on the third floor of the San Antonio Public Library, Market at Presa, is the world's largest collection—20,000 pieces—of circusana. A San Antonio attorney, Hertzberg spent 20 years in assembling the unique collection as a hobby. Many items were gifts from famous circus performers. At the entrance to the collection hall is a bust of Hertzberg which is inscribed, "We love you as you love the circus. Can more be said?" The rooms were dedicated in 1942, two years after Hertzberg's death. In addition to serving on the library board for many years, he was also a member of the state senate.

Jewish Community Center, 103 W. Rampart Dr.

Jewish Family and Children's Service, 8434 Ahern.

Jewish Journal, 8434 Ahern.

Jewish Social Service Federation, 8434 Ahern.

Joske Pavilion, Breckenridge Park and Broadway, is a public picnic ground established by Alexander Joske.

Landa Branch of the San Antonio Public Library, cor. Bushnell Pl. and Shook Ave., was the mansion of Mr. and Mrs. Harry Landa which Landa donated to the city after his wife's death in 1942.

Marion Koogler McNay Art Museum, 6000 New Braunfels St., has the Lang Wing and Lang Collection donated by Sylvan and Mary Lang, and the Oppenheimer Collection of Gothic art in the Oppenheimer Wing, donated by Mr. and Mrs. Frederick Oppenheimer.

New Jewish Congregation, a new chavurah synagogue which holds its worship services in peoples homes, can be reached by communicating with Aaron Konstam, 4202 Modena Dr., San Antonio, Tex., 78218.

San Antonio Battle Marker, on the Main Plaza, is a historical marker commemorating the battle for San Antonio fought Dec. 5, 1835, at the outset of the Texas revolution against Mexico. During this battle Moses Albert Levy tended the wounded after doing his share of fighting. He had come from New Orleans as a member of the New Orleans Greys, a volunteer regiment.

Solomon Schechter School, 1201 Donaldson Ave.

Temple Beth El, 211 Belknap, has the David and Helen Jacobson Gardens, honoring Rabbi David Jacobson, who served as the temple's spiritual leader from 1938-1976, and Mrs. Jacobson.

Temple Beth El Cemetery, Palmetto and Crockett Sts., has three tombstones surrounded by a six-foot wall. On the largest tombstone is a charming piece of early American primitive art—a bas-relief of two men facing each other, one aiming a gun at the other. The strange sight recalls the death of Siegmund Moses Feinberg, who died Dec. 10, 1857, at the age of 30, supposedly in a duel with his friend and neighbor, Benedict Schwartz, also a Jew. They had quarreled over a dog and Schwartz shot his friend. Actually, it was murder and the concept of a duel is the result of a fiction perpetrated by the tombstone maker. The other two graves are those of Elenora Lorch, Feinberg's mother-in-law, and his daughter. Mrs. Lorch gave Feinberg $100 to buy this ground and to establish the first Jewish burial ground in San Antonio in 1856. She was the first person to be buried there in 1856.

University of Texas

Hillel Foundation, 636 Ivy Lane.

Jewish Histo-Wall, Institute of Texas Cultures, is one of 266 exhibits depicting the contributions to Texas history of diverse elements of the population. It highlights Jewish beginnings in the state and portrays the roles of Jewish men, women, and institutions and their achievements.

San Antonio Library, at the University has a collection of over 3,000 Yiddish books, including first editions of Peretz, Sholom Aleichem, and other classics, some works published in Europe in the mid-19th century and one book published in Mexico which was illustrated by Diego Rivera.

SANGER

Alexander Sanger, who settled in Corsicana in 1872 and later became a leading merchant in Dallas, is memorialized in this Denton County town of 1,200 people. The town was originally known as Hulen, but in 1892 some railroad men requested that it be changed to Sanger, under which name the town was incorporated in 1911. Sanger was president of the Texas State Fair in 1894 and also president of the Texas Manufacturing Association.

SAN JACINTO STATE PARK

Site of the Battle of San Jacinto, April 21, 1836, the decisive battle that won Texas her independence from Mexico, now known as San Jacinto State Park, 22 miles southeast of Houston on State Highway 225, was where 785 Texans defeated General Santa Anna's force of twice that number. Among the Jews in the Texan force were Albert Emanuel, a friend of Sam Houston, who served in the 2nd Regiment of Texas Volunteers; Lt.

Kohn, a member of the Texas Spy Company; and Eugene Joseph Chimene, who was also part of the escort that accompanied Houston when he went to examine plans for Austin City.

SCHULENBERG
Temple Israel, which serves scattered Jewish residents in a tri-county area, is not always open. Information can be obtained from Mrs. Maunie Hyman, 508 Baumgarten St.

TEXARKANA
Mount Sinai Cong., 1310 Walnut St.

TYLER
Cong. Ahabath Achim, 1014 W. Houston St.
Federation of Jewish Welfare, P.O. Box 934.
Temple Beth El, 606 W. Shaw.

VICTORIA
Temple B'nai Israel, 606 N. Main St.

WACO
Cong. Agudath Jacob, 4925 Hillcrest Dr.
Jewish Welfare Council of Waco and Central Texas, P.O. Box 8031.
Temple Rodef Sholem, 1717 N. 41st St., resembles the tent of the ancient Israelites in the wilderness, while the roof gives the effect of the sheltering wings of the storied Schechim. The religious school area is shaped in the form of a Star of David.

Waco was laid out as a city in 1849 by Jacob de Cordova, who donated funds to each religious denomination to build a house of worship. De Cordova was well-versed in Judaism and wrote Hebrew with facility. Several *Ketuboth* (marriage contracts) written by him are preserved at the Hebrew Union College—Jewish Institute of Religion in Cincinnati.

WHARTON
Cong. Shearith Israel, Old Lane City Rd. at Highway 60, occupies a building shaped like a Star of David. The congregation serves some 80 to 100 Jewish families in Wharton, El Campo, Newgulf, Edna, and Palacios in rural south central Texas.

WICHITA FALLS
House of Jacob Synagogue,3414 Kemp Blvd.
Zundelowitz Junior High School, 1706 Polk St., is named for Abe Zundelowitz, who settled in Wichita Falls in the early 1900s and gave the city funds to acquire the site on which the school was erected in 1926. Portraits of Zundelowitz and his wife hang in the main corridor on the second floor.

Virginia

Virginia, the oldest and most populous of the original 13 colonies, was one of the last in which an organized Jewish community was established. For almost two generations after the founding of Virginia in 1607, there was no record of Jewish immigration to the area. No permanent Jewish settlement developed in Virginia until the last quarter of the 18th century. The absence of towns of any size, the lack of an independent urban middle class, and the control of economic, political, and social life by large plantation owners who imported the goods they needed from England, made Virginia unattractive to Jews.

Had there been any practicing Jews in Virginia in the 17th century they would have found themselves without any religious or political rights. Not only were they barred from citizenship, but under the Virginia Code of 1611 they were liable to the death penalty for speaking "impiously or maliciously against the holy and blessed Trinitie." A 1705 law excluded all non-Christians, Negroes, and Catholics from serving as witnesses in a court. An act of 1753 banned the employment of Christian servants by Jews. The Church of England was integrated with the civil authority and Jews and dissident Protestants were taxed for the support of the established church. The Virginia House of Burgesses did not naturalize any Jews; nor did any Jews in Virginia become British citizens under the Parlimentary act of 1740. In a colony where Baptists had to fight for toleration, it was hardly likely that Jews would be encouraged to settle and receive religious and political rights, according to Dr. Jacob R. Marcus, noted historian.

The bill of rights adopted by the Virginia House of Burgesses a month before the proclamation of the Declaration of Independence declared that "all men are equally entitled to the free exercise of religion, according to the dictates of conscience." These words, incorporated into the first constitution adopted by the Commonwealth of Virginia on June 29, 1776, did not abolish any of the existing disabilities applicable to Protestant dissenters and Jews, and withheld political rights and citizenship. Under the new constitution, the Anglician Church remained the only legalized religion in Virginia. Jews and certain other groups were not permitted to perform marriages until 1784.

It was not until 1786 that Jews and other groups achieved complete religious and political freedom in Virginia. This resulted from the adoption of the Statute of Virginia for Religious Freedom, written by Thomas Jefferson and adopted by the Virginia State Legislature, making Virginia the first state to give all its inhabitants civil and religious equality even before the adoption of the Federal Constitution in 1787. The Jefferson statute provided that "no man shall be compelled to frequent or support any religious worship, place, or ministry whatsoever, nor shall be enforced, restrained, molested, or burthened in his body or goods, nor shall otherwise suffer on account of his religious opinions or belief; but that all men shall be free to profess and by argument to maintain their opinion in matters of religion, and that all the same shall in no wise diminish, enlarge, or affect their civil capacities." In 1799 the legislature repealed all existing laws that appeared to be in contradiction to the 1786 act, and in 1802 all churches were given equal rights.

Despite the laws aimed at discouraging Jewish settlement, individual Jews were in and out of Virginia in the 17th century. Elias Legardo, who landed in Virginia in 1621, may have been a Jew. A Mose and Rebecca Isaake were listed as residents in 1622. A John Levy received a patent for 200 acres in James City County in 1648. Silvedo and Manuel Rodriguez are mentioned in Lancaster County records for 1652. David Ferrara of New Amsterdam was buying Virginia leaf tobacco as early as 1658. In that same year Moses Nehemiah, Virginia's first known Jew, was involved in litigation in the York County court. In old records, Amaso de Tores, who arrived before 1650, is described as a Spanish Jew, and Albino Lupo, a Portuguese Jew, is also mentioned. There was an Isaac Jacob in Northampton County in 1674 and a Robert Nathan was a member of the militia in 1687. A Colonel Levy was involved in the insurrection of Carolina residents in Virginia in 1711 and was executed by order of Governor Alexander Spottiswood. According to William E. Connelly, historian of Wyandotte County, Kansas, a "Jewish lad" by the name of Samuel Sanders, who was convicted in London in 1760 on trumped up charges of coin clipping, was deported to Virginia where he became an indentured servant. He is said to have escaped and joined Daniel Boone on a journey to Kentucky where he was captured by Shawnee Indians who adopted him.

There is a tradition that after the great earthquake in Lisbon, Portugal, in 1755, a company of Jews sailed for Virginia but their ship was blown off course and they landed at Newport, Rhode Island instead. A scattering of Spanish and Portuguese who may have been Marranos from South America and Europe also came to Virginia in the 17th and early 18th centuries. All of these real or reputed Jews were so few that the authorities ignored them.

One of the earliest known Jews in Virginia was Dr. John de Sequeyra, (also known as Siccari), who kept his Jewishness a secret. A Marrano who was born in London and educated in Holland, de Sequeyra came to Williamsburg in 1745 where he began the practice of medicine. He did not belong to a church and never revealed that he was of Jewish origin. Sequeyra enjoyed a wide and influential circle of friends. On several occasions he treated George Washington's step-daughter, Patsy Custis. Thomas Jefferson credited Dr. Sequeyra with having introduced the tomato as a vegetable to the Colonial dining table.

Following the middle of the 18th century, a greater number of Jewish merchants, artisans, silversmiths, watchmakers, chandlers, and fur and land dealers were engaged in a variety of business enterprises in Virginia. Aaron Lopez of Rhode Island had a Jewish agent in Virginia, Enoch Lyon, who arrived during the French and Indian War. Michael Franks and Jacob Myers served under General Washington in the western Pennsylvania campaign against the French in 1754. David Franks of Philadelphia contributed to a defense fund in Virginia after General Braddock's defeat by the French and Indians. When Washington led an expedition of Virginians that reconquered Fort Duquesne (later Pittsburgh) Franks was one of those that outfitted it. Among the busiest entrepreneurs in Virginia were Joseph Simon of Lancaster, Pennsylvania, and members of the Gratz family. The firm of Simon and Campbell advanced money and supplies for repairing Fort Pitt on the western frontier, and for constructing Fort Fincastle, later the site of Wheeling, West Virginia. Simon and the Gratzes also acted as agents for Virginia in Lord Dunmore's War in 1754.

Michael Israel was a landowner in Albemarle County in 1757 and was a member of the militia. Solomon Israel was a landowner in 1764 in the same county. Hezekiah Levy was a member of the Fredericksburg Masonic lodge before 1771, the same lodge to which George Washington belonged. Isaiah Isaacs, a silversmith from England, settled in Richmond in 1769, having fled from England to escape his debtors. Isaacs became a partner of Jacob I. Cohen and developed what became Richmond's largest Jewish business establishment after the Revolution. He served as a clerk of the Town Market

(1785), as tax assessor, and in the Richmond town council together with John Marshall, the future Chief Justice of the United States Supreme Court. Owner of lands in half a dozen counties, Isaacs wrote and spoke English badly. He wrote his important documents and signed his name in Hebrew script. Isaacs and Cohen dealt in slaves, owned the Bird-in-Hand, Richmond's oldest tavern, and speculated heavily in land warrants, which had been used by the states to pay their debts and as compensation to state troops who had served in the Revolution. Buying and selling these warrants to the western lands became a big business. Isaacs and Cohen twice commissioned Daniel Boone to locate and explore 10,000 acres in Kentucky for which they held warrants. They paid Boone six pounds in gold, and Boone's signed receipts which survive are collector's items. Isaacs noted in Yiddish the transaction with Boone on the back of the receipts.

Jacob I. Cohen, who had come to the colonies from Germany around 1773 and settled in Philadelphia, drifted to Charleston, South Carolina, where he served in Captain Lushington's militia company during the Revolution and then moved to Richmond in 1781. In Richmond he lent money to James Madison while the future President was attending the Constitutional Convention in 1787. Cohen had left Philadelphia because the Reverend Gershom Mendes Seixas, minister of Mikveh Israel Congregation, acting on the advice of synagogue leaders in England, refused him permission to marry a woman who was both a convert and a divorcee. Jewish religious law forbids the marriage of a Cohen—a member of the priestly caste—to a convert or a divorcee. In Virginia, Cohen found no obstacles to marrying Hester Mordecai, whose first husband was also a Jew. Twenty-eight years after his marriage, Cohen became president of Mikveh Israel Congregation in Philadelphia.

Among the handful of Jews in Virginia during the Revolution was Phillip Moses Russell, the surgeon's mate in the 2nd Virginia Regiment, who won Washington's commendation for his role in caring for the wounded at Valley Forge. Captain Jacob Cohen, who raised a company of militia in Cumberland County, may not have been a Jew, according to Dr. Jacob R. Marcus. This Cohen married a Christian. Michael Gratz of Lancaster and Philadelphia, who moved to Virginia, cared for British prisoners of war. He was employed by Virginia as a purchasing agent to bring in goods which the state badly needed since it had few factories. Gratz's ships ran the British blockade with goods and arms from the West Indies. Simon Nathan, an English Jew who was in business in Jamaica, smuggled war supplies from the West Indies to Virginia by way of neutral ports. When the British learned of his activities, he moved to New Orleans where he continued his aid to Virginia. Nathan was a heavy investor in Virginia bonds issued to pay for General George Rogers Clark's conquest of the Northwest Territory.

There were also a number of other Jews in Virginia before the end of the Revolutionary War in 1783. Isaac Levy, a merchant and doctor, was practicing in Virginia in 1779 and provisioning Virginia troops. Henry Lazarus was a merchant in Winchester during the war years. Jacob Cohen, the third of that name in Virginia during the 1780s, was a silversmith in Alexandria, who married a Christian. Ezekiel Levy, identified by Dr. Marcus as a convert, was a vestryman in the Protestant Episcopal Church in Williamsburg in the late 1780s. Marcus Elcan, who owned a store in Richmond in 1782, was witness to the Yiddish document that dissolved the firm of Isaacs and Cohen. Elcan owned a fine library for those times and in his will left $1,000 to the Richmond Charity School. Joseph Darmstadt, who came to America as a sutler with the Hessian troops in the service of the British, renounced his foreign allegiance and settled in Richmond at the close of the war. His knowledge of German enabled him to attract trade to his store from German-born farmers living in the valleys of the Blue Ridge Mountains. Meyer Dirkheim, who came to Richmond in the 1780s, spent his time traveling through the Carolinas, Georgia, and Virginia as the only *mohel* in that part of the country. He also made candles and soap at a shop opposite the state capital in Richmond and worked as a lamplighter for the bridge that crossed a creek at Main Street.

In 1782, three male Jews were listed on Richmond tax rolls. By 1788, there were 28. Among the latter were Jacob Mordecai, who became a partner in 1786 with Samuel and Moses Myers of Norfolk; Isaac H. Judah; Moses Nunez and Abraham N. Cardozo, who were farmers and ancestors of Supreme Court Justice Benjamin N. Cardozo; Isaiah Isaacs; Jacob I. Cohen, who served as a magistrate; and Hyman Samuels, a silversmith, and his wife, who lived in Petersburg in the 1790s. In a letter Mrs. Samuels wrote to her family in Hamburg, she said that Petersburg had 10 or 12 Jews but "they are not really called Jews." She complained that while they had a *shochet*, he bought non-kosher meat and the Jewish merchants in the town worshipped on the High Holy Days without a Torah and no one wore a *tallith* except her son's godfather. All Jewish shops, she reported, except the Samuels' silversmith establishment, were open on the Sabbath. Because of these conditions she said the Samuels were moving to Charleston, South Carolina, where "there is a blessed community of 300 Jews" with a synagogue.

While Mrs. Samuels was complaining about the lack of Jewishness in Petersburg, the Jews of Richmond, who by 1790 were said to have been sixth of the city's total population, established Virginia's first congregation, Kahal Kodesh Beth Shalome, on August 24, 1789, the sixth oldest congregation in the United States. When founded, it was the westernmost congregation in the country. Twenty-nine heads of families were its founders. Beth Shalome's first house of worship was in a building called the Seminarium on Marshall Street, between 5th and 6th Streets. In 1848, it built the state's first synagogue on 11th Street between Clay and Marshall

Streets. Among the founders were Joseph Darmstadt, the former Hessian, who had been captured by Continental troops and imprisoned in Virginia where he remained after the Revolution. He was a member of the Amicable Society, an organization which gave relief to needy itinerants. When John Marshall became Grand Master of the Virginia Grand Lodge of Masons, Darmstadt was named Grand Treasurer.

Pursuant to a request of the Federal government, Beth Shalome met on Thanksgiving Day, 1789. Jacob I. Cohen wrote a prayer for the welfare of the government. In a part alluding to President George Washington, he said:

"O God of Hosts, thou has set peace and tranquility in our
palaces,
And has set the President of the United States as our head.
And in prayer we humble ourselves before Thee, O our God.
Unto our supplications mayest Thou hearken and deliver us.
A mind of wisdom and understanding, set in the heart of the
head of our country.
May he judge us with justice; may he cause our hearts to rejoice
and be glad.
In the paths of the upright may he lead us.
Even unto old age may he administer and judge in our midst.
Pure and upright be the heart of the one who rules and governs
us.
May God Almighty hearken to our voice and save us . . ."

It was Beth Shalome in Richmond, which together with the congregations in Philadelphia, Charleston, and New York, sent congratulations and assurances of support to Washington following his inauguration as President.

Two years before Beth Shalome was founded, Moses Myers arrived in Norfolk from Canada where he had gone after the bankruptcy of the firm of Isaac Moses, Samuel Myers, and Moses Myers in Philadelphia. They had been forced into bankruptcy by post-Revolutionary War economic changes. Samuel and Moses Myers were not related, the former being the son of Myers, the famous New York silversmith. Moses Myers was the son of Chaim Mears, the Dutch-born *shochet* of New York's Congregation Shearith Israel, who Anglicized his name to Haym Myers when he became a naturalized British subject.

Moses Myers, one of the founders of Beth Shalome, had not only risked his neck as the co-owner of blockade-running vessels during the Revolution, but helped finance the unsuccessful American invasion of Cannda in 1775. By 1800 Myers had become wealthy as an importer and banker. He became the Norfolk superintendent of the Bank of Richmond, acted as Thomas Jefferson's personal agent, served in the City Council, represented the

Republic of Batavia (Holland) in Virginia, and served as collector of the Port Norfolk from 1827-1831. When he died in 1835, he was described as the leading merchant south of the Mason-Dixon Line.

Members of the Cohen family of Richmond are immortalized in the famous court case of Cohens v. Virginia in which Chief Justice John Marshall of the United States Supreme Court handed down the historic decision that the Supreme Court had the constitutional right to review a judgment of a state's highest court. The Cohens had been found guilty of selling lottery tickets in violation of a Virginia law. The Cohens appealed to the Supreme Court for a review of the verdict. The Supreme Court decided in Virginia's favor, but Marshall's decision also enunciated the principle that state court decisions were subject to review by the Supreme Court.

In the decades preceding the Civil War, the Jewish population of the state grew. In 1826 it was estimated at 400. Two decades later, when the Reverend Isaac Leeser of Philadelphia visited Richmond, he put the state's Jewish population at 700. The United States Census of Religious Bodies in 1850 listed three congregations in Virginia but there were only two, Beth Shalome and Congregation Beth Ahabah. The older congregation continued to use the Sephardic ritual, although most of its founders and later members were Ashkenazic Jews of German origin. In 1839 Chebrah Ahabat Yisroel was organized in Richmond as a social and charitable society. Two years later it became Congregation Beth Ahabah. A third congregation, Keneseth Israel, was founded in 1856 by Polish Jews. In 1867 there was a move to merge Keneseth Israel and Beth Shalome but the refusal of the latter to give up the Sephardic ritual proved a stumbling block. An attempt to merge Beth Ahabah and Beth Shalome in 1878 was unsuccessful. The amalgamation was finally effected in 1898 under the name of Beth Ahabah.

Next to Richmond, Norfolk has the second oldest Jewish community in continuous existence. A tombstone dated 1819 in the Hebrew Cemetery of Norfolk in memory of Solomon Nones, son of Benjamin Nones, Revolutionary War patriot, indicates there was an early Jewish settlement there. The first congregation was founded in 1836 and later split into Beth El, established in 1850 and Ohef Sholom in 1848. Three Jewish families settled in Alexandria before 1850. There is extant a land deed dated 1844 in the name of Morris Adler. The Hebrew Benevolent Society formed in 1857 paved the way for the Beth El Hebrew Congregation in 1859. Danville was settled in the 1860s and a synagogue was founded in 1877. Petersburg's community dates from 1820 when Abraham Cohen settled there, but the synagogue was not organized until 1857. Worship services were held in Lynchburg as early as 1853 but the synagogue was organized in 1867. The communities in Roanoke, Newport News, Portsmouth, Staunton and Fredericksburg were settled in the 1880s.

The FFVs, the aristocratic first families of Virginia, had their counterparts in the descendants of the early Jewish settlers who remained Jewish and of the German Jews who arrived in the first decades of the 19th century. Solomon Jacobs, acting-mayor of Richmond, 1818-19, was described on the epitaph on his gravestone as "fond as a husband, indulgent as a father and kind as a master." In 1829 his widow had a special law enacted by the Virginia Legislature permitting the sale of a number of female slaves and their children because of "the conduct of said slaves towards their mistress . . . was so very malevolent and very objectionable." Benjamin Davis, Ash Levy, and Samuel Reese of Richmond were leading slave auctioneers. Davis and his partners, Ansley, Benjamin, George, and Solomon Davis, were said to be the largest slave-trading firms in the South, according to Dr. Bertram W. Korn. They are the only Jews mentioned in Harriet Beecher Stowe's commentary, *A Key to Uncle Tom's Cabin.* She refers to the Davises of Petersburg and Richmond as "great slave traders" and Jews "who came to Petersburg many years ago as poor peddlers . . . These men are always in the market, giving the highest prices for slaves." Lewis B. Levy of Richmond advertised himself as "a manufacturer and vendor of servants clothing" and solicited the business of slave traders and masters. On the other hand, Isaiah Isaacs of Charlottesville, who had been obliged to accept a slave as security for a debt, left detailed instructions in his will for freeing the slave. Samuel Myers of Petersburg bought a slave in 1796 with an avowed intention of freeing her. Solomon Raphael and Solomon Jacobs of Richmond also freed their slaves.

Just as there were Jewish slaveholders, there were also Jews among Virginia's Confederate heroes and Jewish sufferers during the post-war years of Reconstruction. Over 100 Jews from Richmond alone served in the Confederate forces. Beth Ahabah's religious school which was suspended during the Civil War was used as a makeshift hospital. Almost every Jewish house served as a military hospital. The women of Beth Ahabah and Beth Shalome organized a Ladies Hebrew Association which used its funds exclusively for caring for sick and wounded soldiers. Synagogue members met endless ambulance trains that entered Richmond and carried the wounded to safe retreats and buried the dead. Rabbi M. J. Michelbacher of Beth Ahabah was untiring in his efforts on behalf of Confederate troops. He visited the encampments around Richmond, composed a special prayer for Jewish soldiers, and visited Jefferson Davis and Confederate generals in a vain effort to get permission for Jewish soldiers to be furloughed for the High Holy Days. When he asked General Robert E. Lee to let Jewish soldiers go home for Rosh Hashanah and Yom Kippur, Lee wrote in 1861 that "I feel assured that neither you or any other member of the Jewish congregation would wish to jeopardize a cause you have so much at heart by the withdrawal of even for a season of a portion of its defenders." The Jewish community invested heavily in Confederate war bonds.

So frequent and venomous were the public attacks on Jews in Virginia during the Civil War, that the Reverend Michelbacher preached a sermon on the subject at a Confederate fast day service in Fredericksburg in 1863, which was printed in many Southern newspapers. In the Confederate House of Representatives, meeting in Richmond on January 14, 1863, Congressman Henry S. Foote of Tennessee charged that Jews had flooded into the Confederacy, controlled at least ninety percent of all its business, and were engaging in illegal trade with the enemy without any official hindrance. He alleged that the Jews had been invited into the Confederacy "by official permission" and charged that they were under official protection. This was an allusion to Secretary of State Judah P. Benjamin who, Foote charged, was transferring all of Southern commerce to the hands of "foreign Jews." Later, Foote repeated his insinuations against Benjamin while other Southern anti-Semites blamed Jews for inflation, shortage of goods, and other economic problems. The editor of the *Richmond Sentinel* admitted that "intolerant and illiberal views and prejudices" against the Jews "prevail to some extent" but they "in no wise affect their (the Jews) individual and personal merits and character."

The two congregations for a time considered some joint action "to vindicate our character as Jews and good citizens, which has been repeatedly and grossly assailed in public prints." At a combined meeting of the two congregations, some suggested that a special Jewish fund be raised to distribute to the poor of Richmond. Letters to the editors of newspapers by Jews were frequent. One Jew, Colonel Adolphus H. Adler, a Hungarian who had served as an officer in Garibaldi's army in Italy, offered to meet the editor of the *Richmond Examiner* in a duel because the editor was printing libelous statements about the Jews. The editor apologized but he probably was unaware that Adler was then in a Confederate prison in Richmond on a charge of being a Northern sympathizer.

In 1880—15 years after the Civil War—there were 2,500 Jews in Virginia—1,200 in Richmond, 500 in Norfolk, and 163 in Petersburg. By 1900, the Jewish population had increased six-fold to 15,000 as a result of some immigration from the North and the arrival of East European Jewish immigrants. (In 1882 the Jews of Baltimore had established an abortive agricultural colony for 73 Jewish refugees from Russia in Charles County.)

There were then 13 cities and towns with one or more Jewish institutions and in 12 cities and towns there were 17 congregations and four towns where services were regularly held on Rosh Hashanah. In the next decade there was virtually no increase in the number of Jews—the 1917 figure being 15,403. There was a big jump in the ten years between 1917 and 1927 to 25,656 and a slight decline in the next ten years. In 1937 Richmond was the largest community with 7,500 Jews, followed by Norfolk, 6,500; Newport News, 1,950; Portsmouth, 1,875; Alexandria, 700; Lynchburg, 520; Roanoke, 470; and the Fairfax-Arlington County suburbs of Washington,

600. There were also small communities in Danville, Staunton, Charlottesville, and Winchester. There were 24 towns with as many as 50 Jews each and 43 each with less than ten Jews.

The upward trend in the state's Jewish population resumed in the 1950-1960 decade, with the end of the ten year period showing 31,200 Jews in the state. Richmond was still the largest community, with 8,750 Jews, followed by Norfolk with 7,750. But the Arlington-Alexandria-Falls Church area in Arlington and Fairfax Counties, suburban communities for tens of thousands of government workers in Washington, moved into third place with 6,400 Jews. By 1974, these Virginia suburbs of Washington were home to 15,000 Jews, topping Richmond's 10,000, and the Norfolk-Virginia Beach area with 11,000. The state's total Jewish population was 48,550.

Rabbi Edward Calisch, who served Richmond's Congregation Beth Ahabah from 1891-1946 was Richmond's leading Jewish citizen and one of the leaders of the entire community. A frequent occupant of Protestant pulpits, he delivered patriotic speeches in both World Wars, lunched with President William Taft in the White House, headed the Richmond Peace Council, and served as treasurer of the English Speaking Union. Once he was named one of the ten outstanding men in Virginia. He got along well with non-Jews but had little following among most Jews except with the old Jewish families. In his last years he gave impetus and leadership to the anti-Zionist American Council for Judaism. Beth Ahabah remained a stronghold of anti-Zionist sentiment until the late 1930s and 1940s when some Jews of East European ancestry joined the congregation. Other Jews of similar origin had founded Congregation Beth El in Richmond during the depression years and this synagogue became a Zionist stronghold. Richmond's Jewish community as a whole was regarded as unfriendly to Zionism until the 1930s because of Beth Ahabah's influence but this changed when the East European Jews took over control of the city's principal Jewish organizations. Lewis L. Strauss, secretary to President Herbert Hoover when he was American Relief Administrator for war-torn countries of Europe after World War I, later became chairman of the Atomic Energy Commission. He was a scion of one of the older Jewish families. Another was David Lowenberg of Norfolk, who developed the Jamestown Exposition of 1907. Charles I. Kaufman was chairman of the Norfolk Redevelopment and Housing Authority which built 3,000 housing units for blacks as part of a vast slum clearance project.

When Virginia became a major battleground in the Southern fight to nullify the 1954 Supreme Court decision calling for desegregation of the public schools, many Virginia Jews felt caught in the middle. While most Jews accepted desegregation in principle, in practice their stand did not differ from the rest of the white population. Many Jews worried about their own status if their white neighbors resented a pro-black stance. In the

1950s, the state was flooded with anti-Semitic literature alleging that desegregation was a "Zionist-Communist plot to mongrelize the white race." In July, 1959, the *Richmond News Leader,* one of the South's most influential newspapers, published an editiorial entitled "Anti-Semitism in the South" which charged that recent manifestations of anti-Semitism "must be traced to the Anti-Defamation League. By deliberately involving itself in the controversy over school desegregation, this branch of B'nai B'rith is identifying all Jewry with the advocacy of compulsory integration."

The paper cited the distribution of "pro-integration" materials by the ADL's Richmond office at a Charlottesville NAACP Workshop as evidence to "embattled whites" of activity that "has nothing to do with defamation of Jews. Such inquiries, once bruited about," the editorial warned, "will be seized upon by the ADL as evidence of anti-Semitic feeling, and having thus stirred up defamation of the Jews, ADL can lustily combat defamation of the Jews," saying "look how much anti-Semitism there is." The editorial then invited the Jews in the South to get rid of "an organization that foments hostility to Jews."

Widely reprinted in other Southern papers, the editorial stunned the Jews of Virginia. A few agreed with the editorial but the majority saw it as a veiled threat of blackmail, a warning to silence the Jewish agencies in the field of civil rights lest the segregationists hit back at Southern Jews. In Alexandria, Rabbi Emmet A. Frank of Beth El Congregation delivered a Yom Kippir sermon in which he charged that Virginia's Governor Almond had brought about more disunity in the United States in the last few years than the American Communists ever had. Assailing Virginia's "massive resistance" to desegregation, Rabbi Frank called on Jews not to remain silent at injustice against anyone. The late Lincoln Rockwell, from the national headquarters of his American Nazi Party in nearby Arlington, demanded that the Jews of Alexandria publicly condemn Rabbi Frank for "slanderous statements and innuendos." Some Virginia papers joined the attack on the rabbi and there were threats on his life. While some Jews urged an apology to Senator Harry Byrd and some wrote letters to him saying that the rabbi did not speak for them.The majority were not susceptible to threats of economic retaliation that worried Jews elsewhere in the state because most of the Jews in Alexandria were Federal Government employees of Northern origin.

In other cities, too, Jews were active in promoting desegregation. Rabbi Malcolm Stern, then of Norfolk, publicly called for a citywide referendum after the city had closed its public schools to combat desegregation. Rabbi Louis D. Mendoza, who had been rabbi of Norfolk's Ohef Shalom Temple for 48 years, and Stern's predecessor, was widely recognized as one of the city's civil rights champions. During the fight over desegregation some of its opponents distributed hate literature in schools and colleges throughout the state. But one member of Congress from Virginia mailed a $50 check to a prominent Virginia Jew "to help pay for the restoration of the Jewish church," (the Reform temple in Atlanta) which had been badly damaged by a bomb blast attributed to segregationists who objected to the militant desegregation stand of the temple's rabbi.

Both Richmond and Norfolk have named Jews as "first citizen"—Rabbi Edward Calisch in Richmond, and Charles L. Kaufman in Norfolk. Alexandria has had three Jewish mayors: Henry Strauss in 1886, 1891,and 1893; Lewis Stein in 1915; and Leroy S. Bendheim in 1957. Herman Funk was mayor of Falls Church and V.H. Nusbaum was vice-mayor of Norfolk. Harry Reyner was twice vice-mayor of Newport News and also served as mayor. When Ben Jacobs of Newport News was appointed judge of the Municipal Court some papers reported that he was the first Jewish judge in the history of Virginia. Actually, he was preceded by Jacob I. Cohen of Richmond, who was a city magistrate in 1790 and acting-mayor in 1819. In 1968 Max O. Laster was appointed judge of the Juvenile and Domestic Relations Court of Alexandria. Lawrence Loewner was mayor of Harrisonburg in the late 1940s. Marx Gunst served as vice-president of the Richmond city council 1905-1908, and Sol Bloomberg was president of the same body in 1902. Michael Umstadter, founder of the Norfolk Library Association, served a term as president of the Norfolk Board of Aldermen.

* * * * *

ALEXANDRIA
Agudas Achim Cong., 2900 Valley Dr.
Beth El Hebrew Cong., 3830 Seminary Rd.

ARLINGTON
Arlington-Fairfax Jewish Center, 2920 Arlington Rd.
Arlington Memorial Amphitheater, a trophy room and chapel containing posthumous decorations and plaques awarded to the Unknown Soldier, is in the rotunda just below the Tomb of the Unknown (sic). Among these are plain bronze plaques bearing the names of B'nai B'rith, Brith Sholom, and the Jewish War Veterans of the U.S.

Arlington National Cemetery, best known of the national burial grounds, where any member of the Armed Forces who died while on active duty or who received an honorable discharge may be interred, if room can be found, is the final resting place of more than 150 Jews. Buried there— Grave 288, Section 12—is Maj. Gen. Orde C. Wingate, a high ranking British army officer who befriended the Jewish settlers in Palestine, taught them guerrilla warfare, and showed them how to create night squads. A Bible-loving Scotsman whose name is cherished in Israel, he is buried in a common grave with American servicemen who died with him in a World War II plane crash in Burma on March 24, 1944. At the foot of the simple tombstone is a small stone from Masada, the mountain fortress where Jews fought off a Roman siege for three years after the fall of Jerusalem in 70 C.E. The stone was placed there by the Orde Wingate Memorial Society, an organization of Washington Jews that holds memorial services for Wingate annually at the graveside.

• The two most celebrated Jews buried in Arlington National Cemetery are Sir Moses J. Ezekiel, the sculptor, whose remains lie at the foot of the huge Monument of Confederate War Dead, which he designed, and Brig. Gen. Charles Henry Lauchheimer of the U.S. Marine Corps.

One of the great sculptors of the late 19th and early 20th centuries, Ezekiel was born in Richmond, Va., in 1848. His father, Jacob Ezekiel, also a native of Richmond, fought vigorously for civil equality for Jews. Writing to President John Tyler in 1841, he called attention to the impropriety of describing the American nation as a "Christian people." In a private reply, Tyler conceded that such an intimation of sectarianism was irrelevant in public documents. The elder Ezekiel also headed the move in 1845 in which Virginia amended its code and granted equality to those who observed Saturday as their Sabbath. When he moved to Cincinnati in 1869, he became active in the movement that led to the establishment of the Union of American Hebrew Congregations and Hebrew Union College.

Moses Ezekiel served in the Virginia Military Institute cadet battalion in the Civil War. In 1869 he enrolled at the Royal Academy of Art in Berlin where his bust of Washington won him membership in the exclusive Berlin Society of Arts. At his studio in Rome he executed the bas-reliefs *Israel* and *Adam and Eve*, which earned him the coveted Michel Beer Prix de Rome in 1873, the first American to receive this prize. While in Italy, he was commissioned by B'nai B'rith to execute a statue for the celebration of the centennial of American independence in 1876. For that occasion, Ezekiel executed the Statue to Religious Liberty, now in Philadelphia's Fairmount Park (see Pennsylvania).

Among his works are busts of Longfellow, Liszt, Shelley, Poe, Lee, Jefferson, and Stonewall Jackson. His religious subjects dealt with Queen Esther, King David, Judith, Adam and Eve, and Cain. Ezekiel is represented in Westminster Abbey by a bust of Lord Sherbrooke. He was knighted by the King of Italy. Ezekiel was the designer of the seal of the Jewish Publication Society of America. He died in Rome in 1917, but because of World War I, his body was not brought back to America until 1921. When the United Daughters of Confederacy, donor of the monument at Arlington, asked to have him buried at the foot of the monument, his family agreed. The late Rabbi David Philipson officiated at the burial service, which was held in the Arlington Memorial Amphitheatre on March 30, 1921. In his autobiography, *My Life As An American Jew*, Rabbi Philipson said that this was the first religious service held in this famous structure. This is quite probable, since the amiphitheatre was not officially dedicated until April 30 of that year. The monument at whose base Ezekiel lies buried was dedicated by President Woodrow Wilson on June 4, 1914.

• The other Jewish notable buried at Arlington, Brig. Gen. Charles H. Lauchheimer, was born in Baltimore in 1859 and was graduated from the U.S. Naval Academy in 1883 when he was assigned to the Marine Corps. After seven years of sea and land duty, Lauchheimer, by then a major, was appointed assistant adjutant and inspector. He applied for front-line service in the Spanish-American War, but the Navy Department decided his services were needed in Washington. In 1903 Lauchheimer was ordered to the Philippines where he established the office of assistant adjutant and inspector in the Far East. Later he was inspector at Marine Corps headquarters, a post he held until his death in 1920. In 1916 he was commissioned brigadier-general. He was posthumously awarded the Navy Distinguished Service Medal.

The Pentagon, the huge headquarters of the Department of Defense, has a room set aside for daily Jewish worship by military and civilian personnel stationed there. The room is 5B-1062. The Pentagon Press Room has a roster of honor containing the names of American newspapermen and news photographers killed while serving with the U.S. forces in World War II, and the Korean and Vietnam Wars. The Jews listed are Harold Kulick of *Popular Science Monthly*, Jack Singer of International News Service, Melville Jacoby of *Time-Life*, and Leah Burdett. In the Pentagon's Congressional Medal of Honor Hall are the names and photos of all those who have received the country's highest military award. The Jews included are: Sgt. Leopold Karpeles, Mass.; Benjamin B. Levy, New York; Abraham Cohn, New Hamsphire; Henry Heller, Ohio; David Obransky, Ohio, from the Civil War; Sgts. Benjamin Kaufman, William Sawelson, and Sidney Gumpertz, all of New York, from World War I; and Staff Sgt. Isadore Jachman, Maryland; and Lt. Raymond Zussman, Michigan, from World War II.

BRISTOL

Former Temple B'nai Sholom, King and 2nd Sts., is now a public

library, the congregation having moved to a new building in the Mt. Tucker
section of Blountville, Tenn., midway between Bristol, Va., and Kingsport
and Johnson City, Tenn. (see Tennessee).

BLACKSBURG
Hillel Foundation at Virginia Polytechnic Institute, care of Dept. of
Physics.

CHARLOTTESVILLE
Hillel Foundation at University of Virginia, 1824 University Circle.
The University's Herz Collection of Greek and Latin Classics, named for
Martin Herz, is in the Alderman Library.

Thomas Jefferson's grave, not far from Monticello, his ancestral estate,
is marked by a simple stone shaft on which are inscribed, at Jefferson's own
direction, these words: "Here lies Thomas Jefferson, Author of the Declaration of Independence, of the Statute of Virginia for Religious Freedom &
Father of the University of Virginia." Throughout his career, Jefferson, the
third President of the U.S., proved himself a friend of the Jews. His Virginia Statute for Religious Freedom, whose effects have been mentioned
above, was the first American law establishing complete religious liberty
for all. It was Jefferson who first proposed the appointment of a Jew to the
Cabinet. Shortly after his election to the Presidency in 1800, he considered
making a Philadelphia Jewish lawyer by the name of Levy, who by then
was already a Christian, his attorney general, but was advised against it on
political, not religious grounds. Jefferson, however, did name Reuben
Etting of Baltimore, U.S. Marshal for Maryland at a time when under the
statutes of that state Jews were still disqualified from holding public office.

So firmly did Jefferson oppose everything that violated the right to ab-
solute religious equality that he protested repeatedly against issuing sectarian proclamations for Thanksgiving Day, holding them unconstitution-
al and violative of the American concept of separation of church and state.

In correspondence with eminent Jews of his time after he left the Presidency, Jefferson continued to champion religious liberty and to oppose discrimination because of race or creed. Writing to Joseph Marx of Richmond, who had sent him a copy of the proceedings of the Sanhedrin convened by Napoleon, Jefferson said that he read them with great interest
"and with the regret that I have ever felt at seeing a sect, the parent and
basis of all those of Christendom, singled out by all of them for a persecution and oppression which prove they have profited nothing from the
benevolent doctrines of Him whom they profess to make the model or their
principles and practice." To Mordecai M. Noah he wrote in 1818: "Your
sect, by its suffering, has furnished a remarkable proof of the universal
spirit of religious intolerance inherent in every sect, disclaimed by all while
feeble, and practiced by all in power. Our laws have applied the only anti-

dote to this vice, protecting our religious, as they do our civil rights, by putting all men on a equal footing. But more remains to be done, for although we are free by the law we are not so in practice; public opinion erects itself into an inquisition, and exercises its office with as much fanaticism as fans the fires of an *auto-da-fe*. The prejudice still scowling on your section of our religion, although the elder one, cannot be unfelt by yourselves. It is to be hoped that individual dispositions will at length mould themselves to the model of the law."

Jefferson was also among the first to protest against the handicaps Jewish students suffered because of the inclusion of courses in religion in school and college curricula. Writing to Isaac Harby of Charleston, he said: "I have thought it a cruel addition to the wrongs which that injured sect have suffered that their youth should be excluded from the instructions in science afforded to all others in our public seminaries by imposing upon them a course of theological reading which their consciences do not permit them to pursue; and in the university lately established here (the University of Virginia which Jefferson founded) we have set the example of ceasing to violate the rights of conscience of the different sects respecting their religion."

As early as 1814, Jefferson suggested the creation of an institution such as the B'nai B'rith Hillel Foundations and even outlined their operation. Writing to Thomas Cooper he said: "In our annual report to the legislature, after stating the constitutional reasons against a public establishment of any religious instruction, we suggest the expedience of encouraging the different religious sects to establish, each for itself, a professorship of their own tenets on the confines of the university, so near as that their students may attend the lectures there, and have the free use of our library and every other accommodation we can give them; preserving however, their independence of us and of each other . . . and by bringing the sects together and mixing them with the mass of other students we shall soften their asperities, liberalize and neutralize their prejudices, and make the general religion a religion of peace, reason and morality."

Monticello, the home of Thomas Jefferson, three miles from Charlottesville, was saved from ruin and restored by Uriah P. Levy, a great admirer of Jefferson, who bought the mansion and 218 acres of the original estate in 1832. While Levy lived there, he restored the historic house to much of its early grandeur and reclaimed many of the original furnishings which had been sold and widely scattered after Jefferson's death. While Levy owned Monticello, he added 2,000 acres to his original purchase. In his will, he left the estate, including the mansion built by Jefferson, "to the people of the United States or such persons as Congress shall appoint to receive it in trust for the sole and only purpose of establishing and maintaining there an agricultural school for educating as farmers the children of deceased Navy officers."

To maintain the school, Levy left the income of his substantial New York estate. His will provided that if Congress declined the offer, the estate was to go to the Commonwealth of Virginia, and if Virginia refused, the creation of the school was to become the responsibility of the Sephardic Jewish congregations in New York, Philadelphia, and Richmond. The school, however, was to be non-sectarian. While Levy's family fought to break the will, which was badly drawn, Monticello fell into ruin again when neither Congress nor Virginia was ready to accept the responsibilities the will would have thrust upon them. Levy's nephew, Jefferson Monroe Levy, acquired the estate from the other heirs in 1881. He, too, did a good deal to restore the famous mansion and to reacquire relics improperly removed. He even went to the expense of having some pieces remade when the originals could not be found. After World War I, when Levy encountered financial difficulties, he sold Monticello to the newly-established Thomas Jefferson Memorial Foundation. Theodore Fred Kuper, a Russian-born Jewish immigrant, who went to work for the foundation in 1923, devoted 50 years to developing fundraising techniques needed to complete the restoration and to make Monticello a national historic shrine. On the wall next to Monticello's summer kitchen, on the south terrace, is a plaque giving a brief history of the estate and indicating the role played by Uriah P. Levy and his nephew.

Born in Philadelphia in 1792, Uriah Phillips Levy ran away to sea when he was but ten years old. After two years as a cabin boy, he was apprenticed by his father to a shipowner. At 18 he was second mate of a brig and at 20 a captain and part owner of a ship. His early career was full of adventure. Once, when the British were harassing the U.S. by impressing her seamen, Levy was impressed into the British navy. On another occasion, when his ship foundered, he drifted in an open boat for five days. He had another narrow escape when his crew mutinied. Levy entered the U.S. Navy as a sailing master during the War of 1812 and served on the USS *Argus*, which spread terror among British ships in European waters. While commanding a prize vessel taken by the *Argus*, Levy was captured and spent sixteen months in England's Dartmoor Prison.

Levy's whole naval career was marked by a series of unhappy incidents, most of which grew out of his not being a regular navy man, his quick and violent resentment of personal insults, affronts to his country, and his Jewishness. He was court-martialed six times, mostly for violating regulations. Although he climbed from the rank of lieutenant in 1817 to the rank of commodore in 1859—the equivalent of admiral—he had difficulty in winning active-duty assignments despite his repeated and passionate pleas. In the interim between commands, he acquired Monticello and built a fortune in New York real estate. He was past 50 when he pleaded in vain for active duty in the Mexican War. In 1855, Levy was one of 200 officers dropped from the services as part of an effort to weed out overage men. Levy bitterly fought retirement, objecting to the secrecy of the proceedings and to the implied slur on his record. There was also some feeling that his ouster was based on anti-Semitic prejudice.

After lengthy inquiries, during which Levy made a famous and eloquent defense and insisted on the right of Jews to equal treatment in the Navy, not only for their own sake but also for the national welfare, he and a third of the dismissed officers were reinstated. In 1859, Levy was given com- mand of the Mediterranean squadron with the rank of commodore. He died in 1862. Over his grave in Cypress Hills Cemetery, Brooklyn, New York, is a full-length statue of him in the uniform of a Navy captain. Levy designed the statue in his will, giving specific instructions as to its dimensions. He also left orders that there was to be a scroll on the monument, inscribed with these words: "Father of the law for the abolition of the barbarous prac- tice of corporal punishment in the United States Navy." The evidence, however, does not substantiate this boast, but Levy was undoubtedly one of those who did agitate for the elimination of flogging in the Navy. Levy was a member of New York's Congregation Shearith Israel and a charter mem- ber of the Washington, D.C. Hebrew Congregation. During World War II, the Navy named a destroyer for him.

About 100 yards from the Monticello mansion, near Jefferson's grave, is the last resting place of Rachel Phillips Levy, Uriah P. Levy's mother, who died at Monticello while her son owned the estate. She was a daughter of Jonas Phillips, Philadelphia patriot of the Revolution (see Pennsyl- vania). Her grave, under the deed of sale by which Monticello was sold, was to be cared for in perpetuity, is marked as follows: "To the memory of Rachel Phillips Levy Born in New York 23 of May 1769 Married 1787. Died 7 of Iyar (May) 5591, ab. (1831) at Monticello, Virginia. Erected August 15, 1859 By her Son, J.P.L. Reerected by her Grandson L.N.L." ("J.P.L." was Jonas P. Levy, see District of Columbia, Uriah's brother; "L.N.L." was L. Napoleon Levy, one of Uriah's nephews.)

Levy St., which runs between Avon St. and Monticello Rd., about 2½ miles from Monticello, is named for Uriah P. Levy.

Arthur J. Morris Library, in the Law School building of the University of Virginia, is named for the late New York banker, Arthur J. Morris, who gave the University $350,000. In the library there is an oil portrait of the banker who founded the Morris Plan.

Old Levy Opera House, on eastern side of Court Sq.

Temple Beth Israel, 3rd and Jefferson Sts.

CRYSTAL CITY

A new town within the city of Arlington is an immense urban complex of 18 buildings containing 2,500 apartments and spread out over 64 acres between the National Airport and the Pentagon. It was conceived and built by the Charles E. Smith Construction Co., whose namesake was one of the leading Jewish communal figures of Washington. The town will house 20,000 people when completed.

DANVILLE
Cong. Aetz Chayim, 168 Stratford Pl.
Cong. Beth Sholom, 129 Sutherlin Ave.

FAIRFAX
Cong. Olam Tikvay, 3800 Glenbrook Ave., is a departure from most modern American synagogues whose sanctuaries are built in auditorium style. All of its seats face a raised bimah at one end, with the seats stretching around three walls. The Ark is against the fourth (eastern) wall with the worshippers facing each other and the Ark.

FALLS CHURCH
Chaplains Memorial Fountain, the National Memorial Park on Lee Highway, is a memorial to the four World War II chaplains who sacrificed their lives when the Army transport *Dorchester* was sunk on Feb. 3, 1943. The monument consists of four 7-foot granite tiers rising from a circular pool of water and supporting a 24-foot basin. The allegory of the design has the tiers immersed in the water, representing the four heroic chaplains. A memorial plaque dedicated on the 10th anniversary of their death reads: "Chaplains George L. Fox, Alexander D. Goode, Clark V. Poling, John P. Washington. The extraordinary heroism and devotion of these four men of God, a priest, a rabbi, and two ministers, who gave up their life jackets to soldiers on the torpedoed *Dorchester* on February 3, 1943, and went down with their ship, is here memorialized as an unwavering beacon of supreme courage and faith."

Temple Rodef Shalom, 2100 Westmoreland St., is designed in a hexagonal shape.

FORT BELVOIR
Jewish Congregation on the military base, housed in the Main Post Chapel, serves both military and civilian personnel. In front of the chapel is a tree planted on *Tu Bishevat* in 1958 as a good will offering from the people of Israel.

FREDERICKSBURG
Religious Freedom Memorial is a historic marker whose inscription reads: "This memorial marks the site of a celebration on October 16, 1932, by representatives of the leading religious faiths in America, commemorative of the religious character of George Washington whose boyhood home town was Fredericksburg; and of the separation of church and state, as the

Virginia 'bill for establishing religious freedom,' was outlined by a committee consisting of Thomas Jefferson, George Mason, Edmund Pendleton and Thomas Ludwell Lee which met in this city January 13, 1777." Not far from the marker is the Jefferson Institute for the Study of Religious Freedom, which houses a library dealing with the facts, circumstances, persons, and events associated with the establishment of religious freedom in the U.S.

HAMPTON
Cong. B'nai Israel, 3116 Kecoughtan Rd.

Fort Monroe's Casemate Museum has a handsome bronze plaque dedicated by the John Ericsson Society of New York to the memory of the officers and crew of the pioneer ironclad, the USS *Monitor*, which fought a historic battle at Hampton Roads with the Confederate ironclad, *Merrimack*, in 1862. Among the 62 names on the plaque is that of William Durst, a coal heaver on the *Monitor*, who was born in Tarnow, Austrian Galicia. When he arrived in New York he enlisted in the U.S. Navy. When he died in 1916 in the Philadelphia Jewish Hospital, he was said to have been the last survivor of the Battle of the *Monitor* and *Merrimack*.

Fort Monroe, which was begun in 1819 and not completed until 1834, had as one of its construction engineers from 1825-1828, Lt. Alfred Mordecai, who wrote a famous *Ordnance Manual*. Mordecai resigned from the U.S. Army rather than fight against the South. His son, also named Alfred, served in the Union Army, rising to brigadier-general.

HARRISONBURG
Temple Beth El, P.O. Box 845.

ISRAEL'S GAP
Michael Israel, a Border Ranger and a member of the militia in 1757, is memorialized in this mountain pass about 11 miles southwest of Charlottesville, at a spot called Cross Roads, between North Garden and Batesville. Israel owned a good deal of land in this part of Albemarle County and was engaged in various business enterprises.

LEXINGTON
Bendheim Physics Library at Washington and Lee University is named for the late Adrian L. Benheim, Jr., a prominent alumnus and a Jewish communal leader in Richmond. Hillel Foundation, 1824 University Circle, Charlottesville.

LYNCHBURG
Agudath Sholom Cong., Langhorne Rd., has an 11-by-18-foot mosaic mural entitled *The Creation*.

MANASSAS

Menassah, a Jewish lodging housekeeper, is believed to be memorialized in the name of this town which was the site of the first and second Battles of Bull Run (sometimes called the Battles of Manassas) during the Civil War. According to an old tradition, first mentioned in an editorial in the *Richmond Enquirer* in August, 1861, after the first Battle of Manassas, Menassah's lodging house was a popular stopping-place for stagecoach passengers bound for Richmond or Winchester. When travelers asked if there was a place to stop, they would be told: "Yes, at Menassah's." Gradually, the junction that grew up around the lodging house came to be called Menasseh's or Manassas. A Jewish soldier in the Union Army wrote a series of anonymous letters to the *Jewish Messenger* between January 17 and March 4, 1862, giving currency to the story.

MARTINSVILLE

Ohev Zion Cong., Parkview St.

MOUNT VERNON

Among the historic items relating to George Washington that are on exhibit at the home of the first President is a collection of Washington's letters to William Pearce, manager of Mount Vernon. They were presented as a Bicentennial gift by Sol Feinstone of Washington Crossing, Pa., a major collector of Washington artifacts. The collection of 128 letters spanning the years 1793-1798, were acquired by Feinstone at a cost of $225,000.

NEW MARKET

Moses Ezekiel, the famed sculptor, is one of the 250 Civil War teenagers, all of them cadets at Virginia Military Institute, who are memorialized in the Hall of Valor in New Market Battlefield Park. In a heroic but vain effort to halt General Hunter's army, the cadets, led by their professors, marched out in a unit to join the Confederate forces. The cadets left ten dead and 47 wounded. Ezekiel executed *The New Market Monument*, which stands outside the Nichols Engineering Hall of V.M.I., as a memorial to his youthful comrades.

NEWPORT NEWS

Cong. Adath Jeshurun, 1815 Chestnut Ave.
Hebrew Friendly Inn (independent transient service), 2126 Oak Ave.
Jewish Community Center, 2700 Spring Rd.
Jewish Federation, 2700 Spring Rd.
Henrietta A. Kurzer Hebrew Academy, 1815 Chestnut Ave.
Mariners Museum, Museum Dr., has among other exhibits on the history of ships and their navigators, a diorama of the building of Noah's Ark and an ancient amphora from Israel, dating from 500 years before the

Common Era. The amphora was the first article exchanged with the Israel Maritime Bureau in Haifa.

Reyner Building, 25th St. and Washington Ave., is named for Joseph Reyner, a former city councilman, whose father, Harry Reyner, was mayor of the city.

Taussig Blvd. in the Naval Station area, is named for Admiral Edward Taussig, who, as commander of the cruiser *Bennington*, took possession of Wake Island during the Spanish American War and later was commander of Guam.

Temple Rodef Sholom, 318 Wheaton Rd.

Temple Sinai, 11620 Warwick Blvd.

NORFOLK

Benmoreell Naval Housing Development, at the U.S. Naval Base, is named for the Jewish-born Admiral Ben Moreell, who organized and commanded the Seabees during World War II.

B'nai Israel Synagogue, 420 Spotswood Ave.

Cong. Beth El, 422 W. 15th St.

Cong. Mikve Kodesh, P.O. Box 1035, Norfolk, 23501.

"Flame of Faith, Flame of Liberty" Monument, on the Civic Center Plaza, bet. Public Safety Bldg. and City Hall, is a stainless steel modern representation of a flame on white cement. It was dedicated to the spiritual freedom on which the United States was founded, as a Bicentennial project of the Interfaith Bicentennial Commission of Norfolk and Virginia Beach.

Hermitage Museum, North Shore Rd., was the original home of Mr. and Mrs. William Sloane, who became wealthy through knitting mills they owned in the industrial suburb of Berkley, which employed a high percentage of immigrant Jews. When Mikve Kodesh's synagogue was dedicated in Berkley in 1903, the Sloanes were given the honor of opening the door. The museum contains among its displays of the religious art, a collection of Jewish ceremonial objects, including Torah decorations.

Hillel Foundation at Old Dominion University, 1411 Melrose Pkwy.

Jewish Community Center of Tidewater, 7300 Newport Ave., has a memorial grove of trees dedicated to Israel dead in the 1973 Yom Kippur War.

Jewish Family Service, 147 Granby St.

Jewish News, 7300 Newport Ave.

Commodore Levy Chapel, at the U.S. Naval Base, named in 1959 for the Jewish naval officer, Commodore Uriah P. Levy, (see Charlottesville), is part of a complex of brick buildings known as Frazier Hall that forms a "U" just inside the naval station's main gate. The right arm of the "U" is the Catholic chapel, the left is the Protestant chapel, and the Commodore Levy Chapel, with its stained glass windows depicting Moses and the Ten

Commandments, connects the other two chapels. The Levy Chapel dates from 1943 when it was the first permenent Jewish chapel established on a U.S. military installation. The commemorative plaque unveiled in 1959 was erected by the United Jewish Federation, the Norfolk Armed Forces, and the Veterans Services Committee of the National Jewish Welfare Board. The Star of David and the Ten Commandments imposed on a ship's helm constitute the symbolism designed for the chapel. The chapel was a project brought to fruition by Marine Corps Chaplain Samuel Sobel.

Moses Myers House, Freemason and Banks Sts., one of the best known landmarks in the city, is a superb example of late 18th century Georgian architecture. Owned by the city and operated as a museum, the house was built in 1791 by Moses Myers,one of the South's leading Jewish merchants, civic leader, banker, and public official. Myers was a Revolutionary War patriot who settled in Norfolk in 1787 with his Canadian bride. The house remained in the Myers family until 1929, when it was acquired by a private corporation which turned it over to the city. Much of the original furniture has been restored, and the house has been redecorated to conform to the style of late 18th and early 19th century living. Among the exhibits in the museum are Gilbert Stuart portraits of Myers and his wife, who was a member of the Judah family of Montreal; a Sully portrait of their son, John; and copies of correspondence between Thomas Jefferson and Myers.

Oldest Jewish Cemetery, Princess Anne Rd. and Tidewater Dr., which dates from the 1850s, is now maintained by the city of Norfolk.

Temple Israel, 7255 Granby St. On the *bimah* walls is a large sculpture entitled *Menorah of the Burning Bush*.

Temple Ohef Sholom, 530 Raleigh Ave., the oldest congregation in Norfolk, was founded in 1848 and built the city's first synagogue in 1859 on Cumberland St. The old gray brick structure, with its parallel flights of stone steps and the dedication plaque on the front, still stand behind the Juvenile Court building. It now houses a black church.

United Jewish Federation, 7300 Newport Ave.

United Orthodox Synagogue, 147 Granby St.

PETERSBURG

Rodof Sholom Cemetery, Center Rd., has some gravestones that date from 1834. Among those buried here is Uriah Feibelman, who while serving with Mahone's Brigade in the Confederate Army, cared for the religious needs of Jewish soldiers although he was not a chaplain.

Temple Brith Achim, South Blvd.

Temple Rodof Sholom, South Sycamore St.

PORTSMOUTH

Cong. Gomley Chesed, 2110 Sterling Point Dr.

Jewish Community Council, 430 Dominion National Bank.

Temple Sinai, 4401 Hatton Point Rd.

RESTON
Northern Virginia Hebrew Congregation holds Sabbath and holiday services in the Reston Catholic Community Church, 1421 Whiele Ave., at Virginia Route 606. Until its own facility is available, the synagogue's office is at 11800 Sunrise Valley Dr. Reston is one of the "new towns" west of Washington, D.C. It was developed by Robert E. Simon, Jr.

RICHMOND
Baruch Auditorium of the Medical College of Virginia, in the Egyptian Building, 1223 E. Marshall St., is named after a famous alumnus, Dr. Simon Baruch (see South Carolina), whose son, Bernard M. Baruch, provided the funds to renovate the building.

Judah P. Benjamin Marker, a stone in the sidewalk at 9 W. Main St., placed by the Confederate Memorial Literary Society, marks the site of the residence of Judah P. Benjamin during the Civil War, when he served as Secretary of War and Secretary of State of the Confederacy.

Beth Sholom Home of Virginia (for aged), 5700 Fitzhugh Ave.,

B'nai Sholom Cong., 9500 Three Chopt Rd.

Civil War Balloonists Memorial, opposite the terminal building at Byrd Field, Richmond's airport, honors both Union and Confederate balloonists. Dedicated by the city of of Richmond, May 30, 1962, "to intrepid and patriotic men, the Civil War balloonists, Union and Confederate, known and unknown, who against ridicule and skepticism laid the foundations for the nation's future in the sky," the memorial lists under the heading "Made Ascensions with Balloon Corps During the War," under the subheading UNION, the names of Capt. Isaac Moses. Under the heading, "Used or Encouraged the Use of Balloons," also under the subheading UNION, is the name of Maj. Albert Myer.

Cong. Beth Ahabah, 1117 W. Franklin St., through a merger with an earlier congregation, is the oldest in Virginia. The Beth Ahabah Archives contain artifacts and documents concerning Jewish history in Richmond and Virginia.

Cong. Kol Emes, 4811 Patterson Ave.

Franklin Street Burying Ground is described as "the first Jewish cemetery in Virginia, in the inscription above the gate to a small enclosure on the south side of Franklin St., just west of 21st St. A Shield of David surmounts the inscription. Deeded to the trustees of Cong. Beth Shalome by Isaiah Isaacs, the cemetery was dedicated in October, 1791 and was last used in 1817.

Samuel H. Gellman Music Room in Richmond Public Library, 100 Block E. Franklin St., is named for a local attorney and patron of the musical arts.

Hebrew Cemetery, 5th and Hospital Sts., replaced the Franklin Street Burying Ground in 1817. When Cong. Beth Ahabah absorbed Beth Shalome, the former acquired all rights to the cemetery. A unique feature of this burial ground is the Soldier's Section where a number of Jewish Confederate soldiers are buried. The posts of the railing surrounding this enclosure are furled flags and stacked muskets, surrounded by the flat soldier cap of the Confederate army. The railing between the posts is of crossed swords and sabres, hung with wreaths of laurel. The claim has been made that except for the one in Israel, this is the only Jewish martial cemetery in the world. On the plaque erected by the Hebrew Ladies Memorial Association, a correction was made in 1863 when the name of Henry Gintzberger was added to replace the name of Henry Gursburg. Research established that Gursberg never existed, but through an error Gintzberger was buried under the former name.

Hebrew Day School, 6801 Patterson Ave.

Hillel Foundation at Virginia Commonwealth, Medical College of Virginia and University of Richmond, in Masada Hall, 113 W. Franklin St.

Holocaust Memorial, erected by the New Americans Jewish Club in 1955, dedicated to 6,000,000 Jews who died in the Nazi Holocaust, is in the Emek Sholom Cemetery, a section of Forest Lawn Cemetery.

Jewish Community Center, 5403 Monument Ave. Just west of the tennis courts is a memorial grove of trees dedicated to the soldiers of Israel who were killed during the Yom Kippur War.

Jewish Community Council, 5403 Monument Ave.

Jewish Family Service, 4206 Fitzhugh Ave.

Keneseth Beth Israel Cong., 6300 Patterson Ave.

Gen. Robert E. Lee Memorial Window, in St. Paul's Epsicopal Church, on the edge of Capitol Sq., depicts Moses going out of the land of Egypt to lead his people to the Promised Land, symbolic of Lee's resigning from the Union Army to come to Richmond to take command of the Confederate Army.

Harry Lyons Building at School of Dentistry of Medical College of Virginia, 520 N. 12th St., is named for Dr. Harry Lyons, for many years dean of the School of Dentistry.

Markel Rd. is named for Lewis C. Markel, prominent insurance executive.

Chief Justice John Marshall Memorial Window in Monumental Church, on north side of Broad St., between 12th and College Sts., depicts Moses with the Tablets of the Law in Hebrew lettering.

Maywill St. is named for Irving May and William B. Thalhimer of Thalhimer Bros. department store, both of whom were Jewish community benefactors.

Roger Millheiser Gymnasium on the campus of the University of Richmond, was presented in 1918 by Clarence Millheiser of Richmond in memory of his son.

Or Ami Cong., 5400 Monument Ave.

Plotkin Rd. is named for Jacob Y. Plotkin, builder and developer.

Richmond Hebrew Day School, 6300 Patterson Ave.

Jennie Scher Rd. was named in 1941 for a local philanthropist, a woman of modest means who helped the Richmond community.

Lewis L. Straus Surgical Research Laboratory, 532 N. 12th St., is named for the former chairman of the Atomic Energy Commission, who spent his boyhood and teen-age years in Richmond.

Temple Beth El, 3330 Grove Ave.

Thalbro St., a contraction of the name of Thalhimer Bros.

Valentine Museum, 1015 E. Clay St., has among its love memorabilia, an "Acrostic for Rosa Cohn," composed and decorated in July 1860, by William Flegenheimer of Richmond, who later engrossed the Ordinance of Secession for the Confederate States of America. Also on exhibit are a number of items of Jewish historical interest. The list of such items is available at the Beth Ahabah Archives.

Virginia Commonwealth University, Cathedral Pl., has a Judaica collection in its James Branch Cabell Library. Theresa Pollak Building at School of the Arts, 325 N. Harrison St., is named for Miss Theresa Pollak who was the school's first art instructor.

Virginia Historical Society, 428 N. Boulevard, has a number of items dealing with the history of Jews in Virginia.

Virginia Museum of Fine Arts, Boulevard and Grove Ave., has in its permanent collection the Charles II silver toilet set, consisting of 16 pieces of 17th century craftsmanship, presented to the Museum by its owner, Albert P. Hinckley, Jr., of Warrenton, Va., "in memory of the Israeli fallen, men, women and children, during the Yom Kippur War of 1973." This inscription, attached to the set, is repeated in Hebrew. Hinckley, an architect and a non-Jew, gave the rest of his valuable silver collection to Hadassah to raise funds for "the care and rehabilitation of the Israeli wounded."

ROANOKE

Cong. Beth Israel, 920 Franklin Rd., S.W.

Jewish Community Council, 15th and Cleveland Ave.

Temple Emanuel, 1163 Persinger Rd., S.W.

STAUNTON

Temple House of Israel, 315 N. New St.

SUFFOLK

Cong. Agudath Achim, 132 Bank St.

VIENNA

Filene Center, the auditorium of the Wolf Trap Farm Park for the Performing Arts, is named for Lincoln Filene, Jewish patron of dance and music. The land—117 acres—and the center were gifts from Filene's daughter, Mrs. Jouette Shouse, who was responsible for developing the park as a major summer festival. The center is the first of its kind in the National Park System.

VIRGINIA BEACH

Beth Shalom Home nursing facility, a branch of Beth Shalom Home in Richmond, is being built in the College Park section.

Hebrew Academy of Tidewater, Indian River Rd. and Tomkins Cove.

Temple Emanuel, 25th St. and Baltic Ave.

WATERVIEW

A short-lived agricultural colony for Russian Jewish refugees was established here in 1882 by Joseph Friedenwald of Baltimore.

WILLIAMSBURG

Dr. John de Sequerya Residence and Office, on the south side of Duke of Gloucester St., near Botetourt St., one of the restored buildings of Colonial Williamsburg, recalls the now forgotten Marrano physician who arrived in Virginia around 1745 and practiced for many years in Williamsburg. Sequerya became the first visiting physician to a hospital for the insane when the first such institution in America was established in Williamsburg in 1773. He compiled an annual record of the diseases prevalent in Virginia and was credited by Thomas Jefferson with having introduced the tomato as an edible food. Among his patients were members of George Washington's family. Local maps refer to the house as "Marot's ordinary," because the building was originally the inn and tavern of Jean Marot, whose successors rented apartments and one of the tenants was Dr. Sequerya.

Temple Beth El, 600 Jamestown Rd., directly opposite the Phi Beta Kappa Hall of the College of William and Mary, is the only synagogue in historic Colonial Williamsburg. Founded in 1959, the congregation was given an old building by Colonial Williamsburg, which was subsequently moved to its present site in 1968. The membership is about 25 families out of the 45 known to reside in the Williamsburg area, but the synagogue is used by thousands of Jewish visitors who come to this restored Colonial town.

WINCHESTER
Beth-El Cong., 528 Fairmont Ave.

WOODBRIDGE
Prince William Jewish Community, meets in the social hall of the Covenant Presbyterian Church, 2281 Longview Dr.

Puerto Rico

Unlike many other Caribbean islands, Puerto Rico does not have a venerable synagogue, an old Jewish cemetery, virtually no native Jewish population, or colorful Jewish history. But this self-governing Commonwealth, linked to the United States by compact and mutual consent, boasts the largest Jewish community in the Caribbean.

In the crew of Christopher Columbus, who discovered Puerto Rico during his second voyage to the New World in 1493, were two or three Marrano Jews. Some think Jews from the Balearic Islands first settled in Puerto Rico as early as 1519. To this day there are old Catholic families in Puerto Rico who observe such Jewish practices as lighting candles on Friday evening, but with no recollection as to their meaning or origin.

Recorded Jewish history began with the Spanish-American War. Jews were not attracted to Puerto Rico while it was a Spanish colony, but the long memory of the Inquisition moved many Jewish immigrants to the United States to volunteer for service in this war. A number of Jews distinguished themselves in the fighting in Puerto Rico, including some who served with Teddy Roosevelt's Rough Riders.

The first known, but short-lived, Jewish congregation was an informal group organized by Rabbi Adolph Spiegel, who served with an American regiment at Ponce in 1899. He conducted Rosh Hashanah and other services in a telephone exchange building from 1899-1905 for Jewish military personnel, a handful of civilians employed by the military, and by the first American civilian government. One of these was Lieutenant Colonel Noah Sheppard, who came to Puerto Rico as an Army sergeant during the war, stayed on, married a local girl, and after his retirement, became an early leader of the Jewish community. During World War II, he was a member of the National Jewish Welfare Board Army and Navy Committee.

From 1900 to the early 1920s, there were individual Jews in Puerto Rico, but no community or congregation. The family of Charles Gans came from Connecticut and established a cigar factory on the island in 1899. Milton Farber, Nathaniel Nemerow, and I. Sachs were also among the early settlers. A number of East European Jews, unable to gain admittance to the United States after the 1924 immigration quota became law, took up residence in Puerto Rico to await entry to the mainland. After learning Spanish, however, some of them stayed on, among them Simon Benus and Aaron Levine, who established a chain of department stores.

While an organized Jewish community did not develop until World War II, individual Jews made notable contributions to Puerto Rico's progress from 1900-1935. After Spain ceded the island to the United States, President William McKinley named Leo Stanton Rowe, later director-general of the Pan-American Union, to codify Puerto Rico's laws. Jacob Hollander, a professor of economics at Johns Hopkins University, organized the island's first revenue system as the first treasurer of the Puerto Rican government. Louis Sulzbacher was a justice of Puerto Rico's first Supreme Court and an early exponent of American citizenship for the islanders. He was succeeded on the bench by Adolph Wolf.

For many years Dr. Julius Matz headed the insular experimental pathology laboratory at Rio Piedras. Joseph Jacobs, an engineer with the United States Reclamation Service, helped plan the island's earliest irrigation system. Drs. William Hoffman and Charles Weiss spent many years fighting the local tropical diseases. Early in the Franklin D. Roosevelt administration, A. Cecil Snyder served as United States Attorney for Puerto Rico and later became Chief Justice of the Territorial Supreme Court. Dr. Robert Szold, a prominent Zionist, was Puerto Rico's assistant attorney general in the Woodrow Wilson administration. More recently, Max Goldman headed the government board of tax exemption, while David Helfield was dean of the University of Puerto Rico Law School.

A Pan-American Union trade report in 1917 listed only six Jewish families in Puerto Rico. Ten years later, when Dr. Charles Weiss conducted a Passover seder in his home, there were only 26 known Jewish families; most were Americans, a few French Jews from other Caribbean islands, and two or three families from Cuba. From time to time these Jews gathered for worship but they were never numerous enough to form a permanent congregation. One such effort in 1937 was short-lived.

By 1942, however, when the number of Jewish families had grown to 38, an organization called the Social Service League was established. Later, its name was changed to the Jewish Community of Puerto Rico. When thousands of American troops poured into Puerto Rico in 1941 and 1942, Jewish chaplains and JWB field workers accompanied them, bringing kosher food, religious appurtenances, and professional leadership.

Small as it was, the Jewish Community of Puerto Rico rallied to the support of the rabbis in uniform by forming a National Jewish Welfare Board Armed Services Committee under the chairmanship of Milton Farber, one of the pioneer Jewish settlers. Mrs. Farber became president of Puerto Rico's Hadassah chapter, the organization's first overseas unit. Rabbi Lavy Becker, the first Jewish chaplain assigned to Puerto Rico, and his successor, Rabbi Bertram Pollans, not only provided a link between the several hundred Jewish servicemen and the handful of Jewish civilians, but organized social, religious, and cultural programs that became the nucleus out of which the present Jewish community developed.

The postwar industrial expansion spurred by the attractive tax inducements of "Operation Bootstrap" to American businessmen and corporations, and the tourist boom that began in the late 1950s, created a sizeable migration of young American Jews. They came as factory and plant managers, entrepreneurs, engineers, scientists, educators, and United States Government specialists. After the Castro revolution in Cuba, some 150 Spanish-speaking Jewish families moved from Cuba to become prominent in Puerto Rico's retail trades and professions.

From 1945, when the chaplains left, until 1952, regular worship services were held in a rented loft in San Juan under the leadership of Aron Levine and Simon Benus. The first religious school opened in 1952. Until 1955, the community's religious leadership was provided by part-time Jewish chaplains on duty at Ramey Air Force Base and the Roosevelt Roads Naval Station, and Rabbi Nathan Witkin, the JWB-USO field director in the Panama Canal Zone.

In 1953, the community purchased an old mansion once owned by a Nazi sympathizer and converted it into the Jewish Community Center and Shaare Tzedek Synagogue (Conservative). A B'nai B'rith lodge was established in 1964, and in the same year the first Jewish cemetery was consecrated. In 1967, a second congregation, the Reform Temple Beth Shalom, was founded. Both synagogues maintain religious schools. There are also several Jewish youth groups and annual campaigns for the United Jewish Appeal and Bonds for Israel.

The Jewish population numbers about 2,000, 90 percent located in San Juan, the principal city. There are about 15 Jewish families in Ponce, and about 10 in Mayaguez.

* * * * *

SAN JUAN

La Casa del Libro (House of the Book), 255 Cristo St., in Old San Juan, is a government-sponsored library of rare books and fine printing founded in 1955 by the late Dr. Elmer Adler, an American Jew who was a noted book collector and typography expert. His bequest of $100,000 to the library in 1963 remains the largest single gift ever made to a Puerto Rican cultural institution.

Habitat de Puerto Rico, off Avenida Franklin D. Roosevelt in San Patricio section (near U.S. Naval Reservation), was designed by the famed Israeli architect, Moshe Safdie, who created the revolutionary prefabricated housing for Montreal's Expo '67.

Jewish Commuinty Center-Shaare Tzedek Synagogue, 903 Ponce de Leon Ave.

Levittown, a major new housing complex on a 500-acre tract, six miles across San Juan Bay in Old San Juan, was created by and named for the American Jewish family of housing developers.

Morris Rothenberg Library, located in the Jewish Community Center, has a large Judaica collection and the only Judaic reference library in the Caribbean.

Temple Beth Shalom, cor. San Jorge and Louiza Sts., was remodeled from a former go-go bar.

Virgin Islands

The history of the Jewish families of the United States Virgin Islands
dates back to the 17th century when early Jewish traders and merchants
from Holland and Brazil arrived soon after the islands were settled by the
Dutch in the late 1650s. St. Thomas, the most populous island at present,
which passed to the Danish West India Company in 1671, and St. John,
which became Danish in 1680, were governed from 1684-1686 in the name of
the King of Denmark by Gabriel Milan, a Jewish soldier of fortune. Related
to prominent Marrano families, Milan was a rascal whose incompetence
and brutality led to his being recalled to Copenhagen, tried, and hanged.

Evidence of a Jewish settlement on St. Thomas during the last two
decades of the 17th century is contained in the contract signed by the
Danish West India Co., and the Prussian Brandenburg Co. in 1685 for the
importation of slaves to St. Thomas. The agreement included toleration for
Jews and Catholics who were allowed to hold worship services in private
"provided they permitted no scandals."

Early Jewish residents included Benjamin Voss, a Danish subject and
leading ship owner, and Emanuel Voss, a trader. Moses Joshua Henriques,
a Portuguese Jew, was the fiscal agent for ships that plied the route between St. Thomas and the then-Danish city of Gluckstadt in the 1680s.

St. Croix also had individual Jews in the late 17th century, but no
community until nearly 100 years later. In 1733 when France ceded St.

321

Croix to Denmark, the aforementioned Emanuel Voss carried word of the transfer to the governor of French Martinique. By 1760, a small congregation had formed at Christiansted, St. Croix, and six years later they opened a synagogue. (Moses Benjamin, a St. Croix merchant, had kosher meat shipped to him from New York!) The St. Croix congregation disbanded some time around 1800.

St. Thomas's permanent Jewish community came into being following British Admiral Rodney's raid on St. Eustatius. Rodney sacked that island in 1781 because its residents were supplying arms and ammunition to the American colonies during the Revolutionary War. The Jewish merchants and shippers fled to St. Thomas and St. Croix.

Under neutral Denmark, St. Thomas' excellent harbor and strategic location in the northeast Caribbean area, brought it great prosperity as a transshipment center, free port, and port of repair for sailing ships. Many Jewish merchants came to the Virgin Islands from Jamaica, Curacao, and the United States.

Although existing records indicate that the first synagogue in Charlotte Amalie, St. Thomas, was built in 1796, an earlier one may have existed.

From nine families in 1801, the Jewish population rose steadily to 22 in 1803, 64 in 1824, and more than 800 by 1850, when Jews accounted for almost half the island's white residents. But when steamships ended the era of sailing ships, the island's economy went into a sharp decline, which worsened following a cholera epidemic and a disastrous hurricane.

Gradually the Jewish chandlers, brokers, traders, importers, planters, and shopkeepers drifted away. The 1890 census reported only 140 Jews. When the United States purchased the islands from Denmark, there were only 40. So few whites remained that the rabbi was the only available clergyman to bless the transfer of the islands.

The synagogue erected in 1796 was destroyed by fire in 1804, rebuilt in 1812, and enlarged in 1823 and 1831. The present house of worship in Charlotte Amalie was the only one in the Virgin Islands until 1976, and was dedicated in 1833 on the same site as the original. The Jewish Community Center of St. Croix opened in Christiansted in 1976.

Buried in the older St. Thomas cemetery are the parents and grandparents of Camille Pissaro, the famous French impressionist, who was born in St. Thomas in 1800. In the same cemetery are the ancestors of David Levy Yulee, the first Jew elected to the United States Senate (from Florida in 1845), and Judah P. Benjamin, Secretary of State of the Confederacy, both of whom were born in St. Thomas.

The St. Thomas synagogue might have suffered the same fate as the one on St. Croix but for Rabbi Moses D. Sasso, who kept the community alive even when it was reduced to six Sephardic families. One of those remaining Jews was Morris Fidanque de Castro, born in Panama of an old

Caribbean family. A career civil servant, he was successively commissioner of finance, cabinet member, and secretary to the governor of the Virgin Islands before he was himself named to that post by President Harry Truman.

Rabbi Sasso, a native of St. Thomas, whose ancestors lived in the Caribbean for more than two centuries, served the community from 1914 until his retirement in 1965. His predecessor, Rabbi Cardozo, served from 1867 until his death in 1914 at age 90. Sasso had left St. Thomas for Panama, but returned to marry Cardozo's granddaughter and to succeed him at his request. Under Rabbi Sasso the synagogue gradually abandoned the Sephardic ritual and Orthodoxy and became a vital Reform congregation during the great surge to the Caribbean after World War II. Sasso's successors have all been Reform rabbis from the United States.

The first European Jews to settle in the Virgin Islands were members of the Levine and Paiewonsky families who arrived from Lithuania in the 1880s. The Levines opened a drygoods store where Isaac Paiewonsky was employed as a boy of 14. Over the years he branched out into varied commercial enterprises that did much to revive St. Thomas' economy. Ralph and Isidor Paiewonsky, sons of "Papa Paie," as the islanders called him, expanded the Paiewonsky businesses and became leaders in the area's economic, cultural, and political life. They helped found the College of the Virgin Islands in 1962, and organized the St. Thomas B'nai B'rith Lodge, named for Rabbis Cardozo and Sasso in 1964.

After several terms in the island's legislature, Ralph Paiewonsky was appointed territorial governor by President John Kennedy in 1961—the first native son to fill the office—and reappointed by President Lyndon Johnson in 1964. Paiewonsky did much to promote the tourist boom, and under his administration the islands made remarkable economic and social progress. Isidor Paiewonsky is the author of *Jewish Historical Development in the Virgin Islands, 1665-1959*, a history of Jewish life on the Virgin Islands based on the date included in *History of the Danish West Indies* which was written by John Knox in 1858.

Today about 200 Jewish families reside in St. Thomas and a scattering live in St. Croix. Most came from the United States after World War II. The majority are teachers, government officials, doctors, lawyers, and a number operate hotels, tourist shops, rum distilleries, bottling plants, and small industries.

A few old Sephardic families remain, and a number of Jews have retired to the islands from the United States mainland. Apart from the Paiewonskys, the best known Jews are authors Herman Wouk, who brought in a Hebrew teacher and has kosher food flown in from New York, and Maurice Petit, a one-time general superintendent of the West India Cable Co. and founder of the St. Thomas Botanical Gardens.

* * * * *

ST. CROIX—Christiansted

Jewish cemetery in the town's western suburb, is adjacent to the Moravian cemetery. Epitaphs range from 1779-1862.

Jewish Community Center of St. Croix, was opened in 1976 to serve 150 residents.

ST. THOMAS—Charlotte Amalie

Altona Cemetery, below the Virgin Isle Hilton, has epitaphs dating form 1837.

Camille Pissarro's birthplace, 14 Main St., is now a shop.

St. Thomas Hebrew Congregation, (Beracha V'Sholom V'Gemilath Chasadim—"Blessing and Peace and Acts of Piety"), Krystal Gade, is up a steep hill from Main St. The synagogue, a Reform congregation, was erected in 1833.

Savan Cemetery, in the peninsula off Waterfront Drive, west of shopping area, has epitaphs dating from 1792-1802.

Simmonds House, Upper Garden St., has a Hebrew inscription from Psalm 107 inscribed on its front.

Virgin Islands Public Library, Main St., has in its archives Jewish historic data and records.

Index

Index

A Abram, Morris, 106
Adams, President John Quincy, 66
Adler, Dr. Cyrus, 55, 62-63
Alabama, 25-38; early Jewish settlers, 25, 27; Jewish office-
holders, 27-28, 31; Jewish population, 31, 33; oldest congrega-
tion, 27, 29-31, 37; public places relating to Jews, 33-36, 38
American Federation of Zionists, 123
American Israelite, 68, 120, 193
American Jew as Patriot, Soldier and Citizen, 161
American Jewish Archives, 40, 120, 133, 209, 223, 229
American Jewish Committee, 63
American Jewish Historical Quarterly, 99-101, 162
American Jewish Historical Society, 63
American Jewish Times-Outlook, 199, 203
American Jewish Year Book, 125
American Jewry and the Civil War, 132, 147, 161, 243
American Overture: Jewish Rights in Colonial Times, 95, 223
Arizona, 39-52; early Jewish settlers, 39-43; Jewish officeholders,
41, 46; Jewish population, 45; Judaica collections, 48; oldest
congregation, 44-45, 52; public places relating to Jews, 48-52
Arizona Jewish Post, 51
Arkansas, 53-63; early Jewish settlers, 54-55; Jewish officehold-
ers, 57; Jewish population, 57; oldest congregation, 54, 56, 61;
public places relating to Jews, 58-63
Atlas, Rabbi Samuel, 32

B Balfour Declaration, 130
Barth, Solomon. 39, 43-44, 51
Baruch, Bernard M., 200, 228, 230, 233-237, 250-251, 312
Baruch, Dr. Simon, 230, 233, 236, 312
Benjamin, Judah P., 30, 37, 75, 78, 92, 109, 145, 149, 152-153,
162, 168, 200, 206, 228, 235, 253, 297, 312, 322
Black Code of 1724, 26-27, 54, 134-135, 159
B'nai B'rith, 38, 45, 50, 52, 60, 73, 94, 104, 108, 115, 165-166,
169, 179, 198, 205, 244, 251, 255, 263-264, 274-275, 299-301,
304, 319, 323
Board of Delegates of American Israelites, 28
Brandeis, Justice Louis D., 123, 129-130
Buchanan, President James, 29

327